DETROIT LIVES

Conflicts in Urban and Regional Development
a series edited by John R. Logan and Todd Swanstrom

DETR🔩IT
L🔩VES

COMPILED AND EDITED BY
ROBERT H. MAST

FOREWORD BY DAN GEORGAKAS

TEMPLE UNIVERSITY PRESS
PHILADELPHIA

Temple University Press, Philadelphia 19122
Copyright © 1994 by Temple University. All rights reserved
Published 1994
Printed in the United States of America

⊗ The paper used in this publication meets the minimum requirements
of American National Standard for Information Sciences—Permanence of
Paper for Printed Library Materials, ANSI Z39.48-1984

Library of Congress Cataloging-in-Publication Data

Detroit lives / compiled and edited by Robert H. Mast.
    p. cm. — (Conflicts in urban and regional development)
    Includes index.
    ISBN 1-56639-225-X (alk. paper). — ISBN 1-56639-226-8 (alk. paper
: pbk.)
    1. Detroit (Mich.) — Social conditions. 2. Quality of life —
Michigan — Detroit. 3. Social reformers — Michigan — Detroit —
Interviews. 4. Social surveys — Michigan — Detroit. I. Mast,
Robert H. II. Series.
HN80.D6D45   1994
306'09774'34 — dc20   93-51007

Over the course of a century . . . [Detroit] was involved in many major historical developments. As the world center of the automobile
industry, it has exerted tremendous social and economic influence. It
has been the headquarters of two of the world's three largest corporations, and it is America's most unionized city. Detroit is the heart of
American industry, and by the beat of that heart much of America's
economic health is measured.

Robert Conant, *American Odyssey*

Neither the ruling elite nor the workers have been able to revive the
Motor City. But hundreds of thousands of people have begun to question basic assumptions about the organization and purpose of their
lives and about the institutions that control them. They have begun to
accumulate valuable skills and experiences necessary to challenge
those institutions and to create substitute or parallel structures of
power.

Dan Georgakas and Marvin Surkin, *Detroit: I Do Mind Dying*

CONTENTS

FOREWORD

Dan Georgakas

DETROIT AT MIDCENTURY, the city in which I was born and raised, relished its place in history as the world's Arsenal of Democracy. Detroiters looked to the future confidently, each generation expecting to live much better than its predecessor. Even a high school dropout knew there was always a good-paying factory job readily available. Longtime autoworkers expected to own their own home, a car or two, and perhaps a vacation home and boat. The public schools and city university were first rate. Detroit's unions were among the most democratic and progressive in America, and Democrats routinely used Detroit's Cadillac Square to launch their national presidential campaigns on Labor Day. Detroit-born Joe Louis was undisputed heavyweight champion of the world, and some years the Detroit Tigers, Detroit Lions, and Detroit Red Wings finished first in their respective sports, making Motor City the City of Champions. Detroit was not the best of all worlds, to be sure, but it represented industrial America at its zenith.

The Detroit of the 1990s, the city that emerges in the accounts that follow, is another place. From being a city representative of nearly all ethnic groups in America, it is now 80 percent African-American, making it the nation's first Black metropolis. Contemporary Detroiters are frustrated and apprehensive about their future. The problematic auto industry has largely abandoned the region, leaving those workers who are still employed fearful of losing their jobs and pensions. The public schools have an enormous dropout rate and a rising curve of violence. Unions strive to stem declining membership and national Democrats flee from any identification with organized labor. The Lions have moved to Pontiac and the Tigers have asked for a subsidy as a condition for staying in the city. Detroit is not the worst of all possible worlds, to be sure, but it embodies all the social plagues that beset industrial and urban America.

The former and present Detroit organizers whom Bob Mast has

assembled to review the collapse of Motor City and offer perspectives for renewal are a rich cross section of the city's progressive traditions. They are too serious to indulge in convenient scapegoating and too smart to offer quick fixes. To a person they believe that reforms at the national level are required to address what appear to be local problems. Within that accord, however, there are distinctive generational differences that reflect the changing Detroit realities and opinions on which modes of change are the most viable.

Those with the longest memories, people like James Boggs and George Crockett, recall a time in the 1930s and 1940s when trade unions were perceived as the prime vehicle for addressing racial and class grievances. While the United Auto Workers (UAW) was always imperfect, its leadership was formally pledged to racial justice and to a social as well as economic agenda. Activists assumed that the steady gain in wages and benefits meant the growing Black working class would have community interests largely confluent with those of the white working class. The operative organizing slogans were "Organize the Unorganized" and "Black and White, Unite and Fight."

The UAW was also a hotbed of radicalism. Both the Industrial Workers of the World and the Communist Party had played a major local role in organizing the UAW in Detroit in the mid-1930s, and radical groups of all kinds retained a presence in various UAW locals through the 1940s. These radicals advanced new demands, worked for racial harmony, and acted as shock troops for change. Control of city government was not yet a viable option, but activists had links to officials in the New Deal and to a trade union movement that had succeeded in organizing nearly half of all working Americans.

The perspectives of the civil rights and New Left activists of the 1960s reflect a different reality. By their time, the UAW had purged itself of its radicals wherever possible and seemed increasingly chummy with management. Although a few African-Americans held higher union offices, the UAW's leading group remained white. Discontent among Black rank and file was so intense that at one famous confrontation, Black workers carried placards proclaiming "UAW means U Ain't White." This political tension was not made any easier by the fact that most activists were vehemently opposed to the war in Vietnam while the UAW national executive was hawkish. As dissident Black workers began to organize themselves within and without the UAW, white and Black activists felt it was essential to support their demands even when those demands upset or alienated white workers. Ideological inspiration was found in the national liberation movements of the Third World rather than in the bureaucracies of eastern Europe.

Local politics turned on a racial axis as well. The police force was constantly embroiled in racial incidents and city government was not particularly responsive to the growing Black population. As white flight from the city accelerated and the civil rights movement blossomed, white and Black activists saw that city posts like judgeships were there for the taking and the mayor's office was not out of the question. The organizing priorities were seen as cultural as well as political. Considerable effort went into creating an alternative press, book clubs, study groups, and bookstores. Affinity groups rather than formal parties were the mode of organization; local rather than national campaigns generated the greatest enthusiasm.

When Coleman Young became Detroit's first Black mayor in 1973, all the economic elements for decline were in process. The Great Rebellion of 1967, the most costly urban uprising up to that time in American history, had proved a watershed event. Investment in the city had evaporated. Aging auto plants and steel mills were not replaced; local commercial firms like Saunder's Candy, Vernor's Ginger Ale, and the J. L. Hudson department store went bankrupt or abandoned their Detroit locales. The UAW remained mired in lackluster leadership, and Detroit's Teamsters were infamous as the home local of James Hoffa, the national personification of labor gangsterism and corruption.

Bucking the bad economic trends were some gains in civil rights. Coleman Young was able to bring the police under control and to eliminate institutionalized racism from city government. But like the UAW leaders and previous white mayors, Young soon found it was easier to cozy up to the industrialists than to confront them. The development plans, good and bad, that emanated from City Hall were mainly short-term public relations approaches that did not address underlying social ills.

Detroit, now sometimes dubbed Murder City USA, emerged as the national reference point for all that had gone wrong in the urban landscape. The growth of relatively prosperous white suburbs in a ring around an impoverished Black Detroit fed the racism of local whites while encouraging paranoia among Blacks.

Critics of Coleman Young featured in this volume contend that Detroit's malaise was accelerated by Young's abrasive methods and toleration of corruption. They picture him as a kind of Black Boss Tweed. A good many Young supporters retort that whatever the economic hardships of Young's era, they were preferable to the racial injustices of the past. What supporters and detractors alike understand, however, is that Young's twenty-year rule has revealed the limits of municipal Black power. Even under the most brilliant and pristine mayor, Detroit would have remained captive to economic, cultural, and political forces beyond its city limits or even the city limits of its suburban neighbors.

Organizers in present-day Detroit remain imbued with the can-do pluck characteristic of their city at its best. They are devoted to myriad grassroots projects designed to aid one constituency or another. But as these organizers go about their daily tasks, they are haunted by questions that haunt all Americans. Why have we so casually forsaken our industrial heartland? What are the ultimate consequences of allowing millions of city dwellers to go uneducated and underemployed? Can we long endure as a viable power if we are divided into the two nations the Kerner Commission on Civil Rights grimly warned against a full quarter century ago?

Only the numbest reader of these pages will fail to see the relationship of the urban realities herein explicated so poignantly to those that flamed so fiercely in Los Angeles in 1992. Given that context, no one should be shocked at the radical elements in the thought of these activists from so many diverse backgrounds, perspectives, and generations. To deal radically means to go to the root of things, the origins, the fundamentals. These Detroit voices insist that the problems of urban Americans have become so grave that nothing less will suffice.

PREFACE

THE YEAR I BECAME A STAFF MEMBER at the Institute of Race Relations in London—1969—Detroit to me was big and Black and complex and riotous. I was part of an institute team charged by the Ford Foundation to uncover the mysteries of racial conflict in urban centers around the world, a popular topic then. Detroit was one of our study sites. Our library was stocked with pamphlets from such Detroit groups as the League of Revolutionary Black Workers and the Dodge Revolutionary Union Movement. The staff at the institute included European and Third World radicals. Rather than an example of negative racial conflict, they saw Detroit as the major center of liberation struggles in the United States: the revolutionary capital of America.

By 1972 I was in a mood to radically change my life and to get into some kind of progressive movement back in the United States. So when an opportunity became available at Wayne State University, I jumped at the chance to move to Detroit. It was about the last year that progressive white émigrés chose Detroit to express their politics. Many saw Detroit as the place where the revolutionary action was, where class and race antagonisms were being dealt with scientifically and practically by a tough and radical proletariat. It also was the year Dan Georgakas and Marvin Surkin wrote their study in urban revolution that resulted in the book *Detroit: I Do Mind Dying*.

By the mid-1970s I had gotten to know some of the urban revolutionaries that Georgakas and Surkin wrote about. Their book, which I used as a text in some of my sociology classes, helped me understand the motion of the Detroit radical phenomenon I was experiencing. By then, I was captivated by the energy and dedication of Detroit activists. There were so many of them from so many walks of life: workers from everywhere who labored in auto factories, proletarian intellectuals, radical artists, Black revolutionaries, white middle-class revolutionaries.

The Detroit progressives had widely different ideologies, theories, and tactics and strategy, but they were deeply committed to the struggles of the day for equality and liberation. They took on the establishment and had a powerful impact on it. They took risks, deferred many gratifications, championed unpopular causes, belonged to "subversive" organizations, proposed solutions to social problems that most ordinary citizens deemed too radical. These folks were inspiring.

The progressives helped me understand better the interconnections of political action with culture and the economy. Most important, perhaps, I was taught the absolute virtue of democratic grassroots organizing. And I know I became much more sophisticated on the question of race, which was one reason I had come to Detroit in the first place.

Sometimes the progressives made mistakes in logic. Sometimes their egos controlled their politics. Though I was very impressed with how creative and productive a disciplined political group can be, I also saw that the very same group could be harmful to members and disruptive of organization goals if there was deep disagreement on tactics and strategy.

During my twelve years in Detroit I watched as factories and businesses closed down and jobs were lost. I observed the exodus of whites and middle-class Blacks from the city as neighborhoods deteriorated, schools declined, street crime rose, and infrastructure decayed. I moved from Detroit in 1984, but my attraction to the city never ended. The inherent validity of most of the Detroit progressive experience, especially in race and class terms, continued to be a model that bolstered me in increasingly confusing times. I determined to keep monitoring the activities of the progressive people there as the city underwent awesomely degrading changes.

How This Book Came About

By 1990 my curiosity about the condition of things in Detroit and the state of the movement there became overwhelming. I decided to begin an oral history project to document the lives of Detroit progressive activists and to learn what folks were doing in the early 1990s. I called the project "Who Cares About Detroit?" I had asked several friends which publishers might be interested in a book on Detroit radicals, and that was always the response: "Who cares about Detroit?" Sure, that made me angry. But in 1990, ten years into supply side, one expected such calumny.

Today scant material for a general audience hails minority and working-class contributions to the development of our society. The ideas and experience of those speaking for the common people are seldom sought out. How, then, do the representatives of the working people in America put their case before the electorate? Democracy does not work well for citizens who do not have a rostrum. I wanted to provide a forum to a cross section of progressives who would tell in their own words something about their relationship with Detroit and who would venture their suggestions for improvement. So, education became a major purpose of this book. I wanted it to be a conduit of information and experience from those who care about Detroit, and who work on its behalf, to those who could not care less or do not know enough to care.

I hoped also that the book might be a vehicle for the exchange of ideas among progressive people. After all, this is the time for new analysis, mobilization, and action. Perhaps the 1990s will prove to be another decisive turning point for the American people, similar to the surge in consciousness and action that was experienced in the 1930s and 1960s. In both periods, millions of progressive people responded to the social and economic contradictions inherited from previous decades. Now in the 1990s the need again exists for ideas to be debated and politics worked out.

Most people who still live in Detroit care desperately about it because it is home. They would be very happy to witness improved job opportunities, better education, reduced crime, less violence, a rebuilt infrastructure. Many would actively participate in the struggles and hard work needed to achieve such a rebirth. Even most of the 800,000 people who left Detroit in the last forty years probably would be pleased to see it grow more healthy and prosperous.

But there is a special group of people who have had a special and intimate relationship with the city and its urban area. They live in Detroit proper, its suburbs, or elsewhere, and they are thousands strong. They have cared more deeply, or have worked harder, or taken more risks, or were more committed to humanity, or were crazier. These are the progressives who I wanted to contact. They are minorities or Caucasians, center-city or suburban dwellers, poor or affluent, Ph.D.s or eighth-grade dropouts, philosophically socialist or capitalist, religious or atheist, oldish or youngish, male or female. Today, some are still active while others are tired out, or getting an education, or raising a family. Whatever the individual case, they constitute the collective body of Detroit progressives. From their ranks came the testifiers for this book.

Progressive people may be quite different from one another, but as I see it, they share some common values and ways of looking at the social world. There is an understanding that the well-being and freedom of the individual are intimately related to the health and well-being of the broader society. Progressives believe that social equality is a central concept for responsible citizenship and social justice. Where social equality is lacking, political struggles to achieve it must be waged. If legal and civil rights have been won, but masses of people still lack life's basic needs, then the struggle for economic justice must be waged.

You might ask what political identity this group of testifiers would have. That is difficult, since the use of left-center-right labels is very confused today. Our national politicians and opinion makers use obfuscating criteria today to label us, like variations in beliefs about the "market," the flag, democracy and freedom, political correctness, and all that. Nevertheless, if averaged out, the testifiers likely would occupy a left-of-center position in 1970 terms.

From the thousands of potential testifiers, I had to cull out a small group to represent the whole. I decided that testifiers should be known for their work, have a track record, be adept at verbal communication, have thoughts about what should be done to improve their city and country, and be willing to take a stab at predicting the future. I tried for a reasonable balance by race, gender, age, neighborhood, and political orientation. I ended up interviewing 100 people, about half of whom were minority and about one-third women. They were community organizers, civil rights leaders, labor leaders, public servants, academic scholars, media people, theologians, agency directors, authors, homemakers, manual workers, and various professionals.

How did I locate them? I started with people I knew, and asked them for names. Then I called or wrote those people, maybe interviewed some, maybe got more names. Although there were a few refusals and some who did not return my calls, overall I was pleased with the cooperation. I sought testimony on three basic open-ended questions: What were the factors in your life that shaped you? How do you analyze the evolution of Detroit? What is to be done to help Detroit and how should it be done? The sessions ranged from one to five hours, and all were tape recorded.

I met with respondents in offices, homes, and public accommodations. For eighty-eight days, mostly in 1991, I drove well over 5,000 miles to reach them in all parts of the city at all times of the day. This travel allowed me to observe the massive Detroit urban area in detail and once again to marvel at the erosion of urban quality of life and deterioration of infrastructure. The travel also was an unscientific, albeit real, test of the Detroit danger factor. Folks warned me about the outbreak of car jackings, drive-by shootings, and general violence. There is a justified fear of the inner city and most outsiders avoid it if they can. I did occasionally wonder whether, if I was to be bashed, would it be because I was a white in a Black neighborhood, a person with possessions to steal, or the driver of a Japanese car in Motor City? But I can testify that not a single hostile act was perpetrated against me. Indeed, much courtesy and cooperation were shown by residents all over the city.

I talked to people from the activist generations of the 1930s, 1960s, and 1990s, including several who spanned the entire period. Nearly all were upbeat, gutsy, staunchly loyal to the city, inordinately busy, thoughtful, and articulate. There was a great sadness about the condition of Detroit. There also was a resolve to dig in and do something about it and a confidence that leaders and programs would emerge to build a new Detroit.

Transcribing some 150 hours of rapid-talking communicators was a monumental task. I then had the tough job of editing the transcriptions into a format and length acceptable to the publisher. I had to make wrenching decisions: eliminating nearly thirty of the testifiers who overlapped with others or did not seem to fit the emerging book format, then cutting more than half from each of the narratives that were selected for inclusion. Sometimes I pieced together sentences that were scattered throughout a transcription when they were making a singular point, but I never changed the respondent's point or added my own words.

Throughout the text I capitalized the word "Black" when it refers to people of African descent. Perhaps I should explain my usage; besides, the etymology is interesting. As late as the 1950s an American of African ancestry was popularly identified as a Negro, though the word often was not capitalized. During the first half of the twentieth century there was a movement to capitalize the word. People like Richard B. Moore—who wrote an early pamphlet called "Why the N in Negro Should Be Capitalized"—argued that capitalization would add some measure of dignity to the people represented. Then in the late 1960s there was a real struggle to replace "Negro"—thought by many to be identified with enslavement and social oppression—with "Black." Though use of the latter word became universal, some capitalize it today and some do not. Standard dictionaries give authors discretion on the subject. Those who favor its capitalization generally are of African descent, and include those with whom I have broadly discussed this matter. The overwhelming practice of the print media is to use lower case. I choose to capitalize the word "Black" partly because it evolved from the word "Negro"; but also because, in the spirit of this book, greater dignity is given to a *people* with a common ancestry and a common oppression in the white world than to a mere color. Of course, this question may be moot with the growing popularization of the term African-American.

Acknowledgments

Many of the respondents in this project gave me names of persons to interview, especially Ishmael Ahmed, Maggie DeSantis, Mike Hamlin, Ron Lockett, Doug Smith, and Hugh White.

Dean John Dwyer provided various amenities for me as a visiting scholar at the University of Detroit Mercy, and Alice Talifer and her able secretarial staff were helpful in a variety of ways.

Technical advice on recording, the loan of transcribing equipment, and general wisdom came from Bill Bryce. Toni Swanger did a great job of transcribing some of the early interviews, while continuing to caution me that I needed more women in my sample. Detroit author and reporter Mike Betzold gave sage advice throughout this project. Dan Georgakas and Herb Boyd were instructive and supportive from New York. Saul Wellman's debates with me from Washington, D.C., were stimulating and helpful.

Ron Glotta, Leonard Grossman, and the late Morris Gleicher helped facilitate a small grant for the project from the Buck Dinner, an annual fundraiser for progressive causes. The *Metro Times* also made a donation.

General support and the occasional bed were given by Mike and Gail Whitty. Norm Goldner, Kevin Moloney, and Dave Riddle, in different ways, provided nurturing. My daughter Cynthia rendered considerable hospitality and a willing ear during the months I visited Detroit to conduct interviews. John King and Emirene Mendosa also provided the hospitality of their home.

Anne Mast—my wife, best friend, and colleague—was a constant intellectual sounding board and personal support in all aspects of this project.

Mike Ames and Micah Kleit at Temple University Press relentlessly demanded rigor, better organization, and parsimony. Jennifer French carefully sheparded the book through production.

I owe a debt to the people who were interviewed but are not included in this book because of formatting or space limitations. They provided great insight. Their absence does not suggest their lack of importance.

My greatest debt is to the unnamed people of Detroit who, by their example, provided the inspiration for this project.

Robert H. Mast

INTRODUCTION

FOR THE FIRST TIME IN THE HISTORY of the United States,
we are in a period when the present generation cannot look forward
to being better off than its parents. Times were bad during the Great
Depression, but World War II came along and ushered in a boom
period that lasted until the end of the 1960s. At about that time,
however, serious industrial competition from abroad was evolving.
U.S. business leaders had short-sighted management strategies and
American-built products became less competitive. Domestic economic
decline facilitated the flight of capital abroad. Plants were consoli-
dated, modernized, or abandoned, or companies just ran away to
more profitable regions. Most workers who still had jobs were required to work harder or longer, usually for less pay. More women
found it necessary to enter the labor market at wages lower than men
for comparable work. The civil rights gains of the previous two decades began to reverse. Unions were broken or rendered impotent by
government and business.

None of this happened by accident. Some time around the middle of the 1970s, a new era of right-wing *laissez-faire* ideology was being
promoted by the upper class, partly as a reaction to the successes of
the progressive movements of the 1950s and 1960s. Progressives had
analyzed the class and economic system and had influenced legislation at all levels of government. Activists organized hundreds of thousands in opposition to poverty, imperialist foreign policy, and discrimination. Progressive journalists and teachers explained the emerging
American system in understandable ways.

Alarmed by their erosion of power and financial control, the
movers and shakers of establishment America mobilized a vast propaganda machine of academics, clergy, and journalists to help usher in
the new era of conservatism. A coordinated attack was launched by
government, business, and an army of propagandists aimed at the
progressive movements. The already vulnerable sectors of American

society—labor, minorities, women, the undereducated, the under-employed, the poor—were forced into stagnation or lower living standards by new laws and tax codes, business investment decisions, and other insidious policies. The net effect of supply-side economic policy was a transfer of a large part of the lower classes' share of the national product to the upper classes, a principally Caucasian and suburban population.

If you pile the total American population into a pyramid-like structure, the base is bulging out more and more today. The majority of people in America have had to greatly modify their aspirations for a better life.

The social problems and human pathologies that have emerged in this country are becoming intolerable. There are, at a conservative estimate, 20 million hungry, 4 million homeless, 35 million workers with no health insurance, 40 million workers with no private pension plan, and 45 million individuals with mental or physical disabilities. Some 35 percent of African-Americans live in poverty; 35 million households experience a rape, burglary, or assault each year. And these figures are rising daily. It remains to be seen whether Clintonomics and right-liberal leadership will make any appreciable difference, but it is extremely doubtful.

About Detroit

Throughout our history, cities have been the focal point of commerce, industry, culture, and social integration. Workers from abroad and from all over this country were lured to the industrial centers by the reasonable promise of a better life. Throughout the long period of industrial growth, both workers and capital interests prospered in industrial cities like Detroit, Pittsburgh, Buffalo, and Cleveland. These cities led the way in modern mass production and the elevation of the working class.

Detroit—our case study in this book—is one of the most dramatic illustrations of boom and depression of any modern industrial city. Known throughout the world as Motor City by car buffs, Motown by Black music aficionados, or the Arsenal of Democracy by patriots, Detroit is in fact a mirror of America.

Detroit was founded in 1701 by the French trader Antoine de la Mothe Cadillac at a strategic location on the straits (the Detroit River) that connected Lake Erie and Lake St. Clair. Windsor, the motor city of Canada, is directly across the river and connected with Detroit by bridge and tunnel. At mid twentieth century, Detroit was ranked third among U.S. ports in foreign trade, with exports totaling $700 million a year.

In the mid nineteenth century, Detroit became a center for capital that was amassed in the lumber industry, and a center for skilled workmen that resulted from shipbuilding and manufacturing. By the latter part of the nineteenth century, Detroit had also established other major industries: iron and steel, foundry, railroad car, boot and shoe, wheel and axle, chemicals, and pharmaceuticals.

Then came the horseless carriage and the predominance of autos. Henry Ford ushered in the era of mass production in his Highland Park assembly plant. In 1914 he introduced the famous $5-a-day wage, which attracted workers from all over the world. By 1972 the average hourly wage of autoworkers was nearly $5.50, one of the highest in the nation. Much credit for this can be given to the aggressive organizing drives of the United Auto Workers (UAW).

Typical of most industrial cities, Detroit throughout its history was a mosaic of racial and ethnic groups. In 1850 nearly half of the people were foreign born; by 1920, only one-third. Then when the restrictive immigration laws of the early 1920s curtailed the influx of foreign workers, people from the American South, primarily Black, moved in to fill the vacuum. Spurred by World War II production, African-Americans came to Detroit in great numbers. By 1960, 482,000 Blacks lived in Detroit.

In the absence of human rights leadership and civil rights laws, the mixing of racial and ethnic groups often caused social tensions in crowded cities where too many workers chased too few jobs and competed for decent housing and where corporate practices pitted worker against worker. Though the enlightened policies of the UAW mitigated much tension, Detroit experienced major racial disturbances. In June 1943 a serious disturbance left thirty-five dead (twenty-nine of them Black) and one thousand injured.

There were more than 1,800,000 people living in Detroit in 1950, the peak population year. Most workers could get a fairly decent job with less than a tenth-grade education. Families could buy houses, cars, and even boats to use on greater Detroit's 3,000 lakes and ponds and 300 miles of Great Lakes frontage. Today the population hovers around 1,000,000. Nearly eight of ten Detroiters are African-American, most of whose parents and grandparents left the Deep South for a better life in Motor City. The remainder of the population is mostly a mix of second- or third-generation ethnic or Appalachian whites and more recent Latino, Arab, and Asiatic immigrants.

Just at the peak of its production and population, Detroit was hit hard by the immense systemic changes in free enterprise that unfolded in the late 1960s. The city has been seriously on its way down for the last twenty-five years, but by the 1980s it was clear to all that production and commercial capital had abandoned the city and de-

3

ployed most of the remaining jobs to suburban, southern, and foreign destinations. In 1965 Detroit accounted for 68 percent of all employment in southeast Michigan; by 1990 it was less than 18 percent. More than 70 percent of business and industry has left Detroit.

The little production remaining in Detroit today continues to undergo automation and jobs continue to be lost. At its peak the massive Ford River Rouge complex in Dearborn employed 120,000 people; now there are 22,000, with higher production figures. A new General Motors Poletown plant that builds Cadillacs and employs 2,200 workers replaced 6,000 workers at two outmoded plants, with greater production. A new Chrysler Jefferson assembly plant produces Jeeps with about 1,400 workers; during World War II it had 17,000 workers.

There has been a mass exodus of population from the city, resulting in thousands of abandoned homes and buildings that joined the hundreds of abandoned factories and stores. The spark that ignited the exodus was economic decline. But as the city grew increasingly Blacker and poorer, old-fashioned racism exacerbated a white flight that had started in the 1950s with the lure of the suburbs and construction of an elaborate freeway system. Detroit's 1967 insurrection—the most sweeping and destructive one in all the country with 43 deaths, 3,304 arrests, and $200 million in property damage—speeded up the exodus of Detroit's Black and white middle classes. People continue to leave the city if they can; those remaining have fewer children and are poorer and older.

Economic decline and population changes have produced astounding contradictions in the everyday life of Detroiters. There are more than 200,000 chronically jobless adults. Nearly half the population lives below the poverty line. Housing activists estimate there are 50,000 people living on the streets in a city with 40 percent of its 10,000 public housing units vacant due to corruption and mismanagement all the way up to Washington. In a city that once boasted the highest rate of home ownership in the country, sometimes just one or two permits a year are issued for new single-family homes. About four in ten people have no car in Motor City. Eight in ten of all new jobs in the Detroit region—mostly low-wage service jobs—are in outlying, mostly white suburbs with no public transportation to them, an a priori case for regional racism.

The infant mortality rate approximates that of Nairobi. There are about 800 murders in Detroit each year, a twelvefold increase from 1940, when the population was considerably higher. More than 300 children are shot each year. Seven out of ten teenagers fail to finish high school. Nearly everyone decries the menace of Detroit's newest industry, crack cocaine, doing about $1 billion worth of business in Wayne County and offering a good livelihood to a growing number of unemployed Black teenagers. At the same time, $100 million of public money is spent annually to house and incarcerate Wayne County juvenile delinquents.

Nearly all department stores and chain food markets have closed down, leaving Detroiters only with the more expensive food and merchandise sold by small neighborhood stores, the majority of which are owned by recent Caldean immigrants. Service agencies like the YMCA continue to close their doors. The Catholic archdiocese recently closed forty parish churches, a particular blow in this traditionally Catholic city where the parish has been a center of social services and education.

If that were not enough, Detroit citizens pay the highest rate of property tax in any Michigan city, in exchange for drastically reduced services resulting from erosion of the tax base. On top of that, over 60 percent of federal financial assistance to Detroit has been cut since the Jimmy Carter years. And very recently, the state of Michigan completely lopped 90,000 general assistance recipients from the welfare rolls, a large portion of whom were disabled Detroit Black males who subsequently became homeless. Many agree with Ze'ev Chafets' declaration in his recent book on Detroit, *Devil's Night* (Random House, 1990)—that Detroit is akin to a Third World city.

Can Detroit Rebound?

As a result of the exodus of basic industry and an unprecedented decline in the quality of life, Detroiters today are underemployed, underfed, underhoused, and undersafeguarded. Most people live every day with some level of fear and uncertainty. Many of them—abandoned by capital, government, and charity—see little hope for improvement.

But with all the pathology and decay, Detroit continues to be an absorbing, dynamic, and important urban center. It has been a bellwether of the social and economic health of industrial America. Its citizens always have been a spearhead of progressive labor, class, and race relations.

Are the people and institutions of Detroit adapting, as in the past, to the economic vicissitudes of a one-industry industrial center that increasingly has become redundant? Can a city that has bottomed out arise and regain its proud place among the large cities of America? Are there movements afoot that have a potential to rebuild the shattered economic base and social structure of a city with 1,000,000 people? Can Detroit become a model for the future in a nation that tends to blame the victims, that is racist to the core, that extols private affluence as a principal virtue, and that is experiencing its worst economic condition since the Great Depression?

The testimonies that follow may begin to answer these difficult questions. But perhaps we might speculate on the logic of the answers in advance. Detroit is a microcosm of all the current problems and contradictions in this nation. Detroit typifies American deindustrialization, racism, and poverty that have resulted from late twentieth-century negligence, greed, and irresponsibility on the part of those who rule. So the condition of Detroit has been *caused* by the political-economic forces in this country that make decisions and presumably benefit by those decisions. These facts are well known by Detroiters, since they have gained wisdom and have become astute analysts through their experience.

Now, the mere fact of *knowing* what causes something to happen does not necessarily provide the wisdom of solution, especially when causality is obfuscated and traditional solutions are demeaned by the movers and shakers. Moral guidelines and structural blueprints of the past—like egalitarian redistribution and central planning—have been debased to the point that they appear to most as implausible, remote, or fraudulent. American free enterprise caused the present Detroit, so *it* has not worked. We are told that the socialist experiments abroad did not work, so we should not ponder *that* approach further. So what is the solution? If Detroiters, faced with this impasse, can come up with a set of priorities, a coherent plan of action, and the political will to make the plan work, then Detroit may be on its way back. Indeed, it may gradually become a model of change, as many Detroiters believe it can.

There are several areas of concern that Detroiters must and will address. First, there must be jobs for the vast underemployed population so that a minimum standard of living can be achieved. Jobs permit spending power, which supports a foundation of small business services, which in turn provides more jobs. Jobs and businesses also provide an enlarged tax base to support the badly needed urban services that governments perform, which in turn provide more jobs. This is perhaps the most critical area of concern and one of the most difficult to achieve. Where will the jobs of the future be located? If in Detroit, how is capital to be generated? If in the suburbs, how are Detroiters to be linked to them? How are Detroit workers and their children, traditionally steeped and skilled in mass production, to be reoriented toward high-tech jobs of the future? Must job creation be tied into traditional for-profit mechanisms, or can it emerge from democratically controlled nonprofit concepts?

Next, everybody knows that Detroit must be made into a livable city for it to have a genuine rebirth. That means that crime, violence, and street drug trafficking must be ended. This is also a most difficult task, since many in Detroit use creative criminal entrepreneurial skills to survive, while many others, frustrated by blocked opportunity, are at the psychological breaking point. Can citizens democratically organize their communities in creative ways for protection, mutual support, and uplift? How are citizens' protection initiatives to be coordinated with traditional government responsibilities?

Then, the citizens of southeastern Michigan must come to terms with racism. Jobs and crime are somewhat easy to conceptualize and measure. The existence of racism is less so, but it is of paramount importance. Twenty-five years ago racism was manifest within the borders of Detroit. With the exodus of most whites and the emergence of African-American political leadership, the locus of racist attitudes and behavior changed to city versus suburb and city versus state. Some citizens of southeastern Michigan claim that the fiscal and social problems of the area are caused by Detroit. Blaming the victims is an easy way out of a difficult situation. Others claim city and suburbs share many things, such as a world financial crisis, local deindustrialization, and conservative, penurious state and federal social policies. Not using race as the key factor in complex economic and technological questions is the great challenge of the times. Can the citizens of southeastern Michigan resolve differences and promote understanding through dialogue? Is some form of metropolitanism the answer? If Detroit was a major player in an enlightened but enlarged political base while retaining its integrity and control of jurisdiction, could there be a revitalized regional political clout that would benefit all?

Detroiters also must come to terms with their democratic process and internal leadership. The great movement of the 1960s for civil rights and Black Power succeeded in establishing a progressive Black city administration that began in 1973 when Coleman Young took office as mayor. That administration inherited a pernicious local mix of deindustrialization and racism in an increasingly inhospitable state and national context. Little help was forthcoming from the increasingly conservative, racist, and self-indulgent national leadership that emerged in the mid 1970s. No ready-made blueprints for economic and urban survival were available to a somewhat inexperienced city administration. So the Young administration set upon a certain economic development course that has provoked a major internal debate, and no small amount of rancor, and this must be resolved before Detroit can embark upon a new course. Much of this debate concerns the extent and quality of democracy. Will the electorate mobilize for broad-based, open debate on priorities for the twenty-first century? Will the astute indigenous leadership spark a new political movement from the legions of displaced workers that increasingly populate the city?

The Detroit urban area holds thousands of sophisticated and experienced activists who are not burnt out or despondent, and they recognize in broad outline what needs to be done. They come from many backgrounds: union, civil rights, antiwar, community, feminism. They are organizers. They are women with family responsibilities. They are union leaders who struggle to represent their members. They are block club members who mobilize for survival. They are community organizers who toil to reconstruct neighborhoods. They are teachers and preachers and healers who strive to upgrade the quality of their constituents' lives. Will they all get together in common purpose to bring Detroit back?

We will find in the following testimonies that vast reserves of talent and energy still remain in Detroit. People are prepared to deal with the tough issues that confront them. They rose to the challenges they faced in previous generations of problems, and they keep alive the hope of this happening again.

PROLOGUE

Grace Lee Boggs and James Boggs

JAMES: We went to work in industry, and industry was a mystery to everybody, poor southern whites and Blacks, because we all had just been used to the mules and wagons and so forth. Suddenly, we're around all this machinery and intrigued by it. During World War II there was nothing you could buy but food—they wasn't making no cars or washing machines during the war—a lot of people saved up some money. So when the war was over, every Pole, Italian, Irish, Black, Belgian, Yugoslavian, Romanian, Bulgarian, which we had all around here at that time, they all bought them a little shack. Detroit became one of the largest homeowner cities north of the Mason-Dixon line. We had more homes owned by individuals than any city in the United States.

We were the Arsenal of Democracy. We made all the material for the war. The war was over and we went back to making automobiles. There was a pent-up demand for automobiles. That boom lasted up to round about '56. We still didn't find out nothing about a serious long-range economy because we thought everything was going to continue. You still had the idea that any kid who did not go to high school, who dropped out, could always go out there and work at the factory. That lasted till '74 when there came a combination of automation and a changing composition of the auto industry. Detroit began to no longer be a place where anybody could get a job. That was the beginning of the end of the blue-collar worker making enough wages that they could afford to get married, buy a car, maybe a boat.

So since '74 there's been an accumulation of Blacks and poor whites who stand on the corner. All across Detroit now there are huge gangs standing on the corner with nothing to do. Looks kind of like the Depression of the '30s but it's not the same, because then there

Grace Lee Boggs and James Boggs are authors, study group leaders, and founders of many community organizations.

was nothing around. Now the stores are full of goods. Everything is there, except the means to get them. So, the deterioration of the industry and the deterioration of people took place side by side.

Strange what can happen in a culture. This was a work-ethic town. Work hard, go to work on a Monday morning, work hard till Friday, have a little boom on Friday to Saturday, and by one o'clock Sunday night until Friday the next week the town was back. But then the town shifted. All these people in the street. We now became a fast-food town, where people eat chicken and stuff like that.

GRACE: In the last forty years we've been developing both a consumer economy and a high-tech economy, both at home and in production. The result is that the kids no longer have chores to do around the home and the community. At the same time, the schools have become more and more abstract and separate from real life, and kids are forced to stay longer in school, presumably at some point to get a degree and get a high-tech kind of job. But everything productive and contributory to the society has been robbed from the kids. They really have become deprived and more and more powerless. They have become more and more separated from real life, and one of the things they do to compensate is become violent. When Paul Goodman wrote that book forty years ago, *Growing Up Absurd,* there was a playfulness about it. Today it's not playful any more. It's devastating. It's murderous.

JAMES: When I first came to Detroit, kids had chores to do. Because you didn't have refrigeration, you had to run back and forth to the store all day long. You had to wash and iron and scrub, dump the water pan from under the old icebox, dig the ashes out of the furnace, if you had a furnace. There was very little gap between living and going to school and everything else.

GRACE: There was a relationship between the things you were doing and the things you were learning. You were being raised. You weren't just being schooled, you were being educated by life. That's changed completely. Everyone is being sort of prepared for the information society. Being a contributor to production, to making things, to utilizing your head and your hands and your heart, all at the same time, is gone.

JAMES: That kind of work is hardly around. Lots of things we used to do at Chrysler when I was there are now being done in other countries and shipped back here to Chrysler. There really ain't no such thing as an American car. They're lying when they say that. Every car out there has got some parts made in Mexico and all through Asia. And something else is happening. When I came to Detroit, Ford Motor Company had an allegiance to the city. Ford no longer has any allegiance to Detroit. Nobody has no allegiance to nothing no more, because everything is transitory.

GRACE: Before they ran away, you could have a sort of Saul Alinsky type of organizing. The company was visible, it couldn't leave, and you could conceive of them as being capable of acceding to your demands. It was possible to think in terms of a different kind of struggle.

JAMES: The only thing you can struggle with like that today is the gas company, the telephone company, and the water board because they depend on the customer. And the other big thing now is schools. Schools today are comparable to the labor struggle of the '30s. The biggest strikes we have today is at schools, because everybody thinks they need them damn schools.

GRACE: And the citizens can always threaten not to vote for the millage.

JAMES: I don't think you would have a struggle about a church any more because churches are just like fast-food places. Churches move everywhere. All churches are drive-in churches now and have no social impact on the community. We've been trying to carry on a struggle against the dope houses. We've got 2,300 official churches in the city of Detroit. Them little storefronts are not counted. So maybe we've got 3,000. We said if we could just get each church to declare a drug-free zone right around the church, we've have it made.

GRACE: If we only had 10 percent of them, we could clean up the crime situation in this city.

JAMES: The deterioration in the society is all through the culture, making inroads in all aspects of a society. Years ago, we used to laugh and say that the white folks ain't got no community. That's the thing we used to brag about, because we all got along down here. Everybody would share. And we used to say white folks don't do that. But when we started to break up, we broke up even worse than the whites broke up. We really fragmented.

GRACE: Much of Detroit was really a community that had been exported from the southern communities, which brought with them all the qualities of the agricultural society. Whole communities, for example, came from Marian Junction, Alabama, where Jimmy was born, and they all lived around here. You could throw a stone in any direction in this area and hit a Chrysler worker and somebody who had come from Selma or Marian Junction. It was like an extended family.

11

JAMES: And that same thing was true with the Irish, who were over on the west side down around Briggs Stadium. The Polish. The oldest community that's left in Detroit now, that *is* a community, that has a sense of community, is Hamtramck.

Up until the late '50s, the bulk of Detroit's Black population was on the east side, with a very small colony on the west side. With the coming of the expressways and the going out from the city of lots of the whites, which made room for lots of Blacks, the Black population shifted to the west side. You have only about 90,000 on the east side now and probably 700,000 on the west side. The largest Black ghetto in the world now is probably right here on the west side of Detroit. Some of those kids out there have never seen a white person. It's six, seven miles deep of just Black folks. In a sense, reverse segregation took place in that movement, and a change in the community relationship took place. As people went to the west side, they lost all the continuity they'd had for years with each other on the east side.

GRACE: We are urgently in need of community for all sorts of reasons. For our psychological development, for our spiritual development, for our physical and mental health. Community is probably the most precious aspect of a human being, and we've lost it. So the question becomes: How do we create it on the basis of what is new? What changes do we have to make in order to create it, because we can't live without it? Community relationships are absolutely essential to an aging population. Community is absolutely essential to young people. How else shall they learn social responsibility except through a community? A community is absolutely critical to infants. Community is absolutely essential for elementary security and safety.

JAMES: When I came to Detroit, every fool in this town, except probably 10,000 or 20,000, was riding a streetcar. Even if you had a car, you left your car at home all week and rode the streetcar to Chrysler or Dodge because it wasn't but seven cents. You could walk out on the street at midnight and they'd be thousands of people on the streets going to and from work. You go out there after eight o'clock now, ain't nobody on the street because everybody's scared to be on the street. We're in fear.

Our presidents and senators in Washington are scared to walk down Pennsylvania Avenue in Washington. Nobody walks the streets. They ride limousines with chauffeurs and armed guards. In the poor community, they ain't got the armed guards, so they just don't go out on the street at all. Old folks sitting behind barred-up doors everywhere. There is not a single house in Detroit or any major city that hasn't been robbed at least once. Most of them robbed twice. So we're at a threshold where we have crossed over the boundary of where human relations was a natural thing, where survival was a commonality among human beings.

When I came to Detroit, I'd walk down the street and wonder, how come folks don't speak to you? I'd been used to saying good morning to everybody I'd meet, and folks here was looking at me like I was a damn fool. You go down the street now and say good morning, and folks think you're crazy.

GRACE: I'm a city person and Jimmy comes from the country. We do a lot of joking about this business that you could take somebody out of the country but you can't take the country out of a person. City people, I have discovered, think that there's something wrong in being involved in other people's business. Country people believe that you *should* be involved in other people's business. That's part of being civil and being civilized. Jimmy's always looking out the window, worrying what this person and that person or the other person is doing. Before crime got so bad, I used to think, why are you being so nosy? But since crime has gotten so bad, I realize how important that is to a civilized society. That people *should* be nosy.

13

JAMES: When I grew up, the reason I didn't steal wasn't because there was police around, 'cause there wasn't no police around. I didn't steal because I didn't want the neighbors to know I would steal. The conscience of the community was your policeman. Now, when you get in the city, because everybody don't have nothing to do with nobody's business, everybody, therefore, can do anything and there's nobody to chastise them. There's no discipline on you.

The alienation took place in the way we live, in production, the way we related to each other. Then as we got all of these refrigerators, those electric gadgets, I don't need the neighbors next door for nothing. I got my own TV, my own movies. I've got my own icebox. I don't have to borrow nothing from them. Now you can't borrow nothing from your neighbors because they don't relate to each other.

This is the thing that bothers me about the emphasis we put on school. I always say that school is where you learn a certain skill, but nowadays people think school is where you learn sense. Sense was certain things we used to be taught in the home. There is no place in our so-called educational system now where you learn common sense.

GRACE: Sense comes from the commonality. That's why it's called common sense. Our educational system has been developed in order to enable individuals to become successful, become upwardly mobile and leave the community. The result is that the community becomes devastated. The American dream, if not completely dead, certainly needs to be reexamined.

Detroit is such a glaring example of the disintegration of a society—politically, economically, socially, spiritually—that has been based upon the dynamics of industry, an industrial civilization. But we also have the opportunity here to create another civilization. That's our challenge. Detroit, we feel, has been a pioneer in the past. It pioneered in the struggle for the dignity of labor. It pioneered mass production. It was one of the pioneers in the creation of Black political power. Now we feel it can become a pioneer in the creation of community which is so desperately needed.

JAMES: But that community is going to have to take some of the facets that are needed in the community deeper than ever before. From the early beginning of the cities, going back hundreds of years, people have always come to the cities where there were all the things they couldn't find in the rural areas. All the ingredients were there, but somebody else was supplying the economic aspect of it. Then the social aspect of it got shaken or lost by the economic aspect.

Historically, most people have worked for somebody else. Detroit is one of those towns where people worked it for somebody, because we had a large enough industry for the people to work for somebody. When you're in agriculture, in a sense everybody's working for themselves. Even if they're renting the property or sharecropping, they're still working for themselves. But when you started working for a private corporation and a big corporation, you get the idea that you're going to forever work for somebody. Today, I would say, 90 percent of the people who go to college intend to work for somebody.

GRACE: I remember when the Ford Rouge plant employed 120,000.

JAMES: Then it came down to 85,000. Ain't but 22,000 working there now. And thousands worked at the big steel mills here. You go to Buffalo and see that big Bethlehem plant. You know who took it over? Seagulls. They sleep in it. You go to St. Paul, Minnesota, and Duluth, and seagulls took over all those big steel mills. What I'm trying to say is, there is no more big industry where people can work for somebody. So now we've got to think, how do people make a living? We're not geared up for that. The educational system is still geared up to train somebody to work for somebody else.

GRACE: Do you know the book by Alvin Toffler called *The Third Wave?* Essentially, what he says is that the first wave was agricultural society, the second wave was industrial society, and now we're coming to the end of industrial civilization and we have to create something new. That's the challenge that faces us here in Detroit. That's what makes us feel that we are present at the creation of something new.

Three years ago, [mayor] Coleman Young, who has been faced with this contradiction ever since he took office and has been trying to resolve it by wooing big corporations to come back with tax abatements, discovered that that wasn't working well, and he decided that casino gambling is what was needed and that it would create 50,000 jobs. We became part of a struggle against this, among other reasons because we saw casino gambling as contrary to the whole work ethic. The kinds of jobs that were going to be offered were jobs that would actually result in the increasing disintegration of our society. It would actually lead to the spiritual and psychological devastation of the community, as it has in Atlantic City.

While we were carrying on this struggle, Coleman said, "What is your alternative?" We thought that was a legitimate question, and we have been trying to pursue that ever since. We're now working to plan a conference that will begin to project a vision for the rebuilding, the revitalization of our city on new foundations. The group that is organizing these meetings to plan the conference is Detroiters Uniting, a coalition of community groups, clergy, professional people, and blue- and white-collar workers who were confronted with this question during the struggle against casino gambling which they spearheaded. They're a very diverse group. They represent the social and ethnic diversity of the city of Detroit, and they are a very free-flowing group, with very diverse views, socially, politically, and ethnically.

We haven't gotten down to the nuts and bolts yet, but we're trying to involve as many people as possible in the planning, because we're sure that it's something that's so significant, such a historic milestone, that it can't be a narrow thing. Right now we're holding monthly meetings. We've created task forces on education, economics, transportation, health, art and culture, on a whole lot of things, to involve people in exploring what the alternative would be.

We're responding to the historical questions that are on everybody's mind: What is the purpose of cities? What is the purpose of people when industry no longer needs them?

JAMES: What a difficult time we're going to have. It ain't going to be easy. We've got problems confronting us now like we've never had before. How do you create an economy with people who aren't just going to come from one aspect and move into another? Because this other one has got to be created. How do you create a new kind of

15

educational system when people are still talking about how we have to make this one more accountable? It's not a question of this one being more accountable. This one doesn't fit in with what we have to do at this particular stage.

GRACE: The crime and the violence that we're seeing in our cities today, particularly on the part of the young, is sort of a cry of crisis, a warning that we have to begin thinking differently. The multinational corporations couldn't care less. The people in government couldn't care less, because our political leaders think of the economic system as the market, that it's magic. All they are interested in is commodity relations. They're not interested in relationships between people. They're not interested in what contributes to the growth and development of people.

JAMES: I think about these poor kids with this Gulf War. They saw that technical war. It's normal in the streets for kids to think they're going to get shot. The people who pressed those buttons and saw all those bombs falling, it was totally impersonal. We killed 87,000-some Iraqis and didn't even touch a one of them. It's like pressing buttons, killing folks, zap, zap. That's in our society now! I bet you in three months, every bit of that will be taking place back here on the streets. These kids are going to be even more unemotional about killing. My grandson got shot two years ago right in front of this house. He's over in the Gulf now. He's got a bullet in his spine, and you know the army took him.

GRACE: This is such a dangerous situation. The arrogance that people are bringing back from the success of high-tech weapons in the Gulf, and the belief that military solutions are a solution.

JAMES: It's devastating. This fits in with what we say that there's got to be some new people. And that fits in with our concept of recivilization. A lot of folks get mad when we use that term, because they want to assume that they're already highly civilized. Everybody thinks they're civilized, and I ask myself, how do you think you're civilized when you're doing all of these things to each other? This can't be civilization. There was a time when I used to think in the United States that each year we were getting a little progressively better. I don't think that at all now.

GRACE: When we begin to project a vision to rebuild Detroit and to recivilize Detroit, we also have to be thinking coherently. Some of the questions that our task forces are facing are: How do we change people as well as institutions? How do we create producers and not just consumers and clients? How do we empower people, especially young people and women whose energy is so needed now? How do we foster civic pride, a sense that I want to live in Detroit? How do we increase participation in decision making and therefore expand democracy? How do we redevelop our area in ways that are ecologically prudent? How do we create cooperation and connection among people?

In the nineteenth century, there was a real conflict between Marx and Proudhon, which actually has been outlined by Martin Buber in his book, *Ways to Utopia*. There's a concept that first you take political power and then you transform the society. Then there's a concept that you begin by transforming society, and as people become transformed, they are able to take power. That concept of political revolution—taking power and then trying to change the people—has been tried for the last seventy years. Lenin tried very hard to do that. He projected a cultural revolution following the political revolution. And we've seen what difficulties the Soviet Union has had in that respect.

17

On the other hand, the concept of creating a cultural revolution among the people which empowers them and makes them able to make good use of power is one that is just beginning to emerge. We are 200 years from the French Revolution, which opened up a huge struggle for rights, for equality, for liberty, and also for fraternity, and we're just beginning to tackle the question of fraternity. You can only begin to tackle questions like this when necessity forces you to. That's where we are today.

JAMES: We are responding to a crisis in the society. We think that Detroit, which advanced so far at one period, is now a reflection of that crisis. We are also aware that every city east of the Mississippi River is in a crisis because they represent the old industrial society.

GRACE: Up to this time, working people, grassroots people, have pretty much depended on the industrialists, the big political leaders and so forth, to come forward with plans for a city. Now for the first time in a working-class city like Detroit, we find people like Jimmy and people from the community like Dorothy Garner, the head of WEPROS [We the People Reclaiming Our Streets], putting forward ideas for creating a new kind of city that's going to be both productive and loving. So we're getting ideas for the building of cities from the bottom, which has never happened before. And it's very exciting.

JAMES: They never thought they'd have to do that before, because up until now, it would take care of itself. We always thought the corporations would supply the jobs. We didn't have to worry about the community because it was a trickle-down thing. If everybody was working, there would be enough taxes paid to pay for the schools, and there would be some houses built, and so forth. People didn't need to talk about the community because the community was a given. Suddenly, ain't nobody working, ain't nobody taking care of housing and here all the houses are collapsing all around us. We ain't working for Ford now so we ain't building houses now. We ain't doing nothing because we ain't working for Ford. The last hope was the government, and the government didn't come through. All levels of government are in crisis themselves, because they were also depending on those industries.

Some in the '60s used to call Detroit the revolutionary capital of the United States.

GRACE: Yes, some gave the impression that we were on the threshold of a revolution here in Detroit. Ken Cockrel [prominent activist attorney] died of a massive heart attack nearly two years ago. He was only fifty. The young people who were twenty-two in 1962 are today fifty years old. Twenty-eight years have elapsed. Look at the difference between their time and our time. A lot of these young people joined the movement because they wanted the opportunities for upward mobility within the mainstream. They joined the civil rights movement and even the Black Power movement because they saw Black people in the place of white people or Black people alongside of white people leading this country. None of us had an idea in 1962 that the system itself was falling apart. It was an expanding economy then.

I have learned over the years that there are very few people who can move from one stage into the next. What happens is that the strategies, the concepts, the ideas that you develop to try to resolve a contradiction within a particular period become fixed concepts which are sort of a vise around your mind and you are locked into them. Actually, ideas and strategies of the past have a tendency to turn into their opposite because history changes. What you struggle for at a particular period, insofar as you achieve something, actually changes the objective reality and you have to change along with it.

JAMES: I spanned the labor movement too. I'm everything the United States has ever been. I was in agriculture, industrialization, and automation. I think, however, it is very difficult for a lot of people to make the transition. The society that they're rebelling against wants to incorporate as many of them as possible. So many people who start out with lots of revolutionary fervor, get it eaten up by being accepted in.

A lot of the people who were very progressive in the '60s have gotten locked in the '60s and haven't been able to move out. A lot of

Blacks, in particular, got locked in because they got hooked on racism. Now, racism is just as bad in the United States as it's ever been, but they got hooked on the concept that the struggle is about racism. There ain't no sense of class in them at all.

GRACE: They also got locked into the concept of power as something that you take, then you can do a whole lot of things. We did achieve Black political power. But what happened when we'd achieved it? How do we evaluate that? Another thing which is very important is that the Black movement is one of the things that brought into being the women's movement, the environmental movement, and all of the other movements. How do you begin dealing with this new reality?

The quotation I use very often is the one from Frantz Fanon's *The Wretched of the Earth*, where he says, "Each generation coming out of obscurity must define its destiny and fulfill or betray it." That concept of historical emergence is very difficult to grasp, and I think we're very lucky that we have lived through so many movements and understood that what was germane, important and significant at one stage, does not remain that at another stage.

JAMES: And in that other stage you may have a down period. We've been in a down period for the last 10 to 12 years. There has not been a viable movement that graduated, escalated right out of one into another one. That means the leap is going to have to be so great because we didn't progressively keep moving as new contradictions emerged, even when we were winning. I don't know now whether each generation must come out of obscurity to do something. That generation may be so shattered as of now. We lost nearly a generation of young Blacks. They're either in jail or dead. And we lost a lot of whites too.

GRACE: It's very hard for our society, which is so youth oriented and so patriarchal, to accept the possibility that the movement for the next period is going to be inspired and triggered by older Blacks, particularly older Black women. Yet that's one of the things I see emerging. There is such a sexism in the Black movement, and such a youth orientation in this country, Black or white. I don't mean we're not going to need everybody, but it's so difficult for young people, deprived as they have been during this last period of life experiences.

I want to go back to what I was saying earlier about where the catalyst can come. I see 1986–87 as a turning point, because in 1986, 43 kids were killed in the city in street violence; 365 were shot, many of them very seriously. Out of that devastation came a group known as SOSAD, Save Our Sons and Daughters, which was founded by a woman, Clementine Barfield, who was at that time thirty-six years old, with four children, who decided that what we needed to do was to go beyond mourning and to begin questioning the values of our society which lead our kids to kill each other over expensive gym shoes and silk shirts, and to begin to struggle for positive change. That was a turning point. I'm involved as the editor of the SOSAD newsletter.

A couple of years after that, Dorothy Garner, the head of WEPROS, began to stand up to the dope dealers in her community and began a project of marching against crack houses to break the cycle of fear in our communities and to reclaim our streets. Both of these women were born in the South. Both of them have some idea of what a movement needs to do that enables people to express in action the yearnings and hopes that they cannot yet express in words. We're beginning to create a movement in Detroit.

Is there any ideology that may attach itself to such a movement?

JAMES: I doubt it very much, but I think what will happen is that there will be new ideologies. The ideology we're going to need for the twenty-first century is going to have to be created. We can't borrow from past ones, because the past ones were in relationship to a certain stage of society.

GRACE: When you come toward the building of movements as a young person, which is the way I came, you proceed from ideology a great deal. When you're proceeding from your life experience, you arrive at ideas in a different way. You begin to share ideas and become involved in dialogue and discussion. And I see people doing that as they're trying to build. They don't get it out of books; they get it out of life and out of the urgency of their life situations.

JAMES: I think there is a different kind of oppression in the country today that provokes people to do things than there was in other years. Used to be maybe just plain old belly hungry, which is what got the unions in the '30s. Naked bread and meat. Now bread and meat did not start the Black movement. Everybody was eating pretty good. In fact, the Black movement came in probably the most prosperous period in the United States. In the '50s and '60s, every plant was working, was nobody unemployed, anybody could get a job. Guys used to sit around and say, "Hell, I don't want that damn job working at the factory." Now we've got probably 30 million or so out there who are oppressed and they ain't done a damn thing.

Most of the people who are beginning to revolt now are revolting on different levels than before. I think the revolt is going to come from the fragmentation, the alienation, the lack of any sense of any place in a society, the gross individualism that is in the society, the dog-eat-dog mentality. I think more is going to come from that than from sheer hunger.

Now it can go certain ways even with that. Some people, because of their physical insecurity, become fascist-like, go get them a machine gun. Lots of whites are doing that, and quite a few Blacks too. We've got more guns here than they probably had in Iraq. Right here in my community, there's at least ten Uzis within six blocks of me. I know the guys. Even got some friends who got an Uzi. We're armed to the teeth and we ain't doing nothing but shooting each other. Now that can drive people either more inwardly and turn them reactionary or fascist inclined, or it can make them mobilized because of that. That's why I say this movement is going to be very hard to see at the beginning because it's going to take place as people try to regain some kind of sense of humanity in a very inhumane situation. It ain't going to come from a big strike. Ain't going to be no big strike. Ain't no place for a big strike to take place no more hardly.

21

Part 1   *Organizing for Survival at the Grassroots*

LIKE OTHER INDUSTRIAL CITIES, Detroit is a place of historic communities where ethnic, religious, and other factors continue to shape identity and politics. Community- and church-based associations can be strong points of political pressure and catalysts of survival efforts. They can form a democratic base of citizen involvement.

Detroit's structure of community organizations is very elaborate and complex, though it is pitifully underfunded and understaffed. Theoretically, one million people have access to a neighborhood organizing vehicle. There is great political potential in such a widespread structure. This fact is not missed by many of today's community organizers.

Secular and religious organizations with economic development initiatives have located small amounts of investment capital from government grants and private sources. A few successful housing, manufacturing, and commercial projects have provided some jobs and homes for neighborhood people. These emerging operations are tiny but they are staffed with people who are fairly sophisticated in business and finance and they have the latest communications and data processing equipment. This modest success gives organizers hope that a phoenix is beginning to arise from the ashes.

Community-based organizations in Detroit have the potential to fashion a new order of democracy that might go beyond the official idea of "maximum feasible participation" that was popular in the 1960s. Organizing theory and methods have not changed since then. Communities still must set goals and objectives to meet their needs. They must formulate a tactical and strategic operating plan. They must develop leadership and an organizational structure. They must garner resources. What *has* changed, compared to the 1960s, is a greatly deteriorated urban condition. To some outsiders or cynical insiders, this is a condition of hopelessness. To most community organizers, it is the foundation for a solid grassroots movement that may be a springboard into the future.

Not a large band of activists for the sixth largest American city, Detroit's grassroots organizers make up in energy and commitment what they lack in numbers. While some organizers are paid staffers with professional degrees, most are neighborhood leaders who have sharpened their talents in past struggles. Many are sophisticated in practical politics and economics. They understand power and capital, so the most energetic are beginning to stand for public office and form coalitions with other communities.

These organizers have a deep empathy and respect for their constituents and neighbors. They work in poverty-stricken neighborhoods that overflow with the human pathologies brought on by industrial abandonment. They work in perplexed middle-class communities where such issues as school quality, racial balance, and security abound. They have a deep affection for the city; they think of it as a loved one who has become sick and needs care and rehabilitation.

The testimonies in this section are from dedicated professional organizers. Some work for multiservice organizations with racial, ethnic, or religious constituencies. Others serve the specific needs of people without homes or who are underhoused or underemployed. Some reflect religious beliefs in their work. Others have political agendas. They are African-American, Arab-American, Mexican-American, Anglo-American. They are female and male. They come to their tasks from vastly differing backgrounds. All do not agree on ideology or strategy, but they all agree on the importance of their work. They are upbeat and dedicated to the core. They work long and hard hours. They realize the great difficulty of building up Detroit from the grassroots, but they know that this is the route that must be taken, and they are in it for the long haul.

Ishmael Ahmed

My father was an Egyptian immigrant who had been a seaman in the Merchant Marines during World War II. He used to distribute Arabic movies; in fact, that's what brought him to Detroit. He started showing Arabic movies here. He had a small record store in Greektown. My mother is third-generation Lebanese. Her family homesteaded in South Dakota in the mid-1800s, probably the first Arab family there. By the time I was six, my mother had remarried a man from Yemen who worked in the Ford plants. My grandfather had worked in the foundry at the Ford Rouge plant. I grew up here in southeast Dearborn and southwest Detroit. My early teen years I was part of a group of young kids from Yemen and Lebanon and southern white kids, all hanging out together.

I wasn't doing particularly great at school, so I moved to Brooklyn, New York, and stayed with my grandmother, who was kind of the mother of the Arab community. She introduced me to Ahmad Jamal, the jazz musician, Malcolm X, and some other people. She had been part of a larger group. I learned a lot from her about my background. She was like the Arabic version of a griot, a musical storyteller for a tribe. She had memorized history going back a thousand years. We'd talk about tribal battles and the warrior history of my family, why people came here, what life was like in South Dakota in the 1800s, how a family helps other families to survive, what things were important.

I joined the Merchant Marines and shipped out. My first trip was to Africa. From my travels in the Third World, I kind of knew that there were poor people and rich people, and the rich people told poor people what to do. There was the same pattern in every country. There was the government house, a nice, wonderful place, and it was surrounded by a ghetto. You saw signs like "U.S. Rubber" or some British this or that, and there was the army. Mostly they were armies of the people in the country, but they were poised against the people. Colonialism or neocolonialism is the word.

Then I came back here and went to Henry Ford Community College for about one year until I got drafted in 1969 during the Vietnam War. After boot camp I ran afoul over an incident of some guy who had punched an officer. They said I didn't have the right mentality toward it. Then I got shipped out. I was supposed to go to Vietnam, but went instead to Korea because my brothers already were in Vietnam.

Ishmael Ahmed is the director of the Arab Community Center for Economic and Social Services (ACCESS) in Dearborn, Michigan.

Korea was supposed to be a quiet place, but there was shooting going on and sabotage and all that kind of stuff. I again ran afoul of folks, having to do with a problem of Korean workers who did all of the work on the base. I'd gotten upset about it, and a lot of pressure got put on me. I kind of dropped out, bided my time quietly, read books. I learned a lot from the army.

The city of Dearborn had started an urban renewal project and had already torn down 500 houses. My parent's house was to be included. *They* were going to tear down my home. Somehow to me all of this was one "they," the powers-that-be. I thought, "they" sent you to Korea; "they" control those countries; and now "they" were tearing down my home. And here it was the city of Dearborn and the Ford Motor Company.

28

I became active in the Southeast Dearborn Community Council. Basically, they'd messed with the wrong people. A lot of the older workers here were people who had organized the union—old Italian anarchists and Marxists—and a lot of people in the neighborhood who had nothing but their homes. There were demonstrations and picket lines. We took the city of Dearborn to court and the city was found guilty on twenty-nine counts of illegal procedure. There was a court injunction.

During the urban renewal fight I met some radicals in West Dearborn. I met my wife there too. They had started a small place called the People's Exchange across from the Dearborn City Hall. I got to know the people and respected them all: the White Panther Party, Black Panther Party, people from SDS [Students for a Democratic Society] who had moved down from Ann Arbor. There was also a big change happening in me. I began to feel that I could walk down the street in this neighborhood and everybody knew me. I was coming here every night to eat, because I didn't care as much for other food as I did for Arabic food. I just felt that this was my home. And that's when we started ACCESS.

I ran into a guy named Nabeel Abraham who was real active on Palestinian questions. He said, "You know, I saw you putting out an underground paper. You talk about all this other stuff, what about the struggles of Arab people?" He gave me a bunch of stuff to read, mainly about the Palestinian question. I began dividing my time between activity in the neighborhood and justice for the Arab world.

Then I met some folks who suggested that I go to Cuba. So I went to Cuba and cut sugar cane. That was my first real look at socialism as a possibility. I was involved in a lot of the antiwar stuff and also a lot of Marxist groups. I guess I was looking for a lot of different answers to how to change things in a big way.

I also went back to work in the factories to get through school, and began working with Arab workers. In 1973, I was the chairman of the Arab Workers Caucus that had groups in fifteen plants. We put forward an agenda of workers' rights, but brought to it our own agenda around the Middle East. The UAW had tremendous holdings of Israeli bonds. We led demonstrations and wildcat strikes in different plants and actually shut down parts of different plants. We led a demonstration of 2,000 workers against Leonard Woodcock [UAW president], who was receiving a humanitarian award at the B'nai B'rith dinner. Most of the unions divested themselves of Israeli bonds.

During those years in the plants, I worked in this neighborhood and with a lot of Marxist groups. But there was a parting of the way at a certain point. This was a very rhetorical time among the left. I would work in the community and see that talking talk about Soviet revisionism didn't make sense. That's the last thing on people's minds. The main difference I had with a lot of the left people was that they called community work reformist. And to me it was the only thing that was real in my life.

So I resigned from the plant and began writing grants for AC-CESS. I wanted to help develop it into a community-based organization that not only provided services but took on social issues and built allegiances with other, mainly minorities, working-class folks. That's what I've been doing for the last ten years. We tried to carve out a "free area," like drug-free zones, where people feel safe, where they feel they can contribute and support each other and get things done.

There are 60,000 Arab speakers within five miles of this center. In Dearborn 20 percent of the adults and 40 percent of the children are Arabic. There are 200,000 in the Detroit area. We're working with a lot of different people in a lot of different ways, trying to preserve art and culture in our community, and through that preserving some stuff about what we're about.

We have a million-and-a-half-dollar budget. We have maybe fifty programs, some major, some real small. In one program alone, we translate 7,000 documents a year.

The Arab-American is overwhelmingly working class, probably about 140,000 of the folks in the Detroit area. In this community of 60,000, we know that there's never less than 30 percent unemployment. There's a 38.5 per 1,000 infant mortality rate. Six out of ten people have been here less than ten years. Most were immigrants with families here. The people coming here are essentially refugees, though they don't have refugee status.

ACCESS has thirty board members who come from just about every Arab group in the community: mosques, fraternal organizations, activist groups in the neighborhood. We have hundreds of regular volunteers. We have food, shelter, and clothing programs that serve about 17,000 people a year, half Arab and half non-Arab. Then we have clinical and other programs—that's another 22,000 families.

One-third of the adults in this community don't speak English, and two-thirds don't read and write English. We talked to people in the Dearborn schools and we came up with a joint program that provided day care for the women and some women-only classes for women who don't want to go to school with men. We got them to hire Arabic bilingual aides—women already respected and playing a leadership role. We now have over 250 people a day in English classes in this building.

People feel that they have a history and a culture worth preserving, and they'll fight to do that. Another thing across the board is the sense that they don't have political power at all in America. Most Arab-Americans believe that the whole society basically has no real idea of who Arab-Americans are. The word is racism, basically. They are willing to organize and fight against that.

We saw that in Dearborn the schools were kind of gerrymandered. You had all of the Arab kids in the east side of town and not enough schools for them, and the west side was relatively empty. So they started busing our kids westward. Well, that works a little bit, but how young do you want to go? The people in the neighborhood felt that kids shouldn't be bused at least before sixth grade. So we decided to support a bond issue that wasn't winnable. We turned out our people and won a $96 million bond. That's the biggest capital bond in the history of the state of Michigan. Almost all of that will go into the east end and benefit Arab kids.

The biggest activity we were involved in was the Jesse Jackson campaign. We provided 12 percent of his state vote, and just about all of the initial money when he came into the city. In response, he gave us a national forum to raise the Middle Eastern question. I was on the national platform committee of the Democratic Party and hammered out the position on Lebanon.

There is tremendous diversity in Detroit, so we wanted to try to see how we could create a positive model that gave us more interaction on a cultural level. So we started sponsoring people from around the world coming in to play music or to do dance. We did that with some Algerian musicians, and got a group of reggae Caribbean-African musicians out of the Detroit area to work with them. We got New Detroit [an elite-based planning and funding organization] to fund a series of traditional presentations, with people from the African-American, Asian, Hispanic and Middle Eastern community each do-

30

ing a presentation together. It might be dance this time, clothing next time, drum-based things the next time.

As a result of all that, we put together a group in Detroit called Earth Island Orchestra, which includes fifteen of the best ethnic musicians in the city all playing together. They now have a CD, and they're playing major venues in Detroit. They play a mix of jazz, rock, Arabic music; it's a synthesis of all of them. And sometimes they play each other's music. It's an amazing thing.

Casa de Unidad is an arts organization that's based in the people of the neighborhood and the Hispanic culture. Every year they have a big event called Unity in the Community that draws all of the groups in the neighborhood together. They put out their tables, they have music, and they talk and work together. They have their own print shops that they've developed. They've taught people how to do photography and a bunch of things in their own neighborhood.

And I'm seeing some other interesting things in Detroit too that we're trying to hook up with. A lot of "old" activists are still activists, but they've gone back into their communities. We're sharing things concretely together and trying to fuse our work. We're not worried about identity as much as we are trying to get things done.

You have an upbeat point of view.

That got shook up a little while ago. We really had begun to feel that we had carved out something free in this community. People leave their doors open in this neighborhood, and in the center we did that too in the evening. We had a children's art show about a month ago, and one of the ladies stayed to clean up. Some people broke in, beat her to death, and set this place on fire. This was the third time. The first time we had a fire, we set up a big tent and we functioned until we were able to rebuild. The other time, we set up a trailer for a year because this building was burned to a hulk. The last two fires, we have no idea who did them or why.

There are always two possible explanations. One, it's just somebody who's crazy or malicious. Then there's the view . . . we do get a lot of hate mail, hate phone calls, that are outrightly racist or linked to the question of the Middle East. We're obviously the most public, vulnerable, Middle Eastern group. You can find us easily.

During this past Gulf crisis, it must have been especially tough.

We were the focus of response to the Gulf War. We opposed the Gulf War. We oppose all wars other than those of people protecting themselves or fighting against colonialism. It's tough to be a war minority, to be the people who are already painted as the enemy. We couldn't wrap ourselves in the American flag, although a lot of people here think of themselves as Americans. There would be a hundred reporters from all over the world all during the war. They wanted us to tell them what we thought. But we don't speak for all Arab people.

But people came out of the woodwork in this city to support us. We had hundreds of phone calls from churches and progressive groups. The African-American community in particular was good. A lot of the Black church leaders helped organize their churches to support us. We went on WGPR-TV and talked about feelings about the war, so we didn't have to hide what we believed.

The Asian-American community came out opposing some attempts in Congress to pull out of the hat the old concentration camps that were being talked about. There had been a plan on the map for "holding areas" for people from the Middle East, and to bring back some laws that would deal very severely with people who don't have citizenship here

Let's be real. America is diversifying very quickly in terms of ethnicity. Ethnicity is a good thing because it's something to hold on to and strengthen yourself with. Part of the strategy here is to build those relationships so we don't end up being played off against each other as resources become less.

Rosa Sims

I'm a native Detroiter. My parents were both from the South. Of all the places I've visited, I prefer to be in Detroit because of the resilience of the people, the kindness, the willingness to work together. It has some small-town features, the way people will open their arms and work with you. In the past it's had a very strong sense of community. I want *that* to be a part of my life wherever I live. I have a dedication and commitment to the city.

I owe a lot to my father. He was active in the community and was an officer in the block club. I remember the block club having clean-up and tree-planting projects, and getting together to help a neighbor to repair their house. My father was a contractor, so he would bring his dump trucks to help with major projects. My mother worked midnights, so he babysat by taking me to the block club meetings. He would sit me in the corner and say, "Go over there and take notes."

Rosa Sims is executive director of United Street Networking and Planning: Building a Community (U-Snap-Bac), a nonprofit consortium of community-based organizations located on Detroit's east side.

When we got home he would ask me what they said. So I had to pay attention at the meetings.

Then I got directly involved in community work. I was president of the junior block club. At about age eighteen my community work was through the church. In 1980, when I was twenty-one, the *Chronicle* newspaper was having an annual Woman-of-the-Year award. A friend nominated me and I came in second.

I've lived on the east side all my life. Sometimes I take a trip down memory lane with friends. We talk about going to Mack or Harper or Van Dyke where the streets were lined with stores. You could buy whatever you needed right there: clothing, furniture, everything. There were pharmacies and shows in the neighborhood. There was a sense of community. On a Saturday you would see all of your neigh- **33** bors. When we were children we looked forward to the time when we were old enough to walk up there by ourselves. I remember going downtown as a little girl with my mother. It was so special. She would dress me up like we were going to church.

It's changed so much. It's been very difficult for me to adjust to not being able to find whatever products and services that I need at the corner. I have to drive ten to thirty miles before I can find a store that has what I need. And taking my money out of the community and knowing that it's not helping Detroit and not going to produce any jobs . . .

When it first started happening I refused to shop any place outside of Detroit. Then it became very apparent that if I was going to have anything I was going to *have* to shop outside of Detroit. Today I usually shop at Eastland and the Grosse Point area. In the city limits there's not a Penney's, a Hudson's, a Winkleman's.

It's been depressing, demoralizing. The decay is a way of getting at the individual's spirit. The more you look at it, the worse you feel about where you live, the community, your neighbors. You even sometimes question the choices *you* make. Does it make sense to stay in a city that does not offer me any of the basic things that I need? And it hurts a great deal.

It probably hurts me more than my children because this is all they know. I've got a son who's twenty-one and a daughter who's nineteen. When you get grown and graduate from school, the answer is just move out. It's easy for them. It's not that simple for me. If I left here it would be like giving up. I would be saying there is no hope and nothing I have done has meant anything. Leaving Detroit would be tantamount to saying my whole life has been in vain. It's not even an option.

My daughter is in college. This past summer she did computer training for the staff here. She has long understood how much this work means to me, but she began to feel the camaraderie and closeness the staff has when she was here. She said, "Yeah, this could sort of wear on you." Who knows, she might come back here and work.

People in Detroit have a resilience and "never say die" attitude that I have not found in any other city. In the face of every problem we have, they still want to work together to bring about change. There are a lot of community activists. It's unfortunate that they get so little attention or applause. You don't have to go and look for the drug addicts or dope dealers, but you almost have to seek out the activists. We're all so busy.

The directors of agencies like mine have a group called Save Our Spirit [SOS] that comes together to work on block grant issues. We try to make sure that the grants are equitable and that the older neighborhoods get their fair share. We all take turns trying to schedule meetings. To get SOS meetings together is a tough job. Who do I call first to see if their calendar is free? You get a good date, and you get halfway down your list. All of a sudden that date's no good because the next fifteen people can't be there, so you have to go back up and start again. It's crazy. But somehow, we all manage to do the one more thing.

A couple years ago, SOS was involved in getting a city charter amendment passed to reduce the number of City Council votes from seven to six for a budget veto. About twenty of us worked on that campaign. We pulled in some volunteers. We had to do the analysis of what polls we needed to cover, get out the literature, work the polls. When I think about some of the things the handful of us have done, it's been pretty phenomenal.

Our job at U-Snap-Bac is to be responsive to the residents and businesses in this community. They're our bosses. Our primary focus is housing and business. If you're going to have housing, you've got to have shops and businesses that folks can go to. That's what makes a community.

We don't directly get involved in issues with the public school system. But if a block club called us and said, "There are problems in a nearby school that we want to address, can you work with us?" we would go and sit with them and advise them on what they needed to do. But *we* wouldn't do it, the block club would. We're developing them as leaders. We would help facilitate them in meeting with the principal or school board to get the issues addressed. Once we leave that block club, we're to leave them stronger than we found them. If an agency has a lot of services, it's a clear indication that the residents of a community are not in control. The residents should hire individuals and decide what services are going to be provided.

The job needed to be done in Detroit, and other cities like Detroit, is one that can *only* be done by organizations like U-Snap-Bac. The top-down approach hasn't worked. In the heyday of top-down Detroit, the corporations were young. They were more committed to the United States, the state, the city. That's changed. Their commitment is to their stockholders, 100 percent. Communities can't survive with that. The commitment has got to be within the community where everyone who lives and works is involved in determining what the problems and solutions are.

We're just getting into business development. The welcome we've gotten from the businesses in the neighborhood has been phenomenal. Business startups are very difficult. In the next five years, if I could see two business startups I'd be happy. We will work with them to help bring together the capital and space they need, to help them select employees and get the technical skills they need.

In twenty years I'd like to say that U-Snap-Bac has a minimum of 250 units of housing. This won't be enough for the needs. There needs to be a lot more U-Snap-Bacs. I'm not into that territorial thing. If there's an organization that wants to join and work in this part of the community, great. I'll help you get started. The more the merrier. I want to see the job done.

People are going to have to get more creative. Resources are always going to be scarce. The question is, how creative can we become as citizens in spending those resources wisely and getting the biggest bang for our buck? As community organizations, that's how *we've* managed. We share like crazy. If one organization gets technical assistance, they'll bring that person in and then call all of us over for a meeting to get the same information.

I would not like to see any programs that are not in the control of the communities. We've learned in Detroit that we cannot sit back and wait and think that government has the answers and can solve the problems. We've found out that they don't know the solutions any more than we do, and probably not as well because we deal with them on a daily basis.

Paul Taylor, Jr.

I was born and bred in Detroit. Upon graduation from high school, I enrolled in Lawrence Institute of Technology in 1964. Out of 3,000 to 4,000 students at Lawrence Tech, less than 50 were Black. Coming off

Paul Taylor, Jr. is director of the Inner City Sub-Center, a youth-centered, culturally oriented, multipurpose agency that provides a variety of services for east siders.

the rebellion of '67 in Detroit, several of us decided that we needed to reevaluate what our aspirations were. I realized that an engineer was not where I wanted to be. I wanted to help my people. Racism was rampant. Police brutality in the Black community was the most obvious it could be. It was like living in a police state.

I got involved with the Association of Black Students at Wayne State. We wanted to take college students into the public schools and organize student-based organizations. We wanted to educate young people as to what their roots were, that we are African people and should be proud of it, that some of the inferiority complex that this society seems to want to heap upon us was all just a ploy to keep us underfoot. Persons who had gone to Africa showed their slides and pictures to the students to give them some real sense of what Africa was, and it definitely was not the Tarzan syndrome we had seen on TV. We initiated a Swahili class and taught them the rudiments of African language. We initiated programs in the schools like African Dress Day where we would wear dashikis and things that depicted our culture.

In 1969 we got a lot of publicity from the media. The contention was that it was the first time that Black students had declared a commitment to go back into the community from which they came to help those who were not as fortunate as they were. The Interfaith Action Council said to us that if we were interested in putting together a proposal to solicit funds for a community-based program that they would support it.

In June '69 we got a grant of $3,000 from United Community Service, which we used to open up our program in a storefront about three blocks from where we are now. That was more money than we ever had before. It still was no money to pay anybody, but it was enough to pay rent, get the lights and gas turned on, a telephone, buy a pool table and Ping-Pong table for the kids, and buy a few arts and crafts supplies. That first summer we had an overwhelming response; 200 to 300 children enrolled in our program. We were getting mainly Wayne State students to volunteer to work with the young people after school and on Saturdays. We parlayed the $3,000 into a much bigger program that gave us a track record.

So we developed a proposal for a more comprehensive program. Our aspiration was to have satellite community centers in four geographic areas of this city. That's how we came up with the name Inner City Sub-Center. Each would be multipurpose, comprehensive, community-based social service centers that would have programs for children through senior citizens. They would have as a backdrop cultural consciousness raising: pride, knowledge of one's history, and a self-help element that would say, We can, we must, and we will help ourselves. So we wrote a thick proposal asking for $4,000,000—$1,000,000 for each center. The Interfaith Action Council and the university wrote letters of endorsement. We took the letters and our multimillion package to New Detroit. They looked at it, fingered through it, and thought it was nice, I'm sure, but made it very clear that they didn't have $4,000,000 to support it. We needed to pare it down, and come back with something more realistic.

Finally, in September 1969, after several sessions with New Detroit, we were granted about $50,000 for one year, which was like a million to us. We were able to compensate ourselves with a little salary for our effort and to bring in some supplies and equipment. In addition to the cultural programming, we added recreational and educational components. We believed then, as we do now, that one needs to develop physically, mentally, culturally, and spiritually to become a complete and rounded person.

From 1970 to 1972 we continued to operate our programs, although we had no new grant money. Because we were still in college, the programs only operated from three to eight o'clock in the evening. In 1972 we went back to New Detroit and got a three-year grant for community development programming that would last until 1975. We knew our storefront facility was not large enough, so we sought another location in the same geographical area.

We found a location at 5457 Fisher Avenue near Gratiot. It was a school building near what was once a Lutheran church. The Lutherans had left and a Black congregation had moved in. The building was six times larger than the storefront. We added a senior citizens' program where we would have seniors come in every day for a hot meal. We provided referral services and senior day care under the city of Detroit Food and Friendship program. We got a grant from the state of Michigan to provide alternative education for adults. We added a half-day day care component and a food cooperative. We still kept the cultural and recreational program for youth, which was the foundation of it all.

In 1976, after we had got things going, the minister came to us and said that he and his congregation wanted to take back the building that we had fixed all up and use it for their own programming. Later we found out that he didn't give us the total truth. We have been, and still are, a very prominently culturally oriented organization. We're Black and proud; we say it loud. "There's no shame in our game," as the kids say today. The minister and his spiritualist kind of orientation thought that was in conflict with what he was supposed to be about.

So again we looked for a place in this community. We came to find out that the school building we're occupying now was going to be closed. We thought it would be ideal. It sits on a major plot of land with Pingree Park on both sides. We set out to get this building, and declared that we were not going to be denied.

We decided to go door to door and have the people in this community sign a petition. We got over 3,000 signatures. We also got the churches, the block clubs, the school community groups, to write us a letter. We held meetings with each of them and explained what we wanted to do. We got over 100 letters. We called a press conference and marched with signs saying that we wanted this building. We overwhelmed the school board. They said to us, "Never in the history of this city had anyone ever come to us with this kind of pressure and support to get a school building." The tradition had always been that once a school building was no longer used it sits there until it becomes an eyesore and the children break all the windows out and then they eventually tear it down. They proposed a purchase on a five-year land contract and the payments would be the same as the rent we paid to the church. So we took the deal and moved into the building in 1977.

This building was a shell when we first got it. The school board had taken out the fixtures, lights, and plumbing. When we got here we said, "Is this what we wanted?" But we got some support from the Kresge Foundation, from Dayton-Hudson, the city of Detroit, and anywhere else we could to put this building into some shape. It's still not where we want it to be, but it's a long way from where it was.

We start off every day with our soup kitchen from 8:30 to 10:30. We treat people with pride and dignity. We talk, we eat, we fellowship, we joke, we laugh, we just "kick it," as they say. They share things with me about problems they have in the community. Many of these are homeless folks who are destitute and down on their luck. It's a free breakfast. We ask for a donation, but most of them don't have it.

We realized initially that a part of our need was going to be economic development. So we set up a store right here in the building. Members of the co-op purchase fruits and vegetables, dry goods, canned goods, household products, dairy products, even meats. We have close to 300 members. That program runs every day from nine in the morning till six in the evening.

In another program we dispense a box of groceries to needy people once a month. It *was* a Michigan Department of Social Services program, and it still is through December 31 until Governor Engler and his people get through with it. After that it's not promised. We have a system that permits our people to come in the building and have a seat. In other places they line them up outside and herd them in like cattle. If our people bring us a letter from any reputable source—block club president, school counselor or principal, pastor, social service worker, Veterans Administration—we'll give them the food.

We have a GED program for high school dropouts who can come right here and finish school. The Board of Education sends the teachers and we help to recruit the students. We offer that service Monday through Friday.

We have a gift shop where people can purchase culturally oriented items: T-shirts, sweatshirts, hats, books, tapes, records, things that depict the culture.

But the alpha and omega is the youth program. It's still the most prominent thing that this center's famous for. It includes tutorial service, a karate self-defense program, an African drill team that does drill to a Swahili command, basketball in the winter, baseball in the summer, a cheerleading team for the young ladies, a weightlifting gym, recreation room with video games, pool table, Ping-Pong table. It also includes a program around Black history and consciousness raising. We try to teach our young people that they can be and must be proud of themselves and their history, and that they need not take a back seat to anybody.

You've been here twenty-two years. With such a great need, do you feel you're on your own?

Our goal still is to have another center on the west side of town. We've never reached the goal of total self-sufficiency and self-support. We'd love to reach that goal. By the same token, we pay taxes in this city, we have been pretty much law-abiding, and we feel that the government and people in society have an obligation to do some of these social programs. We plan to see to it that they fulfill that obligation. We're not going to give them the notion that all social-oriented programs should be on a self-help basis.

We live in a society where capitalism dictates that there's always going to be some poor people. There's people in this society who are doomed from the day they're born, who will never see the good life, or have an opportunity to enjoy the fruits of this society. Some people feel that we should only seek money from our own people to run programs such as this. We certainly feel that we should get money from our people, and we do, but we also feel that we should receive support from private and public enterprise as long as those monies come with no strings attached.

But when they start dictating what kind of program we can run and who it's run for, then we got a problem. Some years ago we turned some money down from a group who wanted to put their members on our board of directors and to volunteer their services in our program. On the surface, I guess, neither of those sound bad, but this is a Black-initiated, Black-orchestrated program that's earmarked for Black people in this community. We used to tell them that they could go into their own communities and teach their own people about the ills of racism and how it has affected this world we live in. There still are people who want to do the old missionary approach to helping and then go back and talk over tea about how they went down and helped in the ghetto. Sometimes they see us as part of their entertainment, or something. We're not going to put on a show for them.

Some young people today are doing a lot of positive things and getting no notoriety for it. The kids who are getting scholarships for college and going back into their community to help others who aren't as fortunate, they never get any ink. There are young people who grew up here in the center who went to college, graduated, and now their children come to the center. They come back all the time and tell me how much impact this program had on their lives. They say, "Paul, we didn't understand what you were trying to say to us back then. We didn't understand this idea of Black pride and cultural awareness, but now we understand it all and we want our children to be involved in the same program."

I don't think we should be duped into thinking that foundations exist for *our* benefit. Monies, and the ability to get those monies, are getting tighter. We'll push forward to get private and public money, but I'm not optimistic about it. There's optimism for those with wealth, for sure. They're doing better now than ever, although they would have you believe otherwise.

My optimism is more in the results of our program. I've witnessed young people who were heading in the wrong direction that we were able to lasso and bring them back home. I've witnessed young ladies who were on the verge of doing the wrong thing who, as Spike Lee would say, are doing the right thing. We are able to salvage or save some of our people, our young people in particular, and I'm *always* optimistic about that.

I think the need for these kinds of programs is more acute than ever with the general assistance cuts. People need somewhere to go, somebody to talk to, someplace they can receive some service without feeling they are at fault because they're in this condition. Is it a newborn baby's fault if she never gets a job? These programs are definitely needed and we hope and expect to continue here for years to come.

Eleanor Josaitis

[*She points to a stack of bound volumes on the table.*] These are computer printouts of the 76,000 people who came in and picked up food from Focus: Hope this month. Last month it was 79,684.

The Catholic church did a good job on me. Feed the hungry meant something to me even as a little kid. I was always trying to figure out a way to translate the gospel message into my life.

Father Cunningham was an English professor at Sacred Heart Seminary. In the late 1950s, he would come and say mass at our parish on the weekends. He had such a gift to articulate the needs and the confusion of our time, the issues that people were struggling with and the changes that were taking place in the Catholic church. I used to go over after mass and invite him to come to our house. Right after that came the civil rights confusion of our time. I became a follower of Dr. Martin Luther King.

Then I watched as people walked out of that church and became more and more distant from what he was saying. But for me he just continued my long-held belief that we needed to be about making the world a little bit better and contributing what we could. When the riots in 1967 hit, my husband and I had been down to the seminary where we had mass. We looked out the windows at all the smoke. The following day I came back and walked the streets with Father Cunningham. When I got home that night, that's the only time my husband ever said a harsh word to me in thirty-six years. He grabbed me by the shoulders and said, "Do you know what you're doing?"

The fear in Taylor, where we lived at the time, was very real. I was asked to join the vigilante groups that were going to stand on the overpasses and wait for the rioters to come across the border. I was asked to go into Dearborn and take pistol practice lessons so that I'd be prepared. I was told to stock my basement with food because surely there would be more rioting. You turned on the television and you thought you were in some foreign country that was on fire.

In 1968, Father Cunningham left his teaching position and Focus: Hope began. We started it in March 1968 at Sacred Heart Seminary. There were three of us: Father Jerome Frazer, Father Cunningham, and myself. Our goal was to train priests to become spokespeople and go out into the community and preach brotherhood and change.

So we hand selected fifty priests who were known for their ability to preach and who were involved in the civil rights movement. We took them away for three days to Lake Orion. We talked about the

41

Eleanor Josaitis is associate director of Focus: Hope, which she and Father William Cunningham co-founded in 1968.

Black Panther movement. We studied the Kerner Commission report on what was happening in our community. We brought in people who were going to talk about Black Power, the term that was frightening everybody to death. And we talked about the fear in the white community.

My family moved from Taylor in April 1968 into an integrated neighborhood in Detroit. It was not easily understood by family or friends: "Why would you want to do that? Why would you want to go back to a city that is having all of this strife? Why would you want to get involved in a civil rights struggle right now, Eleanor, when you've got five children of your own, little ones who need you? What are you thinking about? Are you sure you're even thinking?"

42

We're still in exactly the same location, Seven Mile and Livernois, twenty-three years later. I have a beautiful five-bedroom home in Sherwood Forest that we bought for $27,000. Talk about white flight. As the neighborhood stabilized, we developed a very balanced and integrated neighborhood.

We wrote a mission statement in 1968 that is exactly the mission statement that hangs on our wall today: "Recognizing the dignity and beauty of every person, we pledge intelligent and practical action to overcome racism, poverty and injustice, and to build a metropolitan community where all people may live in freedom, harmony, trust and affection. Black and white, yellow, brown and red from Detroit and its suburbs of every economic status, national origin and religious persuasion, we join in this covenant." I'm sure our intention was not to have an organization that would be in existence twenty-three years later and would be employing 450 people.

We wanted the Black and white community to come together, so we threw festivals in 1969, 1970, and 1971 on the Kern Block in downtown Detroit. We brought in 850 volunteers to staff carnival rides and put up great big signs that said, "Let's get together." In 1972 the ethnic festivals moved down by the river. The festivals featured our logo, which is the Black and white hands reaching toward one another. That logo has not changed in these twenty-three years. People will say it's been a long time, why don't you show those hands clasping? Well, we're not naive. We're still reaching toward one another.

Then we listened to the scientific community that was telling us that babies would lose 10 to 15 percent of their brain power in the first three years of their life if they did not have proper protein. The brain power would never be regained regardless of what the family moved into. So we designed a program to provide food to pregnant women, mothers up to one year after they gave birth, and all of their children up to age six. We started with about 400 mothers and children and built the program up to 17,000 mothers. We depended on volunteers to drive mothers with no transportation to the warehouse to pick up their food, then drove them home. They got involved in seeing some of the shifting neighborhoods of this city and what poverty was all about. Then they began to look for the solution, which is *exactly* what we wanted.

At the same time, we studied the Kerner Commission report that told us the number of stores that had left Detroit. The grocery stores had the same exodus as white flight. The report also noted that city people were being charged more for their groceries, so we decided to check that. We got together 500 volunteers from the city and 500 from the suburbs and we did a massive survey on chain stores and tiny independents to see if Black people were being charged more and if city dwellers were being charged more. We got the volunteers together and sent them out into the stores three times to check the prices of specific items. We found that Blacks were being charged more, and that groceries that wouldn't sell in the suburbs were being dumped into the city. It was not unusual to pay 20 to 40 percent more for your groceries in the city.

Then a woman called and said, "Mrs. Josaitis, I understand you have food." And I said, "Oh yes, we do. Pregnant women, nursing mothers . . ." She says, "I am seventy-two years old. Do I have to get pregnant to get some help?" Creamed me like I've never been creamed before. She was living on less than $300 a month. When I hung up, I thought, Why can't we have a food program for senior citizens?

So we hired a researcher, got enough statistical documentation to fill the room, and went off to Washington for five years to get permission to provide food to senior citizens. In the meantime, I had a waiting list of 16,000 senior citizens. Finally Congress gave Detroit a pilot program to see if the seniors would like it. The seniors *loved* it! They loved the fact that a volunteer would drive them to Focus: Hope where they get about $50 worth of groceries selected off the shelf. I can provide food to three times as many people with one tax dollar than I can for that one tax dollar in the retail community. Focus: Hope has six food centers scattered throughout the area now.

With the help of a lot of people, Focus: Hope purchased the Excello Corporation's vacant building. More and more plants were leaving town and people were looking for employment. A lot of retired people were moving on, and we were going to have a real skills shortage. Excello Corporation had not hired one minority, in the heart of the city. We started a machinist training institute with the purpose of moving people off the food program into the financial mainstream.

With the help of the Defense Department, which has a lot of equipment stored in caves across the country, we were able to get some machinery. With the help of foundations and trust funds, we renovated the building. It is immaculate. It has $10 million worth of equipment in there right now. The machinists training program has operated since 1981. Over 800 men and women have graduated from that program. They are making upward of $12 an hour in 487 shops that have hired our people. Many of these shops hired their first minority.

Then we started a program called Fast Track, which takes recent high school graduates and trains them in math and communications skills. Using computers, we can upgrade their math two years in six weeks' time. If you say "manufacturing" to a young person today, they will say, "Oh yeah, my dad used to work in a factory. He's been laid off ten years." Or "Yeah, I remember when that factory left town." We are saying, no guys, come and take a look at where technology and manufacturing is going today. It's all computerized. You have to know statistical processing control. The Black community had been excluded from that process. If you say technology to the average person now, they'll say, "Auburn Hills, Ann Arbor, Troy." You don't think of high technology in the city of Detroit. That's the perception we want to change. Our Fast Track program has graduated 400 to 500 students in two years, and next year that will be doubled.

We also remanufacture transmissions for General Motors in a plant called Cycletech. That's a for-profit business and it's been very successful. We have won a very high rating with General Motors. We hire mainly from Detroit. We have another little business that does hose and harness assembly for Detroit Diesel and Ford Motor Company that employs all ADC moms, some of them third generation.

Then Ford Motor Company moved out of the city in 1984. Focus: Hope bought the facility which is adjacent to our Excello plant. We now own twenty-five acres of abandoned plants right in the heart of the city, right next door to one of our food programs. One of the first things we did was take one of the buildings down and put up a center for children. There's no greater gift we can give someone than saying, come on, you can bring your child to work with you. So we started a Montessori Learning Center and invested a great deal of money in it so that we could set the tone of the importance of the child. It was one thing to say to a mother that we're going to break the pattern of ADC, but she's got a couple of little kids. Let's deal with the reality.

We've purchased a home with Michigan National Bank and completely renovated that home. We will continue in the housing project. We've been able to take down nine abandoned homes that were absolutely beyond repair. These are only seeds that have been planted. And there are many people out there who are trying to plant seeds.

Focus: Hope now has 40,000 volunteers. We communicate with our volunteers through newsletters. We just celebrated our sixteenth Walk for Justice. It's the old civil rights walk. We walk eight miles, Black and white together. We call on people to come and make a statement. Have we achieved our goals? Absolutely not. Are we still walking? Absolutely, come and join us.

Maggie DeSantis

I'm a native east side Detroiter, born forty-one years ago, and with the exception of a couple of years when I went up to northern Michigan to be a hippie, I've always been an east sider. In 1977 I came back to Detroit from up north, was unemployed, and decided that I wanted to work for a progressive civil rights organization. I picked New Detroit, which exposed me to the politics and the leadership of the city that fed some of the cynicism I was developing about what was happening in the city.

I had to leave New Detroit because it was too difficult for me to deal with what I saw as the great hypocrisy that Detroit was, in fact, controlled by the same corporate structure that had been controlling it all those years. I saw the [Mayor Coleman] Young administration and all of his people as very willing puppets and deeply resented being told there were certain things that I couldn't say.

So I left there and got a job with the Neighborhood Service Organization, which is a very large nonprofit, funded by United Foundation. It was a job I was thrilled to get, because it brought me back to the east side, where I'd been living at that point anyway. I didn't know diddly about community-based planning or really much about neighborhood organizing.

I began to work as a consultant with SECA [South Eastern Community Association]. We put together a neighborhood plan that eventually was instrumental in creating the Warren-Connor Development Coalition, which is the organization that I now am director of.

In this neighborhood plan that we were developing, we put together a couple of concepts which I'm sure are not original, but for us they were important. One was the concept of community investment in land, in the sense of community shareholders jointly owning

Maggie DeSantis is director of the Warren-Connor Community Development Coalition.

real estate and developing it the way they saw fit for the gain of the community.

And the plan also recognized that there were two big new institutions being built right on the border bounded by Van Dyke and Connor and Mack to I-94: a community college and a hospital. The area that Warren-Connor serves is much bigger than that today, but that was the original one. It contained probably 10,000 homeowners. It is a densely populated, gorgeous neighborhood that tends to be very underestimated because the surrounding commercial strips are raggedy.

With the concept of community ownership and with this belief that these two institutions could play a real important role, SECA took the neighborhood plan to these two institutions. The Samaritan Health Center took up the challenge and convened a series of meetings. I began to help put together these meetings and began to recruit people and other organizations from the east side to the meetings. In about a year and a half we challenged Samaritan to put the resources into a separate, nonprofit, community-based development coalition of east side organizations. They put up a cash loan to hire the first director, and I was hired.

Samaritan provided the office space free, the office overhead free. They said, "Stretch this money. You can pay for whosoever's time you want for as long as it lasts, but then you're on your own." So we started basic·organizing, knocking on doors, hitting the streets, going to every meeting we could get to, and we began to put together an organization. The first year we did community-based planning: what were the major problems that we needed to tackle on the east side, and what would our particular approach be so as not to compete with the existing neighborhood councils, but to play a real effective coalition role, and complement whatever work they were doing?

Five months after we started, when we held our first annual meeting in January 1985, it became real clear that people were really ready. They came out in droves, and the feeling in the room that night was absolutely electric. We started a tradition that night that we have our annual dinner in the wintertime, we bring in a keynote speaker, and it's this really upbeat, wonderful night. We always have young people from the community.

Since that first meeting in 1985, we have grown a lot, and I guess we've now become an organization that is viewed as pretty powerful and effective. In a vacuum anything sticks out like a sore thumb. The problem in Detroit right now is that there's not enough activism. Given that landscape, it's not surprising that we're viewed as being very effective.

On the other hand, I don't want to minimize what we've done. I think probably the most important thing we've done is help people on the east side begin to think differently about the east side. We've begun to make the city administration see the east side as something more than just the disorganized wasteland that people think it is. I know they see it now as a place that is pretty decently organized. It's a part of town they have to reckon with.

What is good organizing?

For me, the most important quality of a good organizer is integrity and commitment to the community. I like to hire people of our community. That's very different from some [Saul] Alinsky-style organizations that deliberately seek outside professional organizers. We make use of the VISTA [Volunteers in Service to America] program. We recruit people who have good natural organizing instincts into the organization as full-time VISTA volunteers and then we hire them as organizers. Organizers must also have a great deal of respect for the viewpoints of the people in the community that they serve. They must also bring a certain leadership to the community because they're of that community. What you end up with—and this is where the real skill is—is a blend of the perspectives and priorities of the people of the community and the approaches and leadership that a staff organizer can bring to it.

We have a staff of twenty-eight extremely dedicated, hard-working people. We have a staff of probably twenty full-time equivalents; 90 percent of them from the east side. Probably 75 percent have been there from the beginning. Warren-Connor has a leadership training institute for east side activists. In three years, about sixty people have graduated. Many of them have gone on to leadership positions in their own neighborhood councils. About 75 percent of them have stayed active with us, have moved on to our board of directors.

I have a twenty-two–member board that is superb. We absolutely work them to death. They rise to the occasion and seem to enjoy it. They're all volunteers. Probably half work full time. I think a lot of their activism and sense of political acumen comes from the leadership training. I think it also comes from the very strong role the staff plays at the board table. The board exercises its governance role without hesitating, but it expects staff to have opinions and to be leaders. People on the board are very proud of their independence from the city administration.

We do commercial real estate development. We're building a shopping center on the lower east side in a neighborhood that is viewed as one of the worst in the city. The real estate on which the shopping center is being built is owned by community shareholders. We have 120 resident shareholders who invested their own money in the shopping center. The market value of a share of stock is $25. The

47

average household buys about three shares. We're getting ready to buy our second shopping center right in the heart of our community. It's been owned and milked for ten years by an absentee landlord, and it's in horrible shape. We're commercial real estate developers, and we've had to learn that particular skill. We've had to use conventional methods of commercial real estate development and combine that with creative financing.

We've tapped into the attitudes of people who believe in alternative economics in the sense of community ownership of the land. The corporation they buy stock in has a cooperative voting structure. No matter how many shares you own, you only get one vote. Community control of the land is a very radical concept. We talk about it in the sense of self-sufficiency and community self-determination. Then when we go to the banks and talk about community equity, they eat it up.

48

We also have a youth program. It's viewed as a national model and funded as a national demonstration through the Office of Substance Abuse Prevention of the Health and Human Services Department. We competed nationally with 300 applicants, and they picked 16. We work with sixty young people ages 12 to 18. They are all at risk. The kids are trained and paid to be junior community development practitioners, so they work right with us in the organization and then they go through our leadership training program. We kind of view it as a way of preparing the fourth or fifth generation of staff and board for Warren-Connor. We have no plans to go away. The program was designed by people from the east side to respond to the fact that young people are the primary victims and perpetrators of crime in our community.

We also have community-based study groups. When an issue arises that's controversial, our philosophy is that we cannot tell people what to think. That's sort of arrogant. But we can play a role of educator and information provider. The study group frames the questions they want answered. Then college interns research those questions and bring back the information. The study group sifts through the information, and we produce a report. We use the community-forum approach with that report to do a lot of community education, and we publish a paper that disseminates the information in common English. We've dealt with issues as complicated as airport expansion, casino gambling, prison construction, handgun control.

Does it lead to any kind of discussion on broader political organizing topics?

We got a real clear mandate from our members at our last membership meeting to try to deal with the impact of the state budget cuts on our community, so we are doing that. And it surfaced in past years in relationship to city budget priorities.

In the neighborhood organizing movement in the last ten years, there has been a great deal of reticence on the part of people like myself about getting involved politically. It's dangerous in the city if you're in the difficult position of needing to maintain funding for a neighborhood organization. Without apology, I'll be the first one to stand up and admit that. There are some activists in the city who believe that those of us who do this for a living compromise ourselves because we end up having to be too careful.

I make no apology whatsoever for the need to have to be politically astute in order to protect our funding base. Some of us raise hell anyway and get in trouble anyway, and you end up walking a tightrope. Warren-Connor has a history of always being on the opposite side of the mayor, which has kept us in trouble for most of our years, and has required good organizing and good political acumen to figure out how to attempt to outfox the fox.

At the same time, many of us truly believe that it doesn't matter who holds office. Politics taints people, and regardless of who's there, we still have to be out here nurturing each other and doing good, basic neighborhood organizing, paid or unpaid. Third, it drains energy.

The reality about Detroit in at least the last ten years is that most of the real strong leadership has left. The few of us who are left—who I consider to be the city's real leaders—end up pouring out so much energy on the day-to-day organizing, that for years we said we cannot do this other stuff. We can't do justice to both of them, and we're all going to burn out and that's not worth it.

But about seven years ago, some of us got involved in a citywide coalition called Save Our Spirit [SOS]. Within two or three years of SOS forming, several of us began to get a real serious grip on the reality that we had to fight to change the characters who occupy those elected seats and inject progressive politics back onto the agenda.

More recently, on July 15, 1989, several citywide organizations formed a coalition called the People Coalition. The People Coalition included the SOS Coalition, the United Community Housing Coalition, the Neighborhood Information Exchange, the Detroit Organization of Tenants, the Evergreen Alliance, and several other progressive, activist organizations. We held a convention, and we wrote a progressive platform for change. Every plank was debated and discussed. We had probably 200 or so people at the convention.

We tiptoed into some very unsophisticated, very poorly done political organizing, but nevertheless, it was the first time, in a tangible way, that we said, "We've got to do this." We formed the People PAC. We raised a tiny, tiny bit of money and embarked on the political journey.

Charleen Johnson

My parents came from the South to seek employment. We lived originally in an old cheese factory. We moved into the Pilgrim Village
neighborhood when I was three. It was pretty much an all-white neighborhood. When I was seven, my family joined Twelfth Street Baptist
Church. I graduated from Highland Park High School and went on to
Highland Park College, and then to Wayne State University. After graduation, I taught in the Detroit public school system for eight years.

When I was eighteen I left the church. Folks came to church on
Sunday, and they sang and shouted, and the preacher preached, and
they collected money. And then people went home and didn't do
anything to make a difference in their own lives or in the lives of
other people in the community. I saw people in the church being
powerless to effect any change. At that time we were entering into the
sixties, with the civil rights movement, and I got involved in the revolution. I was looking to overthrow the establishment. [*Laughs*] I was
out of the church for twelve years.

After trying many things and finding that there really were no
solutions, I came back to the church at age thirty, having earned a
master's degree in education. I was an accomplished teacher. I had
married and had two children. I was being considered to run for the
Board of Education.

My background is in the area of family-life education and I
wanted to develop programs that would help to strengthen the family.
I started doing some volunteer work here at the church. I was involved with a mission-type group of women. We started a food distribution program. This is a low-income area with a lot of senior citizens
and single parents living off fixed incomes.

The philosophy of our pastor, Reverend Lee Earl, was that the
church should be using its economic and human resources to not
only meet the needs of its members, but also people beyond the immediate congregation. In 1982 I became part of his Council on Economic Development. Reagan had just come into office. There was this
huge outcry in the Black community about the cuts in social services
and social programs. It was our thinking that the church could use its
assets as a base for capital infusion into our own neighborhood.

I brought the idea of starting a child development center to the
council. I wanted education to be very hands-on and culturally relevant. I believe all children need to be in a school group where they

*Charleen Johnson is president and chief operating officer of Reach Everyone Administer
Care and Health, Inc. (REACH), a corporation that grew out of the Weekday Ministry
of the Twelfth Street Baptist Church on Detroit's west side.*

can progress at their own individual pace. I thought that it was important to start as early as age two because much of the personality of the child is determined by the time they're five.

There was a cocaine house across the street from the church. The owner of the house was a former member of our church who was renting it to some people who were selling drugs. He came to us and asked if we could help. Our response was that we could buy the house and evict the drug dealers and renovate the house and move in a single mom with a couple of children. We could make the community safer, provide jobs for people in the neighborhood, and provide decent housing. Reverend Earl had a background in real estate. He initially taught me housing development and economic development. Now we teach each other.

We incorporated as REACH to get a broader representation on the board and additional financing from other sources. We could have a greater impact if there were entities involved other than the church. Our mission was to provide services to meet the needs of low-income individuals living in this community, to strengthen family and neighborhood, and to revitalize the physical neighborhood. We decided that we had to be comprehensive and holistic in our approach. Our first responsibility is to develop leadership skills, technical abilities, interpersonal relationships, family living skills—all that it takes for an individual to become a contributing member in this society. We identify a problem that we're facing in this community and then chart a plan for solving that problem and getting the resources we need.

We have classes to provide information in job training or home ownership counseling or parenting. We have substance-abuse prevention activities. We've organized a group of primarily older women who do monthly marches against crack and crime. That organization has grown on to form a citywide organization called WEPROS [We the People Reclaiming Our Streets] and now we're doing marches in neighborhoods all over the city.

We have continued acquiring houses. We renovate a house and then sell it to low-income families. We've acquired vacant lots and are now doing new construction. Just down the street we've done a twenty-four–unit apartment building. We're doing transitional housing for homeless families. They need intensive support.

We've acquired several commercial buildings and renovated them. The last one we did was a former restaurant that sat abandoned for about a year. We set up a for-profit S-corporation to actually run the restaurant. It's called Mrs. Thunderbird's Heart and Soul Cafeteria, located on the corner of Puritan and Linwood. We own the building and lease the space to the S-corporation that runs the restaurant.

We're the only ones who would invest in a business in this neighborhood.

We've targeted five sites to build new apartments for rental. Over the next five years we can begin to stabilize and increase the property values somewhat. They're so *terribly* depressed. We started a Small Business Development Center to provide counseling and assistance to existing business owners and to those who want to start small businesses in the area. The development of *our* commercial strip on Linwood Avenue ties in real well with the present development on the Livernois Avenue of Fashion. We've got grants from the city of Detroit, business loans from banks, and subsidized loans through the Detroit Economic Growth Corporation. It's about pooling those different sources of capital.

For our first construction project, we're looking at a $1,700,000 project. Funding is coming from the Michigan State Housing Development Authority for mortgage funding. The Local Initiative Support Corporation will provide the equity financing. Our transitional housing project is about a $400,000 project. It's growing. We started out with a food program with a budget of less than $1,000 a year. Our yearly operating budget now is around $600,000.

We're dependent on local financial sources and on our own initiative to generate program income. We got rents in the first year of the restaurant's operation. That comes back into REACH. Parents pay tuition in the Child Development Center. People who receive food give donations.

The churches are in a key position to use their resources to reinvest in the community. If each church would anchor its own neighborhood, then the revitalization that could take place all over this city would be tremendous. Churches could come together to develop a capital pool to encourage private investment. The Catholics and Episcopalians already have models for this, but it hasn't happened within the Black Baptists to much extent. Now there's more cooperation among the church-based community development corporations. We're getting to know each other better and cooperating on projects. I see minimally a billion dollars emerging.

The community development movement is being seen as a legitimate, professionally run, productive movement in the city. That's exciting. Grassroots organizations are at the table with the city at the highest levels. The lenders are beginning to see that we have learned how to build houses, how to start businesses. It's a different climate. They have as much to learn from us as we have to learn from them. Quite frankly, we *have* to be in business to make money. But we're also in business to help people. And I don't see those two things as being mutually exclusive in this economy. For the first time, the movement at the grassroots level is community development–based. That's really critical.

Nate Thomas

I got a job at Stroh's in 1971 and was averaging $37,000 per year, and the work was very easy. We had a saying, "Working at Stroh's was like finding money in the street." I considered myself middle class and didn't want for anything. I had my home, money in my pocket, two cars—living real comfortable.

When Stroh Brewery closed, my little pension money ran out, then unemployment ran out, and I was forced to apply for GA [general assistance]. The attitude at the welfare office was like, "You're a number, I don't care if you *don't* get a meal tomorrow, I don't care if you lose everything you got, tough!" I'm a disabled vet, so I get enough from my VA disability to pay my monthly house note. But I could not cover my utility bills.

When my light bill reached $3,000, and I had $600 in the bank, I went down to Edison and tried to make a deal with them while the GA case was open. No go! So I took the $600, boarded the house up for security, drained all the pipes, and ended up homeless down here on the street. It took three years to get that GA case straightened out and to get that $3,000 light bill down to where I could make arrangements to pay off the rest. I was homeless from 1987 to 1989.

I used to stay over at the Rescue Mission. They needed someone to watch the place during the night. That's where I got involved with the Homeless Union, and eventually was voted in as vice-president by the members. I saw and heard a lot, and I've been able to help a lot of people. I really began to get involved.

I'm affiliated with People United As One, an organization of concerned citizens. Most of them are homeless or work at low-paying jobs. Our main fight now is affordable housing. Our mission statement is to educate people to things they can do to help lift themselves up and out of poverty. The group started in a sit-in at the Michigan State Plaza Building. The people who were sitting in there felt that with the recall campaign on Governor Engler coming up, this

53

Nate Thomas is a staff person at the Cass Methodist Homeless Drop-In Center on Cass Avenue near the heart of Detroit's high-culture district.

was an opportunity to educate state employees and visitors from southeastern Michigan counties about the state budget cuts.

I'm on a number of boards of directors: Cass Methodist Church Housing Corporation, United Community Housing Coalition, People United As One [Chairman], Wayne County Housing Coalition, Michigan Fair Budget, Michigan Up and Out of Poverty Now. I'm at the point where I have to limit it to two or three organizations because I'm stretched too thin.

Would you describe this place we're sitting in?

If you look at all these older guys around here [*gestures*] most of them at one time were working at Chrysler, GM, or Ford. This is what we call a day shelter. Overnight shelters usually put people out at six or seven o'clock in the morning. During the day there's really no place for them to go. The Department of Mental Health, through Cass Methodist Church, funded this program, which has been in existence for four or five years. The department's guidelines say they do not want a structured program here, they want people to come here and relax, not being encumbered by a lot of antiquated rules. We do have an element that will come in here and try to cause problems. Therefore we search them to make sure there are no weapons, no drugs, no alcohol.

These guys get on that self-pity thing. I say, "Look, man, it's not totally your fault that you're in this situation. You had plenty help from the government. If the government had done some things, you might not have become a drug addict." They see things going downhill and there's no way to stop it, so they've anesthetized themselves to the whole problem. "Yeah, if I get high, if I get drunk, I won't feel the cold, I won't feel the hunger."

Are there jobs for these people in the city?

Not really, but there are many ways that we can create jobs, right now. That's what I'm working on now. My idea is, instead of making those construction companies out in the suburbs richer by bringing them in to do the work on public housing, set up a nonprofit corporation with federal money for training. We have construction companies right here in the city that's willing to train our people. Let's give them on-the-job-training, working on public housing. You're talking about hundreds of millions of dollars that will be kept right here in the city and thousands of people put to work to rebuild the infrastructure. That's building the tax base.

I've been trying to educate the people here that you *must* vote, and don't vote for name people. You must find your ordinary citizens, listen to what they have to say, and look at their track record of community work. You got to get the career politicians out of office. The Homeless Union has a saying: "Can't no one speak for a homeless person *but* a homeless person." We have grassroots leaders who are very intelligent and who *can* set up programs that will work. We have to come up with new ideas, new plans. In 1993 we're planning to run some grassroots people for City Council and a few Senate seats if we can. We feel we have the vote to put people in who are gonna look out for our interests. That's the only hope we have.

It's time for a change. In [Mayor] Coleman Young's first two terms in office he worked for the people. The last two terms in office he's been on a real big ego trip. He's lost an understanding of civil service. When [Governor] Engler first came out with the idea of cutting GA, Coleman knew that the city would lose close to $400,000,000 **55** on just the cuts from GA, but he just kept his mouth shut. There was a time when he would be the first one raising hell: "What are you doing? Are you crazy? You can't do this."

When we put up those tents [protesting Governor Engler's cuts of 90,000 GA recipients] we made sure we called them "Englerville." We weren't trying to attack the city. Instead of coming out in support of the people, Coleman turns around and *attacks* the people. The city said the tents didn't meet the health code and were fire hazards, but we had addressed those issues. Then they said, "There's an ordinance that nobody can sleep in a tent in the city of Detroit." Oh, come on, be for real! When I was a kid growing up here I used to sleep in a tent in my back yard all the time. I do it in the summer now.

We're getting ready to go into a political revolution. First, you got to give a person hope: "Look man, you don't have to be like this, but in order for you to do something about it you must take the government." When I say "take the government" I don't mean by violence, I mean you must start participating and voting. Demonstrations are fine, but you still have to have someone sitting in government. Too many people are hurting, too many people are beginning to question the leadership from the top all the way down. 1993 will be a start here in Michigan. I *have* to be optimistic.

Peggy Posa

I was born and raised in Detroit. My first introduction to the social-issue arena came from a strong religious background. The first issues I was actively involved in were the civil rights movement and the anti–

Peggy Posa is the executive director of the Coalition on Temporary Shelter (COTS).

Vietnam War activities. I was influenced by the activities and thought of my friends, people like Kathy Schultz, Jean and Charlie Rooney, Sheila Murphy, and then a long chain of people. I belonged to a series of political organizations that went from the Alliance [an early '70s coalition of progressive activists], to From the Ground Up, to DARE [Detroit Alliance for a Rational Economy]. I was involved in the Chuck Ravitz and Ken Cockrel campaigns [for Recorders Court and Detroit City Council, respectively]. One thing led to another. It was a hardy group of people who eventually will form a significant part of the thought and activity of the future. These are people who are not going away.

I worked for the Metropolitan Detroit Welfare Reform Coalition, then the United Community Housing Coalition, then a neighborhood citizens district council. I also was a consultant for [Reverend] Hugh White and a number of left-progressive organizations around theology in the Americas and liberation theology, both at the national and local levels. My work life got joined with political activity. Later I worked four years at Mercy College. Five years ago I came to work here.

COTS has been in existence for ten years. It's the state's largest emergency shelter for homeless men, women, and children. We have 140 emergency shelter beds, 55 transitional living rooms for single individuals, and 22 rooms for the long-term, chronically mentally ill. In addition, we have a seven-unit apartment building for mothers with children. We provide a bed with clean linens that are changed once a week, three meals a day, and casework services, which are the linch pin of a good service-delivery program. We have a fully licensed day care center for toddlers (two and a half to five years old). We have a mothers' and infants' room. We have a homeless adult literacy program that operates in the building so that while people are here they can improve their skills.

We have the services of the Detroit Health Care for the Homeless traveling medical team that visits the shelter once a week and takes care of everything from prenatal advice to ulcerated sores from IV drug use, and everything in between. If an individual comes in and self-identifies as having had a mental health problem, or whose behavior shows a need for therapy, we link them with therapists in a neighboring community mental health organization who networks them with the mental health services in the area.

We've been over capacity for the past three years. The most significant change that has occurred over the past ten years is the growth of the number of children in the population of homeless people. The stereotype of a homeless person ten years ago was the wandering wino: a guy about fifty-three years old who allegedly likes his life that way. Now we have families, predominantly mothers with children.

We have some funds, channeled through the city of Detroit, from the Stewart B. McKinney Act, a piece of federal legislation that addresses the needs of homeless people. We write proposals for and compete for these funds. We had a contract with the state Department of Social Services, but with the recent state budget cuts that's going to disappear. We write proposals to private foundations. We do fairly large direct-mail fund-raising campaigns as well. We also have a small United Way grant. This variety of income streams is beneficial because when one source dries up the agency doesn't go belly up. On the other hand, keeping all those streams in the air at one time is tricky.

What might future progressive politics be among you and your colleagues?

I think that we're all standing around asking each other that same question. Until somebody grabs a hold of it and starts something, even if it's the gathering of people in the same room around current political issues, probably nothing will happen. I used to spend a lot of time in political meetings, whether they were discussion groups or activity groups. None of us are hungry to go back to spend a whole lot of time like that, but we all recognize that it will be necessary if any significant political change is going to happen.

In the area of homelessness, when you enter the circle that represents a poor person's life, you run into a whole chain of problems that impact poor people's lives, whether it's poor health, poor education, joblessness, etc., so there's a whole passel of things that need to get solved. I think in addressing these social issues, it has to be solved by more people than political activists or poverty-related issue specialists. It has to be the business community, government, and the private nonprofits. The whole group. Putting that coalition together is tricky.

Between the mid-'70s and the mid-'80s the number of dwelling units available for rent nationwide for under $300 decreased by one million units. During that same period the number of rental units available for over $400 increased by 4,500,000 units. That's not an accident. That's a choice about who we're going to house. At this point the government is pushing the responsibility onto the private sector, either nonprofit or for-profit. There's a finite limit to the number of charitable dollars out there, so there has to be another way to address these problems.

I don't have a vision for the future. But, in the absence of a kind of charismatic leader, we're going to have to develop a vision. Isn't it

57

a fascinating day when George Bush, Pat Buchanan, and David Duke are the significant names on the political agenda? *That*, if nothing else, ought to mobilize us into some action.

We've got to pay attention to the places where people live: the neighborhoods. Unless those are strengthened, people of good will are going to leave. Cut the defense budget, for God's sake. Put some money back into this country. The money needs to get back to the places that need it.

Marilyn Mullane

I was born and raised in Detroit, and spent nearly all my life here. I went to St. Mary's of Redford High School in Detroit. As Catholic schools go, it was fairly progressive. I became involved there in the Head Start program in Detroit which was just beginning, and also with the United Farm Workers boycott in the late '60s, early '70s. Picketing stores that sold grapes was my after-school activity. It was motivated by teachers who had a larger vision of what we should be involved with in social studies classes and ethics courses. We did a lot of progressive reading: Eldridge Cleaver's *Soul on Ice*, Betty Friedan's *Feminine Mystique*, Kate Millett's *Sexual Politics*.

In 1975 I wound up on a fellowship to Columbia University to study ethics. Then Wayne State University offered me a three-year scholarship to attend law school.

I did a work-study program for the Legal Aid Defender Association in the landlord-tenant clinic, addressing public-housing problems. There was a public-housing rent strike going on at the time and cases were coming to jury trial. I lived on the campus in perfectly good buildings that were scheduled for demolition to make parking for Wayne State. Very shortly I became involved in efforts to retain those buildings as housing, and I was elected to the citizens district council for University City. The buildings were pulled off the demolition list and they were repaired.

My work with the landlord-tenant clinic during law school was primarily defending evictions. The courts see about 33,000 evictions cases per year. At that time the clinic was located across the hall from the court and the circumstances under which you came in contact with your clients were pretty intense because they were at the point of

Marilyn Mullane is a staff attorney with Michigan Legal Services, located in downtown Detroit.

eviction. So I quickly got used to a very fast-paced practice. But it *did* feel very much like you were spitting at the ocean, handling this little eviction here and this one there. It seemed like there was a need not only to educate the courts, but, at times, to sue the courts for the way they were handling cases and ignoring defenses.

Also, it seemed there was a need for another legal aid entity where there would be lawyers available to take whole buildings into court. One problem was that the court believed it didn't have authority to order repairs. We eventually got the court rules changed to make it clear that the courts *could* order repairs. It also seemed that it would make sense to take buildings into court and sue owners affirmatively to get them repaired. So I wrote a grant proposal to the city of Detroit to have this project funded. So the Landlord-Tenant Center was born.

Then I went to work for Wayne County Neighborhood Legal Services, where I became involved in much broader litigation and public benefits issues. I worked for the county for five years, beginning in January 1980 when Ronald Reagan took office. The program was severely cut by 1981 from thirty-three attorneys to six. The law reform unit, that focused on impact litigation in the areas of housing, community development, prison work, health law, public benefits, and employment discrimination, was shut down.

I had the opportunity to go to Michigan Legal Services, the backup center for field programs throughout Michigan, that focuses on patterns and root causes of poverty and administrative or legislative advocacy. We primarily handle class-action suits: cases on behalf of groups.

This means that you could represent 90,000 terminated general assistance recipients?

That's exactly what we're doing. We're also representing AFDC [Aid to Families with Dependent Children] recipients who suffered a 17 percent cut in their benefit levels in March 1991. We file a number of amicus briefs. We've been involved on behalf of migrants in Michigan to defend what housing rights they have that have been developed over the years. The growers in the state have filed a lawsuit to have the courts declare that migrants have no housing rights under any of Michigan's housing statutes. Not surprisingly, Ottawa County Circuit Court—a rural circuit court—ruled in their favor.

In housing work I focus more on Detroit. That's where the most sophisticated housing groups are. Outside of the work I do for MLS [Michigan Legal Services], I've been directly involved with nonprofits. I'm on the board of the Cass Corridor Neighborhood Development

Corporation and work pretty closely with that organization, developing nonprofit housing alternatives in the Cass Corridor.

Our office is inundated with calls from people who are homeless or on the verge of becoming homeless and who are absolutely desperate. I had a woman in my office today who was seven months pregnant and was evicted from her apartment by force at two o'clock this morning. She had been told that she had till sundown to get out. We've submitted evidence to the court that they're using cattle prods to evict tenants or evicting tenants at gunpoint and shutting off utilities.

What's the purpose of emptying a building?

60   Burning it down! I don't think there's any way that these owners are going to mothball the buildings for any length of time through this economic period. Many of the buildings in the Cass Corridor were occupied by general assistance recipients who doubled or tripled up in single rooms. The owners of apartment buildings as well as hotel and motel owners are just locking tenants out and shutting off the utilities. Very good judges recently have sided with owners in their efforts to terminate utilities, which is completely illegal. The law is very clear.

It's as though we're living in the Middle Ages in Michigan now. It's a sort of "let them eat cake" attitude. The governor is convinced that those who are supported by general assistance choose that over a minimum-wage job, which would pay more than the $186 a month that general assistance is paying. He thinks persons who are on public assistance are either obtaining money illegally from other sources or they're able-bodied and refusing to work. There's no understanding that this income just passes through these beneficiaries to slumlords and utility providers. The beneficiaries don't see *any* of the money. It basically keeps a very minimal roof over their head.

It's no accident that the governor eliminated general assistance with the support of the legislature. The legislature took a vote at midnight on a Friday night. It's something that could not have happened without the support of the Democrats. There were a number of prosecuting attorneys, police organizations, and local chambers of commerce that were opposed to the elimination of general assistance.

In the long run, the local economic ramifications of this decision are going to be fairly surprising to the [Governor John] Engler administration. In terms of other costs—health care, mental health, institutional, criminal justice—the state's going to pay much, much more. For every dollar spent in income assistance, two to three dollars are generated in the local economy.

The studies that we introduced as evidence in court indicate that the average length of time that half of the general assistance population was on assistance was for less than twelve months. So it really is a transitional program, not a long-term program. No one stays on general assistance if they are able to get off. The income doesn't support any decent standard of living. Those who wind up on it are very often disabled. The department's own statistics show that 50 percent of the population, or more, suffer from some physical disability or mental limitation, or are required to stay at home to care for another disabled household member.

Beyond that, there are serious functional bars to employability. I recently saw a report in the *Detroit News* indicating that only one in four families in Detroit has a car. Most of the jobs that are being generated are in suburban areas. There are virtually no jobs being generated in the city. There is no regional bus system, so it's impossible. The 40,000 general assistance recipients who are able to work aren't going to get to the job. They're locked into poverty and homelessness. The choices they're left with are pretty grim and inhuman.

What happened to the "Recall Engler" campaign?

It crumbled. It was pretty disorganized. A major obstacle was that there was no major institutional support for it. Labor pretty much stayed out with the exception of [UAW president] Owen Bieber who made a few statements. The Democratic Party stayed out. They reached a truce with the Republicans that neither party will recall the other party's elected officials. It really was a poor people's campaign. There were 18,000 petitioners, which is pretty impressive, and over 300,000 signatures collected. When there's no major institutional support and when you're required to collect 700,000 to 800,000 signatures in ninety days, it's a pretty Herculean task. It was by and large organized by welfare rights groups.

At this point I think that the groups that are working directly with the victims of these cuts—and the victims are reeling—are searching for the next steps. We need to organize to take over public housing, to take over HUD [Department of Housing and Urban Development] houses, to go to Washington and complain about what's happening, and there needs to be a campout on the governor's lawn. There are all these ideas floating, but nothing is very concrete yet because the groups are split between meeting the immediate needs of people who are living on the streets, which is something none of us have confronted in this massive way in memory, while at the same time trying to look to some long-term solution.

I'm seeing some very, very desperate people, some of whom are suicidal. There's also been desperate talk of turning to other sources of income—taking houses, taking food. Bishop Gumbleton testified before the House Appropriations Committee that the senior food center at St. Patrick's was broken into last week. [Reverend] Ed Rowe is now the keeper of the food at Cass Methodist. People are now stealing food to survive.

For the sake of Michigan and for the city, I hope we can move in another direction pretty quickly. It's a *terrible* price to pay. The Democrats have taken a pretty cynical position and have not been willing to stand up against these cuts. We're in the mess we're in because there's no opposition. Also, Engler is moving so radically and so swiftly that it's very difficult to regroup and deal legislatively, judicially, and mobilize in an organizational way. The courts have failed, the legislature has failed, and you begin to wonder after a while if the work you're doing is making a lot of difference in the field you've chosen. If we haven't hit it, I think we're near rock bottom. No, I think we're below it, we're in hell! [*Laughs*]

Doug Smith

I'm writing a novel. It's about a person who's obsessed with this one slumlord. Through a series of frustrations with the system, he begins to think that if he could kill this landlord it would scare the rich and the people who make decisions for poor people into doing something about the current crisis that people in Detroit are facing. So he tries to kill this person and botches the job. Instead of being tried, he's immediately put into a mental institution where he's awaiting competency to stand trial.

Is this autobiographical?

Yeah, I think so. A lot of the characters are based on people I know. Obviously, I didn't try to kill anyone, but I definitely felt the same frustrations that this character felt.

I was born in Detroit and grew up in Lincoln Park, Michigan. After high school I was too undisciplined to hold down a job, so I joined the navy and ended up being a radio man in Greece. Being in the service really radicalized me; really taught me a lot about race and class and what our government is capable of overseas.

In the service the Blacks and the "heads," basically hippies, would

Doug Smith is a staff person with the United Community Housing Coalition, located in downtown Detroit.

all hang out together. If you hung out with Black people, or if you have a certain political opinion, you're always being harassed. I ended up being in the brig for sixty days for mouthing off to the superior officers. I was trying to get out of the service at that point, so I told them to stop paying me. I didn't want to get paid by an army that's killing people in Vietnam.

When I got out of the service it took me a long time to get my act together. I was kind of lost. Finally, I got back to school. Then I joined VISTA [Volunteers in Service to America] from '77 to '79 and became a youth worker in Chicago. I organized kids and their parents to pressure City Council to provide a drop-in center for kids. It was an amazing, empowering experience. I found myself doing things that I never thought I had the guts or intelligence to do.

Then I came back to Michigan and did some regular social work in a residential treatment center. You were just dealing with individual problems. Sometimes I thought the program was contributing more to people's problems than helping them. They were taking kids who were basically status offenders and locking them up. It seemed like their behavior got worse over time.

So I went to the University of Michigan for a master's in social work, emphasizing community organizing. I did an internship with the UCHC [United Community Housing Coalition] in '83, and have been here ever since.

For the first fifteen years this organization did housing placement for low-income people and developed relationships with landlords who would take low-income people. In Detroit 60 percent of the people are on some type of assistance. For a long time a multiple-unit building was approached like a caseworker would handle a case. There was no effort to try to link up the people in an area to try to do something on a bigger scale. When we got into building geographical tenant organizations, we had the hope of doing citywide tenant organization.

UCHC has had a kind of schizophrenic problem. On the one hand, it was a welfare agency that fostered dependency. Then there were the organizers who were really pushing for the organization to be more militant, and try to foster more empowerment and tenants taking control over their own lives. We always were having clashes over this. Now we're into public-housing organizing and we've probably become the number one enemy of the mayor and his people. We have two organizers in public housing and one in the private sphere. We used to have six organizers.

I got into the Ajax [an alias name] campaign. At the end of the auto industry's salad days, sometime in the '70s, a lot of people

63

moved out of the city. Ajax bought up houses for dirt cheap and rented them to low-income people. He made all his tenants go on vendor, which means that the rent goes directly from the Department of Social Service right into the hands of landlords. He had a guaranteed income, and no incentive to keep his places up to code. I could drive down the street and the shittiest house on the block would be an Ajax house. That never failed. I spent the next two years going after this guy. We were successful in getting a lot of places repaired, but not in getting this guy to do business differently.

I did some research and found that this guy had just acquired about 150 units. While I was on vacation in Canada fishing, he sold all these houses to the tenants. He got them to sign this quit-claim deed, which meant that if they missed one payment he could take the house back. Since then most of the houses that he sold no longer exist. They burned. They were insured by him. I know of only one family I worked with who still owns their house. That was just a crusher.

Another serious campaign I was involved in was Henry Elrum [an alias name], a slumlord who owned six buildings in the Cass Corridor and who is the model for the villain in my book. That was a two-year organizing effort, and we put the guy out of business. There were a lot of casualties: a lot of people got hurt, some people died.

I got a call from Project Scout, a senior citizen outreach from Cass Methodist Church, regarding a woman with no heat in her apartment in an Elrum building. I went down and told this woman that I could help her, but she would have to file a suit against her landlord. We arranged to meet the next day at the church, but she didn't show up. So I went over to her place. It was in November and the building was ice cold. She was on this mattress on the floor with several blankets on top of each other. She had spent the night freezing and said she was too cold to go to court.

The next day I got another call from Project Scout who had another plaintiff in the building. So I went over and talked to an older Black woman who was really gung-ho. So we filed a lockout case and got the heat turned back on. About two days later, this woman, who drank a little bit, got home. She had lost her keys and couldn't get into her apartment. So she goes down to the manager's office. This landlord had a history of hiring drunks or thugs. People were always getting beat up. This particular manager was both a thug and an alcoholic. She knocks on his door and says, "Woody, I can't find my key; can you let me in?" He goes, "Get the fuck out of here, nigger bitch." There was a bunch of discarded newspapers in the lobby which she put in front of the manager's door and lit. Then she pounded on his door, yelling "Fire." By the time he opened the door, the fire was just about out. In no way was it a threat to his life. He pulled out a gun, shot her five times, and killed her. That was the second time he killed a tenant while he was in the employ of Henry Elrum.

There were these two deinstitutionalized people in their thirties. They were pretty functional. They worked a lot with the tenant organization. They were like a married couple and had lived together for a long time. The manager in their building was always harassing them. One day, he and a male friend made this batch of Kool-Aid and spiked it with some kind of liquor that didn't have any taste. They got the couple really drunk and both passed out. Then they took May down to the basement and raped her repeatedly throughout the night. They threw her into a dumpster in the back. She went into a kind of catatonia after that and never recovered. Within a week, her mate, Andy, killed himself. Stuff like that happens a lot.

Right after the Engler cuts in general assistance we heard about this landlord in the Cass Corridor who was extorting rent from tenants by taking their food stamps. He would put guns to their heads and cattle prod them. These people were so frightened to talk to anybody like me that you'd have to arrange to meet them like ten miles away because they thought there were spies all over the neighborhood, and there probably were. It doesn't cost much to buy a spy in an area where people kill people over fifty cents.

Henry Elrum was our obsession for two years. The Cass Corridor Tenant Association was on his trail. We did demonstrations in front of his office all the time and out at his Southfield home. Eventually we brought Elrum down. We drove him into bankruptcy court and he lost all of his buildings. He had a $200,000 secret account in Windsor, Ontario, and we got that away from him. That was a major success.

That was like a 1960s action.

Yeah, it was very militant, very confrontational. That's what I enjoy about organizing. I enjoy going after the bad guys.

I had some runins with landlords. I'd get calls right before pickets. One guy called and said, "Are you Doug Smith?" I said yes. He said, "You keep this shit up and they're gonna find you in a trash can." Then I heard from a police officer that Elrum had a contract out on me. A couple times when I was in his tenants' apartments, he'd rush in with some of his thugs and shout, "Get out of here, get out of here," but I wouldn't get out. I was more afraid for the tenants because I knew once I'd left they'd be in for some kind of harassment. Anytime something like that happened I'd report it to the police, just so if I actually did get killed they'd have something to go on.

Now I'm staffing PLAN [Preserve Low-income Affordable Hous-

65

ing Now]. It's made up of public housing tenants, churches, community organizations. In the last eight months we've been trying to establish autonomous chapters in each of the housing projects.

Secretary Kemp of HUD is into resident management of public housing. His motivation is to get rid of public housing. This is a real opening in this city to get rid of the Detroit Housing Department, one of the most corrupt and inefficient in the United States. PLAN is for resident management, but not at the cost of government pulling out of their responsibility. In Detroit we're not for ownership because tenants don't have resources for maintenance. Kemp wants them to own the housing. Public housing is hated by the federal government.

There's close to 50,000 homeless in Detroit and 5,000 vacancies in public housing. Seventy percent of those vacancies are occupiable with a little bit of paint and cleaning. Because of our demonstrations, the occupation of Jeffries [housing project], Tent City, those kinds of things, we've made public housing the number one issue in the city. We're forcing both the local and federal governments to intervene. But the same people are still in charge. So we have to get rid of the mayor, his housing department, and everybody else who's contributing to the demise of public housing.

Politicians always talk this good rap about involving the community, but they're not going to involve the grassroots, except some tokenism. If things were to happen the way we would like it, HUD, the mayor, and the housing department would sit down with representatives of PLAN, my organization, Up and Out of Poverty Now, Michigan Legal Services, and any organization that has had experience and a stake in public housing. They would incorporate what we want and take our input. That would be so great!

I think the biggest block to keeping people from building something is that Detroit has a lot of bad history. People don't trust each other. Not all is difference in political ideology; a lot is pure political opportunism and a lot is personality. This city is a graveyard of hurt egos and personalities. That and race are the two biggest things that obstruct people from putting together something really big.

Part 2   *The African-American Experience*

An empty stomach makes you a little more critical of
the things you accept. People awake one day and say,
"These guys have been fooling me with all this nonsense about quotas and affirmative action. I'm really
being done in." It's gonna occur to some suburbanites
one of these days, as they keep getting hungrier and
hungrier, that Black folks, and others who are selec-
tively blamed, could not have done all this damage.

Horace Sheffield, Executive Director, Detroit
Association of Black Organizations

DETROIT IS AFRICAN-AMERICAN. Eight of ten Detroiters are African-American. All institutions except the economy are led by African-Americans. The dominant culture is African-American.

Most African-American Detroiters have southern roots. Their parents and grandparents migrated to the city to work in the auto industry; once they entered the urban area, they became part of an ill-treated minority. Southern oppression was replaced with a northern variant. They endured the indignities of discrimination and prejudice partly because for most, life was better materially. They learned that the harshness of racial oppression could be partly withstood by strong family, church, and neighborhood bonds. They struggled in the early days of unionization for equality in the workplace. They were deeply into the civil rights movement of the 1950s and 1960s and the thrust for Black empowerment that came as a result of their successes.

But times are bad for most Black Detroiters today. They have become the triple victims of race oppression, class exploitation, and abandonment. Something less than optimism pervades the urban landscape. Nonetheless, the Black Detroiters who speak here give voice to a quiet resourcefulness and surprising hope for the future.

The witnesses presented in this section—all African-Americans—reflect the typical occupational diversity of educated America: student, writer, teacher, director, reporter, lawyer, housing activist. Their political orientations are roughly proportional to their lifestyle or the character of their experiences, as is the general case in America. Yet they speak nearly as one voice, with different styles and intonations, on certain key topics that have come from the African-American experience. Chief among these is the centrality of race as a defining feature of life. These are sophisticated people, and they seldom place race as the *single* defining characteristic. Rather, it's one that intersects with the all-encompassing *class* phenomenon in Detroit and this society.

Bill Harris

My family moved to Detroit from Alabama in 1943. My mother didn't want to raise a Black male child in the South. I grew up on the north end where Detroit, Highland Park, and Hamtramck come together. I come from a family of storytellers. My grandmother had five kids. On every Christmas everybody had to be at her house. They talked about their lives in the South: jobs, interpersonal relationships, the joy of being with each other, the struggles they went through.

When I really started to write in the '60s, I wanted to put on paper or stage the sense of the joy of being Black and the struggles involved in that. I wanted to talk about the kind of revolutionary act that simply loving yourself and your "sort" was. At the *base* you have to know who you are and love yourself, and then you can begin to love other folks. There's a ripple effect.

Something that's more defined for me now is to give voice to Black males, on stage, in prose, or poetry. I let them speak through me to other folks. I've just finished a one-act about Bill Pickett, who was a cowboy. He was the inventor of the technique of bulldogging: jumping on the steer's back and wrestling it to the ground so it can be tied up and branded. I want to give voice to his experiences and what the times were like during that period.

A couple years ago I did a play about jazz musicians that premiered in Detroit at the Attic Theater. Music is a large part of my life and informs a lot of what I do. I have always loved music and the men who make this music. There's a kind of creative independent spirit among these men.

Detroit has a real rich jazz history. Jazz musicians tell stories—love stories, political stories, war stories—in music, and they do it on the spot. This comes out of the African tradition of storytelling. Music proliferated in Detroit because of the African sense that the elder passes on his knowledge to the up-and-coming musicians.

During the '60's there was a lot of concentration on the "cultural." There was an understanding that the cultural was an integral part of whatever kind of struggle there was gonna be. One of the failings is that we weren't able to carry that over. There was a lot of theater in Detroit. You could open a door to a theater and people would come in wanting to act. They had no training, but there was the feeling that "I have something to say and I want to be with someone who wants to say something." Part of the reason that broke down

Bill Harris is acting chief curator at the Museum of African-American History in Detroit, located behind the Detroit Institute of Arts.

was because we didn't create our own critics. We could put stuff on stage and please an audience, but we didn't create critics to praise our stuff and analyze it and pass it on.

In the '60s we thought that we could change the world. I'm not sure you can operate on that kind of energy for too long. There are always these folks out there who want things to be the way they are. This system operates on certain kinds of things being, and staying, the way they are. We ran out of steam, and didn't do some of the basic things that should have been done.

If you were in a political or cultural commune, after a while you began to want your own space. You might have said, "I've been with all these folks, now maybe it's time for me to sit by myself for a minute and think." Once you do that, you look back and don't see the *group* any more. Everybody's gone off to think. You don't have the energy to get that group back together. We may have more disappointment and weariness than cynicism. It's like Atlas: "Let me shift the weight for a little bit."

I'm fairly optimistic about a new change that's going to come. It will take a different form because kids have different concerns. The whole rap thing gives me some kind of optimism. At least they're *talking* about stuff, and asking questions like we did in the '60s: "How did the world get in this shape?" I think the rappers are waking up some of the children of the '60s. I think Malcolm X is one of the focal points around which that's gonna happen. Last year the African-American Museum had an exhibition which dealt with Malcolm. A lot of kids came through. I did a one-act monologue for an actor where he talks about Malcolm's education.

Afrocentrism is an idea whose time has come. You see a lot of resistance to it from people who think that it's a movement to change history. It's a reexamination of stuff that we've been told. In almost all my writing there's a character who has to reexamine what he has been told about himself and his history. Kids come in here and ask why we want to just emphasize slavery or the hard times that we have had. They want a different sense of that past. The idea is not that we were slaves, but that we were *enslaved*. Even though the whole idea of rebellion was *there*, we haven't emphasized it.

Part of our charge here at the museum is to reinterpret all of that. Experts in the various fields will have to reinterpret in terms of what the new needs are. Afrocentrism is the thing around which this is going to happen. The world that we get is the world through western European eyes. We're going to begin to get interpretations of history by the *victims*, and it's a completely different story.

I think Black males are an endangered species. Essentially, there's

72

no use for them in America any more. The reason we were here in the first place doesn't exist any more. I read something the other day that said that the powers-that-be in this country have not figured out a way to use Black males for profit. When they do, we'll all be back to work. If there's no need for you, you really have to watch your back.

E. L. Doctorow's *Ragtime* that came out in the late '60s talks about the turn of the century when ragtime music was popular. He describes what life was like: "Ladies wore white and walked on the beach under umbrellas and American flags were everywhere and there were no Negroes." There obviously *were* Negroes. But that's the kind of world where people didn't have to be faced with the difficulties of people whose labor was needed, and were brought here and used, and then discarded.

This whole thing is based on economics, as opposed to race. Race is a subtext. If white folks had been indentured servants, it would be understood more as a class problem than a racial problem. The white indentured servant thing didn't work. So they had to get Africans and it became a racial issue. It's easier to run up a racial flag than an economic flag. If you examine the *economics* of this system, then you have to call the whole system into question. This system is based on the fact that you have to have somebody to exploit.

I think what's beginning to happen is about redefinitions, which relates to the idea of Afrocentrism or the new term "multiculturalism." It's about politics, culture, and other things. I don't separate these things. They're all a part of the same thing. The Western idea that you can separate mind from body and body from soul is stupid. I think there will be a new understanding of that in terms of art, for example.

I think there will be an expansion on the idea of the necessary connectedness of cultures. I think that Detroit is one of the places where that's going to happen. Detroit has always been on the cutting edge of whatever changes there were for minorities, good or bad.

I think there are signs that things have bottomed out, or leveled off, and we are ready to go somewhere else. That's the way things happen in this society. Things have to reach bottom and then some kind of change can be made. It may be wishful thinking, but I think there's gonna be a look at the whole idea of class and privilege.

The spirit of Detroit is still here. People *love* Detroit. They love it for what it was and because it was all that it was they know what its possibilities are. There always have been problems here, but I think Detroit was as good as it has been in this country for several generations of African-Americans. Detroit's history is a model for what's possible in the future.

73

Kalema Hasan

I'm an activist, a performance poet, mother of five children (three teenagers and two under the age of five), life-long resident of Detroit, and basically a Detroiter who believes in the city.

My activism comes from my family. I was talking to my mother last night. She was telling me how she learned how to shoot guns and take guns apart when she was a little girl. I asked her, "Why did your brothers and uncles have guns around the house?" She said, "So that when those white people came down here messing with us . . ." I started thinking, and it reminded me once again that I come from a history of people who believe in struggle, who believe in fight back, who believe in protecting themselves, who don't cater to stereotypes about who they should be, who are positive about themselves. I came of womanhood during the '60s. I read Billie Holiday's autobiography *Lady Sings the Blues* when I was fourteen and that helped me decide what kind of woman I wanted to be. I saw her as being very strong and positive.

Would you call yourself a feminist?

I never use those terms. I've heard Alice Walker say "womanist," but I just say I'm a human being, I'm a woman. I have a particular view on life and reality that is conditioned by the fact that I'm a woman, that I'm Black, that I'm an American, that I'm an oppressed person; you know, from my history.

My whole life has been centered around politics because I have made certain conscious choices about where I want to be, what kind of money I want to make, what kind of people I want to live around, what class I want to be in. I was one of those Black youngsters who was extremely talented, and who was offered the platter through scholarships and things to move up and make tons of money. But I made a decision at sixteen that I might not have made at thirty-two [*laughs*] — that I was going to stay a working-class person, that I was going to stay close to the ground and struggle.

As a youth this led into student organizing, being part of the Black student movement, and then the general student movement here in the city, politicizing youth around issues. Then the rebellion came in '67. I'm one of those people who saw it with her eyes. I went to bed at four in the morning the night before. At six o'clock, Detroit, as we knew it, was not going to exist again. Twelfth Street was

Kalema Hasan is a staff person with the United Community Housing Coalition, located in downtown Detroit.

gone. You were not going to find jazz clubs any more or famous jazz musicians walking around. You were not going to find the colorfulness of the city, the culture, the way it existed before. That riot destroyed not only buildings, but it destroyed a basic foundation and fibre.

The major part of that destruction came *after* the rebellion because drugs were pumped into Detroit. Within a month you could buy heroin at a price that was incredibly cheap. When a large percentage of people became addicted, the price skyrocketed. Heroin destroyed *my* generation in this city, and crack came along for the generations after me. Already crack is playing out. Young people like my fifteen-year-old son are wise to it. Only an idiot is gonna go out there and consciously become a crack addict. So something new will come along. It's apparent to me, from our history, that there are always forces out there seeking to destroy Black people, to annihilate us as a people.

In my development, and getting to know people, and forming friendships and bonds, even though I see it as a Black problem, it's not *really* a Black problem, it's a national problem. It's about national oppression of people based upon race, sex, class, and everything else. Whatever tool that can be used to divide and oppress people is used. We're suffering, we're low wage earners, we're locked out of many economic opportunities, we're locked into communities that all kinds of destructive things are dumped into.

There's no white land, there's no Black land. Historically you find different cultures and different groupings of people that had different ideas and feelings. James Baldwin eloquently expressed it when he said, "Before people came to America they're German and Irish, but once they get to America, they're white. Before *we* came here we were Ashantis, Mandingoes, or whatever. Now that we're *here*, we're Black people."

For so long Black people were in the minority in Detroit. Now they're in the majority. We have a Black administration. There are a lot of things wrong with the city. It is difficult for white people to offer criticism toward that administration. This is a city with a first-generation Black leadership, surrounded by a suburban area that is extremely hostile. We have to know how to criticize this administration and not play into the hands of the racist, reactionary elements.

It's a contradiction based on "We're not going to let these white people in the suburbs tell us what to do, but every dime we get we're gonna use to attract these white people from the suburbs into the city to spend their money." Why can't more money be put into the city to create opportunities for the people who live here, to create a tax base

75

from working people? There are incredible numbers of Black men in this city who are very talented and have skills, who can't find a job. They could build anything in this city that we need. They could *run* anything. But they're locked out, and that's not a white power structure doing that. That's a Black administration that has, in my view, an incorrect analysis of what's going on.

In today's *Free Press* there's an article about the $750,000 renovation going on at the Jeffries projects through volunteer effort, donations from corporations, and so forth, because of their so-called concern for the homeless "problem." Last year when an organization that I'm helping to develop—PLAN [Preserve Low-income Affordable Housing Now]—attempted to do the same thing we met with extreme hostility. It was said that we were outside agitators, that it was something white people were doing to embarrass the administration. I was personally pulled aside a few times and told that I should do certain things and not embarrass Black people; I don't subscribe to the idea that I'd rather have my head beat by a Black man than a white man. I don't want *anybody* hitting me on my head.

PLAN's an organization that's concerned about what's happening in public housing and in the city. It's a group with every race, class, religious, and economic background that's working hard and diligently to turn this city around. One of the commitments that we made was that we're gonna listen to the people who we're supposed to be organizing. They're gonna take a leadership role. Even though sometimes it doesn't seem like the best way to go, we find that they're gonna make the best decision because they're creating change in their own condition. They're being attacked by this administration because white people are participating in it, even though the administration has its *own* circle of particular white people.

Do you see the '90s as a period of building more democratic relationships in activist organizations?

It's important, but it's a struggle. In order to be democratic you have to be honest, you have to be able to deal with your feelings, with people, and with past relationships. So little is studied and appreciated about these past relationships. I was at an event with a mixed group of people and somehow the discussion got on slavery. The remark came out, "Well, I don't understand why the slaves were unhappy; they were fed." And this was a progressive person. It showed me that people were still ignorant and backward on matters of race. If you can have that kind of attitude, how can you be progressive in the '90s?

First, you have to build the new person. If you don't, you get what you have in the city of Detroit right now. We're always making new men and women. The people produced in the 1990s are different from the people produced in the 1890s. New people are made all the time. You have to create the conditions for people to want to be the new man or woman.

It's hard to be a supremacist if you come from very humble origins. It's hard to think that you're better than somebody else when you know that you're not. It's hard to justify the fact that somebody in El Salvador has to die so that you can have a cup of coffee in the morning. It's hard to justify wearing a gold chain around your neck, driving around in a Jeep and selling crack, when your brother in South Africa died in that mine for thirty-three cents a day for you to wear this chain on your neck.

Just this morning I was talking to a friend, and her child who's in fifth grade has been in an Afrocentric educational environment. She's decided that she's taking her child out of that because it's not producing what her child needs. She said, "Afrocentrism is something I can give them at home; they don't need to go to school for that." The love of self that we need is not gonna come from Afrocentric education. There's a lot of Afrocentric young men out there with gold chains around their necks selling crack. They have an analysis. You want an analysis of race in this country, those brothers out there know by their *life*.

Herb Boyd

I was born in Birmingham, Alabama, in 1938. My mother brought my brother and me to Black Bottom in Detroit in 1942. This was the real womb for Black people in Detroit. We were blues people, born and nurtured in the South, who still retained that vital culture of the earth. We were salt of the earth. We brought our culture with us: the love for the music, that feel for the earth, the spirit of adventure, and the oppression that was down there. We thought that Valhalla was north of the Mason-Dixon line.

The first thing that hit me politically was the riot in 1943. I remember my mother coming in with a big can of chitlins and a Virginia ham and a bag of groceries. She dumped them in the room and said she was going back for more. She said that somebody threw a brick through Isaac's Market and the people are ripping them off left and right. Those same memories came back to me in 1967 when the

Herb Boyd is a journalist, New York City teacher, author of African History for Beginners *(Writers and Readers Press, 1992), and co-editor of* Brother Man *with Robert Allen (Ballantine, 1993).*

city went up in flames. She tried to explain to us what had triggered the riot. In 1943 it was just so much mumbo-jumbo about people hating people. So the whole issue of racism didn't come home to me as squarely as it did later.

I grew up in the Brewster and Jeffries projects. We were on welfare a lot. My mother was a domestic, and continues to be today. She's managed to keep the same contacts she's had over the years, working out at Pleasant Ridge, Birmingham, Bloomfield Hills, Grosse Point, St. Clair Shores. She would bring home clothes from her domestic work, and my brother and I would be the best-dressed kids in school. That's the way she held her family together.

Detroit was not unlike Chicago or Harlem where there was a concentration of Black people. But Detroit was unique in terms of the geographical patterns of how we lived—single-family homes, a basement, a back yard. These things figured into the relationships people have that other cities didn't have. Jazz was very important to me as a teenager. We'd meet in different basements and play instruments. We had a certain amount of privacy. We didn't have to go to a settlement. Our *homes* were points of congregation. That gave us a certain control and development that likely triggered the later development of Motown.

My mother was a jazz fanatic. Nat King Cole was like a surrogate father, along with Billy Eckstine, Charlie Parker, and all of the beboppers. She was deeply into rhythm and blues. She had all the records and I wore them out. I got my musical education through her records and listening to her and her friends. She would give these rent parties and gambling parties. She thought I would be in bed, but I always was no more than an ear away from what was happening. My mother was my idol, my role model. She had a tremendous impact on me in terms of cultural awareness and being literate. She read everything. She'd bring home from her jobs all the magazines: *House and Garden, Vogue, Harper's Bazaar, Collier's, Post, Life, Look, Reader's Digest.* I'd read everything that came into the house. When I was about seventeen I decided to become the writer. Richard Wright gave me a kind of ethos about the Black experience: *Native Son, Twelve Million Black Voices, Black Boy, Uncle Tom's Children.* He helped me understand the kind of ghetto experience I was going through as a teenager.

I lived close by two members of the Nation of Islam. They sold us *Muhammad Speaks.* The cultural texture I was getting from Richard Wright and others was being reinforced on a political edge through an incipient nationalism of the Nation of Islam. Elijah Muhammad came to Detroit from Sandersfield, Georgia, in the early '40s to work in the plants. Eventually, he founded the first mosque in Detroit. A number of the nascent nationalist organizations had their beginnings in Detroit.

When people came to the door selling *Muhammad Speaks,* I asked questions. "Well, brother, why don't you come down to the mosque and find out for yourself?" And I did. This was 1959, just out of high school. At the mosque I had the opportunity to meet Malcolm X. As James Baldwin said, "My dungeon shook." I was almost immediately transformed. At that time Malcolm was slowly evolving into a national figure and no longer connected to a small mosque and going around and visiting. My first political perspective came through the Henry brothers, and then James Boggs and Grace Lee Boggs, and individuals in and around the Freedom Now movement. By then I was a stoned Malcomite. The civil rights movement was like the "other side." I was not a devotee of Martin Luther King's strategy.

In 1958 I moved to New York City. I wanted to be a writer and I said writers live in New York City. I lived in the Village since I was fascinated by any kind of counterculture thing. I also lived in Brooklyn and Harlem. Then the army caught up with me and I spent most of my time in Germany. Hardly ever wore a uniform. I was a jock in the daytime and had a band at night. Same as I had done as a kid. 79

In 1964, when my thirty-day leave came up, while most of my partners took off for the Scandinavian countries to get those "long-legged blonde girls," I went to Morocco and roamed around Africa. Ironically enough, it was at the same time that Malcolm was passing through. It's then I decided that when I get out of the service I'm going to go back to college and specialize in African studies.

I went to Montieth College, an experimental college that was set up for people who were interested in doing nontraditional things. The rumor was this was where the eggheads and weirdos and beatniks hung out. Two years later, in 1967, boom—the city exploded. I was living at Fullerton and 12th Street, right in the belly of the beast and right near where much of the stuff went down. That's where Michael Lewis was arrested. They were going to blame him for the whole '67 riot. I got into a letter-writing campaign. That was the first time I was so moved to do something like that. When they grabbed Michael to be the scapegoat for the 1967 riot I said, "No, I ain't hearing that." For the first time I saw my name in print, connected to political action. I got moved by that. Then I did PR for an organization to free Michael Lewis. Some of my partners, like Dan Aldrich and Dorothy DuBerry and Phil Hutchins and Gloria and Stuart House, had cut their eyeteeth in the civil rights movement. I had never gone South. I was a Malcomite and ready to say "by any means necessary." Those were intense discussions.

At Montieth we began to push hard for classes on the Black experience, the African experience, and Third World studies. One of my feet began to ease out of the community and became planted solidly on campus. I said I'd work a little bit in the ivory tower and I'd get back to the grassroots in a minute. I was always straddling and trying to bring the ivory tower and the grassroots together.

At Montieth students were allowed to teach, so I put together the first Black history course on the writings of Richard Wright, Ralph Ellison, James Baldwin. Twenty-five students showed up! I was stunned. I said, "Now I got to teach this thing." That started my teaching career.

Meanwhile, out in the community things were growing all the time: the League of Revolutionary Black Workers, DRUM [Dodge Revolutionary Union Movement], etc. The same people I used to know in the plants are now coming onto campus. I would have classes with 250 students—some Muslims, some people following the ideas of Karenga, some Black Panthers, some Marxists connected with the League. It was a good blend, a grab bag of ideological persuasions in that classroom. It was so exciting and dynamic. Let a thousand schools of thought contend. We contended in those classrooms, and I was like the honorary referee.

From a cultural standpoint, I was trying to see what could be done from the university to effect change for community people, to have their humanity recognized and their music showcased. I hooked up with artists around the Jazz Research Institute at Wayne (Tommy Glover, Ed Nelson) and the Detroit Jazz Center. But it wasn't exclusively jazz. Later I hooked up with John and Lenny Sinclair, who were trying to bring culture and politics together with the *Ann Arbor Sun,* and the *Detroit Sun.* Charles Moore and I commuted for two years to Oberlin, where we taught jazz studies at the conservatory.

We thought there was no division among politics, economics, and culture, and we were trying to bring them all together. Similarly, we thought there should be no division between the academy and the community. We tried to knock the barriers down. All of a sudden you got all these jazz nuts hooked up with these political activists. Maybe the bridge would be Malcolm X to some degree and John Coltrane to another degree. Political and cultural change feed each other. But there was a lot of hit and miss. It's like jazz—we were improvising.

Also, we would read and have study groups. They were mostly political discussions. We would read Frantz Fanon, Che Guevara, Mao-tse Tung, Ho Chi Minh. The Boggses brought in Marx. Without these, these was no context. But there was some undermining of the synthesis that was occurring. The race people stayed over here, and the class people stayed over there. Race was just as important to me as class, though race was the initial thing that you felt. Later on, I saw how important it was to weld the class component with the race component.

I think we all had grown up a bit and recognized the potential power we had. At the same time, we represented a threat to the establishment and they moved to nullify these programmatic thrusts. There were deliberate attacks like running all the radicals off campus. We had a steady funnel of students from various cultural and political groups who saw the university as a meeting place. Then, bam, maybe financial aid fell apart, particular instructors were no longer there. Also, objective reality had changed. The window of opportunity began to come down in about '74. It was just about over. The radical movements began to fade into the general context of things. They were absorbed and diffused of all meaningful power. Or some stayed in there, but they were so small and insignificant that people saw them as a bunch of weirdos.

81

Most of the time, most of us were caught up in a state of flux. Some of us were able to extract ourselves from the general flow of things and tried to make some kind of analysis of what were the next steps. That's really hard to do. Even if you *had* the right notion of the right way to go, there was no guarantee anyone was listening to you. All of the powerful movement personalities of the day had a vision of which way to go. Either you follow them or they just going to go off without you. I was trying to catch up with the masses more than anything. [*Laughs*] It was so dynamic. Things were going in so many directions. Which way should I go? My instincts told me to stick with what I know and don't go running off to these wild-eyed fanatics—like the old John Clare poem, "A fool came to me and said I know the way. Alas, I followed him. He took me to places where I could not see. And then he cried to me that he was lost." Where the hell does that leave me? So I tried to stay close to my roots: that basic little boy who came out of Alabama. Stay with your history. Black history, Black culture. That's your strength. Work, study, and struggle. I've stuck to that pattern and it's helped me shape who I am no matter where I am.

I left Detroit in 1985 and came to New York City.

Gloria House

I was in Paris at the time of the Algerian Revolution. I was in Berkeley at the time of the Free Speech Movement. I was in Alabama for SNCC's [Student Nonviolent Coordinating Committee] movement toward nationalist thought and ideology and the formation of the

Gloria House is a professor with the Weekend College at Wayne State University and author of Tower and Dungeon: A Study of Place and Power in American Culture *(Detroit: Casa de Unidad Press, 1991).*

Loundes County Freedom Organization. And I got to Detroit in the year of the rebellion. I should thank history, or the muse, for putting me where I could get a firsthand understanding of what people were struggling for and to be a part of those struggles.

In August 1966 I married another SNCC worker, Stuart House, who was assigned to Selma in Green County. By 1967, I was pregnant with our only child. The doctor said that if I wanted to carry this child to term, I'd better leave the South and go someplace where I could eat three meals a day, because I was distinctly undernourished.

By this time, SNCC had lost a great deal of its support because of ·
the position of asking whites to work in white communities and because of our antiwar statement, which I had drafted. The $10 that we used to get every week started to come less and less frequently, so we were not eating all that well by 1967.

So, I decided to leave Alabama in 1967 and come to Detroit, which was my husband's home town. He knew that if he came back he could probably find a job fairly quickly. We needed to create some kind of economic base for ourselves. My son was born in July 1967.

I had visited Detroit a couple of times to meet Stuart's family. We came for R&R, and I liked Detroit. I had a sense of comfort and ⌐
feeling at home because the community was so organic. Once you arrived in the core city, Blacks were everywhere. Blacks were in the post office. They were running the City-County Building. No matter what municipal building you went into, Blacks were behind the counters. The bus drivers were Black. The nurses were Black. You had the sense of being almost in a Third World country, and I felt very happy and secure in that kind of environment. The Motown sound! The Black music! It was kind of a feeling of holistic experience.

I didn't know the history of the city. I didn't know the layer upon layer of radical and progressive movements which I discovered after I got here. That's one of the reasons why I'm still here.

I immediately got immersed in various kinds of organizing. My first job was at Cass Tech High School. I taught French and English there, and I got involved in the Detroit Federation of Teachers union, and also in antiwar movement activities.

Then I went to work as an editor at the *Detroit Free Press* and became chair of the Black caucus in the Newspaper Guild. Wherever I worked, I tried to be part of the organizing of the union. I was the second Black person to be hired as an editorial staff member at the *Free Press*. I worked as editor of the editorial page, doing the actual editing of the editorial writings and also the letters to the editor and the op-ed columns. It was my job to edit all that stuff and to oversee the layout of those pages.

While I was at the *Free Press,* I took a position against STRESS [Stop the Robberies, Enjoy Safe Streets], an undercover police operation. A group of young organizers had called for a day's boycott against STRESS. The police had just managed to kill a couple of Black teenagers. So we called a day's work boycott as an expression of outrage against these killings. Well, I did go to the demonstration, and I was fired. There was another demonstration on my behalf by local organizers in front of the *Free Press:* "Black editor fired for participating in demonstrations."

The day of the STRESS demonstration, I met Phil Hutchings, an organizer in the Venceremos Brigade, who invited me to go to Cuba. I went, and was there for two months. Seeing the new society in Cuba, the society of the future, ninety miles off the coast of the United States, had a tremendous effect on me. Cuba was a major turning point for me, or more an affirmation of my vision of what life could be about.

Then in 1971 I came to teach at Montieth College at Wayne State University. Wayne is a very racist institution. From the moment I set foot here, I've been involved in ongoing struggles against the institutional racism here in so many different forms: trying to keep certain minority people here as instructors; trying to get new programs into the curriculum that represent the history of people of color. Five or six years ago, we had a universitywide Black caucus, digging out the data that demonstrated disparities in salaries between white and Black and other people of color. It has meant that my own abilities have gone grossly underutilized by the institution because I've been labeled a troublemaker throughout the Wayne experience, which is now twenty years.

On the other hand, I've had the opportunity to develop some innovative educational programs, like the Third World and women's studies course and the program in humanities at Jackson Prison. I was the first woman to go into that maximum-security prison in any professional capacity to design a program for incarcerated men. I kept saying, What in the world could have any meaning for some of the men who are in here for life? To work with them to create a program that had meaning for them was one of the most exciting and most challenging things I've ever done.

I discovered a new way to organize an educational program. I had pioneered a new way with the Third World and women's studies. The first thing you do is engage the students in designing the program that they want. You challenge the student to really think about the education he or she needs, then to work with you to structure that. I took that understanding into the prison. But the thing I had to do in the prison was to convince these men that I really was going to help them do this, and that I was asking them to be my peer in this process.

For the most part they were Black men. I had to listen, really listen, because their experience was radically different from the experience of a Black woman. I had to face the alienation between Black men and women; the hostility that a lot of the guys had toward women; the fact that many felt abandoned by their wives, lovers, mothers, sisters.

A curriculum emerged which represented their preoccupations. What about the relationship between men and women? What about the philosophical issues of justice and right and wrong and, of course, part of that is the criminal justice system. These were the themes we explored. I had to take all their study material in with me every week. The prison wasn't facilitating this process. This meant my going to the library and finding the stuff and then carting it up there and then carting it back.

The prison work kept me from feeling bitter about the negative part of being a Black member of the Wayne State faculty. I have had my friends and comrades in the community as a source of support and affirmation. That's kept me buoyed against the Wayne State negativity. Even our union has been very insensitive to minority faculty members here. I'm in the union, but I don't have very much good to say for it. I certainly participated wholeheartedly in the two or three strikes we've had, because I know it's necessary. My organizing has been with the Black caucus, an independent caucus of faculty, staff, and students which lasted two and a half years, until the university succeeded in pushing out the chairperson. I was a co-chair.

Outside the university, it's been solidarity work around Cuba, Grenada, the movements of southern Africa, Nicaragua, the Palestinians. I've tried to get my body over to these places and get a sense of what's going on, what people are trying to build. In my course called History and Politics of the Third World I give students the historical development of the Third World movements and talk about how people of color in this country have identified with those movements and began to call themselves Third World people.

In the '60s and '70s, we could think of ourselves as a somewhat homogeneous community, as Blacks or as people of color. Then as the economic gaps between the poor and the fairly well off got broader, it became clear that we weren't sharing so much in common any more, and that people were withdrawing to their comfort zones and trying their best to forget about the poverty that the majority of Blacks were having to face. It's difficult for Blacks in my generation,

especially those of us who've gone through the progressive movements of the '60s and '70s, to face the fact that we're going to have to
say to other Blacks that we must face this rift.

The city of the people is more and more eroded, while the city of
the ruling class continues to thrive in places like the new developments down along the river. They are becoming more and more privatized spaces that are policed and closed off to the general population. We can see the city looking more and more like apartheid
spaces. We can see the gray spaces that are rotting and being allowed
to go, being allowed to be torched or whatever, and the green spaces
that are thriving and being built up. Blacks whom I guess we thought
before would identify with Black poverty are saying, no, I managed to
get myself out of this, and I'm gone. The few progressive Blacks who
are committed to the city are now trying to figure out ways to organize.

Mike Hamlin

I came from poor Mississippi sharecroppers. My mother endured
great suffering. She worked as hard as a human being can work and
got very little in return. I have never gone back to Mississippi. Many of
my relatives go back and talk about how nice it is. I want to remember
it like it was. It's still bad, and I don't want to forget how bad it was.

I was very angry when I came back to Detroit in 1960 from the
army, so I was looking for ways to do something. Most of my ideas at
that time were adventurous. I was interested in terrorist kind of activities. It was a response to frustration. A lot of people at that time
talked about kamikaze or suicidal attacks. You would end your pain
and you would strike a blow.

But then I met John Watson, and through him I began to feel
that maybe a terrorist act, no matter how large, would not accomplish
that much. And maybe there could be a greater impact by organizing
people and focusing on the working class. It was through him that I
began to understand classes and class society. Watson was, is, a super
intellectual, a genius. You could put John Watson in a room with a
machine that he's seen for the first time, and two hours later he
could probably take the machine apart and put it back together and
have it running. John Watson is the most brilliant man I have ever

*Mike Hamlin is on the staff of the Dearborn office of Occupational Health Centers of
America, where he focuses on drug rehabilitation.*

encountered. He's also crazy. I'm told that geniuses often border on insanity.

We worked at the *Detroit News* together. Then Ken Cockrel came, and we constituted quite a trio down there on the docks of the *Detroit News*. I was driving a truck and they were helpers. We kept those folks engaged all the time. Many people were influenced by us. When I spoke at Ken's funeral, state representative Burton Leland came up and said, "You know, I used to work at the *News* with you."

We were all involved in the struggle against police brutality. A Black would be killed in a community, either by a merchant or the police, and the police would plant a knife on the person who was killed. The police would always be absolved of any blame by the prosecutor. We would protest. We'd have these meetings at a church or some place, and people would be very angry. The lawyers in the Wolverine Bar Association [a Michigan Black professional association], the NAACP, the Urban League would be there, and we would say that we were going to have a demonstration the next day at this particular site. When we'd show up for the demonstration, wouldn't nobody be there but the same group of young, ragtag radicals.

Ultimately, that process led to a conclusion that nothing was going to be done unless we did it, because the NAACP and these groups were all gradualists. We were also outraged by what was going on in the South, the beating of those sitting in, the Freedom Riders, the civil rights demonstrations. It was one outrage after the other.

General Baker, John Watson, and others were involved in groups at Wayne State that would meet and fall apart, a lot of times by things like one of the members had a white wife and somebody would bring that up and that would break up the group. John and I came to the conclusion that we had to do something. I was in a better material position than John, and I was willing to make a financial contribution. So we came up with the money to get us started in a newspaper, *The Inner City Voice*. We got an office and we began to develop staff. John learned the technology from *The Fifth Estate,* from the SWP [Socialist Workers Party], and from various people.

The first issue prompted a controversy within the staff because we were publishing stuff by Che Guevara. Some of the nationalists said we shouldn't be publishing stuff by a white man. John obviously had an antiimperialist position and I'd developed it from him. We bought the equipment and paid the rent. We fought them all. We went and got General, because we knew if General was with us they wouldn't mess with us.

At that time, SNCC [Student Nonviolent Coordinating Committee] was moving toward Black Power. White radicals were moving toward mysticism and saying that the working class was too corrupt, could not be organized, wasn't a revolutionary force. Part of our effort was to prove that that wasn't true.

We took our paper, which called for revolution, out to the plants and distributed it and were prepared to fight to the end with any worker, Black or white, or anybody else who tried to stop us from distributing it. If they had attacked us, not only would they have to deal with us, but the Black workers would have joined us. It was a life and death issue for us.

I decided that we were getting very strung out, with a great danger of isolation. We needed to begin to mobilize some white allies. I persuaded people like Sheila Murphy, Frank Joyce, and Jim Jacobs to meet as a core group that led to the Motor City Labor League, to Control, Conflict and Change, to the Alliance [a coalition of progressive activists], and various things. We told them to organize in the white community. What the nationalists did was attack all whites, and in that case they were attacking the allies.

There was a lot of personality stuff. As long as you were strong, people suppressed these tendencies. But sometimes even when there were principled differences, personalities get involved and people made power plays and that kind of thing. I think the main role I played in this period was as a unifying force amongst all these personalities, many of whom couldn't stand each other's shortcomings or flaws as they perceived them.

And there was also the objective situation. We had a lot of external pressures. We had an enormous apparatus. The workload was uneven. Basically, John and I (and mainly me in the end) carried the financial and legal burdens. When it came down to who was going to be the responsible person, who was going to be given up to the Internal Revenue, etcetera, that person was me. It had to be somebody and nobody else wanted to do it. John and I and Ken were the incorporators of all the numerous bodies that we incorporated.

But the situation unfolded in the League to a point where I was unwilling to do that any more. There were, in fact, people who had to go, people who had played important roles in the early development of the organization, but whose excesses were just too much for me and for a large wing of the organization. That's what precipitated the League's split.

The other thing about these splits of the late '60s was that the leadership never wanted a full airing of all the issues. I'm not saying that I'm any less guilty than anybody else. But at no time in any of these splits do I recall a situation where people wanted to have a battle of ideas in front of the membership and let the membership decide.

There were some other legitimate issues about the relationship between growth versus consolidation, and I was on the growth side. My argument for that was that the leadership was so limited. By that time, its size, its ideas, its differences, its energy was limited, plus the forces arrayed against us. We had created quite a stir and provoked concern in Chrysler world headquarters, at the UAW world headquarters, and in the police.

It was so intense. I had lost my job in 1970. I'd been through two divorces. I was just flat out consumed by all of the tasks. And not just me. So was John. So was General.

From the time that I came back from the army, I did not expect a very long life. I was too angry. I was too dissatisfied with the reality of being Black in America and what was happening to the people. For a lot of us, the idea of dying in battle was the desired end. We wanted to educate people to do what was to be done; then it really didn't matter what happened to us. That was my rationale for all of the time I spent doing classes with whites, helping people build organizations, doing all kinds of support things.

Eventually the Black Workers Congress was created, which was a national organization of radical and progressive Blacks around the country who had been part of the SNCC experience and the Panther experience and who would accept the notion that the focus on the working class was the most crucial task.

Joann Watson

I was born in Detroit and am a product of this community. I went to Central High School in the '60s and became immersed in the growing civil rights movement. Mosque Number 1 where Malcolm X was doing his work was right across the street from the high school. I was greatly influenced by Martin Luther King. I was influenced by the Motown sound. Much of the music was a real anthem for many of us.

The year that I graduated from high school, 1968, was the year that left a permanent mark on my life. I really had not gotten over John F. Kennedy's assassination in '63 nor Malcolm X's assassination in '65. These were riveting pieces for me. But to have Martin Luther King killed on April 4th, right in the middle of my senior year, was a traumatic assault on my social consciousness. And then Robert F. Ken-

Joann Watson is executive director of the Detroit branch of the National Association for the Advancement of Colored People (NAACP), one of the largest branches in the country. It's located on West Grand Boulevard, just a stone's throw from the General Motors world headquarters.

nedy was assassinated two weeks before my graduation. I was propelled toward human service work.

I majored in journalism at the University of Michigan and spent most of my waking hours in the student movement, the civil rights movement, the peace movement, the women's movement. I got married while in college and had children.

I was blessed with an opportunity to work with the desegregation of the Detroit public schools. My work for the YWCA for many years in Detroit and at the national level combined many of the ideals that are very dear to me. That institution prioritized the elimination of sexism *and* racism, so I was able to work on all the things that I believed in. Plus, it was a social service organization. I helped to start women's shelters, job centers for the unemployed, pantries for the needy.

89

I was the vice-president of the Michigan NAACP before I left to go to New York to work at the YWCA. It was a thrill and an honor to be asked to come back home and come into the challenging position I now have.

I think of the NAACP as being blessed with a legacy because we're strong and old and traditional. We've done our job so well that a lot of individuals and organizations take us for granted and don't always see us as being as relevant or as visionary as we ought to be. Some of those critics are people who have earned degrees that have been wrapped in an affirmative action sheepskin. They owe a debt to somebody that paved the road.

I've always been fascinated by the civil rights movement and the selflessness of so many people. I'm not happy that most of our children don't know Ella Baker or Fanny Lou Hamer, women who really gave so much to the movement, including being jailed, assaulted, and abused, and putting themselves and their families at great risk.

This generation that has come along since the '60s has not been given the kind of awareness they need. We've not mainstreamed the issues and the priorities that drove the civil rights movement into the hearts and minds of America's youth. That's why so many of their souls are up for grabs. The White Aryan Resistance and the neo-Nazis and Skinheads would not be attracting the white youth to their movement if we were collectively doing what we ought to be doing with our youth.

I think there's a great potential for positive growth. Regrettably, there's also just as much potential for disaster in the country. It depends primarily on how much people who are champions of justice are willing to put themselves out. I don't call people who are advocating the annihilation of populations as conservative or even right-wing extremists. I think they ought to be viewed as what they are: treasonous. They're using technology and cable and hotlines, proclaiming that every state west of Illinois ought to be reserved for whites only. There are some in this country who don't think there's any place for Black, Brown, and Asian people *at all*, despite the fact that native people were the *first* people here.

There's a guy in this area who made the public statement within the last month that he believed that half the people in Detroit ought to be interned, and the other half incarcerated. That's a blatantly fascist statement. There aren't enough good people who are repelled by that insane racial baiting.

If blue-collar, low-income whites who are victims of classism could ever understand that they've been manipulated into believing that they've lost privilege because of those "other" people, if they could see that as the bill of goods it is, then we could really organize around basic issues related to justice and empowerment for *all* people. Therein lies hope for the country. What so-called liberal, human rights groups are all about is really the most patriotic activity going on in this country.

You meet very few whites in America who understand that the elimination of racism is in their own self-interests. I'm not just talking about racial understanding and multicultural appreciation, but I'm talking about power. The real void is in white leaders committed to justice who are brave enough to become a lightning rod. We need some white Martin Luther Kings around who will stand up and say, "I am not going to allow my community, my children, my city, to be dominated by this kind of narrow-minded oppression that does not serve any of us well."

We must nurture in our young people a proud legacy that goes back to the kings and queens of Africa. The pyramids were built by African people: the first scientists, architects, and mathematicians. If that's instilled from a perspective of power, along with past struggle, I think then you have a real potential for movement that does not *just* respond to injustice, but in which people set their own norms and define their own destiny.

When I speak out strongly about the incidence of violence in our community, as I did on the day we commemorated Martin Luther King's birthday this year, I did so not because I had been a personal victim, but because the level of death and violence in *any* urban area is an abomination to the legacy of Martin Luther King. There is no way we can just celebrate the recitations of "I Have a Dream," and have those feel-good sessions for one day, and not have that make a difference in how we conduct our daily lives.

People in Detroit, despite the fact that there's been economic siege for more than a decade, give more per capita to the United Way than any other community. This is a giving community. Whenever someone is in distress or a family is in dire trouble, Detroiters from all backgrounds dig deep. We take care of our own, even though we're very hard on ourselves. Sometimes we're our worst critics about the city. We don't want anybody else talking about Detroit. We're fiercely loyal. We're deeply devoted to the work ethic.

In Detroit we sit on the waterfront, and with the backdrop of organized labor being rooted here, and the natural combination of working-class people of all backgrounds, we have great potential, despite the steady diet of bad news that gets communicated in the media. We have more potential for lifting up the inherent greatness of American people here than in any other city.

91

We've shown we can come together. We do that in times of crisis and in times of greatness. The community came together to celebrate Nelson Mandela. It took New York City three days to raise $1 million to help Mandela. Detroit did it in one day. People who suffer the highest levels of unemployment and underemployment came together and gave him a welcome that was unprecedented, across all lines.

I love Detroit. The greatness of the city is embodied in its people who are tough, who've had to go through a lot just to make it. Therein lies what America is all about.

Ron Lockett

In 1968 the whole notion of Black Power became a magnetic field for me. I really felt good about it. I read *Malcolm Speaks*. It was like a spiritual thing. Everything that I was feeling, he was articulating. My parents were very conservative, very religious. I told them that this thing was just like Jesus Christ. They said, "Oh, my God, you're talking about a Black Muslim revolutionary leader that you're equating to Jesus Christ." By that time I was on my way.

My mentor was Dan Aldrich. He was on the mayor's staff and also a writer for the *Michigan Chronicle*. He had come out of SNCC [Student Nonviolent Coordinating Committee] and was a disciple of Grace and Jimmy Boggs. We had a different worldview. We saw ourselves as Marxist-Leninists. We developed an organization called the All-African Peoples Union, which was similar to Kwame Nkrumah's organizational structure in Ghana. Grace and Jimmy were theoreti-

Ron Lockett is the deputy director of youth services for the Wayne County Office of Health and Community Services, located on Cass Park near downtown Detroit.

cians who had a worldview different than the League of Revolutionary Black Workers, who saw the leading force being Black workers. Jimmy and Grace, we thought with clairvoyance, saw that technology, which already had reduced the working class, was going to reduce the working class further.

Then I went to Wayne State. Wayne was so fertile. There were the cultural nationalists, the nationalists who embraced socialism, the Marxist-Leninists, the communists. It was just an incredible time. I didn't get involved in school for about three years [*laughs*] because I was so involved in the movement. My writing and reading was greater than it would have been if I had been just a normal student.

The Vietnam War kept the left together by providing a focal point. And there were some things happening economically that we just weren't paying attention to. Some of the analysis became so sterile. It wasn't looking at the evolution of the American economy or even looking at America. The notion of racism was so pervasive that we paid attention sometimes to the wrong things. We tended to be very international and in some ways not national enough to look at exactly what needed to be taken care of at home, such as housing patterns and school issues.

The Black *petit bourgeoisie* said that we had had enough of Black history. The Black studies programs that we got started in high school were dismantled. No one thought about the fact that we had a whole generation of kids coming up that knew nothing about Martin Luther King, or the civil rights movement, or the Scottsboro boys, or the wave of independence of African nations, or of colonialism.

A lot of people started focusing on careers. America just didn't fit the concept of proletariat versus the bourgeoisie. Some things that we thought were immanent just were not happening. The idea of socialism springing from the ashes just collapsed.

With the wave of Black consciousness and the exodus of whites from the city, the numbers were there to elect Black politicians. You saw that first real wave start in the early '70s: Gibson, Stokes, Young [the first Black mayors of Newark, Cleveland, and Detroit, respectively]. As Blacks we got caught into the pride thing so much that we gave these leaders carte blanche. They had a free period to do what they wanted to do because we knew it was tough, and we didn't want to judge them by the same standards that white mayors had been judged. We felt that they would open up resources that had been closed off to our communities and they would make the police departments more humane. We felt that the quality of life would improve in our communities because we would have someone there who looked like us.

It was like a mild high, but it was temporary. After we came back down, reality was still slapping us in the face. We rejoiced at times that whites were leaving, but whites also were taking away the tax base. The overwhelming majority of the Blacks still were poor and living off social services. We weren't doing the type of in-depth analysis with the skills that the movement had afforded us.

Not having that type of Afrocentric apparatus that was built in the late '60s, our kids got involved in the pop culture more than ever. As a result, we have Black kids who don't know about themselves having, not only a very oppressive history, but a glorious history, and that their people have always fought to make themselves better and to make things around them better. These kids have really bought into the me, myself, and I syndrome.

Then we had this phenomenon that came up in the mid-1980s called crack. It followed the heroine drug piece in the mid-'70s that was real, real strong. There's always been a network, a system, an ingenuity in the Detroit street culture to take something and make it in this very tough town. The adage is that if you can make it here, you can make it anywhere. So we had some very brilliant entrepreneurs from the street who got involved in drugs. They developed a corporate system. Their plans included using kids, because kids go to juvenile court if they're caught, but come right back out, as opposed to someone age seventeen or older who goes to adult court. They developed a courier/messenger system, used technology with beepers and cellular telephones, etc. The same people who society said were learning disabled and illiterate and couldn't do chemistry in school, could take baking soda and cocaine, light it, and make that into crack cocaine, which is a very sophisticated chemical experiment.

The drug dealers believed in the kids in the negative sense because they knew the kids could make them money. And it just exploded! Conservatively, a billion dollars was made in Wayne County in the late '80s just in crack alone. Abandoned houses were taken over and people started selling drugs there. It became very, very violent with rival groups. It hit so hard here in the city that the market became saturated. Detroit became so good that they ran the drug industry in Fort Wayne, Cleveland, Columbus, Dayton, Lima, all over.

It's known that many people invested just $10,000 in crack cocaine and, working hard, became millionaires. That's a Horatio Alger rags-to-riches story. One can criticize them and say they're petty criminals. But if one makes the analysis, what's the difference between them and a corporate giant that takes over a company and then rapes the company and cuts loose 10,000 employees, that then causes alcoholism, crack abuse, spouse abuse, and child abuse because the economic supports of that family have been destroyed? Tell me the difference. It's the same! Drugs is free enterprise. The markets are everywhere.

Crack has added to the demise of the city just as great as the loss of jobs. Crack is such a drug where one starts out recreationally and in such a quick time one can lose absolutely everything. I've been involved in drug-abuse counseling and running substance abuse programs, and I've seen a person lose it all in ninety days, from being a well-established member of society to being out in the streets.

Do the kids in the crack business use it themselves?

Most don't. That makes it different than heroin. Many heroin dealers were also users. These kids basically don't even drink; it's totally about money. They have bought the American dream totally. They drink and use drugs less than some corporate giant. They have a cardinal rule: do *not* mess with the merchandise.

My job as deputy director of youth services for Wayne County is to be the architect of prevention programs to stop the kids before they enter the criminal justice system. Once kids enter the system the costs become prohibitive for the county. We're spending between $50,000 and $65,000 a year per juvenile to, in essence, lock them up in residential facilities. We spend $100 million in federal, state, and county funds in Wayne County alone on juvenile delinquents. The overwhelming majority of these are drug youth that the judge has committed to the custody of the state of Michigan until they become adults or display worthwhile conduct. These youth are Black, in the ninetieth percentile, and male, in the ninety-fifth percentile. They're bankrupting the county. We're literally hemorrhaging as a result.

It's so sad. Part of the blame is on all society, and part is on African-American leadership. They've shied away from responsibility. The key thing is that African-American leadership, in addition to having ethnic pride in themselves, must learn to cooperate, negotiate, and bond with white suburbanites. I don't say that in the sense of "Black and white unite" or "we shall overcome," but we're pressed. We have no choice but to come together.

Linda Jones

Coming to Detroit, after being in south Florida, was like moving to a Third World country. Some people have problems with referring to Detroit as a Third World city. I'm talking about seeing people who look like me. Some of them are screwing up, some are doing wonderful jobs.

Linda Jones is a reporter for The Detroit News.

I remember when I came here and drove through Boston-Edison, Rosedale Park, and neighborhoods like that, and seeing Blacks working in the yard, and thinking that they've been hired to clean the yard of the white owners. When I took colleagues from the South around, they asked, "Do they live there? Do they own those houses?" We didn't realize how much living in *that* racist society down there had affected us. When I set up a Detroit bank account I went into a bank and asked to see the manager. A Black woman came out. That impressed me. When I first came here and heard people complain about racism and segregation, I chuckled and said to myself, "Detroiters don't realize how little they tolerate racism here." To me, it wasn't as intense as the South.

When I tried out for the job, the boat races were going on. They assigned me to go to the yacht club on Belle Isle to get a color story, to write about what's going on around the race and how people are preparing for it. And I said, "Oh God, the yacht club, of all places." I was thinking of the Miami Yacht Club, scrutinizing me, checking my credentials to see if I'm a reporter. When I went to the Detroit Yacht Club a white woman took me by the hand and showed me around. I was surprised to see an integrated environment. In Florida when I saw Blacks on the boats, they were working the boats. Here they *own* the boats.

Detroit is a powerful place. I found that the Black community is extremely powerful and maybe doesn't recognize it as much as it should. I've become a Detroit booster.

Errol Henderson

At U. of M. I gave speeches that said we must speak to the needs of our community. If you become a doctor and work at a hospital where poor folks don't have insurance and can't afford to get sick, you're not helping anybody. If you organize a clinic in the *projects* or in one of the Detroit public schools, OK, now we can talk. But don't tell me that just by you getting a degree you're making my people better because you're making yourself better. Be for real! Go join the Republican Party.

We went around to the schools to talk about why students didn't do well in school. The curriculum presented subject matter that was foreign to them. When I was in high school some cat's telling me

Errol Henderson is a Ph.D. candidate in political science at the University of Michigan.

about Shakespeare, and I'm walking home to the projects. It just didn't make any sense, so I wouldn't do the work. When we go to the schools we talk about developing and getting control of the curricula to infuse it with Afrocentric understandings and get the racism out of it. I tell the kids, "I have complete faith in your ability to process information, but I question the information you're being supplied with."

I've been writing my dissertation on Afrocentrism. We think that different cultures of the world have a right to develop and articulate their view of the world, without an imposition of which one's right. This is a pluralistic worldview. The worldview that came out of Europe has been glamorized and valorized as *the* worldview, the one all others should aim for. But there should be an Asian worldview, an African one, a North and South American one, an Australian one.

We also think that history should be reconstructed in order that people could see their humanity. Europeans questioned the humanity of Africans, in particular, on the basis that they had no history. Afrocentrism demands a reassessment of the historical contributions of African people. That's one level. The other is to cast history in our own image and interests, not in someone else's. So it's right that we look at Africa as the basis of our identity. Afrocentrism also attacks racism at its roots. This type of analysis also will attack sexism at its roots. It calls into question the legitimacy of *any* hegemonic culture. Europe is implicated for its racism, what's called the "holocaust of enslavement," and for the colonization of damned near the world.

I accept that Egypt, in a meaningful sense, was the classical Black, or African, civilization. Egypt is to Africa and the diaspora what Greece and Rome is to Europe. I *don't* subscribe to the claims of sociobiological preeminence and the seminal importance of melanin in your basic humanism. Our history suggests that color is very important, but it's not definitive. It did lead to a commonality among those who were so oppressed because of their culture.

Cheikh Anta Diop in his *Civilization or Barbarism* knocked off so many Eurocentric racist tenets. He translated parts of Einstein's theory of relativity into Wolof [Senegalese language]. He exploded the idea that African indigenous languages couldn't encompass highly developed theoretical formulations.

Are your professors able to relate to you?

[*Laughs*] Harold Cruse and I argue. He's not sympathetic to Afrocentrism, with good reason. He says, "Afrocentrism must do for Africans what Marxism has done for Europeans." He's talking about the idea that you can materially change certain social relationships. I agree with that. He says that Afrocentrism must come out of Eighteenth-Dynasty Egypt and we've got to stop proclaiming antiquity and start talking about what are the necessary relationships between Africans in the diaspora and a liberated South Africa.

But I've made enemies among *some* Black professors. There's a lot of collective guilt there, like people used to talk about white guilt. I used to call such people super-Negroes. I make it clear in my talks at U. of M. that the people who looked down on us in the projects were white folks and "super-niggers" who came down there to do something *for* us, like the social workers at the welfare office. Now we have generations of "us" who have just got to college, and we have these "old-school" Negroes, with their middle-class values. They're a *perfect* example of E. Franklin Frazier's *Black Bourgeoisie*. They want to keep us in check.

Can Afrocentric thought be adapted to the current community development efforts in Detroit?

Yeah, it only makes sense. We're talking about community control: the people in the community understand best. Community economic development is not a glorification of capitalism, but a utilization and management of resources for the betterment of community. The community, city, state, country, and world are inextricably related.

Coleman Young's economic policies from '73 to '80 were very positive in the sense that he had a plan for economic development in Detroit. His shortcoming was that he didn't understand the national politics of the time. Just like in Africa, Detroit has a gerontocracy— rulership by the elders. That leadership has to move over. The patronage politics of communities, whether nations or cities, is so lucrative that novel ideas and people get sucked into the patronage system. Criticism is construed as condemnation. There's no such thing as a loyal opposition. This reduces any type of free-flowing ideas.

At the local level we have to provide resources and jobs for the people who are here. Part of that is attracting outside business. The *immediacy* of the problem suggests this. I'm not talking about the theoretical accuracy or propriety of capitalism. We don't have a lot of time for that. We can't afford to wait on some theory that shows us how this really works and gives us a plan for the betterment of everybody while our people starve.

Black folks have never been taught the value of our culture in any meaningful way. We have to be able to utilize the best aspects of our culture. Will it persist? Yes! Why? Because youth is being infused with remnants of it. This is most evident in rap music. If you look at progressive music, it went from jazz, with people like Coltrane, to Jamaica, with Bob Marley and reggae, to rap music. Rap is the most current progressive thing.

The present generation gap in the Black community is *really* manifest in music. The nationalist sentiment is expressed in rap music. Young people said to hell with what the civil rights leaders say, we're going to follow and support Jesse Jackson. That's the nationalism in the youth. Here you have the national culture, Afrocentrism, and a major aspect of the popular culture, the music, coming together. That was absent in the '60s.

Part 3   *The Struggles of Women*

In the block clubs, when you do alley cleanups, ain't
but two men and all the rest is women. Women's struggle for survival is closer to the family than ever before.
Today, they hardly look for another provider. The
struggle for food, shelter, and clothing is compelling
them to fight. And they're standing up. They don't
have a whole lot of hope no more that someone's
gonna come and help them. The women's movement
as we've classically known it hasn't represented that section of the working class. When that section enters the
women's movement then you're gonna *have* a movement.

General Baker

DETROIT IS A CITY where just getting life's essentials puts a great number of people to the test. Women are forced to bear much of the shock of deindustrialization and the government's antifamily policies. As the traditional nurturers of the family, women have an enormous responsibility to sustain dependent children and the men who become victims of faceless economies. Detroit women are strong. In a city where the Black male is considered by many to be an endangered species, women are taking up the slack.

Thirty percent of Detroit households are headed by women with no husband, but only 6 percent of households are headed by men with no wife. Detroit women are four times more likely to be widowed than Detroit men. Detroit women are three times more likely to be heads of households than women in neighboring McComb and Oakland counties. These facts mirror national trends, but they are exaggerated in Detroit.

Women are showing us the politics of survival. They are leading grassroots initiatives in community-based organizations and planning electoral campaigns for local offices. They are organizing demonstrations and advancing women's protective programs. They are developing theory that's pertinent to the needs of women.

Then there's gender politics. Detroit women are putting together ideas that come from their struggles to break loose from historic male dominance. This is more than women's liberation vis-à-vis men. It's liberation from some of the myopic thinking that got the United States—and Detroit—in such a mess. Detroit women don't have a tidy formula all ready for implementation, but they are passionately engaged in the search.

The narratives that follow are generalizable to the condition of most women in this country. They depict the problems faced by women in male-dominated situations or their engagement in struggles to overcome burdensome conditions. These narratives reflect an essence of Detroit, where the quest for solutions to problems can bring out the best in people.

Marian Kramer

In the late '60s I worked for the West Central Organization [WCO] in Detroit. It was a community-based organization modeled after the Alinsky style of organizing. It was in the Wayne State University area, around Grand River and Trumbull, where urban renewal was happening. I was one of the people who was heavily involved in the fight to save that community, and make sure that the city, state, and federal governments respected the community's plans. It taught me how to be a community organizer.

Around 1967, folks like General Baker and Glanton Dowdell who worked at Dodge Main started coming around to WCO. Dowdell painted the Black Madonna, that beautiful picture that hangs in Reverend Cleage's Shrine of the Black Madonna on Linwood. They were putting out leaflets from DRUM [Dodge Revolutionary Union Movement].

We also had started to read *The Inner City Voice* [*ICV*]. I got recruited to help type up articles for the paper and started hanging out at the *ICV* office on Grand River across from the Trade Union Leadership Conference. The printers in the city refused to print the *ICV*. They'd get the "blue flu." So a decision was made to take over *The South End*, Wayne State's student newspaper, and continue to get the word out concerning the situation at the plants, the communities, and the students in the inner city of Detroit. Some of our people enrolled at school and became staff of the paper. People all around wanted to read the paper. Women like Cassandra Smith, Edna Watson, Dorothy Duberry, Diane Bernard, and Gracie Wooten played tremendous roles in the paper. We were forceful, but we were played down.

We were not the typical women in the NOW movement. A lot of us got pulled into the League of Revolutionary Black Workers and we were its backbone. But male supremacy was rampant and we never got proper credit. We were always in the streets, fighting urban renewal, organizing against slum landlords, forming tenants' unions, protecting people against police brutality, and so forth.

A lot of the men in DRUM were catching hell from their wives for participating in the struggles. The wives were concerned about their husbands being fired. General Baker and others formed a committee to politicize and get the wives involved in the fight. There were peo-

Marian Kramer is the president of the National Welfare Rights Union and co-president of the national Up and Out of Poverty Now! campaign. She's a Louisiana native with a long history of activism in the civil rights struggles in the South.

ple like Arleen, Gracie, Cass Smith, myself, Edna Watson. We endured a lot of name calling and had to fight male supremacy. Some would call us the IWW: Ignorant Women of the World. I was thought of as one of the grouchiest women. In meetings we attended to form a Black liberation party, there was debate [as to] where the struggle had to be. One faction said that the focus should be in the plants, at the point of production. I said, "Yes, but all those men got to come back into the community; they live somewhere. We've got to be organizing in both places."

A lot of social struggles were right there in the community. Women had developed a lot of skills and were becoming central in the organizations. We asked, "Why is it that we always get the work and get shit upon in the process?" Also, a lot of Black women were getting into the plants and into the union. We thought that women should have been on the executive board of the League of Revolutionary Black Workers.

The city of Detroit was increasing the rent of people in public housing. In 1969 some people in the Jeffries projects came to my house and asked me to help organize the tenants against rent increases. On a Sunday we had a *big* meeting and we decided to do a rent strike. We forged a unity between the seniors and youth. Ron Scott, who was in the Panthers, lived in the projects. We set up a picket line and used the young people from the Panthers and the League to help man it. We spread to Brewster. The city gave some concessions. It did not raise the rent and it formed tenants' councils in the projects. They still have those councils, but they've been coopted. Some people who serve on the councils are nothing but lackeys for [Mayor] Coleman Young. Some people who were active in the housing struggles of that time now have been coopted into city government and are people we had to confront last year [1991] when we pitched Tent City. They get bribed.

I love my history in the sense that I had the opportunity to participate in the development of a Marxist-Leninist party in the '70s. It came off from lessons I learned from my involvement in the community, in welfare rights, and all that stuff. I treasure that. I was asked to sit on the preparatory committee to struggle out the party's line. I had *never* studied like that before in my life. I never learned to read real good in school. But I *have* learned to read real good in dealing with the "science" and dealing with my community involvement. In those preparatory groups you could see a lot of those people were all armchair revolutionaries, just studying the stuff so they could be popular at the time. But this was life and death for me. I wanted a future for the child that I had birthed and for the many kids that we were taking care of at the time.

Then I got requested by Beulah Sanders, a former president of the National Welfare Rights Organization—I had met her in '65 at the Poor Peoples' Conference in Syracuse, New York—to help to re-organize the organization. She had seen one of our comrades at a meeting, and she liked the way the young man blew. She said, "We need folks like you to help us."

I was known then as being part of the Communist Labor Party. I was working constantly to organize welfare rights. Some of the old welfare rights women tried to do some red-baiting on me. Beulah said, "I wouldn't care what she is. If there's anybody that's helped build this organization historically and now, it's been Marian. If I hear that any more, and using that as an excuse to cover up the fact that *you* are not doing anything, then I'm gonna kick your ass."

I was on public assistance at the time. Working with women like Beulah and the others helped me deepen my development. These were the true fighters. These women stood in the forefront. They always were willing to give up more than what they had. They only had a welfare check. They always were willing to fight for decent child care as a support mechanism for people who are working. They fought for education. They nurtured a movement. I learned a lot. I was always in and out of the welfare offices. I went to New York for two and a half years and found myself being back in a network of welfare rights people.

It was time to come back to Detroit. General Baker and I got married. I started working directly with Westside Mothers, a welfare rights organization. We started grinding in and taking positions against workfare programs. We studied around that and looked at workfare as a program that was used in the economic ebb and flow. It was a slave program. We organized at least ten organizations through-out the county, helped throughout the state, and rekindled connec-tions around the nation. In the mid-'80s we held a national confer-ence in Chicago against workfare. The "advocates"—those who had been making money off the backs of people living in poverty—felt that they were better equipped intellectually to determine how the conference should be set up and what direction it should go in. We were sick and tired of them. They had taken the bribe of the '60s. Our thing was that the victims of poverty should take over the boards and determine their destiny. A split took place.

Some women from Boston went back and started a campaign "Up to the Poverty Line." It started with six organizations and developed into ninety. But some said that our children are hungry *now*, we are homeless *now*, our kids need an education *now*, we need to be talking about up and *out* of poverty *now*, not tomorrow. There was a three-pronged approach: the streets, the courts, and the legislature. Some of us wrestled the question about who should lead the fight around hunger in this nation. We set up the foundation to reorganize the National Welfare Rights Organization. We held our first meeting at Georgetown University in 1987 and named our organization the National Welfare Rights Union. I was elected president. At the board meeting in Ohio in 1988 we decided that we were going to join a national Up and Out of Poverty campaign.

There was a joining together of activists in welfare, hunger, and homelessness. In July 1989 we had a summit in Philadelphia with over 500 people. Annie Smart said the theme had to be Up and Out of Poverty Now. We had representation from the Black Belt of the South through Albert Turner, Wendell Parrish, Jerome Scott, Annie Smart, Vernon Bellecourt, and many others. We put on a $90,000 conference with $11,500 seed money. Even with the heavy budget cuts here, Michigan came with a busload of people. Local groups played a hell of a role: Michigan Welfare Rights, the Homeless Union, Cass Church, Local 600 and General Baker, Flint United WRO [Welfare Rights Organization], groups in Lansing, Ann Arbor, and others.

We took this thing to the streets in Detroit. There was a media blackout, so in October last year we took over Channel Four and the *Detroit News*. Sixteen of us were arrested. We needed a coalition to maintain our campaign of Up and Out of Poverty.

The women I've had the good fortune to work with in the homeless movement, the welfare movement, the trade union movement, etc., have understood one thing: in order for our children to have a future we've got to eliminate poverty in this country. We've got to participate politically in this fight. We've got to run the victims themselves for public office.

The purpose of our survival summit is to debate how we can bring those various sections of the working class together around a common agenda: the question of survival, the question of coming up and out of poverty. Even though we understand our differences, the more and more we fight together to come up and out of poverty, the more and more we will become one. This working class has to cease fighting within itself and become a working class to fight *for* itself.

We've had several survival summits in the South. We've had a youth survival summit in Minneapolis. We've had many survival summits, and every one has been a jubilee. In May we had one of the most profound things that took place in this country: a poor women's survival convention. Over forty-seven cities alone in California were represented in Oakland. Two busloads came out of southcentral Los Angeles. The significance of this is that we had just gone through the L.A. rebellion. These women from southcentral L.A. had never participated outside their community. The Bloods and the Crips have been fighting each other for twenty-two years. The young women who came to the poor women's convention said, "Before we came here, we were gang-banging each other. Now we've learned we've been gang-banging the wrong people. We got to gang-bang this government from now on." They are determined to be a part of this fight. People are doing things all over this country. These young people represent our future.

We're understanding politically that this working class is in motion. Even the National Organization for Women reached their hand out to us and for the first time we participated in their march, at the *front*, and had a meeting with their national board.

Here in Michigan we've been through some struggles. We've fought the legislature, the executive, the judicial. They all turned against us. Both the Democrats and Republicans ripped 90,000 people off the welfare rolls. We put Tent City up. We exposed the city of Detroit for not fixing up public housing. The city spent over $2,000,000 in homeless shelters and warming centers last year rather than in public housing. Diane Bernard designed the program Operation Michigan Storm, coming off Desert Storm. We said there's a storm raising in this country and we were forced to be a part of this army because of our economic plight. We didn't declare this war, but damn it we're going to carry it to its fulfillment. So we *fought* Coleman Young and fought Lansing over Tent City and won a court case.

Back in June, I was a speaker at a meeting of the National Organization for Women. The question of a third party came out of their conference. They've been working on this Twenty-first Century thing. Even though we're gonna fall out with them sooner or later, they want a change in this country. They've done a tremendous thing this year in trying to get women elected. We've seen the need to elect the victims, and we're still doing that.

There's got to be a party that's going to spearhead the general strike. One part of it can be electoral, but it's gotta be the fighting in the streets. People are not talking about no Republican Party, or no Ron Dellums, or no Twenty-first Century Party. They want a party of a new type. *We* represent the revolutionary section. I did not come to that conclusion by myself, because I don't claim to be nobody that's original. It's through collective analysis and theory.

Amy Good

I was born in Pittsburgh and my family moved to Farmington Hills, Michigan, when I was eleven. I went to the University of Michigan in '74 and got an undergraduate degree in psychology and a master's degree in social work. Then I moved to Detroit where I've lived since 1981.

As an undergraduate I was a youth care worker in a residential treatment facility and did some volunteer work at Jackson Prison and a couple youth centers. That was my first introduction to the idea that the system around us isn't working. I grew up with the notion that a really good system operates in this country. When things go wrong, it's because there's a glitch in the system and it needs to be fixed.

Then I took this class in corrections, and read the book *Weeping in the Playtime of Others,* which was about children in correction facilities. The author wrote of his attempts to make changes and how he ran up against the ferociousness of a system that was dedicated to sustaining itself. I was appalled at the level of corruption I learned about. I started becoming more and more aware that many things needed really serious change. One of my field placements was working in Children's Protective Services. I was very disillusioned by the lack of interest in real change on the part of my co-workers.

When in graduate school I learned about family systems theory and how it doesn't make any sense to just try to fix an individual who's hurting. You need to look at that person in the family context. And you also had to deal with that family in the context of its neighborhood and the neighborhood in the context of the community.

My first social work job was with a child welfare agency in Detroit where I worked for seven years as a caseworker. We worked with families who were referred to us by Children's Protective Services because of abuse and neglect of kids. I became director of that program and helped develop a respite care program. The idea was to provide an opportunity for parents who needed a break, for whatever reason, to voluntarily place their kids with us. The parents could participate in counseling and avoid the intervention of the state and their kids getting sucked into the foster care system.

Alternatives for Girls was incorporated in '87. Our staff is twenty-

Amy Good is the executive director of Alternatives for Girls, tucked inside St. Peter's Episcopal Church sanctuary in Detroit's near southwest, across the street from Tiger Stadium. She has been involved in Pax Christi, an international Catholic peace movement involved in Central America, and in the Central America Solidarity Committee.

six full-time and seven part-time persons. We serve homeless teenage girls and young women, living on the street, particularly those involved in substance abuse, prostitution, and other street activities that threaten their health and their development and sometimes their lives. One of our clients was murdered on the street in August by a drug dealer. We had worked with her a lot and she really had made great progress.

We have five programs. The first is shelter. We have a thirty-day shelter program and a transitional living program. Generally, there's a young woman, mostly from age sixteen to nineteen, who is homeless and comes to us. She checks into the thirty-day program and we work out some goals with her. She is required immediately to start putting in forty hours a week of school or work or volunteer work, just to get busy and to start marking off some accomplishments and successes. These are folks who don't have much of a history of success. There are ten independent living skills modules. Each young woman works her way through each of the modules: budgeting, banking, nutrition, physical fitness, career planning, job readiness training, housing, etc. We have educational forums most every night in the shelter. It's very exciting. It really works.

We also have an after-care program in which we follow up on everybody who's left the shelter. We help each young woman maintain independent living and help her keep a job or stay in school. We have specialized support groups around pregnancy and parenting. We have a *very* active corps of about eighty volunteers who act as mentors. A mentor is a woman or a couple in the community who are self-sufficient and agree to work on a one-to-one basis with a young woman.

Then we have our street outreach program that began in '88. You may have seen the van on your way in. Two staff people and a team of volunteers drive through the streets of southwest Detroit six days a week from two P.M. till two A.M. and make contact with young women on the street. We pass out sandwiches and snacks and warm clothing. We do a lot of AIDS education and pass out a lot of condoms. We provide transportation to health care and make lots of referrals. The phone in the van has been really great. For those who are ready to exit street life and come to the shelter, we're here for them. People know who we are. They trust us. Our first contact is very laid back. We tell them who we are: "We're not the police, we're not church; here's one of our fliers." Recently, a young girl took our flier and didn't say a word. It was the first time I had seen her. She listened to us, but didn't say anything. Finally, she said, "I *am* the police." [*Laughs*]

Is there any danger?

We haven't had a single incident so far. There *definitely* have been times when it was time to leave the scene. We do *serious* self-defense and conflict-avoidance training. If somebody is getting beat up on the street the van might park across the street and honk its horn and use the phone to call the police, but they're not going to jump in the middle of it. We have had pimps come here. We've had more than one scary situation. We have security guards at night and everybody knows they're very good.

Last March we started the residential substance-abuse treatment program. It's a four-bed program for thirteen- to seventeen-year-old girls who are addicted to anything and do not have private insurance. It's the only program of its kind in southeastern Michigan. There's no such program for boys.

Our fifth program is really neat. This is our neighborhood prevention group program. It deals with girls age five to fifteen from the immediate neighborhood. They're high-risk kids from a home that experiences serious problems like prostitution and drug dealing. One hundred and thirty-five kids participated last year. They meet weekly in small groups of four to six kids, mostly run by volunteers. The object of the program is to build self-esteem. The groups do all kinds of activities, like arts and crafts and tutoring. We have a big emphasis on staying in school. We look at their report cards, and when they show improvement in grades or attendance—it could be bringing an *F* up to a *D*—they get a reward, and the reward is $10 to spend on a one-on-one outing with their group leader. That's *really* effective.

We write grants every week. The Skillman Foundation pays for three of our programs. The city of Detroit pays for four. The Department of Social Services pays for street outreach. Health and Human Services pays for drug prevention that goes throughout four of our five programs. Every one of our grants is distributed differently. It's incredibly complicated. I really love my job. Sometimes it's difficult, but it's not depressing. It's rewarding.

Our current concept is to develop leadership in the most functional families in the area. The kids have trouble in school. The parents, who may be illiterate, have had terrible failures in their *own* experience with the school system, and feel totally powerless to deal with that system. So we try to bring them together to learn how to act as effective advocates for their kids.

A huge problem is housing. Our kids get through a transitional living program and they're *ready*, but can't find decent, affordable, and safe housing. Only in the last month, a church in Royal Oak decided to work with us. The parish owns a two-family flat locally and is leasing it to us at a very low rent. We will sublease it to four women and a baby or two, while the women complete college.

We struggle a lot over jobs for our clients, especially with general assistance being cut off in Michigan. What they usually find is minimum-wage, part-time jobs. It's been frustrating to work one-on-one to help people move toward meaningful employment. One of the biggest barriers is the lack of self-esteem. Many don't imagine themselves doing something that's worth being paid.

Agnes Mansour

I was born and raised in Detroit. My parents both came from Lebanon and met here in Detroit. My family was very concerned about the needs of other people. I went to St. Charles grade school and high school on Detroit's east side. Then I went to Mercy College and upon graduation entered the Sisters of Mercy. Right out of the novitiate I went to graduate school at Catholic University and received my Ph.D. in biochemistry. I returned to Mercy College and taught chemistry. I was president of the College from 1971 to 1983. My thirty years with the Sisters of Mercy obviously helped shape my values, especially since Vatican Two and the movement of the Sisters of Mercy to challenge their own goals of concern for the poor.

What motivates women to go into the sisterhoods?

In the past, if a woman wanted to play a role in society that was more direct than simply being married and raising a family, she didn't have many options. If you add the dimension of dedication, and not just a job, then a sisterhood was an avenue for that. Today the opportunities for women are much greater. They don't have to demonstrate a concern for the poor by associating with a religious community.

In the summer of 1982 I ran for Congress. [*Laughs*] I had spent twenty-five years in higher education and I was getting tired of it. I wanted other experiences since I was becoming more politically aware and I thought terrible things were going on in foreign and domestic policy in the early Reagan years. I thought women were falling through the cracks and the poor were being totally neglected and demoralized. I figured it would be good to spend the last phase of my

Agnes Mansour is the founding director of the Poverty and Social Reform Institute, incorporated in 1988. The institute is lodged in the Mercy Health Services complex in Farmington Hills, a suburb northwest of Detroit.

professional life *directly* with the political sphere and focus more of my time and energy on public policy that impacts women and children, especially the poor.

The religious community supported my candidacy and canon law permitted it, but the church didn't like it. Detroit Archbishop Edmund Szoka didn't like it, but he was sure I wasn't going to win. Still, he said I needed *his* permission. He was invoking some of the new philosophy of John Paul II, who didn't want Father Drinan to run again for Congress and didn't want priests or religious in any elected positions. The Pope thinks you must stay above partisan politics. I don't think that's legitimate. As a citizen you have a right and obligation to become politically involved. It's especially legitimate for religious women because they are secondary in the hierarchical church. They're considered three-dollar bills, falling outside of the laity and outside of the clergy.

I didn't do well in the election. [*Laughs*] I hadn't held any political office or been involved in local politics directly. People in power positions knew me because of my position at the college, but the broad voting population didn't know me. I also was competing against well-known politicians like Sandy Levin, Doug Ross, and Maryann Mahaffey. I didn't expect to win, but I figured it would be a good experience and I'd meet a lot of people and find out what the political process was like.

When Governor Blanchard was elected in 1982, he invited me to be the director of the Michigan Department of Social Services, a Cabinet position. Most people said I needed my head examined. The Sisters of Mercy approved my appointment at both the province and national levels. The archbishop said he wasn't going to stand in the way and, in a sense, gave tacit approval. My appointment got off on the wrong foot. At that time the state allowed Medicaid funding for abortion. Since I would be administering that, the dirt hit the fan [*Laughs*] as far as the archbishop was concerned. He was under pressure, including Rome. There were big ads in the *New York Times* and *Wall Street Journal* saying, "How can a Catholic bishop allow a nun to direct the Department of Social Services?"

Szoka called me in and asked that I change my position on Medicaid funding for abortion. My position had been that as long as it was legal it was inappropriate to penalize poor women. I held that abortion was wrong, and that we should help people to understand that. But we also should help with problem pregnancies. We should dialogue, rather than try to change people's consciences. As Catholics, we need to respect other people's religious traditions. We live in a pluralistic society and people come to different conclusions legit-

112

imately. Catholics act as though we possess the total truth, and everybody else ought to march to the Catholic drummer.

He asked the religious women in the Detroit province to request me to leave the director's position. They would not do that; they wanted more dialogue. Then it moved to the national church leadership in Washington and they refused to ask me to step down. Then I got a direct letter from the Holy Father through one of the bishops. I either had to leave the director's position or become subject to a process leading to dismissal from the religious community.

I couldn't spend all my time and energy on that while directing the department where we had over one million people receiving some kind of assistance. So I just left the Sisters of Mercy, a very difficult decision. I'd been in the religious community thirty years. It's like a divorce or a death. It was just *wrong*. It was a contradiction that I would have to leave membership in a religious community in order to carry out what is often the number one role of religious communities on behalf of the church: service to the poor, the sick, and the uneducated. Totally unbelievable! Blindness!

The church hierarchy thinks it can control everything. The church ignored the leadership of the religious women's community all the way through. That was a slap in the face when you consider the contributions that religious women have made to the church. This was a glaring example of hierarchical and patriarchal church control. I think today the church is just as hierarchical and just as sexist and authoritarian as it always has been. My relationship with God isn't going to be determined by a bishop or a pope or anybody else.

Did you have problems in your state job?

Oh yeah! You get all kinds of political types, and bureaucracies are difficult to manage. I had 13,000 staff. I pride myself on good administration. I'm very demanding and conscious about the use of resources. I do not like money to be wasted. With those kind of desires, managing a bureaucracy is very, very difficult. And I was a strong spokesperson on issues relating to the poor. I had a lot of power because every day there was so much publicity surrounding the church thing.

I watched my budget like a hawk. I made demands. I tried to get policies loosened so they were more humane; tried to make people treat the poor with dignity and respect. I spoke out. I never knew from year to year how many staff I was going to have. I never knew whether the staff was committed or whether it was just a job. Whatever I *did* get was never enough. We were always in crisis management. It got harder and harder to get [Governor] Blanchard to

113

commit dollars to programs for the poor. I was usually the only department director who challenged the budget.

Blanchard supported me in the beginning, then there was the recall of two Democratic senators as a result of his tax increase. The Republicans played that for all it was worth: Blanchard raising taxes and giving the money to these shiftless people who don't want to work. We had a 10 percent unemployment rate. Blanchard got much more conservative in his agenda. They played politics. That became more and more obvious, and it became more difficult to associate myself with it. That's why I left after the first term. I wanted to try and do more creative things like we're doing here at the institute.

There's a lot of waste and politics in government. The poor are the ones who are constantly caught in all of this and the services just aren't being provided. You can't be creative in government; it's so clumsy, and complicated, and topheavy with costly staff. Much of government money goes to nonsense at every level.

We have to set our priorities right. I think most people are ahead of the politicians and the politicians don't know it. The public are not opposed to paying taxes, they just don't want money *wasted*. People want a humane society. They want the poor taken care of reasonably. They don't want children growing up in poverty. We don't build on that, nor do we design systems that are efficient. It has to get to a crisis situation before anybody does anything about it.

If politicians had guts, there would be two issues they could capitalize on: health care and child care. We've *got* to overhaul the health care system. All we're doing is Bandaiding, and it's costly. A year down the road we'll cut back again, and the most vulnerable will get hurt. The politicians are afraid of ruffling the waters. The second is child care. If a majority of women are going to be working, how are we helping them? How are we helping families? We don't provide adequate child care for poor families. What is desperately needed is quality care in those early years. You lose those early years, you're just *always* behind.

I do think we'll be getting more courageous leadership. I also think that will be challenged and encouraged by grassroots groups. They're doing some wonderful things. We need creative approaches. I see a lot of hopeful signs from community groups still plugging away in Detroit. The whole purpose of the Poverty and Social Reform Institute is to encourage and catalyze those new models and approaches. *All* of our people should have a right to food, clothing, shelter, health care, education, and employment. At the same time, people should have a responsibility of providing those things for themselves where they can. Other industrial countries care for their children far better than we do. We can't even get a family and medical leave act passed for a worker to care for a newborn child or an ailing parent.

Our value system is skewed. We don't care if we waste money on war, but we care a lot if we think we are wasting money on human needs. It's ridiculous! When General Schwarzkopf came back from the Gulf he thanked the former president and Congress for giving him the best tanks and aircraft. We need to ask when Congress and our leaders are going to give us good health care, good housing, and good child care. Aren't they more important than tanks?

Sharon Howell

People ask me what makes me radical and I say I was always a radical. Growing up in industrial Pennsylvania you could see class differences all over the place. You could see the lie that poor people don't work hard. You could see perfectly well that people were working very hard and still poor. It was clear to me that there were some terrible things wrong with the country, whether it was closing of the coal mines and foundries and people thrown out of work, or strikes, or selling from one company to the next. That was a constant part of life that helped shaped what I understood to be inequities in the world.

I got a debate scholarship to Marietta College in Ohio, where I had a wonderful radical professor who introduced me to Simone de Beauvoir. That helped to change my life. I read every word she wrote. It was the first time I had ever seen such an explanation of the world. I was at Marietta from '64 to '68. My debate partner was a young African-American man from Washington, D.C. We were the first inter-racial debate team in the nation. We took hell.

By '68, particularly with King's death, it seemed to me that we must respond to what was happening in the cities. So I went to Ocean Hill-Brownsville in New York City to teach. That's where they fired all of the union teachers and the community hired the teachers. I thought that the answer was community control, and in the abstract I still believe that. But it was just as corrupt with the community running it as anything else. You couldn't get chalk in your room, but the principal was getting wall-to-wall carpeting and a TV set in his office.

Then I went to work for the welfare department and allied myself with the welfare rights folks. I was not equipped to handle New York

Sharon (Shea) Howell is a professor at Oakland University.

City. It was so dehumanizing. I had never seen such harshness between people who didn't know one another.

Then I went to Northern Illinois University in the early '70s and
got involved in the struggles there against the war and closing down
the university. I was known as a radical on the campus. One of the
professors who was a leader for antiwar stuff was fired and we organized a support committee. Angela Davis came to campus with a
bunch of folks to assist in this activity. That's the first time I saw real
organizing up close. The Illinois Bureau of Investigation held hear-
ings to find the cause of the rebellions on campus. Eleven women
were on a list of people who were troublesome and we all were fired.

I drove a cab in Chicago for a while, as one of four women cab
drivers there. I was a good driver but had a lousy sense of direction so
I'd get lost all the time. I met some great people, and learned how to
play pool. I learned about the Chicago police's corruption. They
would stop you all the time and say they were going to give you a
ticket. I was too dumb to realize that they were asking for a bribe.

Then I did some substitute teaching, which was a terrible experience. There were fifty third graders in my class. I never had seen
anything so wild and vicious. The school was set up to encourage
viciousness, particularly on the part of teachers to kids. But I learned
how structures shape us. The second day I was there I saw a teacher
take a giant board and knock a little boy down to the floor because he
didn't stand on the line right. I stopped her and for a hot minute was
a hero to these kids. Two weeks later in my classroom a little girl
threw a pair of scissors at a little boy and I found myself picking her
up and smashing her into the wall. I had regarded myself as nonviolent. I'd been at camp for ten years and had never touched a kid
in my life. You know what frightened me? It felt good. I could have
smashed her forever into that wall. I walked out and never went back.

I got a flier about an antiracism meeting in Detroit that Angela
Davis was part of. So I packed up my car and came to this meeting in
1974. I was looking for some way to connect politically with people.
The closest thing that made sense was Angela Davis and the Communist Party. But they didn't seem to be doing anything. I was really at a
loss. Then I ran into a debate coach at Wayne State who said he
would get me into graduate school.

I was at wit's end, really groping for something. Then this African-American woman in one of my classes, Pat Coleman Burns, would
say these things. I would ask myself, "Where did she get that? It's so
true." Pat and I became friends. She was being recruited by what
ultimately became NOAR [National Organization for an American
Revolution]. She was part of a study group in Detroit called the Advo-

116

cators, which was based on the book by Jim and Grace Boggs called *Revolution and Evolution in the Twentieth Century*. This brought together a lot of what I'd been thinking about: change takes time, there's a relationship between you and the system, change yourself to change the world, an emphasis on Black leadership and the central role of race in the country, learn from other revolutions. I thought this was the best thing I had read in years. I asked Pat how I could get to work with these people. She said that the only problem was that I was white. The group was all African-American except for Grace, who was Asian-American.

NOAR was beginning to discuss whether they were going to bring whites into their organization. They began to invite me to their meetings. I found them fascinating. There was a sensitivity to cultural questions. They always tried to balance an understanding of where we are with an openness to new ideas. We went through an eighteen-month recruitment process. It was worse than giving birth to get into this thing. Some of it was coming out of the underground mentality, and part of it was the effort to develop people before they came into the organization. I was with NOAR for the next eleven years.

Part of what NOAR was about was an assessment that all the movements that had been propelling people toward change were disintegrating. Our responsibility was to try and create an organization that would clean up the mistakes of the past and help propel another movement in what we then hoped to be the late '70s. Then we hoped for the '80s. Now I'm ready for the '90s. [*Laughs*] There was the belief, which I still hold, that there were many people out there looking for progressive change. We began on a national scale to try and build a cadre organization rooted in communities around a body of ideas.

So much of what we did came from what I now think is the male belief that you controlled a lot more than you do. We were much more oriented toward having the right idea than our processes, our development, and listening to people. We *were* touched by the feminist movement and we *were* responding to notions of ecology and technology that nobody else in the radical movement was looking at. But a lot of what led to our demise, aside from the times, was our real inability to see how profoundly the world had changed. We weren't really able to talk with one another in ways that opened us up for that. As racism in the country got worse, race tensions in NOAR got worse. As homophobia got bigger, the question of lesbians in the organization got bigger. Black men feeling like they were the endangered species held on to the rigid, least productive ways of male leadership.

NOAR was becoming more and more rigid and defensive. We

had a lot of criticism and self-criticism. We never really figured out how to deal with race, class, gender, and homophobia. There were times when we would reach across these differences and connect on a human level. But there were other times when those differences just tore us apart. We tried to deal with those differences ideologically, rather than personally. That devastated all of us. It was the male "prove your idea" thing or "what is your principle?" Sometimes it really wasn't about principle, but about emotional pain people had.

Over the last five years I've learned so much from feminist processes and things that were developed by women in women's community to confront these differences in more holistic ways. I was just reading Gloria Steinem's book about self-esteem. She says the sense of self is often covered up by political argument. At the end of NOAR I posed the question, "How can it be that we do to one another the very thing we say the dominant culture does to us?" I've been struggling to answer that. I now work with Margo Adair in California, who was in NOAR, on multiculturalism. I think we have been so afraid to talk about difference and have been so dominated in our politics by middle-class culture that we've created political forms that are without humanity. Public life is set by the values of the white middle class.

In workshops I do and in my classes I consciously try to create a different context for the exploration of ideas. One of the things I trust about women is that women by and large are not removed from the urgencies of community life. Very few women are into self-development outside of the sense of community and what is needed for life to continue. Most women are poor, most have kids, most are struggling. I would argue that the leadership of activities in Detroit is essentially women. They *do* do things differently. You see here the creation of SOSAD [Save Our Sons and Daughters] and the leadership of Clementine Barfield. I march with the crack-house people, WEPROS [We the People Reclaiming Our Streets], and it's primarily older women. They have a stake in the community and aren't just interested in it for themselves.

Lavelle Williams and Brenda McCain

BRENDA: If you look around at the powerful grassroots leaders in this city, you see that they're women. Women have bigger views and are willing to do bigger things. They're home nurturing the kids. They

Lavelle Williams and Brenda McCain both have been ADC mothers and past presidents of the Michigan Avenue Community Organization (MACO).

want a *whole* loaf of bread; but if they can only get two slices they'll take two slices. We're nurturing people, we're heart tenders. We want our neighborhoods to survive.

I think there needs to be a recruitment of men and force them to take some leadership. I was really impressed when I was in a small village in the mountains of Nicaragua a few years ago and heard women say that they had to stop all activity for a year and force men to take a leadership role. You look at the traditional Black family, the women have always been the leaders. They're the ones who aren't too good to wash the steps in order to get money. You're left with women in the city of Detroit who have children at home. I was out doing all this crusading and traveling all over and going through all this training, but I had to go home and do fourteen loads of laundry, wash the kitchen steps, cook the meals, and take care of my children.

As far as Lavelle and me looking at the bigger picture and being different kinds of leaders, I think it *does* have a lot to do with our MACO experience. We were networking on a regional level, and looking at Europe and the way they do plant-closing legislation. In 1980, total catastrophe had hit the city of Detroit and I think that we were blessed in having people who challenged the shit. We used to sit around in the back office with two sixpacks of beer and everybody throwing in the last of their cigarettes and played "what if": What if I was the mayor, if I was the city lawyer, if I was on the council, what would I do?

When we look at who the next mayor of the city will be, we have to choose from men who are playing the political game, all lawyers in suits. From their totally different roles, they will come out and kiss our babies, talk about our schools, and talk about our lives. I read an article by Susan Watson saying that if the mayor had ever gotten married or had a family, he might look differently on the city of Detroit.

LAVELLE: I think that when you compare MACO's style of Saul Alinsky organizing with most of the other organizations, the whole style is different. The others will go down and talk to the city and compromise and all that kind of stuff, and they'll do that for a long *time.* We at MACO went down there twice, and told them if they didn't do what we asked we'd come with 500 people and make a whole issue out of it by using the press and whatever else is available.

BRENDA: It's important to be able to say, "Look, don't tell us the money's not there because on page 35, subparagraph two . . ." You have to know what you're talking about. The Alinsky style of organizing has been *hated* all over the city. Even when we were closing banks, people all over the city participated in that action, but a lot of them went away saying, "Well, we agree with your goals, but we don't like your methods." Too confrontational.

Look at what happened in Kansas City with the Right-to-Lifers. I'm pro-choice, but they're doing some of the best confrontational organizing. Those are Alinsky-style confrontational methods if ever I saw them. They work! They're not the end, but they're what brings people to thinking and acting on particular issues.

LAVELLE: MACO came out of a cry in the community to do something about the problems that the city was not addressing and the only thing we had was some Jesuit priests that came in—

BRENDA: We were church-based organizing that initially came out of the West Side Community Organization, which came out of the first Alinsky organization in the '60s. [Detroit member of Congress] John Conyers came out of that. I have a picture of him addressing the group. The ideology is that we create our own forms of government to represent ourselves, whereas the social work organizer style is to shift what's already there, to reform. They've been in the way because they tend to play the same games as the elite—pacifying needs—as opposed to going to the roots and engaging the people in participation in change. That professional social work style took over the MACO staff. In the past few years you saw the staff operating without the leadership and direction of the people, without a real interest in going out and finding and developing local leadership. They're into what I call this résumé-building, self-glorifying, social work kind of attitude.

LAVELLE: The theme of the next MACO convention to elect a new board is "going back to the basics." There are the basics of working on community needs such as garbage and whatever, as well as looking at the larger picture. There hasn't been a convention in a couple years. When I came back to MACO I went to what I thought was a board meeting, the first one I'd been to in a couple years. I went in there looking for the board, but what I saw was staff. There were organizers there who were not being given any kind of direction, and there was a person who had no real good idea about what organizing is all about. I just went on a total rampage: "Hey, this is bullshit, this can't happen. We need a convention, we need to elect people, we need to set some *goals.*" They can't stand my guts. The present director is totally upset that I've come back. I've raised all these hells, like if there's a board meeting the staff comes in and gives their report and then gets the hell out of there. It's a *community* organization and the community has to run it.

BRENDA: About four years ago I started working with Witness for Peace and Justice. I had this idea that we needed to create a training institute in Detroit. Now, as then, there is so much untapped leadership in this city that if we could get them in a room, past their staffs, past their social workers, that we would begin to find solutions. If we did a clearly designed analysis of the city we would begin to raise the kind of questions that would ultimately lead to a charter change. At one time we had thirty-five people in a room. Unfortunately, that fell apart because egos got in the way. Somebody wanted to put it under their flag and call it *their* name. Whenever people get together someone wants to try to corral that energy. You *cannot* do that.

We have to allow dialogue and freedom and creativity to come to fruition, and then the answers will come. It's not just a matter of Lavelle or me walking into a room and saying, "This is the plan we want you all to buy into." People have to develop that on their own. In my opinion we first have to find some nonturf, truce-based way to bring people to the table to just dialogue under the auspices of doing a power analysis. You *represent* that part of town—what's going on there, what are the threads, how does it work? We have to know who's on both sides, who's out there against us, who are we, who do we have and who don't we have, who do we need, what kind of resources do we have or don't have, and where can we get them? 121

How are the participants chosen?

We go to the knowns and ask for names. That's tough, though. I might go to a leader and say, "Give me the names of your two *best* leaders. We want to do a leadership training session that's gonna take three months. We want to do a citywide power analysis of them and us. We're going to try to understand what the political, economic, social, and cultural ramifications of this analysis are. We're gonna try to come up with a platform and strategy moving toward the next election." I would bet the farm that this leader would not give me these names, but she would come herself.

It's that thing of self-protection, afraid of taking the risk. Maybe we don't want to admit it to ourselves, but we hold our people back with that attitude. MACO did not do that. When I was there I was going to groups all over the country by myself. I didn't have a staff person whispering in my ear telling me what to say. When I sit down with the city attorney on industrial revenue bonds, I gotta know how it works, why it works, where it works, how I can improve it. There's an attitude, and it's this maternalism shit, particularly among the women religious who have found themselves in positions of authority in community groups; people who fall just under the noblesse oblige.

You see it with the Black Baptist pastors who have decided that they're their own pope, and they know what's best for their congregations. They'll take the direction of their congregation when it comes to a new parking lot, lighting, or whether they get a new car this year, but they don't really foster people to move beyond what they're able to give them. When you get into that shit you hamper, you stop, you gum up the works.

LAVELLE: They're part of the administration. Whatever Coleman [Young, the mayor] wants, most of them will agree to.

BRENDA: There was a significant split in the Black Baptist Pastors Alliance around the time that Jesse Jackson was running for president. Coleman refused to back Jesse, he went with [Democratic candidate] Mondale. That was the first crack in what had been a *staunch* support of the Young administration. There's also been splits around the gambling issue. But the alliance doesn't take a stance on alternative solutions and actions for the city.

LAVELLE: The only group that will do that is Detroiters Uniting, the Boggs' group. They'll go up against the administration aggressively. A lot of them are pastors from what we call renegade churches.

BRENDA: The past alliances have been chipped away. We no longer have a strong union base that we can draw on. We no longer have the NAACP. It's not been out there talking about human rights violations in the city of Detroit or the fact that we have a Black infant mortality rate equal to Honduras. The fact that we have a governor that is allowed to take away indigent health care and cut general assistance benefits in Wayne County says that the conservatives are gaining ground in the state.

LAVELLE: You can hear NAACP yelling and screaming that they can't run around the park out in Dearborn, but you don't hear NAACP talking about the homeless out here in the street, the hungry, or none of the problems that we face and have to fight. I think what is so crazy is that we go out and do that stuff for free while these folks are getting paid to kill the city.

BRENDA: New Detroit will *rent* you a bus for an action. Used to be the unions would give you sticks to put your placards on. You can't even get *that* out of them any more, so you certainly aren't going to get any damned leadership. But they also have a choice. I don't have a choice. Lavelle doesn't have a choice. Where are we gonna go? What are our options? We have to stay here. These folks can *talk* all they want to, but they get into their cars, drive to their safer neighborhoods, go to Sherwood Forest, put their kids into the Friends School at five thousand bucks a kick . . .

LAVELLE: To me it's like going to church. You go to church and the preacher gets up there and tells you how you're supposed to love your neighbor, and folks say, "Oh, you preached a good sermon," and all that garbage, and they go home and lock their doors, lock their bars, and don't come out till the next morning to go to work. There is nothing, nothing in the city of Detroit that is happening constructively through these big-time organizations like the unions and NAACP.

When the Cadillac plant over there was closing I went to several meetings that the union was hosting about Cadillac. I thought these folks were gonna figure out how to keep this stuff alive. Here were people at the podium talking about rights, but they weren't addressing the problem that these people were going to be out of work and gonna be part of ADC and the welfare line. They had no training. Where the hell are they gonna go? They're gonna close the damn doors and leave a great big huge-ass plant sitting up in the middle of the neighborhood. They weren't even *addressing* any of that stuff, and then they had the nerve to *march*. Damn! That pissed me off.

Part 4   *City Life, Scenes, Feelings*

My participation in Detroit is peculiar to what a core city has historically offered and what few suburbs anywhere in the country can replicate. There's no way that you're going to find a French Quarter in suburban New Orleans. You go *down* to the French Quarter, *down* to Greenwich Village, Chinatown, or a little Italy. That's where it's at. That's why I'm in the city more.

Mike Whitty, University of Detroit, Mercy

DETROITERS NEVER ARE PASSIVE about their city. There's a deeply felt love that has many roots and complex interconnections. It's not the kind of love that might, with some turn of events, turn into hate, as in a marriage. Detroit residents and boosters don't hate their city. They may fear the danger in the streets or grieve for the suffering of the unemployed, but this is different from hate. The love of Detroit is the kind that overlaps with sympathy and sadness, as in a parent's love for a sick child. Those whose emotions have turned to hate have long since left the city.

Contemporary Detroiters have an abiding respect for the dynamic city that used to be, that provided opportunity for families with humble origins to fulfill the American dream. This backdrop adds a wrenching dimension to the reality that tens and tens of thousands of city people today can't begin to fulfill the dream of their parents.

Everyday Detroiters live everyday lives. Like most everybody else, they experience the strains and confusions of life in rudderless, often heartless, everyday America. In Detroit, "normal" American life is often made harder by the difficulties of earning a living, finding food and shelter, and avoiding violence. That's the downside. But there's an upside, and that's the spirit of survival and rebirth. It's the strength that comes from the pioneer experience. In Detroit it's not the spirit of individualism as much as it's the spirit of community: building confidence and creativity, in cooperation with one's fellow human beings. Not only does this process begin to build solidarity, but it facilitates political mobilization. For this process to jell, Detroiters must be tough and wise.

To portray some of the spirit of Detroit and cityscape scenes, this section presents an eclectic set of Detroit participants who are serious players in the Detroit drama. Their statements include the pathos and humor, the frustration and hope that emerge from daily life in Detroit. Though their personal life situations are quite varied, they share an involvement with Detroit that tells its own story.

Jeanie and Bill Wylie-Kellermann

JEANIE: I moved to Detroit to work for the Associated Press. I was miserable in that environment. It was the most racist and sexist place I ever had the lack of pleasure to work in. I fell in love with Detroit. My involvement in Poletown started in 1981. The first time I visited a Poletown neighborhood council meeting, the people really won my heart. They were hard-working, working-class, union people who were gradually putting together a pretty sophisticated analysis of what was being done to them in the destruction of their community. I wanted to put my skills at their disposal, so I don't think I missed another meeting after that.

The resilience of the people in Poletown is one of the things that I found most striking. People were having their neighborhood decimated, houses were on fire, there was construction dust. People would come into the church center and say, "I can't breathe, I can't sleep at night." The folks in Poletown invited the daughter of the chairman of General Motors to have her wedding at the Immaculate Conception Church [scheduled for demolition] when it became public that she was getting married. They rented a bulldozer and took it out to the house of the chairman of General Motors to let him know how it felt to have bulldozers pull up on his lawn. Once the church had been taken over by the police, they wove flowers through the fence that was between them and the church demolition. Police officers were put every twelve feet along the fence to keep people from scaling the fence to stop the demolition. The ladies went and got red vigil candles from the church that they had saved and put them beside the feet of every police officer.

The neighborhood was not saved. The Cadillac plant was built. It's not been a very productive or worthwhile plant, even from GM's perspective. Ironically, the analysts have said that the plant's too big. [Laughs] Shortly after opening the plant, they permanently laid off 17,000 Michigan workers. The City Council was quoted as saying that was a real slap in the face after all they had done for GM. But I wouldn't say the struggle in Poletown was for nothing.

Initially I worked on a documentary film, *Poletown Lives!* When we

Jeanie Wylie-Kellermann is author of Poletown: Community Betrayed *(University of Illinois Press, 1989), which exposed the destruction of a viable community in Hamtramck and Detroit to make room for a General Motors Cadillac plant. Bill Wylie-Kellermann, a Methodist minister, formerly pastored at Cass United Methodist Church and is author of the book* Seasons of Faith and Consciousness *(Orbis Press, 1991). They live in a working-class neighborhood in southwestern Detroit.*

were working on the film there was only a very, very small number of people who would give *any* credence to what we were saying. Most of the left was solidly behind the mayor because he had at one time been associated with the Communist Party and had not renounced it, he was the first Black mayor, he had a good track record on civil rights, he had sort of a gutsy, street-talk profile that made him seem real appropriate for the city. To suggest that he was selling out the city's resources for a song to corporate interests was untenable. You just could not do it. You got laughed at in any forum. And to criticize the archdiocese was a difficult thing to do. A couple years later the archdiocese closed forty-two churches in the city and made its intentions real clear.

130   If any of these institutions for a moment had said, "Let's stop and look at the plant configuration and see if we can save the neighborhood and also build the plant," they'd have found out that they could. GM put a lot of pressure on them and said that it had to happen immediately. All these institutions said that GM was being civicly responsible. There's a more sophisticated sense among people in the city that "No, you can't trust the courts, you can't trust Coleman Young, you can't trust the archdiocese." If you care about your neighborhoods it's gonna be a solo fight or a fight along with other neighborhood groups.

BILL: Being a resident of the city, a pastor, and a parent, my commitments to nonviolent resistance have more and more bridged what would be global issues and local ones. Nonviolent resistance is more urgent than ever. With changes in the Cold War and recently in the Soviet Union, there's going to be a very different shape to things. The new world order is really going to be a totalizing—I was going to say totalitarian—one-system order with alternatives probably not permitted. In the past, on a global scale everyone was forced into choosing sides, East or West, but now it's really going to be First versus Third World.

JEANIE: The irony is that Detroit's probably not the place where people want to build. If corporations are going to be attracted to build in the city of Detroit it would be because there were decent schools and a strong infrastructure that made it a tenable place for their employees to work. But that's not the way the City Council and the mayor have viewed it. What the mayor in particular sees is a lot of underused land that he's perfectly willing to clear regardless of who lives on it. So they continue with these megaprojects. All these new developments along the river are touted as this tremendous boom to the city of Detroit. But those office buildings are not occupied. They lure people out of the old office buildings to become tenants at reduced rates in the new ones, and then the old buildings are operating on one-third occupancy, and eventually go under, and then need to be torn down. It's a pathetic idea.

I don't think there's any guarantee that we get to keep the standard of living that we've become accustomed to. As the jobs get exported from the United States to Mexico, I start to wonder who's going to be able to afford to buy the Cadillacs that get put together in Mexico. Most Mexican workers couldn't buy them. If U.S. workers don't have a union wage income they're not going to be able to afford them either.

Detroit doesn't have any alternatives whatsoever. There's a whole echelon of people, probably including representatives in the federal government, who don't care if you throw Detroit away. Suburban people are often quoted as saying, "Nuke it!" Use the neutron bomb, get rid of all the people, and save some of the buildings. Given that there is very little corporate investment, I don't think Detroit has an alternative except community-based economics. Get people mobilized and independent of the current economic structure in a way that is really promising.

BILL: I think we're involved in a kind of spiritual struggle. Fundamentally, it's hope versus despair. I think despair isn't a free-floating issue of spirit, but very focused. It's the main method of political rule and economic power in Detroit. Poletown is really pivotal in that connection. I think many people live in neighborhoods around the city where large projects are slated, hovering as a sort of shadow over the neighborhood. That shadow casts a huge spirit of futurelessness on a neighborhood. You can say that about City Airport, the Bridge Neighborhood here, and a number of places where these projects are hovering. We lived in the Briggs Community neighborhood, north of the expressway, off Trumbull Avenue, where a new Tiger Stadium had been proposed—

JEANIE: It reached a point there where there were all the signs of Poletown all over again: the arson, the real estate blockbusting. No one said, "We want to buy your house because it's going to be condemned and then we can sell it for more money than it's worth." But we began getting fliers saying, We want to buy your house. One block over, an apartment building went up in flames and sparks went over our house and caught the house behind us on fire. The area was unlivable so we got out. This was a deliberate demolition policy of the city of Detroit.

BILL: At the time we were there, a church on Martin Luther King with a day care center set about to build a playground. The community actually built it. It was one of those nice playscapes that the kids had designed. Well-placed sources told the church, "Don't do it; you're wasting your money because that's where the stadium's gonna go." Now, there's an example where you're being urged not to do something because there's a plan for your neighborhood. In 1986 or '87 the newspapers were trying to get information on where the city of Detroit owned land within the city boundaries. The administration refused. The papers filed a freedom of information request. The city refused. The judge found the city in contempt. Emmett Moten, the city development director, went to *jail* to try to prevent that information from getting out. When it *finally* came out, our neighborhood was where the city owned more land than anywhere else. They'd been land-banking. A house would become available or vacant. Someone, a neighbor, would try to buy it and, boom, it would not only be unavailable, but it was *demolished* immediately and you'd have an empty lot. When we left, there were only four houses on our side of the block and two on the other side.

JEANIE: The *dangerous* houses were allowed to stay, so those would stand and be a hazard for your children. The viable houses were destroyed.

BILL: I believe, at least at an unconscious level, maybe at a calculated one, that crack is used to clear neighborhoods that the city wants for development. I've talked to people who are part of WEPROS [We the People Reclaiming Our Streets], the crack movement. Folks who had lived in the State Fair neighborhood experienced that years ago with heroine. We were experiencing it in the Briggs Community neighborhood. At that time I was pastoring in the Cass Corridor area. At a community meeting we asked Emmett Moten a number of questions about neighborhood development. I heard him describe what he called a police strategy, "to corral the crack houses into one neighborhood," so they could drop the net over them. Now that's not a serious police strategy.

You can see places in the city that have come to be called the "hole," where crack is very concentrated. The city wants to extend City Airport, and suddenly you have a neighborhood that's riddled with crack. Now I'm not saying that downtown in some office people say, "All right, put the crack in there." At an institutional level, almost at a spiritual level, there's a kind of collusion. If the cops know that this neighborhood doesn't have a future they're not gonna risk their asses for the sake of a neighborhood that isn't gonna *be* there in a year.

Poletown was a situation where arson was actually systematic and financed economically. The suggestion in Jeanie's book was that the folks who were demolishing houses would pay kids on the street to light fires cause it's easier to demolish a burned-out hulk than a full-standing house. Well, there's an economic pressure to burn the houses, but that also works to create despair in the neighborhood. I think *Devil's Night* goes back to Poletown where arson had a targeted economic base. [*Note:* Ze'ev Chafets in his book *Devil's Night* (1990, pp. 3–4) writes, "It was in the fall of 1986 that I first saw the devil on the streets of Detroit. . . . Three years earlier, in 1983, for reasons no one understands, America's sixth largest city suddenly erupted into flames."] Landlords use the occasion to do insurance fires.

In Detroit the spirit of the city is part of political discourse. Where is the spirit of the city? Who has it? Where is it alive and well and where is it fallen and corrupted? Those are the theological issues. The City Council gives out the Spirit of Detroit Award. The mayor uses the Spirit of Detroit as an emblem of the renaissance, or whatever. On the other hand you have a coalition of neighborhood groups that fights the city over block-grant priorities. It's called SOS, Save Our Spirit. The Spirit of Detroit statue downtown is a symbolic political space in the city. Demonstrations, vigils, press conferences, etc. happen with that as a backdrop. There is a sort of a power to it.

133

JEANIE: There was a real passivity in 1980 after we had been in a recession for several years. It took several years for people to realize that this is not our average recession. This is something permanent that's changing the nature of the city.

What came from that since then are these voices of hope throughout the city. The one that's clearest and most distinct for me is SOSAD [Save Our Sons and Daughters]. To have the parents of kids who've been killed, and the parents of kids who are in jail for having done the killings, stand on the same platform and talk about the importance of our youth in the city of Detroit, is a tremendous reversal of this huge sense of despair. These small movements and voices of hope are setting up a countervailing momentum for the city of Detroit.

At a certain point, having been treated so badly and abused for so long, some of the people of Detroit, those who aren't part of an addiction cycle, have finally been able to come together and say, "We don't need the economic growth corporation, we don't need the urban planning master's students who arrive in Detroit because they couldn't make it into a more glamorous city. We don't need the experts at General Motors or the folks at community economic development who say what's best for the city of Detroit. They've made a shambles of it."

The biggest question is whether or not people are going to be able to capture the imagination of the youth. The youth in Detroit, young African-American males, die of murder more often than anything else. That's to be born with a death sentence. I have a good friend whose father was surprised when he made it to eighteen and said, "I thought you'd be dead or in jail." And he writes periodically about what it's like to have watched all his friends end up dead or in jail. If that's your inheritance, you know it real well by the time you're five because you've been to a variety of funerals and you watched the mothers of your friends cry. It's going to take a significant spirit to reverse that. There's always been a battle between hope and despair. Hope and despair are manipulated by the political and economic interests.

134

BILL: Our block here has been fighting crack houses for some time. The worst time was when we had five crack houses on the block. They were infrastructure for a sort of open drug bazaar going on in the park. There was a lot of traffic. At one point the block came together. People who had lived here for thirty years and didn't know one another's names sat around and met and undertook some public acts of solidarity as a block. Some of the houses had been burned down and empty hulks or empty lots remained. A decisive thing in changing the spirit of the block was that a number of Puerto Rican families from the same village in Puerto Rico had moved onto the block. They have a very public culture. They sit on their front porches at night or on weekends and sing. There's an ongoing fiesta. They have lots of kids. Suddenly the life of the block is a public life. The street just had a different feel to it.

JEANIE: The national media comes to Detroit to look at the city that's the furthest gone, the most destroyed, and asks, "Is this the future of the American city?" Either this city will be totally eaten alive house by house by crack, addictive psychology, violence, abandonment, poverty, or there will be a change. There aren't any alternatives in Detroit, so community economics and community life either will, or won't, save the city because there's nothing else that's going to, short of a radical change on the part of the federal government.

Given the grip of the current institutional arrangement of power and money, politicians don't have enough power and enough imagination to be able to make the kind of changes that are needed. They would do so at the sacrifice of their own career, and very few are willing to do that. What needs to be done instead is that people in the community set the tone and agenda, and eventually the politicians will follow. With any luck, later there will be bank loans. Eventually the establishment will say that's the bandwagon they've been on all along.

If we waited for Washington, D.C., we would give up in despair.

There was that brief moment when there was gonna be a peace dividend because the Cold War was over. I think people had a moment of hope that they would be able to get some of those resources back into the city and create a better way of living. In no time, that money was used in Iraq. This is another opportunity to be disappointed. If there is a groundswell, if there is a community revolt, if there is a new sense of survival among people in Detroit, it would probably most quickly influence local politicians, but it eventually would affect congressional representatives and senators. They wouldn't *not* be able to be influenced by it.

Brian Carter

I work in the Third Precinct. Hispanics and Appalachian whites have been there for a long time. That's where I grew up. I lived there when we first came from Washington, D.C., in 1945. It was an eastern European area, like Hamtramck, where the people scrub the streets and wash their houses. Everyone worked in the factories. All *those* people are just about gone.

We did a survey in our precinct to locate the vacant lots and abandoned houses. Because there are so many vacant lots, the wildlife's coming back, and there are a lot of pheasants in the city. So they had a project to capture a bunch of these "urban" pheasants for interbreeding purposes.

They survive even if beer bottles are thrown at them, cars run over them, smog, and all that stuff. They said it was unsuccessful because the pheasants were *so* wily that they couldn't catch them. [*Laughs*] I don't see how they can survive, because there are a lot of wild cats and dogs that'll eat their eggs and chicks.

I run into a lot of situations in the precinct. One was in all the newspapers. I went to a house and talked to a woman who said that someone had stolen her kids. She said she had left them in her car when she went into the store. When she returned to the car the kids were gone. She was a frail, dope addict–looking lady living with a guy. She was in her thirties. Her boyfriend was in his sixties. He's half drunk. I asked,

"Where did you leave your kids?"
"I was up at McKinley and Buchanan and went into the store—"
"What did you go into the store to get?"

Brian Carter is an attorney and a sergeant with the Detroit Police Department.

"Just went in to get some things."

"What kind of things?"

"Well, you know, milk, ice cream, stuff for the kids."

Now, *that's* where the dope houses are. [*Laughs*] I asked,

"You weren't going to get some of that stuff that helps keep those fingers and hands fat as they are, were you?"

"What are you talking about?"

"Look at them hands, they're as big as Mohammed Ali's."

She weighed about 110 pounds, but had those dope-addict hands. When they use *up* their arms they end up shooting their hands, feet, vagina, everywhere. Their hands and feet swell up.

The one daughter's age nineteen, and retarded, and the other's an eighteen-month-old baby. The woman said that she had left them in the car and somebody stole them. The car belongs to the old guy who came to the door with her. It's the kind of car that nobody would steal, and nobody would steal a car with an eighteen-month-old baby and a retarded nineteen-year-old in *any*way.

Later on, the kids show up at another precinct. The police happened to walk by, saw the kids, and took them to the station. She had left the motor running and the car ran out of gas. The retarded nineteen-year-old didn't have sense enough to get out of the car. The kids had been sitting in the car for like two days in front of a dope house. She got the kids back. The system doesn't have any alternatives or options. What's the system gonna do with the kids? It's cheaper and fits the books better if they give the kids right back to her and send her check on time.

A thirty-three-year-old guy comes into the station and tells me, "A guy just shot me and my brother. My brother's in the hospital." I asked,

"Who shot you?"

"Well, he's a security guard someplace."

"Why would he do that? He just walked up and shot you?"

"Yeah, he just shot me for no reason at all."

"He wasn't trying to rob you or something?"

"No, he's a *security* guard."

"Do you know him?"

"Yeah, I know who he is."

"And he just walks up and shoots you for no reason?"

"Yeah!"

Later I went to the hospital to see the brother. I asked,

"What happened? Why would this guy shoot you?"
"He was getting smart, so me and him and my brother was fighting. He pulled his gun out and shot us."
"Who was winning the fight?"
"We was kicking his ass."
"Well, when you're kicking someone's ass who you know has got a gun, ain't the next move to be they *shoot* your ass? Why would a guy stand there battling with you tooth and nail—*two* of you—when he's got a gun with him? Why would you jump on a man with a gun? You *caused* this. It seems like by the time you get thirty years old you should *know* this. Do you know *now* not to do things like that?"
"I'm a *man*, man! No one's gonna mess with *me!*"
"You're semiparalyzed and you're *still* saying that. That's funny as hell. You've got your manhood and you can't walk."

A guy came in to the station with a wound that was straight down. His heel was shot off. I asked,

"How'd that happen?"
"I was walking down this street and I heard a shot. I kept on walking and noticed my heel's hurting."
"You're lying. You had that damn gun in your waist. You was going up there to rob the shrimp place. When you pulled out the gun you shot your *own* damned self in the foot."
"No, it didn't happen that way."
"Well tell me, if you're walking, no matter how you're stepping, how can a bullet come straight down?"
"I don't know. Bullet's ricochet, or something."

You can't outsmart them and you have to go back around other people, *today.* If you put too much of your life into dealing with them, then you become part of that. Then you have to do the big schizophrenic switch on your way home from work. *That's* the stressful stuff in my job. The part about people pulling guns and shooting, or threatening to jump on you, there's not much of that. You can get by on the *physical* side. It's the frustration of there being no resolutions to *any* of it.

These are situations that you can't straighten out. You can't walk them back to some "normal" home situation where it's right and nice, and they say, "We'll take care of him; he won't do this again." It's so interwoven in the way they do things, all you're *really* doing is getting some paper off from desk to desk, and getting them the hell away from you till the next time they show up. When I was back in detec-

CITY LIFE, SCENES, FEELINGS

tives, the saying was, "Today's complainant is tomorrow's defendant."
Today he got cut and lost. Tomorrow he'll win: *he'll* be the cutter, and
he'll be the defendant.

These people who get physical with each other and call each
other a racial name, I imagine that you could probably mobilize them
to kill whatever group they're not into. While they're heating their
hands on the gas stove and opening up a can of Franco-American
spaghetti, they probably tell their kids, "Well, at least we're not like
them niggers on TV with the flies walking on their eyelids." You know,
the Sudanese and Ethiopians that they want you to send money to.
"You keep messing with me, kid, and I'm going to send you over
there." [*Laughs*]

138

I heard that the crime rate is down in Detroit.

One way to look at *that* is that they already stole everything. There
ain't shit left to take. I guess the murder rate is down. We're not first
any more. But these things are situational: they come in spurts. The
kind of crime that bothers people mostly is that they can't leave the
house without a dog or somebody constantly coming or going from
your house.

We went on vacation for a couple days and they tore the bars off
the windows of *this* house. The guy who broke into the house lived in
that abandoned building over there. [*Points*] The guy who built this
whole block of stuff still owns *that* house as well as a whole complex
up on Van Dyke. We had been complaining about that house. I'd
seen him in the middle of the night dragging in TVs and stuff. We're
not supposed to get involved in neighborhood stuff, you know, so I
called the police and they caught the guy. He got convicted and got
three to seven years.

My wife said she saw him in the old neighborhood where *she* used
to live. I called the Department of Corrections and learned that he
was in the Woodward Center by Wayne State. It used to be a motel.
He was supposed to go to Jackson Prison, but he never left the city
and never got to Jackson. That place is like one of those adult foster
care centers that say, "Get the hell out of here at eight o'clock in the
morning, be back at five o'clock, don't get in no trouble." [*Laughs*]
So they *walk.* There aren't many jobs, except washing cars. They'd
do better with hubcaps. Someone would give them five dollars for a
hubcap.

The kind of crime like that woman who was raped in New York is
committed by people who usually have some kind of serious problem.
Murders are between dope men and within families. Very few people
walking down the street are murdered by someone who says, "I think

I'll kill somebody." The police can't control the drug fights, nor husbands killing their wives and wives killing their husbands. And then there's the stuff that these young kids are doing where they shoot at one and hit three others.

I don't think the people at the top who are making all this money give a damn about racism. It's economics they're concerned with. When the owners of Mitsubishi and others go home at night in Japan they might say they don't want Koreans living next door to them, or those "slimy" Filipinos, or something like *that*, but it has no impact on what they do in business.

This auto production stuff is all shifted from Detroit to some other place, like Mexico or Indonesia that pays lower wages. The people who shifted are not saying, "Those people aren't as black as the people in Detroit. At least they got straight hair and they're tan, so we'll give *them* a break for a while." They're saying, "Those people over there haven't been exposed to all this union crap. We can pay them a *penny* a day, so we'll make the stuff over there." **139**

Then someone might say, "Well, if you're making a product that's gonna be sold in America, if you put everybody out of work in America who's gonna buy it?" The response is, "We're not selling that kind of low-class shit. The kind of cars we're making that get shipped back to America aren't bought by the lower class anyway. They're not a market."

I think about Black leaders who focus on issues involving more of this or more of that for Blacks, and they have to include women and other minorities to make it palatable to someone else. We Blacks are a population of maybe 30 million people, and it seems to me appropriate that Black leaders should be representing *all* that group. But they just don't seem interested in the things that are beyond their *own* personal interests in getting to the same level as white leaders in the community. The "trickle down" of Reagan will take a couple thousand years at this rate. [*Laughs*]. We need a *Niagara Falls.*

Moira Kennedy

I think the Detroit community is very well developed. In *my* community on the Detroit east side I trust my neighbors. We're together, Black and white. In some ways, my moving to Detroit was almost a political statement. I did not want to live and raise my kids in white

Moira Kennedy is a family therapist and political activist.

suburbia. I wanted to live in congruency with my politics. When I decided to buy a house—a large financial investment—I decided to do it in Detroit. My neighborhood is aesthetically beautiful. My neighbors are very close. At any point we can have a party just by calling all the neighbors together. [*Laughs*] I just can't see living anywhere else.

I'm involved in politics partly because I'm so angry. Last night [November 7, 1990] some comrades and I watched that terribly one-sided ABC TV show "Prime Time" that focused on Detroit and Mayor Young. It said nothing about the good side, the good people, the positives, of Detroit. I get so angry and so frustrated by such things that I feel like if I'm not involved there's no place to go with that anger. I guess the alternative would be to say, "You just can't fight City Hall." But that would leave *me* with a lot of anger. My way of dealing with that is to do something.

I've thought about why I have this indignation and what drives me and my brothers, sisters, and other comrades to continue activism. I was raised in a progressive family. My father was a member of the Communist Party and a writer for the *New York Times*. Although he was not a big part of my life, I knew he had suffered from the blacklisting of the McCarthy period.

I remember one of my first political experiences. It produced a feeling of *rage* in me and the reaction that "they can't do this!" As a way, I suppose, of politicizing the kids, my mother gave me *The Rise and Fall of the Third Reich*. It had all those pictures of the camps and the people in the boxcars. I remember clearly in early grade school looking at that, taking it to my mother in the kitchen and, with tears, saying, "What is *this*? Are these *people*?" And my mother, crying, said, "Well, this is what people can do to each other." All I could say to myself was "My God!"

In Detroit we're blessed because there's a lot happening. It's pretty well organized, not scattered. People know how to organize here. I spent some time recently in Cincinnati attending meetings. When I went to some of the events, I said to myself, "These people need to *learn* a lot more about how to organize." In Detroit there's an immense amount of expertise and the people are still active.

Dr. Alex Epthim, a professor of social work at Wayne State, who recently passed away, was an icon and psychic mentor of mine. One of the things I learned from him, and from other activists a generation older than me, was that, you keep at it, even in the face of adversity. And why do you keep at it? Because this is what you love to do. There's no point in doing it with sadness, or malice, or frustration. This theme was repeated at his memorial, attended by many of the people he touched.

In 1968, shortly after the rebellion in Detroit, I started working with New Detroit, Inc. around race issues. New Detroit had spawned a group called PACT [People Acting for Change Together] that had a strictly *nationalist* analysis. I read Malcolm X, and others, and concluded I was a racist. I felt guilty. I remember in New Detroit we would go around and have these consciousness-raising circles where everyone would have to admit their racism. I felt terrible.

I'm not *sure* when I became politically aware, but I think it was when there was some movement toward *doing* something about our racism. So we went out, as Black and white trainers, to inquire of whites why they were so racist. [*Laughs*] It was a fairly antagonistic kind of approach. I remember going out to Warren to the Social Security Administration office with Smitty, who's since passed away. We ran this long line on them: "If you're white, you gotta be racist, and the best you can do is to be an antiracist racist." [*Laughs*] Well, *that* really went over well in Warren. By the time we left they were calling us commies, and this and that.

Bob Terry [a PACT trainer], more than most, tried to gear the training toward the self-interest piece. Bob tried to move us from a guilt and adversary perspective to one that raised the question, "Why is it in our best interests to fight together?" The PACT experience was a movement away from feeling my awesome guilt. I really took this whole thing hard. I would end up weeping and being real self-mutilating about it. This isn't too empowering. I think it's more empowering to ask, "Why shouldn't we work together?"

Mary Sue Schottenfels

GRIN started five years ago when I was a staff person at the Michigan Avenue Community Organization. I've become very immersed in this neighborhood. I can't tell you how much I love it. It's very deep inside me. I often wonder what we'll be doing in ten years. My husband says, "We'll be right here," and he's probably right. This neighborhood really does get inside you. I know a lot of people who feel this way. You're just not going to find that anywhere else.

Five years ago my husband and I realized that a lot of people were thinking about moving. We both feel like pretty empowered people and had credibility in the neighborhood. So we decided to

Mary Sue Schottenfels has been an activist and organizer throughout her adult life, and is a leader in the Granmont-Rosedale Integrated Neighborhood (GRIN), which includes four community associations in northwest Detroit.

pull together twenty or so people we knew, an all-white group to start with. We knew white people better and the people who were thinking of moving were white.

We had a meeting and asked people to come and talk about their feelings. It was an incredible experience. We went around the room—nobody could talk twice—and talked about what would make you stay, what would make you leave, why are you here? Every one of us could afford to live in the suburbs and everyone knew the schools were better there. Why are we here? It was such a warm, wonderful experience helping each other tune into the feeling of trying to live in an integrated neighborhood, trying to make it work here, trying to be a part of the city, trying *not* to walk away.

142

After that first meeting most of the people went out and had another meeting just like it. Probably twenty groups of twenty people met in the next year. We went to most of those meetings and facilitated them. Some worked out better than others. The first meeting was all white, including people who were comfortable enough to have the discussion. It takes courage to have such a discussion, and it takes a lot *more* courage to have it in an integrated setting. Chuck Wilbur came to the meeting and wrote a cover story article for the *Metro Times* called "They're Staying."

The later meetings were integrated. We really did stabilize things. Of that initial group, almost everybody is still here. Who can say for sure that they're not moving? If somebody gets shot in their house they're gonna move. "Short of something horrible happening, I'll stay here" is so comforting in an atmosphere where you're just not sure who's staying and who's leaving.

Now we have come full circle. It's been five years and we've done a lot in the interim. We've done Martin Luther King days, we've had a couple of real estate open houses where we've advertised and had Realtors come in the morning and home buyers come in the afternoon. We've had 500 families come through the area looking at houses. We had Father Cunningham [Focus: Hope] come and talk to a meeting. We're wondering again if people are going to move. It's *exactly* where it was five years ago, which is why we're now planning another meeting in January where we talk again. Now we have an integrated steering committee, though it's mostly white.

Five years later it's a more difficult problem because there's been a couple horrible crimes. A very active guy in North Rosedale was shot at six A.M. in his house by an intruder. That just did people in. Then there was a rape during the day in North Rosedale. These incidents have really rocked people. Also, the city and the state are just going down the tubes right now. There's the sense that maybe this *is* the time to get out. Some of *my* good friends are thinking of moving. I really don't think race is an issue in the neighborhoods. I know people personally who are real frustrated right now. But this is *not* an all-Black city. If middle-class whites and Blacks leave and take the remaining tax base, the city's going to close the doors.

I've talked to friends—and this is one of those things that you'd do if you ever had the energy—about getting a citywide stayers' group together. I'd get a rap group of people together to talk about those struggles. The experience of bonding and finding out that "I'm not really isolated" is incredibly important. When you get anxious about whether you should stay, the most important thing is knowing that other people are staying. I go through this all the time.

143

When times get hard—and they are that way now—I have to click off in my head the people who aren't leaving. And that's exactly what I'm going to do in January. I'm going to go around the room again and ask, "Who's staying?" We need to know that. We need to know who our frame of reference is. If you could do that citywide, it wouldn't solve most of the problems but it would be real important to have people like that hold on.

Osvaldo Rivera

In 1898 the U.S. took over Puerto Rico. The Jones Act gave U.S. citizenship to Puerto Ricans in 1917. The first migration to the mainland was in 1918 when about 100 single males came to New Orleans to work in the shipyards. The South was very much Jim Crow at the time. The Puerto Rican males tended to be very dark in complexion and probably were *immediate* descendants of freed slaves. They went as far north as they could. Some ended up settling in New Jersey and New York, but about 100 settled in Black Bottom in Detroit. Because there were no Puerto Rican females, and because they settled in a Black neighborhood, they intermarried with American Blacks.

I was born in Puerto Rico in 1953. When my mother was pregnant with me, my father came to Detroit to do labor. His entry to Detroit in the early '50s was part of the *second* migration of Puerto

Osvaldo Rivera is the director of Latino Family Services, in the southwest section of Detroit.

Ricans to the mainland. This was part of Operation Bootstrap, which included a major exportation of labor from Puerto Rico.

The second wave settled in an established Mexican community in the Corktown area, the Holy Trinity area. That's where I was brought up. The second wave was more reflective of the island as it is now: a rainbow of colors.

I came to Detroit when I was five years old. I was an altar boy at Holy Trinity Church where Monsignor Clement Kern was the pastor. He was a community organizer in the Latino community. All the good stories about him are very true. We were in one of the most progressive churches in the city. They ministered to the poor. Skid Row used to be located close to Holy Trinity, and Father Kern and his people ministered to those folks.

Under Father Kern's guidance, the Puerto Rican Club was formed in the early '50s in response to police brutality against Puerto Ricans in Detroit. At that time Puerto Rican nationalists had attacked President Truman at the Blair House in Washington and shot up the Congress. In Detroit and throughout the country there was a backlash against Puerto Ricans, irrespective of their political views. Males would be dragged out of public places and beaten up.

As a teenager I was grappling with the Vietnam War and the civil rights issue. I clearly remember the day Martin Luther King got shot. Classmates who I grew up with would say, "You know, I believe in Malcolm X." I had no reason to doubt that these were real good students, and good individuals, and they talked about reading radical things.

By age seventeen, I began to form some clear ideas about the fact that people of color were oppressed. I began to believe the Vietnam War was wrong. Latinos and Blacks started organizing around cultural clubs, youth activities, and pride. A lot of us started to read and send for information from the Young Lords Party in New York. It was similar to the Black Panther Party but less adventuristic.

Then I became a student at Wayne State University in Chicano Boricua studies. Prior to 1971, it was estimated that there were only 25 to 30 [Latino] students on the campus. Those classes were very progressive. We used a systems approach to look at the oppression of minorities, particularly Mexican-Americans and Puerto Rican–Americans, the two primarily Latino populations. El Grito de Mi Raza, a radio program for twenty years, was a Latino affairs, music program on WDET. It was a project of that group.

1970 to 1972 was a hotbed of activity for this community. The Latino Students Association formed an alliance with the Association of Black Students. We studied political theory, economic issues, and particularly the history and culture of our own people. We're still struggling around those issues.

One of the things that has to be done in Detroit is to admit the extent of the problems. This is the first time there's been consistent and significant African-American political power in a city in this country. We are proud of those achievements. But there's a flip side to that and it's racism. That escalated people running into the suburbs. Racism is very alive. A lot of activists moved out of the city, including myself. This is one of the most segregated metropolitan areas in the country.

I think [Mayor] Coleman Young has encircled himself with a machine that's very effective, but is stifling grassroots empowerment. A lot of it has nothing to do with city politics, but with the national economic state of affairs. We're in a mixed bag. How do you criticize an administration which *needs* to be criticized, but not go overboard and blame it for things that are not of its doing. That's the dilemma that a lot of progressives are in.

In the Latino community there's real dissatisfaction. We're not considered an important community. We're not a big enough grouping to ensure elections. A lot of metropolitan Detroiters don't even know we exist, and the administration has condoned that attitude. That can cause tensions between people of color. It's all a question of turf.

The Latino community in Detroit has very specific interests, and it has to fight for those interests: upgrading the services to this community, electing or appointing Latino leadership to key positions of power, an increase in cultural sensitivity, fighting as a community against racist immigration laws. If we can't achieve these without building alliances with the African-American community, then we must build alliances. Building coalitions is a very fluid thing. It's not long-lasting in the sense that conditions change and interests change. We're going into the twelfth year of a Reagan/Bush counterrevolution, and we have not changed our tactics. That's not good leadership.

We must build an alliance with members of the white community based on combatting racism, and saying that we have common interests. White progressives have to stand up and build alliances with the Black community. We have to launch a cultural war against racism. There has to be a struggle with the media. As disgusting as you might think those media representatives are, we must say, "Let's struggle around this Detroit bashing." We must turn the enemies into reluctant supporters. We have to do some education to get to the white folks. We cannot have this war situation.

Frank Rashid

I've lived in Detroit since I was born in 1950 and I've watched the neighborhoods change. The first neighborhood I lived in, where my parents still live, was in the area of Lothrop and West Grand Boulevard. It's made up of all kinds of flats and duplexes. It was a middle-class neighborhood in the 1950s. There was one Black family when I was born. By the time I was fifteen it was almost all Black. I grew up with the advantages of a multicultural background. On my block there was a German family, a Japanese family, a Polish family, an Irish family—all first generation—along with two Arab families: mine and another of Lebanese background.

146   Then Black families moved in. The second Black family on the block was Roger Short's family. He's now the auditor-general of the city of Detroit. When I moved here onto Parkside Street, I was one of the last whites to move onto *his* block. We had divisions in the neighborhood, but they were geographical, not racial. Roger Short was the big ally on my block. He was the kid who scared away the gangs from the other blocks, all of whom were white. He was protecting us.

Another formative thing was working in my dad's store. We were the Lebanese store owners. This was before Caldeans became the store owners. The experience with the customers was wonderful. Of course, the *one* formative experience was the riot in 1967. My dad bought his first store on Linwood in 1935. It had been an A&P at one time. Then he bought a liquor store on 14th Street in '54. Both stores were hit in the riot of 1967. When the grocery store was broken into and looted, the Black customers in the neighborhood called us. I owe my life to those folks. The clientele of the grocery store was very middle class. The customers helped us clean up. One of the customers who I later found out was a cop told my dad that we had better get out. The customers walked with us to the car. As we drove off, the car was pelted with rocks.

Because of my attachment to Detroit I developed a sensitivity to literature about cities. One thing that makes a city work is its landmarks; its continuity with the past. Detroit has systematically destroyed its past. It's not new to the Coleman Young administration, though he has carried on that tradition. We tear down buildings and put up plaques. It's all so wrong because it just makes no economic sense. A few rich corporations and individuals profit from the constant tearing down and building up. But most people end up paying more taxes. We subsidize this all the time because of the illusion that it's doing us

Frank Rashid is a leader in the "Save Tiger Stadium" movement and a professor at Marygrove College in Detroit.

some good. We go along with the gospel of business. Combining that with the deep seated racism of this area, it's pretty much destroyed this town.

Look at Hudson's. They built that Northland complex with the profits they made from the downtown store. They built Northland with all that parking around it and put it into direct competition their own business with no parking. They drew all the business to Northland. The downtown department store was a distinctive shopping experience. They didn't do a thing with that. They let quality deteriorate and said, "Hey, you know, it's just not a profitable store." Hudson's downtown was an anchor.

Our stupid willingness to be seduced by the auto companies has subverted any mass transit which a viable city needs. They talked us out of building a subway system when one was on the books in the 1920s. They talked us into selling the streetcars to Mexico City and they're still in use. Apparently they still say Detroit on them. How many generations of buses are we on now, those ugly, wasteful, polluting, expensive, inefficient buses?

We built these damned spoke freeways *parallel* to the main commercial arteries instead of building beltways like Washington, D.C., or Baltimore. Detroit's main commercial arteries are ghost towns now. It's nuts! We were the first with freeways because we were the automobile capital, so we made the first mistakes. The auto companies did direct harm.

During the '20s, '30s, and '40s the car companies drew massive numbers of people from the South. Poor whites and Blacks, who had been segregated from one another in the South, came here and there's not enough housing. So they fought over the same housing and the working space in the plants. So, in 1943 everything erupted. That was the real harmful riot that brought out the modern racial tensions in Detroit, and was ugly, and was personal, and polarized the generation before me.

Unfortunately, the preservation groups in Detroit, like Preservation Wayne, tend to be white and that makes the majority population suspicious of them. We face this in the Tiger Stadium issue. Here is a landmark that is linked with the racist past. Major league baseball didn't integrate until 1946. The Detroit Tigers were the second last team to integrate. The stadium is seen as the *symbol* of racism. I see it as a place where segregation fell in a truly remarkable, wonderful way. Ozzie Virgil was the first Black player for Detroit. In the first game he played, the Blacks came in large numbers for this historic event. This guy was a mediocre ball player. He never did anything in his life that was noteworthy, except for that day: he went five for five.

We have Black members in the Tiger Stadium Fan Club, but not as many as we should have. We have a lot of support and interest, not just for preservation, but because replacing Tiger Stadium would be taxing the people of Detroit to support another rich white man's business. But I think also there's a hunger for continuity. Walter Briggs, whose family is associated with Tiger Stadium's past, has an idea for buying the stadium, selling stock, and having the people own the stadium.

It's wrong to replace the stadium. If you're a baseball fan you're going to get screwed. You're going to pay more money for an inferior product. You won't have all the advantages that Tiger Stadium has. A new stadium will be a copy of a modern stadium which is inferior. It will just increase the profits of the team owner and the costs are borne by the people.

If you're not a baseball fan it's even *more* wrong because your tax dollars are supporting something you don't even give a damn about. The Black majority in Detroit should be up in arms, and they *are* up in arms unless they're connected to the political machinery in town.

The stadium links old and new leftists, and people concerned with social and economic justice, such as myself. Even some conservatives and people outstate [outside the tri-county area] are concerned. It's proposed that there be a restaurant food tax to pay for the stadium. This would only make [team owner] Tom Monaghan richer.

A lot of people say we can't win this because the powers that be are too strong. If we can't win this, we can't win anywhere. Tom Monaghan who owns the Tigers is one of the least popular people in the world. He has an absolute disregard for the true needs of this city. Baseball's tremendously profitable. I think Monaghan has made a profit on the Tigers since he's owned them. In some years, the profits have exceeded those of all of Dominos [Monaghan's pizza chain], a much bigger operation. He also owns the cable network PASS.

How can they be talking about a pleasure palace for an upscale clientele to profit someone who's already one of the state's four billionaires when we have the kinds of problems we have in this town? It's unconscionable. It's a thing that's been done over and over in this town, but never so baldly.

Fighting the power is so draining, and that's what they count on. So far, we've not given in. When they hit us one way, we hit them from another. The Tigers have said the stadium is structurally unsound, then we get the experts to say it *isn't* structurally unsound. Then they say it can't be renovated to meet their needs, so we take the needs that they publish and we came up with the Cochran Plan that *meets* their needs. Then Wayne County gets into the act and looks at our renovation scheme since the Tigers won't. The county hired a firm that pretty much scuttled renovation as an option. Then we got an initiative on the ballot to force the city of Detroit to enforce its lease with the Tigers. Tiger Stadium is public property. We're doing this part time and I don't know how long we can keep it up. We're fighting against people who are skilled, intelligent, and have lots of resources.

Alternative points of view are marginalized here. I hold a lot of us activists responsible for this. There's a real fear of success among activists. Sometimes we do those very things that will keep us from being successful because we don't want to dirty our hands and do the fighting. We want to remain ideologically pure. We won't get into a political campaign because politics is so corrupt; the ballot is corrupt. I sympathize with that. On the other hand, damn, we've got to do something! The people I criticize are elitists in reverse: they want to be able to spout their own lines and point the finger at society or the institutions and say, "Look how corrupt that is." But in doing so they're satisfying their own need to feel pure, a kind of masturbatory approach to issues. Until we can get over that and build alliances and coalitions, we're not going to overcome the force of those institutions that are destroying the quality of life in this town.

Lee Carter

In the middle '20s I hung out with a group of Jewish kids who formed a little gang here, just like boys do, which later came to be known as the Purple Gang. It was one of the most feared gangs in Detroit in the early '30s. Matter of fact it was the only gang that Al Capone and his henchmen didn't ever want to tangle with. When a bunch of us would go out and get into a fist fight with other boys, you couldn't hardly tell one from another, and you ended up sometimes hitting a member of your own gang. So we put a purple band around our arms to know each other.

Most of the merchants in Detroit at that time were Jewish, with stores on Hastings Street. The neighborhood was predominantly Jewish, mixed with Italians and Black folks (they called us colored or Negroes then). The younger Italian fellows were sort of aggressive. They'd go up and down Hastings Street and started extorting money

Lee Carter is the president of the Island View Association, a community development group on Detroit's east side, where he lives.

from the Jewish merchants. So, some of these boys decided they'd form a gang to protect their parents.

But, as with any gang, there's somebody who said, "Hey, we can make some money out of this thing." It seems that when you organize something to combat one evil, you create another one. These fellows that was money-minded decided that *some* of the merchants were giving us money, but we were protecting *all* of them and some of them ain't giving us nothing. So they went to *all* the merchants and told them that if they want protection they should give us a couple dollars a week. So one type of extortion replaced another type. This was *really* the beginning of the Purple Gang in Detroit.

I go back to these underworld cultures that developed because I think they did more to form the destiny of Detroit than any other force. I say that because they got so powerful until they controlled the politicians and then the administration and the courts. They had the money that made it possible for people to get in office. Most big cities operated about the same way.

I lost my newsboy about a year ago. He dutifully delivered my paper every day rain or shine for a whole year. And then suddenly I'm getting a new newsboy, and I'm wondering what happened. And the new boy told me, "John got him a better job." I had overlooked the fact that about four or five months after John had stopped carrying papers, his mother's house across the street there had aluminum siding put on, a new garage was put up, John was walking through the neighborhood here with a pit bull and with gold chains on. I called him in here once and said, "Look, what the hell happened? Now you tell me." He said, "I got two friends who made more money in one day than I made in a whole year. If my momma's monthly check was a couple days late, I had to take my paper money to help her pay the rent." Need meets opportunity. You know what kind of results you're gonna get.

This boy went into crack?

Yeah, they're dealing crack in the neighborhood. But they do it in such a quiet way, it doesn't bother anybody, so we don't say anything. But we know what's going on. That type of situation surrounds us and he became contaminated by it. You can take one situation like that you know about, you can multiply it by many others you don't know about. Some kids will do it through need, and then there's always some people who will do things through greed.

A fellow in the neighborhood got shot three times, and I said, "You're still dealing?" He said, "Yeah, Mr. Carter; I don't know no other way." I said, "You've been shot once in the telephone booth, you got shot at the Coney Island, and you got shot on the street corner. How many times do you think you're gonna get shot and keep on living?" He said, "Well, when I think about the way me and my family and my brothers and sisters was living before I got shot, I just decided I had to make myself some money. If I didn't make myself no money, it didn't make no difference whether I was dead or alive."

If everybody would just stay in his own little given territory and just sell his little stuff there, and let everybody else do their own little thing, there wouldn't be no gang fighting. But wherever you have a lot of money floating around you always have some guy who wants to be king of the island and set on top of everything. He wants this street, that street, and as many streets as he can get. Well, you eventually have to kill him to get rid of him. And that don't do very much good; it's just like cutting an arm off of an octopus. You kill him and you got another person you have to kill. So you got guys running around shooting at each other.

How does the Island View Association approach the needs of Detroit people?

We're trying to make a little bit of difference. Sometimes I think it's almost like spitting in the blast furnace to try to put it out, but then I begin to wonder how much worse it would be if you didn't do the little bits that you *are* able to do.

The area covered by the Island View Association is 740 acres, from Mack Avenue to Jefferson, from Baldwin to Mt. Elliott. Many of the houses in this area are run down. When we repair a house, you repair the dignity and uplift the spirit of the people who live in the house. You help to keep family life together. The longer you leave repairs go, the more the house deteriorates. And how long will a family live in a house that continues to deteriorate? One day Henry will say to his wife Mary, "We can't stay here no longer. We've got to move somewhere else. I ain't paying no more taxes on this old shack. We can stay here three years for nothing and I'll put that money in the cookie jar." It takes the city about six years to foreclose on it. So they patch it up here and there.

In a destitute neighborhood where every little bit helps, then you've got the fellows with shopping carts going through the neighborhoods in broad, open daytime to scavenge. If you got a brickyard giving them ten cents a brick, you get about ten or fifteen carts going up and down the streets every day picking brick out of the brick

151

houses, and taking doors and lumber from the other houses. Pretty soon the area looks like a war zone. These scavengers aren't violent. They just take anything that's not nailed down if they can get away with it.

I saw a sign in the area—"This House Is Being Watched."

Yes, we organized that through the block clubs. There's an eyesore over there, and we know the city cannot get around to tearing it down, so we decided not to let the scavengers tear it down. If they know that they're being watched, they'll go on to somewhere else. We don't care where they go as long as they do it away from here. You also keep out the drug addict who's looking for a place to sleep. When he gets in there, he might drink, and smoke a cigarette, and set the mattress on fire, and the house will catch fire, and it might burn *yours.* So it's to *your* benefit to watch the house like you would watch an orphan child.

We did twelve homes this year, fifteen last year. I wonder what would have happened to the people if we hadn't repaired their homes. The houses would have been demolished and the families would be gone. All the families are still here. Nobody moves. We screen them before we repair the homes and we monitor them after the repairs. We want them to keep their homes up.

The federal government have shown, with all they try to do, it's ineffective. Any time you get involved in a program that's *big* enough to serve the needs of the people, you're going to build a big bureaucracy with so many incompetent people in there, that the purpose for which the program was designed will go down the drain. A perfect example is the Brewster Housing Project. When that was first built it was the most beautiful building we saw in this city in a long time. They were substantial structures, not matchstick wood like they build houses out of today. A young Negro architect from the housing department was made manager of that project and remained manager for twelve years. And that project was kept up. I got my family a place over there. You had to meet certain conditions for your behavior pattern. You had to keep your place up. It was regularly inspected. If you didn't come up to those standards, you'd have an eviction notice. No fooling around. The place was kept beautiful.

Then the politicians started meddlin' in: "I'll make this guy housing director who gave me $100,000 to help me get elected." All he's got to do is sit up there and shuffle paper around. Soon as they got the paper shufflers up there, it began to go downhill. Jeffries is the same way. It happened to every project in the city. They're living skeletons. Those buildings didn't deteriorate by themselves or just because the people who lived in them abused them so much.

Vicki Kovari

I was born in Detroit, raised in the northwest side, went to school here and in Ann Arbor. Except for a year overseas, I spent my life in Detroit.

The major force in my life that led me to what I'm doing today was spiritual. There's a book called *The Religious Roots of Rebellion,* and I think that sort of applies to me. I grew up a Catholic. There was always a value put on taking care of the poor. My two years at Immaculata, an all-girls Catholic high school, had a great effect on me. It was in the late '60s, and there was a lot of activism on the part of the students, both Black and white, and a lot of participation in antiwar stuff.

In the community organization program at the University of Michigan I first found out about Saul Alinsky and his work. I wanted to concentrate on the community as a way of intervening in making people's lives better. I met a group of women there who had a great influence on my life. We all wanted to change the system. But the ground was already fertile because of my belief that living a life that was true to the Gospel meant working to make the world, as Ken Cockrel put it once, "less inhospitable to the poor."

Every year I seem to get more radicalized; you're supposed to sort of settle down. [*Laughs*] I seem to get more angry or more convinced of a need to change the system, which I find very oppressive to people, particularly poor people. I've worked as a social work organizer in Detroit for eleven years. At some point I decided that this was the way it was going to be, that burnout was not really an option for me. It was going to be for the long haul.

I was married in 1985 to an organizer in Detroit, a former Jesuit priest. We nurture and sustain each other in a poor neighborhood in southwest Detroit. We have two very young children. The ethnic diversity of the area is tremendous. But there's a definite fear. It's not an easy decision to raise your kids in Detroit because of the crime factor. Last summer the fifteen-year-old brother of a friend of my four-year-

153

Vicki Kovari is a staff person with the Detroit Organization of Tenants and part-time instructor at the Wayne State University School of Social Work.

old son was shot in the stomach in the alley right behind our house a half hour after my child was playing in the back yard. It was a dispute while they were coming home from school. Such violence happens regularly. Having children here, I have a very personal stake in wanting the carnage to stop.

Many people I know moved out of the city over the last ten years. I used to get very angry and felt like they were selling out. I don't think the same way now. I know very well how hard it is to live in a city with as much violence and poverty. And I know that some circumstances demand that people can't survive in this environment.

When I started organizing around housing, homelessness wasn't even in people's vocabularies. In 1980 we started the Detroit Tenants Union, a first attempt at a citywide union for people who lived in private housing. There had been attempts to organize public housing tenants on a citywide basis in the '70s. We also tried to start a rent-control initiative in the city, going after a charter amendment, but we weren't successful in getting enough signatures.

So we started to build a core group of leadership. In '85 and '86 we got tenant leaders from all over the city together. Out of that was born the Detroit Organization of Tenants. The core of that group were people who were organizing through the United Community Housing Coalition.

We started a group called Fair Rent Initiative, which tied rent increases with code violations for the first time. We circulated a petition to put a city rent control ordinance on the ballot. We received 12,000 signatures in six months, and we put the initiative on the ballot in August 1988. Three weeks before the election the state legislature passed a law that prohibited municipalities in Michigan from passing their own rent-control ordinances, and the governor signed the law.

The landlords then went to court to get the issue off the ballot. But we were successful in court in keeping it on. The rent-control initiative passed by almost two to one. Now we have an ordinance that the city administration refuses to implement because of the state law. We weren't able to get enough attorneys to challenge the law. It was really a crucial blow to the organization. We won the battle, but lost the war.

Ten years ago I thought Detroit couldn't go any lower. I was wrong. [*Laughs*] The cuts in general assistance are probably going to have about a $300 million impact on Detroit's economy because of the multiplying effect. For the first time since I've been working in the city do I see a real challenge to the powers that be; a real desire by a lot of people to want change and to see an end to the violence. I

154

don't see any political figure on the horizon right now who promises major reforms without getting into the probusiness mentality: the trickle-down effect to the citizens. We still need to do a lot of work at the grass roots so that people won't fall for the same stories and promises as in the past. The major hope I have is what happened in Louisiana around [ultraconservative candidate] David Duke: they were able to register large numbers of people who have been traditionally disenfranchised from the voting process and get them to turn out for an election.

A lot of leadership is coming from people who work in neighborhood organizations and agencies in the city, for example the people who are part of SOS [Save Our Spirit]. We've been successful in uniting a large number of organizations around block-grant funds. In other cities, groups have fought each other tooth and nail over these dwindling funds. In Detroit, we've been able to organize a *large* coalition around a common purpose without major divisive results.

155

We came heartbreakingly close to pulling off the recall of Governor Engler. Six hundred fifty thousand signatures were required in ninety days. We got five hundred thousand signatures with no money and hardly any organization. That gives me hope. What we have is people. But we have to do a better job of mobilizing more people. We have to be much more disciplined about a strategic plan.

The magnet schools in Detroit are the models for the city. They have waiting lists of years for kids to get into those schools. Their dropout rates are minuscule. All of our public schools should be like those magnet schools. There has to be a way to say, "This is what we want for every public school in the city." I think we can do that if we involve the teachers and the parents more in developing those kinds of priorities.

Most people who live in Detroit shop in the suburbs because of the selection and the quality. What we need in the Hudson's Building downtown is a Meyer's Thrifty Acres that has auto supplies, lawnmowers, and salami. You would see tons of people shop downtown. If the future of the economy is in service, then we have to be about creating a climate where people can shop and work in stores and laundromats in their city. We've had two or three grocery stores close down since I've been living in the southwest side. Fort Street now is a ghost town. There needs to be a massive public works program that will give people hands-on employment in service-type jobs like carpentry. Most of Detroit's housing stock is prewar and so it's falling apart and people don't have the money to fix their houses. There aren't people around who are carpenters or plumbers as there was before.

The money and energy that's gone into things like revitalizing the theater district is a good example of the energy and capital that's there. Nobody I know can afford to go down and see a show at the Fox or the State. It's been so unbalanced. We're just asking for balance. We have to be ever-vigilant at the grassroots in asking for that kind of accountability. We have to fan the flames now.

Ed Hustoles

I worked for Vilican, Leman and Associates from 1957 until 1976. We did general, comprehensive planning and landscape architecture. Our practice was concentrated in Michigan, Illinois, and Ohio. We worked with sixty-four communities in our local seven-county region and did master plans for Southfield, Farmington, Farmington Hills, Bloomfield Hills, and a lot of other places.

We used [urban planner] Howard Bartholemew's analysis of existing cities across the country. The average city of 50,000 to 100,000 people had 15 percent of its land in industry. So that was our benchmark. The geographic center of our region is at Ten Mile Road and Middlebelt in Farmington Hills. The population center of the region is about at Eight and a Half Mile and Greenfield. Southfield is literally at the center, so it was the logical location for offices. It was all farmland in 1960.

Another study had been done by [financial and urban consultant] Constantine Doxiadis who projected a population of seven to eight million people in our region. Nobody really argued with the Doxiadis assumptions. It was still post–World War II boom times. Families were having three to four kids. The suburbs grew. St. Clair Shores went from 18,000 to 70,000 in the '50s. It was three bedrooms and bath and a half. The feeling then was that the city of Detroit wouldn't suffer. Physically, downtown Detroit couldn't absorb all the commercial, so it would be logical to have a satellite of offices in Southfield.

Detroit industry was the heavy, smokestack type. The idea of having an economic base in offices—as opposed to some big assembly plant—was very appealing, so Southfield developed that way. This was before the freeways were built. People say that the cities helped to empty themselves out by building the freeways. But we were talking of a population of 8,000,000 people. The thought at the time was that

Ed Hustoles is deputy executive director for planning at SEMCOG (Southeast Michigan Council of Governments).

156

the freeway was going to make it easier for people to go to downtown Detroit. Downtown would prosper and grow, and we'd still have development on the outside. They would reinforce each other's economic activity.

A lot of things happened that I wished hadn't happened. It turned out that we helped to empty out the city of Detroit. We didn't expect to do that. We didn't anticipate the almost complete elimination of public transportation. Everyone was going to have to drive a car. We laid out 120-foot rights of way for the mile roads in the middle of nowhere because they may end up being four-lane roads. We anticipated a lot more traffic. Many of those communities developed exactly as we thought they would, but not nearly as nice as we thought they would.

157

One of our problems now, because of sprawl and the cost of housing, is to get people to recognize that people can live together on sixty- or eighty-foot lots. You don't have to have two-acre lots. We often get the response, "Well, if I had wanted to see my neighbor, I'd have stayed in Allen Park." That was an exact quote by one of the township commissioners.

SEMCOG has just completed a study called the RDI [Regional Development Initiative]. It was our concern about sprawl. The Detroit area has not grown by one person since 1970. We have more households because there's fewer people per household. The city of Detroit has dropped from 1,500,000 in 1970 to just over 1,000,000 now. So we're having to build all these new utilities and roads in the suburbs. There's a taxpayers' revolt.

In the last ten years we have closed 140 schools in this region and we've built 210 new ones. Some were very old and needed to be closed, but some were built in the '50s on thirty-year bond issues and weren't even paid for by the '80s. St. Clair Shores is a classic example. It grew quickly and they built a lot of schools. Next door to St. Clair Shores the township is asking the people to build new two and three million dollar schools, and St. Clair Shores closed six of the schools they built in the '50s.

According to the Michigan Department of Transportation, to serve that spread-out population, six-lane roads like the Lodge Freeway would have to go to ten lanes. The Chrysler Freeway, which is eight lanes, would have to go to sixteen lanes. The 1990 census said that the average automobile trip increased 27 percent between 1980 and 1990. San Francisco concluded that all their freeways would have to be twenty-four lanes wide. Florida came out with the estimate that they'll need forty-four additional lanes of freeways between Miami and Orlando.

If communities like Detroit, Highland Park, or Hamtramck lose their tax base and still want to maintain services, the only way is by raising taxes, and *that* drives people out. They can cut services, but *that* drives people out. Highland Park is soon going to lose part of its tax base when Chrysler moves 7,000 people out into Auburn Hills. Highland Park can't roll up one-third of its sidewalks, sewers, and utilities because it's losing one-third of its jobs. It's still got to maintain all of that. Meanwhile, up the road in Auburn Hills they're putting in $35,000,000 worth of new sewers and new utilities to service the *same* jobs.

Another of our recommendations was that we need an areawide tax for public transit. We're maybe the *only* major metropolitan area that does not have a dedicated source of revenue on an area-wide basis for public transit. We've *gotta* do something about public transit. Historically, it's been *heresy* in this region to say that we've got to get people out of their automobiles and into public transportation.

We also talked about the social issues. SEMCOG has been vehemently criticized, to the point where many of our 140 member communities are threatening to quit. We had headlines: "SEMCOG says racism is the cause of sprawl." The study really said that racism was the dominant *social* issue among *other* issues of economy, etc. That really pricked some people. *Nobody* wants to admit they're racists. The very fact that people were so sensitive to it illustrates that perhaps there's a lot of truth in it. SEMCOG has the city of Detroit, the suburbs, and the rural areas as members. The best sign of doing your job is when everybody's a little mad at you.

There's a group of churches that's been lending their facilities to the homeless as temporary shelters. When homeless advocates wanted to use the basement of a suburban church for some of the homeless to sleep in, the township used the zoning ordinance against it. The township supervisor said, "Homelessness is not our problem; homelessness is the problem of Detroit."

We did a study at SEMCOG that indicated that in the last ten years three-quarters of all new jobs in this region were in areas where there was no public transit. And yet 28 percent of the households in the city of Detroit have no cars. The chronically jobless who need the jobs the *most*, can't get to the jobs. It's another catch-22. We talked to the manager of a major shopping center in Oakland County about setting up a bus line between Detroit and the center. Every other store in that shopping center had a "Help Wanted" sign in the window. His reply was, "No, we don't want those people because they'll arrive by bus and they'll leave by car." He meant that the whole central city Black population are thieves.

Ron Williams

I was born in Royal Oak, Michigan, and graduated from Royal Oak–
Dondero High School. With the exception of the period of 1969 to
1979, I spent my entire life in the Detroit area. My formative time
politically was when I went to college at Central Michigan University
in Mt. Pleasant from '69 to '74. I was swept up by the antiwar movement of the time and radicalized in that process. I've continued political work in one way or another, mostly through communications.
Music and politics are my passions and journalism is a way to enjoy
and share them.

I'm a veteran of the underground newspaper wars. I published a
paper from 1970 to 1974 in Mt. Pleasant with an ever-changing collective of people. Everyone got an equal vote. No one ever received a
penny of salary. All of us did all the things necessary to put a newspaper out: wrote the stories, laid the paper out on the kitchen table,
sold ads, took photographs, drove the paper to the printer, and distributed it. It was part of a political movement of the time that was
creating a network of counterculture institutions. In Mt. Pleasant that
included the food co-op, the free concert committee, and all sorts of
other things. It was clearly tied in to saying, "We're opting out of a
very sick society, and we're going to create the seeds of a new society."
The glue that kept this together was the music as much as the political movement.

Then you saw a diversion: certain cultural folks headed down one
road and political folks headed down another road. I think that hurt
the movement that we felt we *were* part of. Alternative papers were
tapping into the explosion of youth culture, fueled by alternative living which included the use of certain drugs—LSD, marijuana, things
like that—that we called "life-affirming" drugs, rather than heroine
and speed and downers that we believed killed people.

So, there was a political movement and a cultural movement that
were seminal at the time. It was an American period of renaissance.
Those newspapers were the expression of all that enthusiasm and
naiveté in tying into many of the developing political movements that
have now gone into a thousand different directions, from the farmworkers to the Panthers to women's liberation to the environment,
and certainly anchored by an antiwar movement.

Then Laura Markham and I started the *Metro Times*. Our great
interest was to utilize journalism as an agent for social change. This

Ron Williams is editor and publisher of the Metro Times, *Detroit's popular alternative
newspaper.*

also was an interest of Toni Swanger, Herb Boyd, and a lot of other talented people who participated in founding the paper. We began publishing at the dawn of the Reagan era in a very conservative, repressive atmosphere. No city was hurt harder than Detroit in the early '80s recession/depression. We struggled along, we missed payrolls, we had staff turnover, we had a lot of turbulence, and we made just about every mistake in the book.

Laura and I believed that what was needed by the left in America, going into a Reagan-Bush era, was outreach. Though we had a compelling story to tell, the left was not being successful in telling that story. We attempted to ground the *Metro Times* firmly in popular culture. At the same time it was important to integrate into that package an alternative political viewpoint of what this city could be and what this country could be.

In publishing and journalism the issue is effective communication. It really doesn't matter how good your story is or how strong your newspaper is if people aren't going to read it. The exciting dimension that the alternative press brings is that we are engaged in outreach. We are taking many new ideas and reaching people who don't think of themselves as being political.

I don't confuse organizing with journalism. Those are two very distinct things. There have to be the people who get out there and do the hard work and raise the issues. The *Metro Times* and papers like it are open to exposing the issues being raised by progressive people in the community and broadcasting them to probably the most likely people to be open to that issue. Here's a classic example that we've done a thousand times. A local group will bring in a speaker. The group may have fifty or a hundred people show up to hear that speaker. We'll send a writer who will interview the person and somehow take the essence of what is being said and put that into the *Metro Times*. Sometimes we do it prior to the event to build attendance, sometimes after the fact. Instead of that group reaching 100 people they've reached potentially 250,000 people.

The alternative papers speak to the "baby boom," that "pig going through the python," according to the demographers, which is working its way through society. They will continue to dictate the trends, fads, and marketing interests of America. This is the largest group of consumers that America has ever seen. As they mature into their thirties and forties now, they are able to make purchases way beyond what they were able to do ten years ago. They have grown up reading the alternative newspapers around the country. The alternative newspapers have an unusual relationship with them that goes beyond the relationship of a reader and a local daily paper. It's sort of like, "It's *our* paper, the voice of *our* generation."

Probably one of the major impediments for Detroit ever revitalizing itself is that the people who are entrenched are operating on antiquated assumptions. They are making decisions and operating on how things *used* to work, and things don't work that way any more. Time is overtaking Detroit. By the way, time is overtaking America. For Detroit to have the kind of future many of us want it to, it will have to figure out what role it is going to play in the global marketplace. It is a *global* problem that Detroit has. It's only a national problem in part. We're talking about an internationalization of culture, of technology, of economy. Detroit has got to find a vision that is consistent with that within which its residents can flourish.

But also there's a certain alternative vision shared by an awful lot of people in southeastern Michigan of where this city can head, where this nation should head. What our paper does is take all these people who sometimes can't sit in one room and talk to each other, and mix them into the pages of the paper. We take these disparate tendencies, concerns, organizations, individuals, and issues into one central place. Then we're able to reflect all those things back out as some kind of whole thing; as one kind of unified vision. That's how you provide leadership as a journalist. You're taking all the different tendencies and creating a way for them to be packaged.

My intuitive sense is that the city is on the threshold of major change because we have been disintegrating as an urban community for so long now. So much of what Detroit has to deal with relates to what goes on at the national level. I don't believe there's another city in America where the stakes are higher on this upcoming presidential election. On the other hand, the answer isn't in Washington, D.C., it's in the neighborhoods of the city and it's within the people. But we have diverted resources away from investing in the *people* of the city. In the last ten to fifteen years, the largest sums have gone to General Motors and Chrysler.

It's OK to have state-of-the-art factories, but in a time of scarcity, what you have is a mayor and administration who's operating on a paradigm that was somewhat functional in the 1940s, 1950s, and even in the 1960s. It is absolutely inappropriate to follow that paradigm in redeveloping the city and addressing the needs and the future of the city. The year 2000 is around the corner. Where are the jobs going to come from? Not from multinational corporations. Small business creates jobs in America and is a way to get minority entrepreneurs. Some of our most talented entrepreneurs in Detroit are involved in the crack trade or other elements of the underground economy.

There's a pent-up desire on the part of many, many people who are readers of the *Metro Times* and residents of the suburbs—many of them former residents of the city—to cross the bridges back to Detroit if they are built. While respecting the distinct differences of each community, our paper does not accept the myth that there's the city of Detroit and a hundred other cities in the metropolitan area. We call this the "metropolitan community." One of the greatest barriers that we must overcome as a community is to understand that everything is connected. We have an incredible fight going on right now in transportation. We've always had two transportation systems: D-DOT [Detroit Department of Transportation] and SMART [Suburban Mobility Authority for Regional Transportation]. The folks in the suburbs would rather close down SMART, and have no regional transportation system in the suburbs, than merge with D-DOT and create one transportation system. There's an element of racism and an element of fear operating here that is unbelievable. We have an apartheid system in Detroit.

Part 5   *The Trauma of the Politics of Race and Class*

Mayor Young says that racism is behind many Detroit-suburban issues.

He's absolutely right. He may not be cool in the way he says it and he antagonizes a lot of people, but it's the literal truth.

In some suburban areas you don't run against your opponent, you run against Mayor Young. I teach a class at the University of Michigan–Dearborn where a good part of the students are suburbanites. They don't think they're racist. They think *Coleman's* racist. They may say that some white politician is a corrupt son-of-a-bitch, but Coleman Young, wow, he's the devil incarnate.

Part of the problem is the idea that *any* mayor in Detroit could fundamentally change things. How could a mayor prevent all the Chrysler plants in the city going down, the economy from going down, the auto industry going down?

Marty Glaberman, professor emeritus, Wayne State University

NOTHING IN DETROIT'S RECENT HISTORY excited and united its citizens more than the acquisition of Black power. When Coleman Young won the mayoral race in 1973 it was viewed by the Black majority and their white supporters as a victory of major proportions. But the victory had its costs. Existing racial antagonisms were exacerbated, more whites left the city, capital continued to vacate. Politics in Detroit is nothing if not racial, nothing if not about who has the power.

Prior to the Young administration, the city was in the hands of white power brokers who possessed racist tendencies, whether or not they are aware of them. As some of the testimonies that follow will show, Detroit in the 1950s was not a mecca for African-American freedom and dignity. As some said, it was the promised land of economic opportunity in the postwar boom days. Compared to what? Compared to sharecropping. But it was not the land of *equal* opportunity, a postwar trademark of liberalism. "Equal opportunity" is often hollow in multiracial situations when only one group controls the means of production and access to jobs.

Then when capital abandons an area, leaving behind many underemployed workers with few prospects for improving their lives, people begin to blame each other for their plight. Today, there is bitter disagreement in Detroit over who's to blame for the city's woes. This is a fairly pointless exercise, in light of the great need for political cooperation and creative problem solving. The insidious use of race as a whipping boy detracts from building common political agendas within the city or between the city and the suburbs. To greatly compound the problem, within a racial group there is the American-as-apple-pie division by economic class. All this can lead to hostility and political stagnation. Detroit is a model of this process, a "mirror of America."

Many major players on Detroit City Council, in the Young administration, and in Wayne County government are deeply concerned about their city. So are players who may not have been on the inside political track, but who agitated and organized on the outside for change. These perspectives are represented in the testimonies that follow. There are both optimism and pessimism. Opinion is divided on policies of the city administration and on Mayor Young. There are assorted proposals for change. But there is near unity on the prospects of a new Detroit emerging from considerable political struggle.

George Crockett

In 1944, I was with Roosevelt's Fair Employment Practices Commission in Washington, and the agency sent me to Detroit to look into employment discrimination against Blacks in the Detroit street railway system. Subsequently, I became consultant to the UAW on race relations. Blacks were just beginning to feel their political and economic significance, but there was intense discrimination against them.

It would be difficult to find any other city where you had a greater impetus of organizing of labor, particularly among Blacks. There was a large influx of Blacks coming into the CIO. At the same time, some so-called Black leaders in Detroit were literally bought over·by Ford Motor Company to oppose Blacks joining unions. Outstanding among the Black leaders who were encouraging Blacks to join unions was Reverend Charles Hill, pastor of Hartford Avenue Baptist Church, the church that I subsequently joined and became a trustee.

It was in the framework of the trade union movement that Detroit's Black leadership got its start in politics. They learned their political ropes in being elected or influencing the election of trade union leaders, and from that they went out to organize the community. They worked with groups like the NAACP. Those were the activists that were tapped in later years when Blacks became politically prominent in Detroit.

During the war, there had been a no-strike pledge with General Motors, but right after the war, Walter Reuther, who was head of the GM department in UAW, headed up a strike against GM I discussed with Walter making fair employment practices one of the goals of that strike because we were having more trouble with discrimination in GM plants than in any other plants. We had a no-discrimination clause in the Chrysler and Ford contracts. Walter said, "I thoroughly agree with you. This strike will not end until we get a no-discrimination clause in the contract."

I traveled throughout the country preaching about the issues in the strike and that we had to hold fast. The day before the strike was called off, Walter had one of his lieutenants call me to tell me that he was sorry but the strike had gone on long enough. I said the equivalent of bullshit. We didn't have a no-discrimination clause. I never forgave him for that.

Then Walter ran for president of the UAW. In the course of cam-

George Crockett recently retired after ten years as a member of the U.S. House of Representatives from Detroit.

paigning he or his henchmen called a meeting of just the Black delegates. I heard about it and went to the meeting. Walter got up and made his spiel about race relations and improving conditions in the plants and the locals. Then when he sat down, I asked for the floor and told the story of the GM contract and our failure to get a no-discrimination clause, and compared that with the Ford and Chrysler contracts. Well, Walter never forgave me for saying that to that group of delegates right to his face.

After Walter was elected, he sent me a "Dear George" telegram which said that he felt it would be better if he became director of fair practices in UAW with the assistance of Bill Oliver. That wasn't the end of my tenure with UAW because immediately I was appointed administrative assistant to the international secretary-treasurer. My chief responsibility was to do exactly what I'd been doing before: watchdog on discrimination in UAW locals and plants.

When I came to Detroit, the best way you could describe me was apolitical. I wasn't interested in the left or the right. I was very conscious of the so-called Black issues since I had organized a branch of the NAACP in West Virginia where I had my first law office. I suppose the way I got interested in politics in the broad sense of the term was my contact with Maurice Sugar who was general counsel of the UAW and one of the leading labor lawyers in the country.

The first time I talked with Sugar it had to do with whether the bowling alleys in Detroit were going to permit mixed teams. All UAW teams were mandated to be integrated teams. Sugar and I decided that the International had to take that on as an issue and let the American Bowling Congress know that the union was going to advocate a boycott of all their places and, if necessary, set up our own bowling alleys.

UAW became interested in the portal-to-portal pay issue, and Maurice Sugar as general counsel was the one heading that up. I had been with the Wage and Hour Division of the Department of Labor in Washington before I came, and I was considered the department's expert on portal-to-portal issues. So Sugar asked me to take a leave of absence from UAW and come with him to work on these legal issues. Technically, I'm still on leave from UAW.

Sugar remained on as UAW general counsel during the first year of Walter's presidency, but when Walter got control of the international executive board, he bought up Sugar's contract. He went to New York, and the rest of us who'd been associated with him stayed on in Detroit.

Sugar called me one night and asked if I would come to New York and join the defense team in the Smith Act trial against the leadership of the American Communist Party, the charge being that they had conspired to bring into existence an organization that would teach and advocate the violent overthrow of the government. I knew that if I went to New York I was going to be labeled. McCarthyism was just beginning. I also knew that what really was involved was the First Amendment. We have a canon of legal ethics that says you do not refuse any man's cause because of considerations personal to yourself. Well, I debated it a long time. I had practically no practice in Detroit. I had just left UAW's payroll. I had a wife and three children. Anyway, I took the job and went to New York.

We had a trial that lasted the better part of a year. It was replete with arguments between the defense lawyers and the judge, the late Harold Medina. At the end of the trial, Judge Medina accused all of the lawyers of engaging in a conspiracy to bring the administration of justice into disrepute. He sentenced all of us to prison for contempt of court. Because my client once stood and I couldn't make him sit down, Judge Medina also decided that I was guilty of contempt of court, and on that charge he sentenced me to four months in prison. The case was appealed to the U.S. Supreme Court eventually. Though Frankfurter, Black, and Douglas dissented, all of us went to prison, and I did my four months.

When you come out of prison, people don't line up to have you represent them. For the most part, the cases that came to me were people who were being persecuted for their political beliefs. They were people who had been naturalized, whom the government contended were members of the Communist Party and should have their citizenship taken away. I represented Billy Allen, who was the editor of the *Daily Worker* in Detroit. That's one of the few cases that I won. I took another case, a woman named Smith, to the Supreme Court and argued it twice, but eventually we lost. In those days, you just didn't win those First Amendment cases.

Then we had the whole business of the House Un-American Activities Committee coming into Detroit, subpoenaing Coleman Young and the more vocal trade union leaders. My office represented most of them. I represented Coleman Young, Reverend Hill, Stanley Novak.

I don't think most Blacks in Detroit perceived me as a leader. After all, I was a guy who just came out of prison and was labeled as communist-oriented. But you fight your way back step by step. Finally, I was elected president of the Cotillion Club in Detroit, the place for aspiring young Blacks in business and the professions. At just about the same time, Jerry Cavanaugh decided he wanted to run for mayor, and it was important to him to have the support of the Cotillion Club.

169

Jerry met at my home with the leadership of the club, and we got his commitments to appoint an acceptable police commissioner and to upgrade Blacks in the police department. There was one Black sergeant, the highest Black officer in the police department.

I appointed my law partner, Bob Millender, as chairman of the Cotillion Club political action committee. That was Bob's beginning in politics. He went from that to become the Black kingmaker in Detroit. He handled John Conyers' campaign for mayor, Coleman's campaign for mayor, and my campaign for Recorders Court [Detroit's criminal court]. In 1960, John Kennedy was committed to passing a civil rights act. He called a meeting of civil rights lawyers from all over the country to meet with him in Washington. Charlie Diggs, who was in Congress at that time, suggested my name and John Conyers' name. So the two of us met at the White House with President Kennedy and Attorney General Robert Kennedy and Vice President Johnson. When I got back to Detroit, I found that people no longer crossed to the other side of the street when they saw me walking on Woodward Avenue.

Meanwhile, something else was happening to me individually. I became fed up with the practice of law. Now I had a good law firm. It was, I think, the first interracial law firm in the country with actual partnerships. I was one of the senior partners. Our firm was committed to handling civil rights cases. But you didn't make any money handling civil rights cases. So we developed a specialty in personal injury law, and that's where we made our money. Well, personal injury law is basically a question of who's going to gyp who. I got tired of that, and that's when I decided to run for public office.

In 1966, I got elected to Recorders Court. I look back at my FBI file now and see the exchange of telegrams between J. Edgar Hoover in Washington and the Detroit office about what should be done to make sure George Crockett isn't elected to Recorders Court. I have all that documented.

All hell breaks loose after that. First, there were the riots in 1967, and the arresting of almost all Blacks. They didn't have any place to incarcerate them all, so they kept them in city of Detroit buses lined up around Recorders Court. They'd call bus number one, and that bus is assigned to Judge Crockett's court. The police just marshaled all of them in, all of them charged with some misdemeanor.

I came into the limelight because I refused to set high bail to keep these people locked up. I let them go on their personal promise to come back when I got ready for them. The other judges were fixing bail at $10,000. To show you how brash I was, I sent a letter to each of the judges telling them what the Eighth Amendment of the

Constitution required and what the Michigan Constitution required on reasonable bail. I was mad as hell.

I think the result of that experience was to make Blacks in Detroit conscious of what could be accomplished if they got their own people in a position to use the power of the state. They finally had a judge who was not reluctant to say, "The law says they cannot hold you." One reaction to this was, Why don't we get more like that? Well, how do you get more like that? By registering and voting. As a result of the riot, you had this beginning of political consciousness on the part of Black Detroiters.

Then there was agitation for Blacks to run for mayor. Richard Austin became a candidate. Then Martin Luther King was assassinated in 1968. Then in '69, with the New Bethel Baptist Church situation [confrontation between Detroit police and members of Republic of New Africa], Blacks came of age politically and they really felt their strength. Either fortunately or unfortunately, much of that centered around the one Black judge, Judge Crockett.

I served on Recorders Court for twelve years and retired at the end of 1978. Then I became acting corporation counsel in Coleman Young's second term of office.

Coleman had made an outstanding record as mayor of Detroit. But he and a lot of Blacks resented the fact that many whites who had moved out made their living in Detroit but took their earnings to the suburbs. A lot of the large corporations didn't want to invest capital in Detroit. They built in places like Southfield and Warren rather than in Detroit and carried jobs to those areas. Coleman wanted a subway to connect Detroit with the suburbs. The suburban areas were opposed, saying they didn't want to facilitate criminals coming into their communities.

Coleman's policy was to bring about an integrated administration. Where he had a white person as head of a department, he tried to have a Black person as the deputy. If a Black person was head, he tried to have a white person as the deputy. In many instances, the white person felt that the Black person had easier access to the mayor. That's one aspect of Coleman's administration that I think could have been improved.

I don't think Coleman surrounded himself with the best brains available in Detroit. He was anxious to have Black representation, but I don't think he got the best Blacks that were available. He should have scoured the country. I think there was a bit of the buddy-buddy situation.

You had on a small scale in Detroit what the African nations had. Countries like Great Britain and Belgium moved out without having trained the natives to take over the government. In Detroit people who had absolutely no prior experience in government were appointed heads of major departments.

But now notice the difference between Detroit and Atlanta. When Mayor Andrew Young took over in Atlanta, he surrounded himself with the best brains he could find. I think in large measure they were whites too. He want abroad to influence companies to locate in Atlanta. The relationship between the races is excellent, though it flares up every once in a while. He had a good motto: "Atlanta is a city that's too busy to hate." I was never aware of any concerted effort in Detroit to go out and bring in capital. You had Henry Ford heading up an advisory group on developing Detroit as a port city, but it never got to first base.

172

How should the people of Detroit organize for the future?

Following the riots of '67, some of the top leadership in Detroit industry and community life, Black and white, formed New Detroit. Its primary concern was to sort of quiet things down and it didn't have too much grassroots confidence. Some of its programs were naive. But I think all in all it did a pretty good job. I think you need something like that in Detroit today. You've got to bring together a cross section of the Detroit community—top leadership in business, community organization leadership, grassroots leadership, labor leadership, the different ethnic groups—to sit down and discuss the plight of the city and what needs to be done. There's got to be a continuing organization. It's got to consider both the political and economic situations.

What should the role of the federal government be?

Right now the tendency of the federal government is not to aid cities and metropolitan areas. The feeling is, let them fend for themselves. A few years ago, we used to have a fund that we would divide between the cities and states based on the size of the population. Most of that went out during the Reagan and Bush administrations. Instead, the government has been taking a larger share of the tax bite and leaving less for the local communities. If you're looking to the federal government to help bail out communities like Detroit that are on the verge of bankruptcy, forget it. The metropolitan areas are going to have to fend for themselves. It's awfully important that we bring together people to sit down—I suppose something like the old town meetings—and let them work out their own salvation.

I'm in a turmoil myself with respect to most of these issues. You serve in Congress for ten years, you're right there at the base of power, you see what *can* be done if only there were a will to do it, you know that we have the resources with which to do it. But you ask yourself, why don't we do it? Why is it we can give money to everything else except to solve the problems we have here at home? And, of course, you know the answers too. You know that there are certain interests and that those interests control what happens in Congress and throughout the federal government, for that matter throughout state and local governments. And not until you get some administration that's willing to go to the mat with that kind of interest will you get any changes made.

I'm not opposed to foreign aid. I think there's an obligation to aid our brothers and sisters in other countries who are less well off than we are. But it's the old saying, "Charity begins at home." My gosh, the money we claim we're giving to foreign aid just goes around in a circle and comes right back to the monied interests in this country. And the government is not concerned with taxing them in order to get that money back to use for housing, education, and health. You've got to get people in government who are responsive to the needs of ordinary Americans.

173

Maryann Mahaffey

The analysis of Detroit is pretty simple. The National League of Cities has told us that three out of four cities are in trouble. Increasingly, the cities are the repositories for the seniors and the poor. Outsiders are trying to distance themselves from the cities. [Mayor] Dinkins is having the same trouble in New York as we're having in Detroit. There *are* poor people in the counties in Michigan, but everybody wants to blame Detroit and everybody wants to blame New York City. It's a national problem.

I think that the Detroit corporate sector—and it's not different elsewhere—is probably struggling with the development of the international market. That becomes a good excuse to get out from doing certain things here. General Motors wants backslaps because they're moving a plant out of Lake Orien back into Detroit, but they closed so many plants already.

The corporate sector is trying to figure a way out of the fact that they don't like the Japanese system of government investing in research and development and delaying an immediate high-profit re-

Maryann Mahaffey is the president of the Detroit City Council and a professor of social work at the Wayne State University.

turn for a longer-range return down the road. They have this feeling that government shouldn't be involved: you know, the pure market. It's *not* a pure market for the corporate sector; it's far from it. We're constantly giving them abatements. Now that's welfare for the rich.

They love to deal with a dictator who gives *his* word and everything gets done. The problem they're finding now in Detroit is that the Mayor is the dictator but he ain't living up to the promise. In the beginning, they went to him and he took care of it. He said, "I'll see that you get this money." He had enough votes on City Council to get it.

The people are increasingly angry as they see their homes destroyed by absentee landlords. The mayor consistently vetoes putting in more inspectors for housing, even though at the end of the year they earn their own pay and benefits and a little extra. That means there's nobody to go out there and make sure that these absentee landlords are keeping the houses up. Houses are deteriorating that never should have.

Coleman has never cared about social services, recreation, people services. He controls the police department, which is in violation of an ordinance on how the secret service should be handled. But it's *his*. Departments can't come before the City Council and tell us what they know. *He'll* decide when they come and what we should know. As a result we learn through *press* conferences.

Coleman is desperate. He operates from crisis to crisis. He didn't want to do any real cutting when he brought us the budget because then we would be able to review it. He does his cutting afterward and then sends it to us piecemeal, which is in violation of the Michigan Uniform Budget and Accounting Act. So we have to take him to court. It's very clear to the business community that you're on the list of cronies or you're not. Corporations used to hire someone out of city government with the idea that they'd have an "in" to the administration. But even *that* isn't working any more. The little businessman is also getting upset.

Because Coleman concentrates on getting the *big* employers, the small industries feel left out, like the pattern makers around the airport. Nobody gives a damn about it. Coleman goes after Poletown with 3,000 jobs and that's back into the mentality of manufacturing as it was in 1950, still producing to make up the war deficit. We've known from our own studies that we get more compliance with hiring people and retaining people and expanding employment from the small and medium-size than we do from the GMs and the Chryslers of the world.

Coleman *is* our first Black mayor and nobody wants him to go out

174

under a cloud. He *is* what we needed and he *did* a good job his first term, and not too bad the second. Then it began to deteriorate with the power move. The mayor is relying on others to tell him what to do and how to do it. Nobody is pulling people together to ask, "What needs are you meeting, what should be done, how do we pull together to do it?" It's top down instead of bottom up.

Color notwithstanding?

That's right! It has *nothing* to do with color. It has to do with power: the conception of where the power comes from, how it's exercised, and how you hang on to it. They *think* you don't hold on to it by sharing it.

As we look at Detroit and the United States, we have to have an historical perspective. The U.S. is in the second decade of the Reagan era, which really began when Jimmy Carter laid the psychological base for "government's too big and shouldn't be doing services." So we have these incredible cutbacks because Reagan was advised that government should basically do foreign affairs and military. Underlying that, of course, was the classic "anybody can be a millionaire," and you'll have more chance to be a millionaire if you are free of regulation. You have an increase of greed and selfishness fitting in with economic theories which blame the victim: it's *your* fault you're poor.

There's a big fight going on in that outer ring of suburbs like Canton Township and Auburn Hills where they want a growth policy. They don't like the Southeast Michigan Council of Governments suggesting that, instead of permitting further growth, we should start filling in where we already have development, existing sewer systems, etc. Children who grow up in Auburn Hills, etc. may not be able to afford to live there when they reach maturity because of the prices.

Then you have the race problem. I learned today that there's been a 100 percent increase in open manifestations of racism. Ku Kluxers and White Aryans are recruiting in the suburban malls and going into the high schools. You have a president who campaigned on the basis of Willie Horton, who fought the civil rights bill, and obviously wants to use quotas as his campaign theme in '92.

You have an increasing number of poor. Then you have someone like Governor Engler who's out of the Reagan mold whose attitude is that government shouldn't do services and government is wasteful. So he cuts general assistance and health care while increasing his own personal staff. I'm absolutely flabbergasted at people who pretend to be educated and come forth with myths.

A lot of state representatives and senators think the problem is only in Detroit. What percent of *their* constituency is suffering? Ultimately, in my experience, the only change comes not because some lovely person on top with a warm feeling for people *gives* you something, but because people organize and demand it.

In terms of the future of Detroit, I think we're reaching a point where there are going to be some moves away from some of these extreme positions. The only way you counter that is to do the constant education and organizing at the grassroots level. Organized people are more likely to vote.

Engler is gonna have to shift a little bit. The question is, how far? It will depend on how much organization and knowledge there is so that people are prepared to insist on him going further than he wants to. The Recall Engler campaign was a watershed! It failed, but never before did we have so many people from so many walks of life from so many places in the state signing petitions.

I don't really see a new political movement. I think this country is too wedded to two parties. One of the things they're so damned scared of is socialism. Some of them see socialism in what we already have and they're pressuring Canada and other countries to reduce *their* benefits. Ultimately, *that's* the direction it has to go in. The best chance is by working at the grassroots level. Upset as the business people are at what goes on and eager as the Chamber of Commerce is to grab a ball stadium, or whatever, they *too* can't ignore a city that's deteriorating. They're caught in a vise between their economic interests and the charge of racism. They'd like to ignore the latter and deal with the former.

I think there will be a resurgence. Right now Detroit's property is the cheapest and we have a lot of the infrastructure that's not out there in the suburbs. Part of what holds us back from development is the racism and what's happening in the neighborhoods. I think Detroit will turn around. There's a guy in Lansing who points out that everything goes in cycles and if you're going to do economic development you also have to have an infrastructure. One of the selling points for Detroit might be, we've already got the sewers, the electric cable, streets and sidewalks. Here *is* an opportunity.

Whether or not the mayor runs next time, he's *not* going to get reelected. My plea to the press is to concentrate on the programs and digging out the facts; leave out the labeling and the personality stuff. Then it will be harder to say, "Oh, you're attacking him because he's Black." Now, he's using that line. I've already had Black people want me to run. I say, No, I'm not going to be a devisive force. You've got Black people out there with the capacity to do it. I'm not sure Dennis Archer has the heart or the commitment to organizing and involvement at the grass roots, but he's surely going to have the money. The corporate types will be delighted with him, and they're already back-ing him.

I'm sort of that left-wing, loose cannon. They cannot get over the fact that in the last City Council elections I came in with 12,000 more votes than the next guy. So they can't ignore me. An executives' asso-ciation is giving me an award next week, the first time they've ever given it to a woman. I'm not quite sure why they're selecting me. I guess I represent a counterforce.

I can be *radical*, like going out to the Jeffries public housing ac-tion yesterday. I was out in support of their civil disobedience. I'm *radical* when it comes to social programs. Fiscally, it makes more sense to have a Canadian health system than the one we have; it's less ex-pensive. Also, when you have a universal program it's harder to cut it out. They'd like to get rid of Social Security, but they can't because it's universal. Until we have a universal children's system, they'll keep whittling away.

What am I conservative on? Money! Fiscal matters. I don't like giveaways. We're doing remodeling now and I'm saying, no new furni-ture. I do most of my own driving because I'm capable of doing it. There *is* a security person and a backup person who are assigned to me if I need them. I try *not* to need them. The mayor has God knows how many. These people who complain that they have to pay a tax on a boat that's longer than 100 feet, shit, they've been getting away with murder for years with free service from the Coast Guard and the Army Corps of Engineers, and then they complain about poor people getting $183 a month to live on.

Bernard Parker

I was born and raised on Detroit's east side near City Airport. The community was working class. People there worked at local factories: Chrysler, Eaton, Cadillac. There wasn't a lock on my back door dur-ing my young life and I had no fear of going out at midnight and walking around the block. I went to East Catholic High School and later married a girl I went with since tenth grade. I went to a commu-nity college and then to the University of Michigan in the late '60s and majored in secondary education.

At the university I got very active in the Black Panther Party. I

Bernard Parker is a member of the Wayne County Board of Commissioners and founder of Operation Getdown, a multiservice agency on Detroit's east side.

hung out in the Center for Afro-American Studies, where I was continuously reading and discussing. I began to understand my African roots. I went to every event where someone like Rap Brown, Stokely Carmichael, or Huey Newton was talking. The Panthers had a free breakfast program and an after-school tutorial program at a local church. I got actively involved with those programs for about one year.

I believed the U.S. Constitution, that every man should be free to live his own destiny. I believed that people should not be judged by the color of their skin. My framework was not to stand back and let anybody walk over us. We were going to defend ourselves and attack, if necessary. We were going to do everything we could to show that the police were brutal; that the government was not in our best interests and needed to be overturned. I had a revolutionary concept.

My mother disagreed and said we must cooperate with people and try to understand that it's their ignorance that makes them violent. My mother was a typical Christian who was a great supporter of Martin Luther King. Her view was that we're all people, we're all Christians, and we all should love each other. I love my mother, but we had a real battle over this. She got involved in community activities in the neighborhood church, and tried to pull me into it.

In 1970 I came back to Detroit and began to get involved with the local church. By then, James Foreman had received reparations from various churches that would go to neighborhoods.

I began to see the teenagers acting out violent solutions to their problems. I found myself trying to justify to them why they shouldn't do it this way. Of course, *I* had been that way a few months back. I began to question the value of violence in trying to solve anything.

I got into sensitivity training sessions. I became more comfortable with the philosophy of direct service. In a study group again I read *The Autobiography of Malcolm X* and began to understand that he was never talking about a revolution. He was always talking about dignity for Black people. We should do for ourselves. We should all unite. I became a nationalist, one who believes that we're the only ones who can solve our problems. That does not suggest hatred for anybody else, just love for ourselves.

Then we started Operation Getdown. We identified a small area on the east side of Detroit for intense work. Its boundaries were Connor to Van Dyke to Harper to Gratiot. Within that area we began to deal with all the basic needs: housing, crime, jobs, education, food. We adopted the philosophy of Malcolm X, and it's still our philosophy: if you give people a thorough understanding of the problem that confronts them, people will create a program which will get action.

The community should direct which way we go. It was a real grass-roots effort.

Right now we're a United Way agency with about a $2,000,000 budget. We have emergency food programs, a program for pregnant teenagers, a health clinic, a day care program, an after-school youth program, an adult education program, a homeless warming center. We have a caravan that goes out every night to feed about 400 homeless on the streets all over the city. We have a staff of about seventy people. We're the largest community agency of that nature in Detroit.

We have monthly meetings with the community. People come in and direct us. They tell us what the problems are and what we should be doing. We have a fifteen-member board of directors that sets policy, and we have advisory committees over each of our programs that give day-to-day direction.

I was elected to the Wayne County Board of Commissioners in 1990. I represent a constituency on the east side right around Operation Getdown. I ran on my experience in Operation Getdown, and said that I wanted to take that experience down to government: self-determination and helping people to solve their own problems. My campaign was very grassroots.

In my first year in office I opened up the first community office of any Detroit commissioner. Half of my staff is out their in the neighborhood where we concentrate on constituent concerns. Anybody with a problem—cutoff of utilities, complaints about tax bills, and so forth—can come in and we try to solve that problem. In the tax season, volunteers do taxes free of charge. A lawyer comes in voluntarily four hours per week and helps people with legal matters. We register people to vote. Blocks clubs meet there on a regular basis.

Governments have financial problems because they're still trying to do government the way it was done thirty years ago. We have to look at that completely differently. Eighty-five percent of Wayne County's budget is spent on staff, mostly sitting in their offices pushing paper. We don't need that type of intense staff. Government has to get out of these downtown buildings and get into the community.

Privatization is a bad word to many people. We have to look at that another way. I'm not for privatization that contracts out to a private business to make profit. If all motivation is to make profit, then services eventually will deteriorate. If privatization is to ask a community to collect their own garbage, or to do other services, and communities are paid to do that or their taxes are reduced, then I think that's the way to go.

People recognize that the quality and quantity of services have gone down tremendously. They're concerned about basic things like

179

safety, increases in utility costs, jobs, transportation. Community people recognize that government has not responded to their needs. That's why voting is so low and apathy is so high. When I talk about communities solving their problems, and giving them resources to do it, people get excited. I *know* there are communities—perhaps 100 blocks, or one square mile—that would be excited about being a "mini-city" and being responsible for some of their own services.

Maybe people's taxes would be reduced 30 percent, and that 30 percent goes into an authority in a particular area. They take that money and provide maybe garbage collection, maybe security patrol, maybe emergency home repair, maybe take a vacant lot and make a garden or playground, or paint a senior citizen's home. I *know* it would work. There will be development of pride and a sense of true democracy.

Security is really important in my neighborhood. They don't feel comfortable leaving their house. I know homes where no one ever leaves their house without someone staying home. That's their security system. It would be unrealistic to think of having police patrols to drive in that neighborhood every day, but it's not unrealistic to think of a citizen's patrol to do it.

What's your conception of the safety net?

Nonprofit agencies can provide the safety net. We need a different approach. Government's approach is an individual type of safety net: "You need some services; we'll provide them." The better approach would be from the nonprofits: "If you have a problem, let us see what caused that problem, and let us see if we can get to that cause." If people walk in and say they're unemployed and hungry, just to give them food stamps and a check doesn't solve their problem. Is there mental illness? Is there a character problem? Is there a transportation barrier? Is there spouse abuse or a family problem? Is it drugs?

We need to get people jobs and then be about trying to reeducate them. If I could push a button and blow the whole educational system up I would. It is completely unrealistic in today's economy. Yesterday I learned that out of 8,000 students who graduated from Detroit high schools last year only 500 passed the SAT at the national average. Of those 500, 90 percent were from Renaissance High School and Cass Tech. We're failing.

I liked what they did in China. When they began to reeducate their people, every student got two books. One book was left in school and one they took home, with the assignment that they teach their parents what they learned that day. We have to reeducate the people who we have failed to educate in the last twenty years or so. In Opera-

180

tion Getdown's recreation program the fifth and sixth graders come in and say, "My momma can't help with this; she doesn't know this." Parents aren't going to go back to school, so we need some system where the children will help do it.

Detroit is going to have some rough times, even after we get out of this recession. Then I think there's going to be a real commitment to change and a real desire to do things differently. I really think that Detroit is going to show the country that you *can* solve urban problems. I'll continue to speak out and try to educate people so that we can bring change. I'm committed to Detroit. I'm gonna be here the rest of my life and I'm going to do all I can to improve the quality of this city for my children.

181

Sheila Murphy Cockrel

I grew up in the Detroit Catholic Worker movement. My father opened up the first House of Hospitality soup kitchen in 1937. He was a conscientious objector in World War II and drove an ambulance with the American Friends Service Committee during the war. My parents had two Houses of Hospitality: St. Francis House, where the soupline was and where men lived, and St. Martha House, where families and single women lived with *my* family. So I grew up in a collective long before the 1960s approach to collective living.

I separated with my parents quite early on the question of pacifism. I did not grow up in a community where being pacifistic made it easy as a teenager. I was operating in a context where kids were organized into gangs—the Bagley Boys and the Bagley Girls; the Stilettos and the Stilettoetts. These were the baby versions of adult gangs and that was a part of the culture. I see civil disobedience as an important organizing tool, not a stance about life. As I grew older I began to see that my parents didn't fully understand that they had created a family with the inherent idea of class conflict. I began working in '66 for the WCO [West Central Organization], which was the first citywide attempt at community organization that was rooted in the concept of self-determination, using the Saul Alinsky model. My parents were active in the formation of WCO and were on the board of directors. It was at WCO that I first worked with Ken Cockrel. WCO's community-based organizing strategy was "You can take control and make politi-

Sheila Murphy Cockrel is an assistant superintendent with the Detroit Building Authority, City of Detroit, with offices located in the Cadillac Tower downtown; she is the widow of Ken Cockrel, the prominent Detroit lawyer-activist.

cal and social decisions that determine the direction of the neighborhood." WCO took on issues like land use policies, how landlords took care of rental property, police-community relations—that whole set of local, daily-life issues. There were lots of confrontational demonstrations like sitting in front of bulldozers to stop the University District No. 2 expansion. The Elijah McCoy housing development exists because of the standoffs on Hobart Street to stop urban renewal by Wayne State University.

At that point there was pressure and urgency for the creation and expression of Black Power. That was coupled with the fact that this city was a union town. When Alinsky's people were trying to make the deals to come into Detroit they never got the buyin from the unions. I think that in order to have been effective in Detroit in the late '60s, organizations like WCO would have had to take on organized labor, given the nature of racism in the unions. There was no way Alinsky, with a national agenda, was going to get organizers operating in a city where the unions were going to be a target. And the churches, which were the funding base for Alinsky-model organizations, also got real nervous. So we never got a full-fledged Alinsky organization in Detroit.

When it came to the workplace, however liberal people might be, it was bedrock racist.When there was one supervisory position open and there's two people contending—one Black, one white—and the Black has more experience, the white usually got the job. That *was* the experience in the plants in the city. And that's why the League of Revolutionary Black Workers was such a threat then.

The police in this city were unbelievable. It was a predominantly white police force. Police brutality was as common as abandoned houses in the city now. It had a racial character and was a political act of terror by the police establishment on a daily basis in the Black community. In '67 a seminal event that set a course for the city's history was the rebellion. At that point, race became a very critical issue in how people organized politically.

The Poor Peoples Campaign came to Detroit in 1968 and was *welcomed* by the mayor and permitted use of Cobo Hall. So we were at Cobo Hall getting people registered and moved in for the night, and the mounted bureau of the Detroit Police Department was present. For some reason that was never clarified, the horses were ordered into the crowd. This was an outrageous example of police brutality which had been stirring after the rebellion in 1967. The level of police violence in the city was unbelievable. I was outraged and I felt that I had to take a stand.

So I organized the Ad Hoc Action group to protest police brutality at police headquarters. The cops were outraged. I'm twenty-one years old and leading a group of older people and people my age who are protesting police brutality. It was good TV. That began a very intense two-or three-year struggle with the police department and the mayor. We had a two- or three-day sitin in the mayor's office, demanding that he do something about these cops.

In '69 there was the New Bethel incident [shooting of police] and I was very active in the stuff that came after that: the defense committee for George Crockett; the defense of Ken Cockrel when he was cited for contempt. In terms of fundamental self-respect in the Black community, vis-à-vis cops, that contempt case will be seen in history as having been absolutely seminal. Ken was defending two members of the Republic of New Africa who were accused of shooting a police officer. The judge wouldn't permit cross-examination at the preliminary exam, wouldn't entertain a motion for reduced bond, just bound them over. Ken stepped out of the court and announced to a 99.9 percent white media that this judge was a "racist-honky-dog-fool, a bandit, a pirate, a thief, and didn't know as much law as Judge Crockett had in his little finger." People were unable to believe that they had heard this in a court building, about a judge, let alone a young Black man against a middle-aged and respected jurist. Ken was cited for contempt.

There was a heavy-duty organizing effort around that. We had Harvard linguists coming in to provide interpretations of all the words and say that this was appropriate language. I believe it was a profound experience for the Black community in Detroit. We took over Kennedy Square and had people's court every day, with no permits. Ken would come out at the noon hour and talk about what had happened in court that morning.

Ad Hoc was around from '68 to '70ish. I was kind of conscious that this could be a personal trip. If you really want to deal with making social change, other kinds of organizations need to exist. So I began to work with other folks to build the MCLL [Motor City Labor League]. One of the things we wanted to do was break down the tensions and turf divisions that existed among the various white, left groups. There was the old left, the "fringe" left, and the indigenous Detroiters who were trying to make social change, while we had all these "crazies" loose in the city. Detroit was Petrograd, these idiots were in town for it to become Leningrad. They were a serious problem. They would come to Detroit prepared to relate to the Black Panthers like they were *the* important left political presence in the Black community. That was not the case here. It was the League of Revolutionary Black Workers. One thing that constantly happened was that white left groups or individuals, through well-intentioned but misguided actions, were constantly creating issues amongst the various Black organizations. On top of that, police *agent provocateurs* were loose in all of this.

I never perceived of myself as in the left. I thought of myself as an activist who wants social change. I thought of the left as playing games about criticism/self-criticism, and who's reading what, and doing stupid stuff like standing on a street in downtown Detroit and throwing a rock at a cop. Nobody who throws rocks at cops has a fundamental understanding of the nature of police power. Even if you do understand police power you don't throw rocks. If you're not a white, middle-class kid from out of town or some wealthy suburb somewhere, you're gonna get shot and killed. If you're throwing a rock and you're one of these young whites, you're taking advantage of your position in the culture.

One of the realities at the time was that as organizers our relationship to our white, working-class base was *not* parallel to what the League of Revolutionary Black Workers had to *its* base. Since that didn't exist with us, petty jealousies, turf battles, and raging ideological abstract debates about correctness came to the fore.

When I knew that MCLL had hit upon something real was when we ran Chuck Ravitz for judge of Recorders Court in August 1972, and he won. The minute he won, the MCLL began to break up. The people who I no longer harbor intense emotional anger toward, but who I genuinely thought were really in this stuff for personal growth, had to get out; they couldn't deal with it. In the late '60s and early '70s a lot of young people who came out of the Catholic religion didn't go into the seminaries or religious nun orders, but into left groups.

The process of splitting began in September. I know it was because of a combination of the Ravitz win and the presence of [police] agents in the group. This was a very strange experience to go through. You know, the Murphy group, the Joyce group [leaders of factions in MCLL]—oh my, what a colossal waste of energy. I don't know who in the leadership of MCLL were agents. That there were agents in that group, I will take to my death, believe me. At the time, I said to Ken, "We win, and now we're starting to split?" This was an effort to derail the Ravitz campaign and it was *clear* that anything significant happening in the white community from a left perspective is *not* going to be tolerated. The security measures we took on Chuck were enormous.

In '78 Ken ran for City Council. That permitted a regrouping of a socialist-oriented, community-based structure. DARE [Detroit Alliance for a Rational Economy] was organized around a number of local

184

issues like economic development, tax abatement, and downtown versus the neighborhoods. Ken perceived of himself as operating as part of a collective, though his voice *did* carry more weight than the others. Our position in DARE was that we had to function as a part of some collective apparatus in order to be effective.

Coleman Young was elected in '73 primarily on the issue of STRESS [Stop the Robberies, Enjoy Safe Streets]. Most whites voted for John Nichols. There was a racial character and a significant police dimension to that election. The liberal white vote for Coleman Young was between 12 percent and 16 percent. Young's pledge for a fifty-fifty [racial ratio] administration in 1973 did not reflect the way whites in the city responded to him in the election. A fifty-fifty administration wasn't required based on what whites did electorally.

185

It was crystal clear by then that one of the consequences of Coleman Young's election had been to create a possibility for genuinely progressive people to have good jobs. A whole layer of political leadership was in the administration and not leading assaults from the outside.

Not just in the city but also in the suburbs, people are basically comfortable with the idea of Coleman Young being the problem with the city of Detroit: "Detroit would be OK but for the Blacks taking over." That's a comfortable analysis for people to make about the last thirty-five to forty years' worth of economic history in this city. You don't have to take responsibility for leaving the city. You don't have to look at the role of corporations and what it meant for them to leave. You don't have to look at what the real nature of multigenerational poverty has been in the Black community.

I work for the mayor, so clearly I'm not going to be here running a negative thing on him. However, after twenty years in office any political organization has issues about administration and organization. There are some of those and they're legitimate. But the political discussion about the mayor is shaped and framed by the media and accepted by people in the main as the way to talk about the Young administration. As long as that's the case it's a fundamentally racial discussion, and it's wrong.

People keep telling me, "Maybe we should do a book club." [study-discussion group]. What the hell do we say? Since Ken has died the Berlin Wall's come down, communism as we've known it has collapsed, multigenerational levels of communist leadership are embracing *this* [U.S.] economic system. What's the intellectual framework in which we operate? I don't know! Do I believe that capitalism's a viable economic system, a humane economic system? No! But that's sort of abstract. For me it gets real practical. What *is* the legitimate expectation that a city should have from its corporate members? What's right? As a political activist, what should I be able to demand of a corporation? I guess that I'm personally seeking a framework that I can function from politically to create in this country and city an economic structure—with the attendant political and social institutions that are necessary—that is more fair and equitable than what we have now.

I believe that Ken left a political legacy that belongs to whomever can claim it collectively. He stood for something. His death created a political void that I would like to help fill in some way. But I don't see what it is or where it is. That's what I look for. In the interim what I'm doing is finding issues that I think are really important to the daily life of people in this city and trying to work with them.

Morris Gleicher

I've lived in Detroit for seventy-two of my seventy-four years and watched the city through all of the various phases. My first major political involvement was over the Spanish loyalist cause in 1938 when I took the Oxford Pledge along with a gymnasium full of Wayne State University students vowing we would never go to war.

The 1950s was a period of very difficult times in terms of McCarthyism. All my friends were being called to appear before the committee. I was called, but never went. I said, in effect, screw you, come and get me. I was lucky because it was at a time when the committee was in disarray. But I had been harassed by the FBI, and a lot of my friends had suffered a much worse fate. They were fired, forced to move out of town, forced to give up their business, had broken homes, and so on. That made me much more of a radical.

My closest friend at the Michigan Employment Security Commission where I worked in the '50s was a Black who was head of the counseling department. He and I would pal together. We were both single. We'd go to the nightclubs and listen to the music, and I began to learn what was happening to the Black community in the city of Detroit. That was an eye opener. Here we were in the '50s, and people were still with outhouses and wooden shacks and unable to buy homes anywhere else in the city even if they could afford them. When

Morris Gleicher is head of M. G. Associates, a political consulting and public relations firm, and president of the Metro Times.

186

my friend traveled in the state, he would have to sleep in the car because no hotels would take him.

From 1960 on, I've been involved with more political movements and candidates in this area—I don't say this immodestly, just as a fact—than anybody in the state. I've been in many campaigns, for every office you can name. Through all of it, my values have never changed. I have also had feelings of tremendous social responsibility and involvement, and kind of a natural sympathy for the poor, the oppressed, the minorities. And I think it's grown stronger through the years despite the fact that successes have been relatively few.

I've never represented a candidate with whom I did not have some sort of ideological association. I would never take a candidate with whom I disagreed. I have never solicited a candidate. There was always the hope that the candidate would do something for the community, and do something for our society. That has been one of my biggest disappointments in the last thirty years. There are so few candidates who, once they reach office and are supposed to do the things for which they were elected, actually fight for them and really perform.

Coleman Young was one of the brightest guys I ever met, politically very committed, very effective. Charismatic is the word they always use, and it's true. He can move people. And he was always involved in the most social of causes. When I first met him in 1946, we were attending a convention in Chicago of a new veterans organization, the United Negro and Allied Veterans of America. It was a reaction against the American Legion and VFW, which had segregated posts. We've had a friendship, and association, through the years. When Young ran for the state senate and for mayor, we were there.

I had an extraordinary time with Young one day. It was at the beginning of his campaign for mayor. Each day one of us would spend the day with him. The day started with an eight o'clock meeting with the Chamber of Commerce in a downtown bank building. They didn't know him; they didn't like him. He was very Black. He was a radical. He sat down with them, casually having a cup of coffee and a sweet roll, listening to their introductions of the problems of the city of Detroit. Then they asked him to speak. In half an hour, he had them so enraptured, so impressed. To every question they asked, he gave responses that were so knowledgeable. He was a state senator. He said, well, Senate Bill 502 examines just that problem. Whether it was trade on the waterfront or the school system, he was brilliant.

Then, at nine o'clock, we had to race out to a Baptist church on Dexter and Davison. I sat in the back, the only white there among thirty to forty Black ministers. They had their meeting and they're ranting and raving and all that. Then very reluctantly, and not in a receptive kind of attitude, they called on him to speak. Coming from the earlier upper middle class, establishment meeting, where he was expounding very clearly, no cussing or anything, he gets up on the platform in that church and goes into a rap about the city of Detroit, about the police, about the crime, about the schools, about our children. He had them wrapped around his finger in about three minutes. He was extraordinary! Two totally different personalities adapting to the environment. And that's Coleman Young. Brilliant!

I had great hopes, as did all of my friends, for what he would do in this city. He would go to the people and educate them. He would generate activity. He would move them to demonstrate and raise the level of understanding, not only of the Black community but the whole city. Of course, this followed the riots of 1967, and he was certainly limited by conditions, and then by the undermining of the whole industrial structure. He had plenty of problems, and one can sympathize with those.

But as time went on, I didn't see support of the labor movement. I didn't see any effort to stimulate activity from the grass roots. What I saw was a growing favoritism toward the big developers in this city, toward fixing up the downtown as opposed to low-cost housing or federally subsidized housing. I saw no efforts to generate funds from Washington to help the poor. I tried to involve him in such urgent matters as hunger in Detroit, without success.

You've seen patterns like this in other elected officials?

Oh, yeah, it's almost universal. It happens so often you grow to expect it. There are some tremendous exceptions, like George Crockett. He's an example of somebody who never varied from his principles. Maybe the lowest common denominator of what happens is that the candidates get in office and want to stay there. They accommodate to the political situation. They fall into a pattern and are no longer willing to strike out to new paths. The bottom line is that the system overwhelms them, as it does all of us. It's the power of capital, the power of what is called the establishment, the power of incumbency, of the ability of those who have the money and have the power to control the whole political process.

I teach frequently. I go out on behalf of the American Civil Liberties Union and talk about the Constitution and the Bill of Rights and so on. We're talking to a generation of Reagan-bred students. Their knowledge of history is almost nonexistent. Their appreciation and understanding of America is nothing. Their prejudices are frightening. We have had twelve years now of this kind of right-wing ideology, which really denigrates education. And as far as its moral standards are concerned, it's a disgrace.

The '60s were different. It was sort of a miniature revolutionary period when people progressed a great deal in their social understanding. The problem was it wasn't buttressed with an economic understanding. So we had on the surface a tremendous social gain, but underneath, the core was rotten and it got worse.

I think we're headed toward a period of economic unsettlement. We're in a recession now, and I think the recessions are going to come quicker and deeper. Although I never subscribed to this before, I'm beginning to think *that* may be the only thing that really will shake people up and make them understand that they have been taken.

189

No one ever anticipated that so much of the wealth would be in so few hands. In the '30s it was different; the Depression hit everybody. There's a class distinction in this recession. You can go to the suburbs out there, Somerset Mall or wherever, and a lot of people are spending an awful lot of money, and they don't give a damn about the rest of society.

I'm certainly optimistic about what will eventually occur, because I think this underclass, these various elements of our society, are ready, or should shortly be ready, for expressing some kind of effective opposition to the national administration. Every city in the country is in trouble. Why? It's the federal budget that's got all our money and that pisses it away. They're telling the people that government is not responsible for social services or taking care of its citizens. What a turnaround since the Roosevelt days! And people are buying it. Well, they're not going to buy it for long.

How radical can ideas be in Detroit at this time?

Extremely! I think you would turn people on with a very radical program to turn this city back to the neighborhoods, reorganize our priorities so that the low-cost housing and public housing is supported, give support to our hospitals, and rid ourselves of the high infant-mortality rate. Obviously, the first problem is crime. Let's help the neighborhoods themselves mobilize the community against crack houses. There are a lot of radical positions you could take, and I think the people will be responsive.

I think the problems of Detroit can be solved in only a small way by the local elected representatives of the people of Detroit. We are pawns in a national game. We are victims of a system which clearly does not give any sort of priority to our inner cities. Until the attitude of the country is changed toward its national administrators, toward its budget allocations, toward its social priorities, Detroit is never going to come back. There will always be a Detroit, but it will continue to shrink as people with money move out. I think we're going to melt down to a semi-busy financial, legal center, with some residential activity along the riverfront and with fragmented communities that somehow survive, but not in a healthy way. We are a tremendously segregated city now. That's not going to change until the national system changes and there's an enormous commitment to sort of a welfare state. We're back to the beginning. We're back to 1932.

190 Charles Butler

I grew up in the delta region of Arkansas, the son of a cotton farmer. I attended college at a small Christian college in Little Rock with a major in chemistry and intended to go into medicine. I ended up going into the military service and came out convinced that I should go into the ministry. So I went to Union Seminary in New York in 1947 and then did some graduate work at Columbia University. Then I taught at Morehouse College in Atlanta for three years. I came to Detroit in 1954 and have been here ever since. I pastored two churches: one on the west side and the present one.

At the west-side church, I followed a pastor who had been somewhat progressive. There were about a couple hundred forward-thinking people in the congregation, which grew to 800 by the time I left. They accepted me and the social ideas I was wrestling with. Most people assumed that the plants would always be there, and there would always be a need for a vast labor pool. There was no great incentive to go beyond high school because the high school graduate could earn as much as the college graduate teaching school or other occupations available to Blacks at that time.

I remember talking with a family about their child, who had good academic credentials in high school, going to college. After I'd finished, the father took me to the door and said, "You see that car out there? It's bought and paid for. You see this two-family flat? It's bought and paid for. I did all this with six grades of learning. My son has twice what I've got, and he's got to make it on that." [*Laughs*]

Coming from the South where there were certain ideas of what was valuable and what was unimportant, and spending some time in Atlanta, as prejudiced as it was in many ways, it was still a mecca of

Charles Butler is the pastor of the New Calvary Baptist Church on Detroit's east side.

education for Blacks in the Atlanta University system there. I found myself feeling that there was more ignorance per square inch among the folk that I met in Detroit than any place that I had ever been in my life. There was such little motivation, I thought, to move in the direction of preparation that I thought we were going to need in the coming years.

What surprised me at first was the disillusionment with being up north, and what that means in terms of social liberation and freedom. I soon found the truth in the words of Malcolm X: everything south of the Canadian border is south, and that we're probably more up south than up north in terms of attitudes. In the South the saying was "Come close, but don't go high." In the North it was, "Go high, but don't come close." [*Laughs*] There was no problem ever in the South of Blacks and whites mingling in certain ways. In the North, reach what you want to reach, but there was very little cross fertilization, culturally and ethnically, to enrich and enhance each other.

Comparatively, however, there was very good income in Detroit. For many years Blacks were better off here than any other place in the country. It became a magnet that drew many Blacks. The plants were a gold mine.

One of the things that was inbred in us in the South is that land is extremely important—a home and some land. My parents used to say to me, "Get some education because that's the only thing anybody can't take from you; get you a piece of land because that's the only thing nobody can move you off." It was that kind of mentality that many Southerners had who formed the background for small-parcel acquisitions of housing in the city of Detroit.

As to the politics of the city, there evolved a degree of sophistication with the political process in Detroit, especially after the 1967 revolt. There was a growing sense of the strength of Blacks, especially fueled and fostered by the union movement and the fusion of Blacks with the union, and the kind of education in politics that was gained through union activities. Some of our strongest and best came from those union activities, and from the great desire on the part of many Blacks who voted once in four years in the South—and had to pay a poll tax to do that—to become a part of the political process and to exercise the franchise which was seen as a very valuable right. As that grew, the rest is very well known history: the acquisition of political power and the concomitant removal of economic power that is necessary to support a good political base.

That brings us to one of the bottom lines of the whole thing: the economic shortfall. We witness a city surrounded by thriving communities on all sides. You drive across the city limits of Detroit and it's

191

like going into another world: no vacant storefronts, the lawns are green, the houses are occupied, and all the things that reflect affluence and well-being. This drainage of the heart of a city seems impossible for it to have been accidental. It had to be a planned, deliberate effort against persons who would be bold enough to seek political liberation and the exercise of political power to the extent that Detroit has done it, especially through its top administration here. It appears to be a way of saying, "Look, we will teach you; we'll give you a real flogging; you slaves gonna have an uprising and control the slave quarters, so we'll teach you how well you'll be fed, and housed, and schooled, and what your health care will be like in the slave quarters."

So whites who left Detroit engaged in racist behavior?

I certainly saw it that way. I saw no other reason for them to leave. The businesses were *not* having a problem. They certainly were damaged by the [rebellious] activities of July '67, but, God, Berlin and Frankfurt and Naples and all the other places were bombed, but it depends on how determined one is to restructure and redo things. I think 1967 was the excuse used to justify the escape. Yes, we see it as an act of racism.

Of course, New Detroit grew out of the 1967 rebellion. What was most amazing about that was that the persons who started New Detroit were the same persons who most of us had learned to be the power brokers anyway. So what we ended up with was the same persons who exercised power, then came to the rescue, at least titularly, to fix the thing. The *fixes* came from the persons who we felt had caused the problems in the first place.

I sit on the board of directors of New Detroit. I was most surprised about two years ago when one of the directors, at the end of some expression of concern about funds for adequate policing and school and social services, stood and began to walk back and forth and to harangue that there was absolutely no shortage of money. He said that all the money that Detroit wants it can have. All that was necessary was to develop metropolitan government.

To most of us, that's the worst kind of blasphemy because the only power we have right now is a little political power. That would mean submerging again in a larger population. That's another way of saying, "OK, natives, if you behave and we walk back in with full control, you got all the money you need." That's a matter of swapping a little sense of freedom, liberty, and self-respect for money. I don't think the concession needs to be made. It's too much to give up for what we're going to gain. You're gonna still have your hungry [people] and other problems. There is a kind of awakening that we have *nobody* but ourselves that we can ultimately depend on, except God.

I am part of an evolving group called the Michigan Nonprofit Forum. It is the first such experiment in the nation and is an effort to bring together all possible providers of service by nonprofit agencies—universities, United Foundation, churches. I'm not sure what the basic philosophy really is, but I know there's been a lot of talk about privatizing social services and removing them from government, with a heavy emphasis on getting foundation funds to flow back into the communities. It's believed by some that there would be some savings in the whole process because of the heavy bureaucracy of government.

There's been some effort to prove that the private sector would be more efficient and cost effective in terms of the number of people employed, or that it wouldn't be quite as political. Of course, nobody believes that because, I don't care how privatized you make a thing, politics is gonna be there. [*Laughs*] I *do* know that there are very large corporate structures at the head of the thing in Michigan. Generally, corporations don't enter such a thing without very clear self-interest. It's being funded by the Kellogg Foundation. That speaks volumes. 193

I understand that you are close to Mayor Young.

I have a *long* relationship to Mayor Young and strong support and admiration for the man. I know the mayor to be an extremely brilliant man. Some folk think that he is uninformed, blunt, and stupid because he doesn't mind using some choice words from time to time. The mayor is an extremely well-informed man in the areas of his profession. He *knows* what he's about. He's unintimidated by the challenges of the office because he's confident in his information and his skills, except when he might be ill advised, and that can happen. I might be oversympathetic about him.

I also find him an extremely compassionate man, despite his gruffness and everything. I remember once being around him when he had just fired one of the persons on his staff, and he was telling his secretaries what they had to do to find the person a job. And I said to him, "Mr. Mayor, you just fired the man." He said, "Yes, I fired him, but he has a family. By my firing him, all I'm saying is he can't work for *me*, but I don't want him to be without work and I'll do all I can to help him to get work." It was *that* kind of sensitivity.

He spent a lot of money building a scholarship fund that he was solely responsible for. He has over sixty kids on four-year scholarships right now. He doesn't talk about that at all. There are a number of private things that he wants to do, and he doesn't publicize it. He *loves* his people intensely. He's a gregarious person; just enjoys being around folk.

The first year of his administration there was instituted the Board of Police Commissioners. I was named as one of those commissioners. I remember how the police department opposed his efforts for integration and the upgrading of Blacks. He said, "I want to hire women equal to men, fifty-fifty across the board, and I want the complexion of employees to represent the complexion of the city." A case went all the way to the Supreme Court to get some relief and equity, to allow for some catchup on the part of Blacks. I remember testimony before the Board of Police Commissioners in which one of the white officers talked about how this disrupted the system of promotion. One person, haranguing against the mayor, said, "Well, the last one out of the city turn out the lights." I've heard that many times since.

194

Roger Robinson

Detroit was the future in terms of Black politics. Because of Henry Ford, Detroit was the first area with a developed industrial Black working class. The children of that Black working class became teachers, management people in the post office, professionals. By World War II there was a sophisticated Black industrial working class earning adequate money, and a sizable, true middle class. This was a generation before anywhere else in the country. It was no accident that demands for Black empowerment came out of the UAW before other unions.

There was a major Black empowerment movement with the CIO upsurge in the UAW, in which Coleman Young gave leadership to the National Negro Labor Congress. He was then an organizer, I think, for the UPW [United Public Workers]. Then he became secretary of the metropolitan Detroit CIO council when the CP [Communist Party] was dominant. The UPW was then thrown out as a communist union, put on the Attorney General's list, and Coleman fell upon hard times.

When the Black movement inside the UAW succeeded in its demand for access to the international bureaucracy, when the major cadre of Black leadership that pushed that demand became international representatives, in one swoop most of the talent pool was co-opted, and they were put into the equivalent of a civil service bureaucracy. The insurgent edge was taken away. There were some incredibly talented and impressive people. They didn't have access to becoming

Roger Robinson was a union organizer for several service workers' unions and the UAW.

foremen. The only route for advancement of a Black was through the union.

The importance of Detroit and the Black community is inter-woven with working-class organizations. In 1964, Detroit was the first urban area that elected two Blacks to Congress. Relatively propor-tional complements of Blacks were elected to the Michigan state legis-lature. That's not an accident. That election had to do with the so-phisticated forms of the Black political subculture based on the Black working class, *and* the weight of the Black middle class, which was organizationally attached to historical left forms.

Detroit was a generation ahead. Detroit was the future. When there was a white male walkout at the Packard plant during the war—I think it had to do with Black males and white females working to-gether—the UAW ordered the white workers back to work. It was one of the few unions that did not abide with that kind of racist behavior.

There was economic integration going on in Detroit, but then Fannie Mae gave the white working class the ability to finance homes in the suburbs while denying Black people that same mortgage money. Then the hard rails were taken out of Detroit as the result of GM doing it all over the country. Then the freeways were built. Then J. L. Hudson developed the first major suburban shopping center in Northland, then came Eastland, Southland, Westland. A peripheral commercial culture was built that was not dependent on the core. Concurrently, Ford shut down the Highland Park plant, leaving no facilities in Detroit. All their stuff went out Van Dyke, Mound, Michi-gan Avenue. All of GM's new capacity in the '50s and '60s was built outside of Detroit. By the time of the civil disturbance in '67, the seeds of destruction were already sown. The Black revolutionary movement just accelerated the process.

In a lot of cases it was rational to build new industrial capacity. It was a political decision about where to locate that capacity. It could be in the peripheral suburbs where there were transit lines or it could be beyond the transit lines. A convergence of a lot of things brought about disinvestment. There was no countervailing tendency in Detroit corporate culture to prevent disinvestment in industrial capacity in the city or the immediate urban-suburban circle.

But the exodus was so complete: auto factories, Hudson's, super-markets.

It's sort of like there's a renegade ruling class in Detroit. Cincinnati still has a central business district which functions, a merchant section in its ruling class which still cares to do business downtown. Pitts-burgh has a viable downtown. When they built satellite stores it was to

195

expand the market, not at the expense of the fundamental base. In Detroit they decided not to reinvest. The next generation of the auto rich just didn't care. In other communities there is a traditional form of conservatism which still values the institutions of the city. They have some sort of commitment to their geography. In Detroit that seemed to be weaker. That may be based on the brutality of the auto industry where the management cadres don't give a damn.

The ascendancy of Colemen Young into the mayor's office is a complex thing. It's a historic Black victory. It was a coalition. If you analyze Coleman Young in the tradition of big-city politics, even to this day, and compare him with the historic white mayors, you'd say, "Boy this guy's very skillful; built a machine; enforces his will; is able to win elections; he's like a Daley." In the tradition of American politics, Coleman Young did the job.

If you use a separate yardstick—insurgent Black politics—to analyze Coleman Young, well, maybe he didn't do the job.

You can use a much more complex yardstick: here's a guy who came with the left and Black movements, and had the opportunity to pull together the Black community and the labor movement. When Carter was president, Young could have mobilized an entire city. He could have taken a quarter million people to Washington to demand justice for Detroit and urban America. He had that skill, and clearly had the roots and analysis to have done something like that. He *could* have, in fact, put together a *class* and urban coalition that went across many lines, and used Detroit as the example. But he didn't, and that's the failure.

Another analysis by a fundamentally white intellectual cadre concluded that the same thing that was afflicting Detroit was afflicting the immediate suburban ring. They did a class analysis. The disinvestment, reduction of population, loss of services, and increase in the transfer-payments population were also apparent in the contiguous suburban ring. They concluded that there should be a coalition of forces between Detroit—*barely* a Black majority in that period—and the immediate ring of suburbs. Ken Cockrel couldn't buy that, so he basically destroyed his own organization, DARE [Detroit Alliance for a Rational Economy]. Cockrel built electoral forces for his own support, and understood the tactics of coalition, but strategically was not a coalitionist.

Detroit is a benchmark indicator for a lot of political sociology and political economy. When the city went up, it was indicative of certain aspects of expansion and growth. When it contracted, it was an advance warning for America. It was the first city I can recollect that had bulletproof glass in taxicabs and in all these little neighborhood stores. In a period when Detroit had 5,000 public police, there was a private army of 25,000 rent-a-cops.

In Detroit, over 50 percent of the kids don't graduate from high school. If there was a full-employment economy the majority of people growing up in Detroit would be vocationally unable to participate in the economy. They are almost structurally incapable of disciplined vocational activity. To a greater or lesser degree, it's the same in every major city. In a democratic society, the last institution that was the partial guarantor of access to the rewards of the society was the public school system.

I think the brutality of the auto industry caused people in this geography to recreate community. Even with the racism and the craziness, you go into most auto plants and the Black workers and the white workers generally look out for one another. There are also complex political coalitions. In a plant where the white tendency is Polish, you have a Black-Polish coalition. Where it's Italian, you have a Black-Italian coalition. Or a Black–southern white coalition. There's a political subculture in the industrial unions where coalitions are made based on real power. And they don't even necessarily *like* each other.

Given Detroit's present population, what are the organizing bases?

I don't see any organizing bases that are exclusive to Detroit. There are caste and class relationships. Obviously, there is oppression based on being Black. But the fundamental abuse now being heaped upon people has to do with class: access to jobs, who controls investment decisions and their effect. Until you obtain collective control over investment decisions, you have no future. That suggests a political coalition with others who are incrementally being frozen out of the rewards of the society. It also suggests that you have to bring in shock troops and ferocious amounts of money to start correcting things. You never will correct the damage that's been done based on the miseducation of the population of Detroit. You can only see that it doesn't continue.

The basis for organizing in Detroit is a Black-white coalition, with the older working-class suburbs being attached to the power base of the urban core. That has to manifest itself as a political movement in the state political bodies and hopefully a valid coalition in national politics. Americans are operational liberals and cultural conservatives. How do you form a legitimate, honest coalition in which spokespeople of the white working class, in their own self-interest, come into political consciousness where they see a common purpose with the Black working class and the Black underclass? Unless you have a political culture that articulates that, it won't happen.

I don't see community organizations as the basis of a political movement of consequence. They are not class based. A community organization objectively is a populist organization that is looking for legitimate, conservative improvement of their own political geography. This is not the basis for some sort of radical adventure. There is right-wing populism and left-wing populism, depending on the world-view or different kinds of overarching problems. Welfare or homeless groups are legitimate parts of a possible coalition, but they don't have the staying power. Even though contracted and weakened, the industrial working class is still the fundamental backbone upon which all the other things have to be added.

I assume that inevitably leadership will develop, though I'm not a spontaneous socialist. The working class and the working-class political parties, by themselves, cannot take power. Therefore, they must have a coalition with the culturally advanced sections of the population—the educated middle class. There are unions entirely composed of such people—teachers' unions, broad bodies of government workers, called "new class" in European parlance. The National Education Association, which is culturally correct on race and other questions, the Service Employees Union, and AFSCME [American Federation of State, County, and Municipal Employees] still are growing.

Then there is a set of issues which have to do with movements. There's still a women's movement, very weakened, though still a movement. There's an ecology movement which cuts across hard class lines, especially in the suburban rings. How you thread together a left politics, or anticorporate politics, or a popular politics which empowers people, is complex. But there are ways of doing that.

Arthur Johnson

When I first came to Detroit I thought of it as most southern Blacks did: it had to be better than what we were living in. And Detroit was a very important city with a wonderful national reputation. When I arrived I immediately was struck by the racial segregation and racism that existed here. Job discrimination was rampant. In Hudson's Department Store downtown no Black person could sell anything. A Black person could not drive a Checker cab, and a Checker cab would leave Black people standing in front of Hudson's and pick up

Arthur Johnson is vice president for community relations at Wayne State University, and former executive secretary of the National Association for the Advancement of Colored People.

white passengers. Discrimination in hotels was common. All the better restaurants and bars downtown generally refused Blacks service.

I became involved with NAACP volunteers that we called the Restaurant Discrimination Committee. We actually conducted the first sitins in the United States in 1951 and '52. It was a period of the most active attack on discrimination in public accommodations in the city. We would meet every Friday night, organize where we would go to test discrimination, and then send teams out to those places. We didn't have any money, so we got the cheapest thing on the menu. If you ordered a drink, very fine places wouldn't hesitate to say, "You've had too much to drink." If you ordered food, they'd say, "We're closing." In many cases, particularly during the day, places would *actually* close rather than serve a Black person.

199

The ugliest part of the problem in the '50s was police brutality against Black people. Nothing was done about it. For years, the *Detroit News* identified crime stories by race. The city of Detroit maintained segregation in public housing projects. The Detroit NAACP sued the city and went to federal court on that issue, and we *won*.

When people talk to me today about what Detroit has lost and how bad a shape the city is in today, I am quick to say, "If you're thinking about Detroit in the '50s, what you call the good old days is a question of who's talking." I could not possibly want to return to the Detroit of the 1950s. In spite of the tremendous burden of economic deprivation that exists here today and the hollow shape of things here, I have to tell you that I'd rather see *that* than go back to the Detroit of 1950. Whites walked away from this city, literally abandoning all they had built, rather than make a reasonable accommodation. As a result, we have seen a pattern of economic disinvestment in this city that cannot be matched by any other major city in the United States. When I say it rides on race I absolutely mean that.

And Coleman Young is correct when he says that?

Of *course* he is. The mayor and I are good friends and I have tremendous respect for what he has done here. And I know his mistakes; he's not been perfect. But his achievements, his gift to this city, the best of himself, is difficult to measure adequately. I've said to the mayor, "You are the victim today of a lot of white bitterness and resentment and it's primarily because you would not let the city commit suicide. You stood in the way. You kept this city on the conscience of the white population that's been on the move. And they hate you for that."

Last week I told a reporter from *USA Today* who visited me, "You must know that we are tired of you media people dealing with Detroit as though it's somehow detached from the main. You look at all its scars and problems and you hold it up as though it's separate from the rest of the country when what you're *really* seeing is a mirror of America. But you never want to interpret that. It's easier and makes a more dramatic picture for you to hold Detroit out as a failure, not that it's a mirror of America. You call it a failure of this administration and the people who live in the city, whereas the people who *left* are without blame."

As much as people want to communicate the image of Detroit as a Black city, there are more whites living in Detroit than any other city in Michigan, and they are just forgotten. Any picture painted of Detroit today will not give any recognition to them, and most of them are here because they *want* to be here, just like the middle-class Black people.

I've not yet seen a single chronicle of the positive things that are going on in Detroit. But that story is there, nevertheless. Because I love this city so much and am involved in it so deeply—emotionally and otherwise—I *know* that story. I have to keep looking for it to keep my *own* sanity and hope.

This city simply is being remade. It never will be 1950 Detroit again. And I celebrate that. I'm willing to wait for the other changes to fall in place. We're in the process of building a new city. We're building, in the words that our President George Bush misused, a "kinder and gentler" city; at least, a city that will be more hospitable to the interests of *all* of the people.

Adam Shakoor

Unfortunately, I think that we traded the activism of the 1960s for a certain kind of political activism in the traditional political process and began to stake all our indicators of success based upon who we could elect and how successful we could be in that process. Not to undermine that process—I'm very familiar with it, being a participant in it—but there was something greater in that period, in the civil rights era, where leadership arose out of the churches, colleges, and universities, and factories. It was a leadership that had a sense of the rightness of the cause, and there was no compromise. But the nature of politics is the art of compromise. I mean, you've got to count votes.

Adam Shakoor is deputy mayor of the city of Detroit; he participated in the work of the League of Revolutionary Black Workers and in the 1960s became a Muslim.

In the Black community we passed the mantle of leadership from those idealist civil rights leaders over to our successful elected politicians. That sense of urgency and commitment began to become a part of a political process. But I think that really kind of reverses what the political world is about. I believe they are the leaders, but they lead from the standpoint of those who fuel that cause with the concerns and the desires for change. In many respects, that has not been translated yet. It will, in time. I think it comes through a certain sophistication. I think it comes through a certain period of time. We are in the first generation of successful political leadership in this century.

I think the primary struggle I focused on was pragmatic. What can be gained in my lifetime through my efforts and what can be gained where some more practical solutions can be offered in my community? If people are hungry, we need to find ways to feed them. If people are improperly educated, we need to begin to take whatever skills and knowledge we're gaining in these universities and go back into our community and begin the process of education, supplementing the failure that may exist in the public school system.

I think the lessons of the '60s point to the need for an active community of progressive-minded people. I think the '50s showed an active movement in a more conservative right pattern—the McCarthys and John Birchers, etc.

The '80s, I think, have fueled a similar situation. But the lesson is, that where there is no active, progressive element, then the right begins to experience greater success. The '60s experienced some points of success, then we got lax. We felt we had done something. We felt we had won. Then some of the people got involved in other things. They began to be concerned about how they're going to pay for their kids.

The lessons are that we have to maintain vigilance; that there is no victory until people have all of their needs addressed. Quite frankly, I just don't see that occurring. People, regardless of their condition of birth or their race, are entitled to basic standards of human dignity, health care, housing, jobs, job skills. Many believe that government has no interest and no right; that it's all a matter of the individual's access and free will. Why is government there if it's not to serve?

As close as I can sense, we're in a period where a resurgence is going to take place in people's concerns about each other. Maybe this is wishful thinking, but hard times sometimes breed some very tremendous movements. Whether it occurs in the '90s or the early period of the turn of the century, I think a new leadership will rise up and its going to create a new wave of thinking in the nation that focuses in on the problems of the majority of its people here.

Politicians are not the answers. They are not the leaders. They are the people who do the people's will. If they know what the people's will is, politicians will do it, because they must get reelected. That's the fueling drive for most political leaders. It's going to have to arise from those campuses, from those service organizations. It's going to have to arise to a point where perhaps some business leaders begin to say, well, this is good business.

I don't expect future leadership to come from the political arena. I expect it to come from the grassroots elements, whether it's SOSAD [Save Our Sons and Daughters], or the churches, or the masses of homeless people who are increasing every day. As they put the pressure on the service-delivery components of cities like Detroit, as they put the pressure on the institutions that have the responsibility to regulate activities within areas like Detroit, then there will be greater pressure on the political leadership of the state, of the city and of this nation to begin to address those concerns. And as they gauge the mood swing, the winds of change . . . then it happens.

Clyde Cleveland

One of the reasons my father left the South was that he was unable to vote. He came to Detroit in 1923. Never missed an election up until he died at the age of eighty-four in 1980. He worked for thirty-eight years and nine months at Ford in the foundry. He was active in the union movement, so I grew up in an atmosphere of politics. I've been active in politics since 1944 when I was nine years old.

The North was just as segregated as the South when I was growing up, particularly in terms of housing. The experiences I had of not being served at a restaurant were not in Georgia or Alabama or Mississippi—they were right here in the city of Detroit.

In the '50s the dances on the Boblo boat cruises, Mondays were reserved for blacks. In fact, Mayor Coleman Young couldn't even go to the island when he graduated from high school and his class went there for a picnic. Blacks could only go to the Graystone Ballroom and skating rinks on Woodward one night a week. If you saw a bar or

Clyde Cleveland has been a member of Detroit City Council since 1973, twice a delegate to the Democratic National Convention, and co-chair of Jesse Jackson's successful 1988 Michigan campaign.

any eating facility that said "Black and Tan," you knew that Blacks were welcome to come in there.

The Orsell McGee family bought a house over on Sebolt, and the neighbors sued because the restrictive covenants said the houses in that area could only be sold to peopleof the Caucasian race. That case was taken all the way to the U.S. Supreme Court in 1948 or '49 and restrictive covenants were struck down. You could be the richest Black person in the world, but you lived on the north end, the old west side, in Black Bottom, or the east side.

In the '20s, a Black doctor by the name of Ossian Sweet moved over on Garland near Charlevoix in what had previously been an all-white neighborhood, and a crowd gathered out in front of the house. A shot was fired from the house that killed one of the mob outside. They arrested all the adults in the house, about eleven people. Clarence Darrow tried the case and won.

203

The political objectives of civil rights were met; also the economic objectives in places that we picketed—AAA, banks, supermarkets and so forth—to hire Blacks. The only chagrin I have now is that with the demise of the automobile industry, Blacks are worse off today economically than they were years ago. When I graduated from high school, any kid who wanted a job had a job, because you had Ford, Chrysler, Chevrolet, Murray Body, Packard, Fisher Body, Continental Motors. Subsequently, Detroit has lost 65 percent of its business and industry. It's moved out of the city, out of the state, out of the country. This year will probably be the worst year we've had since I've been on City Council.

Twenty years ago, one-third of the SEV [state equalized value] was located in downtown Detroit. The city was growing in the '50s at a rate of almost $1 billion a year in new construction in those day's dollars. Now the construction and jobs develop outside of the city of Detroit. I'm chairperson of SEMCOG [Southeast Michigan Council of Governments], the regional planning body for the seven-county area. One of the committees we have is looking into finding transportation for the jobs that have gone outside of the city, through van pools or buses. Finally, it was determined that the people who moved out there didn't want Blacks out there too. This is today, not something forty or fifty years ago. Racism is alive and well. As Rosalyn Carter said, "Ronald Reagan makes us feel comfortable with our prejudice." To think now that the best opportunity for Blacks is in the military service.

Blacks working in the automobile industry were able to live a middle-class life. With the loss of jobs in the city of Detroit, a horrendous thing has happened. In the 50's, the state of Michigan had 20,000 employees and the city of Detroit had 29,000 employees. Detroit *was* Michigan. Now this has all been frittered away. We've lost almost 800,000 of our population. We've lost 65 percent of the business and industry, the bedrock of employment and the tax base.

Last year we had a budget deficit of about $34 million, but we were able to take money from a rainy-day fund of about $74 million. This year we anticipate a deficit of $40 to $50 million, so the rainy-day fund will be wiped out. And the governor has these horrendous cut-backs. The state had a budget deficit of about $1 billion, and he's cutting social programs. He's talking about cutting welfare for single people, cutting back on drug programs, day care programs. All of the social programs are being cut.

Another thing that could be very harmful is Bush talking about turning community development block-grant funds over to the states for the states to disburse. With the guy we have up in Lansing now, he might be giving it to Grosse Pointe when its needed in the city of Detroit. So at this particular point it's a very, very glum picture. It's the worst economic crisis I've seen in my eighteen years on City Council.

When Carter was president, 30 percent of our budget came from the feds. Now it's down to 12 percent. It's been cut by 60 percent. Under the Carter administration, we actually turned around. In 1980, we had 5,500 police officers. Services were good. Housing was being built. We built almost 3,000 Section 8, low- and moderate-income houses under Carter. The last Section 8 housing was built over here on Trumbull and Bagley. When you lose 60 percent of what you're getting from the federal government, you're in deep trouble. In the city of Detroit you probably have 40 percent of the people trying to support 60 percent of the people.

What's to be done?

I wish I knew. I think a change in leadership at the national level would start some things going. Detroit needs to develop a replace-ment for the automobile industry in terms of a service industry. I would like to see Detroit develop more as an international trading center. We've been very derelict with that. The Detroit River is one of the busiest inland waterways in the world.

There's been a tremendous falloff of Black participation in the electoral process. Only 54 percent of the eligible Black voters both-ered to vote in the 1988 presidential election. Governor Engler won by only 19,000 votes, and you had 19,000 Blacks standing on the cor-ner at the bus stop that day. The weapon that we have is the ballot box. King preached that. When you have seen things that were gained through the political process now being stripped away through the political process, I think cynicism and apathy probably set in.

Although we have problems of decay, crime, and so forth, you still have many blue-collar and low-income neighborhoods where people are still cutting their lawns and keeping up their houses. You're going to have to start tapping into this grassroots leadership and have them come forth as it was done in the civil rights days. A coalition for better living or something. I can't think of a catchword for it, but there is a need. We're all in this boat together.

Being chairperson of SEMCOG, one of the things I want to do is to bridge the gap between suburbia and Detroit. We're meeting with people from Southfield and Oak Park. There are empty buildings out in Oak Park, because what's happened is they've left Oak Park and they've gone [further out] to Troy. Then they're leaving Troy and going to Farmington Hills and Novi. And the horrendous part of it is there's no growth. There has not been any growth in the area in the last twenty years. What's happened is it's just transferred. You build twenty new houses, and nineteen of them are people moving from one neighborhood to another. Only one is actually a new arrival.

It's very chilling and very frustrating to be an elected official in the city of Detroit. You know what the needs are, but the resources aren't there, and that's the frustration. It's not like the needs are there and the resources are being mismanaged or not put into the right place. The resources are just not there.

There are no magic answers, and I'm not one to come up with flip responses that have no depth to them. But I do say it's a very frustrating feeling at this juncture being caught in this whammy of the state cutbacks now and the national situation for the last ten years. And I don't know what's taken people so long to wake up.

Part 6   *There Is Power: The Dilemma of Organized Labor in Motown*

ORGANIZED IN 1935, THE UNITED AUTOMOBILE WORKERS
was a potent force in the history of Detroit and Michigan. It restrained the power and excesses of the auto companies and forced them to share more profits with their workers. Its militant bargaining improved the standard of living of thousands upon thousands who had come to Detroit to better themselves.

At the peak of its power under Walter Reuther, the UAW was respected nationally as a progressive union. It influenced the institutional life in the Detroit area. It successfully lobbied for higher standards in the quality of life of workers. Its political clout forced expansion of government programs in human services. Michigan has been a national model in facilitating the rights and protection of the working people.

The UAW was crucial to the advancement of African-Americans and other national minorities. It called for solidarity in the ranks of a multiracial labor force and fought for racial equality in labor-management negotiations.

Like the union movement in general, the UAW has been engaged for years in a rearguard fight for survival. Its auto-related membership is drastically down, but there are organizing drives in nontraditional labor markets, like the Hudson's department store chain, that give hope for growth. In some places a fight-back stance is evolving.

Detroit has been a strong union town for over fifty years. Economic pitfalls and deindustrialization notwithstanding, a gutsy, class-conscious, struggle mentality seems inbred in the working class. Many call for an expanded, empowered union movement to help slow down or stop the degradation of the American working class and the cities in which they live. Echoing the refrain of an old labor song, their cry is still, "There is power, power, power in a band of working men [sic]."

Yet the differences among union activists on tactics, strategy, and theory may be deeper today than they've ever been. Capital's anti-unionism is as deep today as it was in, say, 1930. Additionally, the current international battle of capital has produced a new ballgame in which the losers are the workers. Detroit workers have been really hit hard in this newest thrust of capital to maximize profits and consolidate advantage.

So, how do UAW leaders in Detroit today analyze the crisis, and what do they think should be done? The five testimonies that follow from two working and three retired UAW officials show the difference in points of view. They represent many collective years of service to advance the union cause. They represent both the union establishment and the loyal opposition.

Bob King

I graduated from the University of Michigan. After getting out of the army I hired into Ford in 1970 at a parts depot. While working on my law degree I went through the UAW-Ford electrical apprenticeship program at the Rouge complex and got my journeyman's card. I've served almost every step in the UAW: standing committees, recording secretary, general council delegate, district committeeperson, bargaining committeeperson, local officer, local president, and regional director.

Early on I decided I wanted to do something about hunger and suffering in the world. I had a chance to become active in the labor movement and it seemed to be a real vehicle for impacting human suffering and raising dignity. I wouldn't give this up for *anything*. I think I'm really blessed to be doing something I enjoy and get paid more money than I thought I ever would. I have the opportunity to be in a position where I can use resources and power to try to make changes that are better for our membership and our society.

Recently I read a prediction that the labor movement would slip to 2 percent of the work force by the year 2000. I said, "Ah, that's just antiunion propaganda." But the more I looked at the factors contributing to the decline in the labor movement, the more it seemed possible that we could go down to 2 or 5 percent unless there's a major shift in this country. Those 2 or 5 percent would be without any meaningful power and would have their contracts gutted, their pensions and long-term security taken away. We would become like many Third World countries where the labor movement is meaningless or they're just company unions.

Percent unionization hit its peak in the early '50s, about 35 percent of total. We shrank down to 25 percent by 1980. Nobody got concerned, though, because actual numbers were the same or larger. The population was bigger, the workforce was bigger. What's shocking is to look from 1980 to 1990, when there was a horrendous drop in percent unionization and also a drop in actual numbers. We're millions less today, even though the population and workforce is bigger than in 1980. In private industry we're down to about 12 percent. If we lost the same absolute numbers in the next ten years that were lost in the *last* ten years, we'd be down to 2 percent. What's worse is what I call the shark effect: the corporations, wealthy, and anti–working-mentality people in this country are like sharks who smell the

Bob King is director of UAW Region 1-A, consisting of 42 union locals, 500 workplaces, 93,000 members, and 50,000 retirees.

blood of the labor movement. They're taking us on more than they ever have in thirty or forty years.

You can put your neck out to take the boss on and win some justice, or fight to bring a union in, and it can be tied up in the courts for years. The NLRB [National Labor Relations Board] is toothless. It says, "Yeah, XYZ company has violated the law and committed these unfair labor practices," but it has no injunctive power, no power of fining or imprisonment. You have to wait till you get to the court of appeals and that can easily be two to four years. A Montgomery Ward case was tied up eight years in court and when they went to have a new election *nobody* who was there when first they voted was there eight years later.

Things were good for a number of years. We got contract after contract with improvements in wages, benefits, pensions, and better health and safety in the plants. We were good grievance administrators and good arbitrators, but everybody got lulled to sleep. We became bureaucrats. Members would have a problem and they'd come and say, "Here, Bob, here's a problem, take care of it." And I'd go charging off and take care of it. For twenty years I viewed my job as servicing the membership by taking care of their problems. If you'd ask me for a job description I never would have thought of the word "organizer." I realize now that the *greatest* responsibility we have is to organize our *own* members. Instead of letting them come and dump problems on our desk, we all have to be fired up to take it on *together* to get a resolution from the boss or company. Though we'll still use them, grievance and arbitration procedures are all legalistic methods that are disempowering.

We're trying experiments in a number of different workplaces. We had one case where a company said it wasn't going to recognize someone being on medical after twelve months and, boom, that person no longer had employment. It's crazy. Five years ago I would have filed a grievance for that person, but it would have taken up to three years before we got it to the arbitrator because of the number of grievances in the system. What did we do this time? We went around and asked every member in the plant to sign the grievance. The company knew we were going to fire up every person in that plant, and we *did* and they were angry. This is direct workplace action.

Today if we relied on the NLRB to help us in organizing, we would never organize or turn around the trends. It's too slow a process. The old saying, "justice delayed, justice denied," is absolutely true. In 1960 there were over 3,000 workers fired for union organizing. By 1987 that had grown to 16,973 people. There are even more now. It's just unbelievable what's happened to the law in this country. We have a real job to do.

212

Compare Canada and the United States. They have similar economies and deal with the same multinational corporations. In Canada in 1955 they were 32 percent unionized and in 1985 they were 37 percent. The laws in Canada are tremendously different than the laws here. Canadian workers understand they've got a common political agenda. In the USA we've bought into the corporate line that if you're a retail worker you're different than an industrial worker, different that a service-sector worker, iron worker, auto worker, steel worker, electrical worker. We've allowed ourselves to be so divided that we don't see that we've all got common interests.

We're involved now in an organizing drive at Dayton-Hudson department stores. The company managers tell their employes, "You don't work for General Motors, Ford, or Chrysler, so how can you expect to make the kind of wages or benefits they have there?" Dayton-Hudson's is an extremely profitable corporation and makes a hell of a lot more than the Big Three. They have more profits per square foot of store than anybody else in this country. But the retail workers *believe* that they're different than auto workers. American workers don't see themselves as workers. They see themselves as retail or auto. My simplification is that all companies are in business to make money. Ford doesn't care whether they're making cars or running a financial institution. Same thing is true of Dayton-Hudson's, McDonald's, or anywhere else. We need to have workers understand that unless they stand together everyone will get squeezed by their individual corporations. They have to understand that we're all working class.

I think that people are going to wake up and we're going to turn around. I see new spirits of solidarity. I went down to Ravenwood, West Virginia, last weekend. We had a convey of over 300 cars. We raised almost $100,000 in a very short time to help workers who had been locked out for about a year. When we make the proper call to the membership I see a response. We have more organizing going on now in this region than we have had for twenty or thirty years, and it's very, very difficult to organize today.

How do you raise consciousness in this period of great conservatism?

A couple months ago I started visiting every local union, doing plant tours, and holding leadership meetings. We discuss this very thing when I go to the locals. I say, "I don't know how to do it. How do we raise people's consciousness? How do we get involved?" How do you eat an elephant? You do it one bite at a time. I think you've got to do it a hundred different ways. The president of Local 387 is doing focus groups where he's going out and meeting with each department and talking about issues and problems. Some have done different incentives to try to get more members out to membership meetings. All of our representatives are swamped now because the problems are .huge in all the plants, but we're trying to get them to understand that they'll never be successful in their job if they don't get more people active.

It's tough enough to organize a new place, but sometimes it's five times as difficult to win a contract. The companies pay antiunion consultants $2,000 to $3,000 per day. They pay antiunion attorneys huge fees to keep unions out. They do surface bargaining because they know the NLRB is toothless. The focus I'm trying to set here is, what direct-action things can we do and what ways can we impact that company without relying on the law or the NLRB?

214

We had a recent case with a supplier for a big automotive company. We openly told the company, "If you don't get the supplier turned around in terms of antiunion activities we're going to find a way to shut you down." Within two weeks the key union organizer that the supplier fired was back to work and within another week a letter was on [UAW president] Owen Bieber's desk saying, "We've reconsidered our position, we're going to negotiate with the UAW." Henry Ford said he'd be dead in his grave before he would recognize a union. What changed his mind? When he couldn't make cars, when the workers stood up. A strike isn't the only method to do that. You can take public actions like consumer boycotts, but those are *tough* and you really got to think them through. One of the big hurdles today is that employers make a hell of a case in their antiunion drives by saying that joining a union is meaningless because unions don't have the power to make a difference. So we need to demonstrate in open, public ways that we have the power to make a difference.

Where the labor movement is expanding you see every index of fairness in society becoming better for working people: taxation, health insurance, unemployment, workers' compensation, labor legislation, and on and on. It's fairer and better when unions are stronger. When unions are shrinking, as has been happening in the United States, what happens? The corporations and rich get billions and billions in tax breaks. Unemployment compensation is *much* worse today than it was ten years ago. Workmen's compensation has been squeezed and benefits taken away from workers. Health insurance in this country is horrendous. Public school systems are deteriorating. Any criteria of the quality of life of the middle or working classes has gotten worse.

Frighteningly, it could go in the wrong direction: you could have a David Duke, an Adolph Hitler type. I see the frustration level being really high among common, working people today. David Duke is created by Ronald Reagan's and George Bush's racism in their campaigns. Our government has supported military dictatorships, deprivation of personal rights, and torture all over the world. That mentality is out there. If we don't keep people actively involved in the democratic process, that right-wing mentality could take control of this country.

Many people see that the present system isn't working and that they're losing ground. They see, hopefully, the danger that it could be much, much worse in a very short period of time, so they're motivated to become involved *in* the system to make it work fairly for all people.

Well, that means a redistribution of wealth.

Sure it does. We had minor redistribution of wealth in this country until the '70s. Now it's going in just the opposite direction. There's a lot of documentation of that, including Kevin Phillips's *Politics of Rich and Poor.* The key to approaching workers on this is to show that it impacts on them personally. When I'm talking about the need to organize or go to Ravenwood, I always try—sometimes successfully, sometimes not—to make the direct connection: "Your pension isn't going to be here, your wages aren't going to be the same; not in twenty years, but in five or ten years." I try to get them to see that they and their families are threatened.

Part of the problem is that we in the labor movement have not properly exercised our power and resources in the state of Michigan. Frank Garrison, president of the Michigan AFL-CIO, says that if all union members and all their family members voted for *a* candidate in the state of Michigan, that candidate would never lose. We go sixteen different directions or we don't vote. It's shocking how many of our members are not registered to vote or, if they're registered, it's shocking how many of them *don't* vote, and it's shocking how many of them vote for candidates who work in their *worst* interest 99 percent of the time. Governor John Engler is an example. Bush and Reagan are examples. There are some figures saying that 45 percent voted for Reagan. That's *horrendous,* that's *unbelievable.* We have to wake up our members.

215

Doug Fraser

The new Poletown plant was to have generated about 6,000 jobs, but the market dictated otherwise. The Poletown plant replaced the Clark Avenue Cadillac assembly plant and the Fleetwood plant that built the

Doug Fraser is a retired president of the United Auto Workers and instructor at Wayne State University.

bodies. I do not think GM would have built the new Poletown plant absent Coleman Young's influence because they could have gone to a greenbelt without all the problems attendant to a workforce in an urban community. He also was very influential in having Chrysler build the new Jeep plant on Jefferson Avenue where they expect to put out something like forty to forty-five an hour. We still lost a lot, but it would have been in even worse shape had it not been for Coleman Young's political influence.

Chrysler and GM had a sense of community responsibility in building those plants. Their decisions were contrary to why most economic decisions are made: to maximize profits. Industrial leaders took an interest in the city basically after the 1967 riots. Before then they thought a manager's job had the single focus of maximizing profits without regard to what happens to the communities. Now there's a greater sensitivity, I must say. They're active on various commissions like the Renaissance and New Detroit. These people don't view their roles as one-dimensional any more. For years, Henry Ford was the exception to the general rule.

There are minimum-wage jobs in the suburbs. We've got to find a way to match up the unemployed in Detroit with those jobs. The suburbs might be forced into this out of economic necessity. Before the present recession, there were jobs above the minimum wage because they couldn't get anybody at the minimum wage. If you're an entreprenuer in the surrounding communities and you're looking for help, and that help happens to be Black, I don't think that would make any difference.

People argue that there's going to be a labor shortgage in the 1990s. A case can be made for that if you look at the birth rate and the number of people coming into the workforce, and the expansion of the service industry. But the premise is based upon a healthy economy. I was the chairman of a committee that was trying to develop mass transit in the Detroit area. We developed a good plan, but we didn't have the resources. We talked about increasing resources through increasing the sales tax, but everybody runs when you mention the word tax. The president of Stroh Brewery said, "That's a mistake; we should not provide mass transit and we'll force businesses to come to Detroit because that's the only place where manpower will be available." I said, "Well, you're dreaming. You're talking about a lot of industries which are gonna locate where their customers are, and their customers aren't in Detroit." I don't see economic development in Detroit.

More and more of the economic responsibilities for services are pushed back to the states and the states push it back to the community. The sum of it is, we're in a hell of a mess. There's no Detroit solution or Cleveland solution. There has to be a healthy economy and a national government that understands the problems of the communities. Detroit certainly can't tax itself any more. It taxes itself more than any other city in Michigan and more than most other cities throughout the country. The basic solution is national.

The purchasing power of people for the last twenty years has either stagnated or declined. When the mills shut down most jobs earned about $12 an hour. Now these people are working for $6 an hour. Then their wives are forced into the workforce at maybe minimum wage, even though they're quite happy being a homemaker. Together, a couple earns a dollar or two less per hour than what the man did as a single earner. That's a shocking development in a family's life. Their standard of living is *shattered*. People are devastated.

That's happening all over this country. Some of it is a natural evolution. Students ask me when are we going back to the glory days of the '50s, '60s, and '70s. I say "Never!" We're engaged in fierce international competition. The economic ballgame has changed. Perhaps for the first time in our history, the current generation is worse off than the predecessor generation. When I was a young person I just worked in the shop, and I could buy a house. Most young people can't *dream* of buying a house now.

People haven't exhibited sufficient anger at this situation. The genius of a democratic society is that when the people are aroused they can change things. There are countless examples in history. The power of the people is enormous if you can just mobilize that power. You can move mountains. I see signs of us in this country reaching that point.

What's the role of organized labor in this process?

I'm prejudiced, but I watch the labor movement and they've still got enormous political clout. Last week all six presidential candidates came to an AFL-CIO meeting in Detroit. It was a tough question-and-answer session. Obviously, they think the labor movement is still pretty important. At the peak, 35 percent of the labor force was organized; now it's around 16 percent. People overlook the fact that the number of people who belong to unions has been absolutely constant at 14,000,000 for the last eight years despite the fact that we lost 2,000,000 manufacturing jobs. People aren't turning their backs on the labor movement. It has some problems and some bad image, but it's not dead. And it's very influential in the Detroit area.

Good labor leaders today must take some risks and try new approaches. Ninety percent of industrial workers still want their unions.

217

We lost membership not because members turned their backs on us but because of the erosion of jobs and the great difficulties that archaic U.S. laws make for new organizing efforts.

AFSCME [American Federation of State, County and Municipal Employees] is now up to 2,300,000 members. The Service Employees International Union is growing by leaps and bounds. The government union is growing. In the United States we generated 25,000,000 new jobs in the '70s and '80s. That's almost a miracle. There was no growth at all in Germany during the same period.

There are some other good signs. Some businessmen who are pure free enterprisers and want no government involvement at all, used to say, "It's socialism," but now they're saying, "Wait a minute, we've got to work with government." Industry in other countries—France, Germany, and particularly Japan—has formed almost a consortium with government. Government helps in research and development, targeting of markets, etc.

This afternoon I'm meeting with the Mazda people in Flat Rock. An example I'm going to present is the effect the airbus has had on our jobs with McDonnell-Douglas and eventually will have on Boeing. I ride on the airbus all the time. They're good planes. They have maybe 30 percent of the American market. It's a consortium between the United Kingdom, France, Germany, and Spain. They poured *billions* of dollars into it and lost money every year until last year. There's no company in the world that could have generated that much capital to start a business. I always point out there would not be a Chrysler Corporation today had it not been for the government. Lee Iacocca was not a folk hero in those days. We pushed the legislation in the executive branch and in Congress. Everybody made sacrifices and we saved the company.

Industrialists have been shortsighted and somewhat arrogant. Steel, more than auto, fell behind the technological curve. In autos we got sloppy and careless in the '70s and produced some bad cars. We lost our reputation and are still paying for it.

Pete Kelly

There's been a tremendous change in technology. What traditionally was done on the bench, is now done by computers. You'll find UAW model makers now sitting in front of computers all day long, never

Pete Kelly is president of UAW Local 160, which represents hourly employees at the General Motors Technical Center (known as the Tech Center) in the northern suburb of Warren.

lifting a tool to cut a piece of wood. We're operating with fewer people. At the Tech Center we're an industrial elite. All the engineering goes on there. It's the cutting edge of this corporation.

When I first heard Walter Reuther speak I thought the sun shone out of his ass. He was a very impressive orator. He was probably the most progressive labor leader in the country at the time.

My problem came in 1967 when the cost-of-living factor was given up. I couldn't understand why the greatest protection that had been won was being given up at a time when profits for General Motors, Ford, or Chrysler were enormous. The Japanese competition was *minimal.* The GM president then was C. E. Wilson, who purportedly said, "What's good for General Motors is good for the country."

In 1970 I went to the national convention with a group called the United National Caucus. We set up a headquarters right beside the convention. It irritated the hell out of the union leadership. One great organizer of this was Arthur Fox of Local 600. I have nothing but the highest respect for his memory. Reuther's state of the union speech was very clever. He rose and said, "There are those saying that we've made a mistake in putting this cap on the cost of living. If you want to blame somebody, blame me. But by God we're gonna get it back." People at the convention gave him a thunderous ovation: "What a man; he can admit to a mistake." Walter died the following month in a plane accident, so the whole thing rested on Leonard Woodcock's back. We had a long, ten-week strike and they came to terms. We got six cents of new money and got the cost of living back, a tremendous achievement. More than half of UAW wages today is the result of getting that cost of living back.

Woodcock was a hawk on the Vietnam War. I led a demonstration to the Chrysler Tank Arsenal. When we got there, Donald Lobsinger [right wing populist] and his group were waiting for us. I was told after the demonstration that somebody had left the plant to go home and get his rifle to take care of me. If I had stood for election the next day, I wouldn't have gotten two votes out of this Tech Center. We had a lot of people who had fought in World War II and the Korean War. I was called a communist, and I never belonged to any political party in my life.

When I came here in '55 it was during the McCarthy period. I admired the Diego Rivera murals in the Detroit Institute of Arts so much. Mary Beck, a Detroit councilwoman, wanted to paint over the murals because Rivera was a known communist. We went down there to demonstrate to stop her from doing that. I thought it was ridiculous for somebody to paint over a work of art. This whole nation had a mania about anticommunism.

A lot of people today realize that what I did was up front and several years ahead of what people later came to their own realization about. The Vietnam War *was* a calamity. I don't know many nations where a people can actually force the government to withdraw from a war. What happened in the '60s in this nation has had an indelible imprint.

What about the Reagan-Bush '80s?

Oh, it's been terrible! What's going on in Detroit is going on throughout the entire country. I travel on this job a lot. I've been in the major cities and they *all* have major problems. Detroit is a whipping boy, but it has a lot of problems. Racism is the divisive factor in this nation. Today, I am as leery as anybody to go to Detroit. But I feel as apprehensive in Chicago or Philadelphia or Pittsburgh or New York or anywhere when I get off the main drive. Our cities tell us where our society is. Our priorities are all screwed up.

I find a lack of consciousness among American people. They've been robbed of their history. Most young people haven't been exposed to the history of the CIO. That's unbelievable. Labor history is revered and honored in other nations. If you asked anybody in my shops who is Lynn Kirkland, I would guarantee that less than one-half of 1 percent would know that he is the leader of the labor movement in this country. We're watching labor getting its ass kicked up and down this country and brutally bullied by corporations. The modern-day robber barons use goons and union busters to achieve their goals.

The most tragic mistake made by the labor leaders in this country is that they've consciously declared that the best interest of their membership can be met by *total* cooperation with the corporations. The only organization to stop the abuse of corporate America is the labor movement. I'm talking about *power*. I was quoted yesterday in the paper: "A lot of people pose as union leaders, but they're basically company men."

I brought Mexican workers here to speak to my people. I made appeals to Owen Bieber [UAW president] and the entire executive board to raise the Free Trade Agreement at the 1990 summer negotiations. I have yet to get a response. The Democrats have succumbed to Bush and joined the fast-track thing. The impact of this is going to be phenomenal, not just for workers in the auto industry, but for the overall welfare of workers in the United States. General Motors is the largest employer in Mexico, outside of the Mexican government. Workers in Mexico make seventy-five cents an hour. There is no way that the American worker can compete with that. Our problems and programs are *here*. We have a unique set of circumstances and we're not the same as the Mexican workers who have circumstances unique to *them*. How they organize is going to rise or fall on the kind of leadership the Mexican labor movement can produce. The same thing here.

These corporations have got the world and are able to play off one nation against another. There's a lot of resentment here, but it manifests itself wrongly in racism. What has the labor movement done about it? Nothing! This guy Bieber, my president, he's in love with Washington. He *loves* to go there and testify in front of the senators. He's forgotten his own history. At conferences and conventions when somebody talks about a national strike, people stand up and give ovations. And that damned podium is scared shitless of it.

Is a new leadership emerging?

No. There's a lack of education. There's no consciousness of what trade unions are about. There are careers in unions. The turnover in secondary leadership in the union is phenomenal. They don't have any background in union history or anything. It's a popularity contest. It's just, "Hey, let me get my nose in the trough for a while; it's *my* turn." They fall in bed with management. They're told not to rock the boat. It's not a very pretty picture.

You can't have solutions to problems when you've had an agreement at the top that the best interests are served by total cooperation with corporations. That only leads to corporate abuse. The leadership of the labor movement is circling the wagons, continuing to protect this shrinking organized group. They are not addressing the needs of the $5-an-hour people. We've got to be a whole lot more vocal in relationship to the problems of the unemployed and the underemployed and the question of health care. We only give lip service. Are we using the full power of the labor movement? No! Is Kirkland using the power of the organization? No! He's relying on the politicians in Washington—who, by the way, now perceive organized labor as being weak. The solutions to the problems confronting us today lie within our own history.

Marc Stepp

I came to Detroit in 1941 from Evansville, Indiana, and was hired at Chrysler in 1942. For twenty years I worked in the factory as an arc welder and machine operator. In 1946, after discharge from the

Marc Stepp is the director of the Institute for Labor and Community Affairs at the University of Detroit Mercy, former vice-president of the United Auto Workers, member of the national board of the NAACP and of the National Committee of the Democratic Party.

army, I attended classes in collective bargaining, parliamentary law, and public speaking that were held by the UAW Workers Education Program. In 1952 I enrolled at the University of Detroit's downtown campus, majoring in accounting and minoring in economics. I felt I needed to know *something* about economics if I was going to be effective in collective bargaining for the union. It took me eleven years, all at night, to complete the degree.

In 1967 I accepted Walter Reuther's invitation to come to Solidarity House to work as an international representative, negotiating contracts with small companies and Chrysler plants. Then in 1974 a Black vice-president was killed, and I got elected to fill that spot. The UAW has four vice-presidents for North America. Vice-presidents become directors of different departments. At one time I had twenty-three departments and Chrysler was just *one* of them. I became the director and chief negotiator for the union at Chrysler, and I had constant contact with Lee Iacocca. When Chrysler almost went bankrupt in 1979, Lee and I brought together a commonality between the union and management. This resulted from a desire to survive.

Detroiters are resilient people. Workers have generated self-respect by not allowing the boss or anybody else to push them around. The labor movement has protected the workers' dignity and self-respect. There's been that daring, that stick-to-it-iveness, that stand-up-ish kind of attitude that workers have generated. It's made this a *tough* town. Because of the peaks and valleys of the economic system in Detroit, people have learned how to adjust. You don't find too many people committing suicide over some economic loss.

Our social and political problems here are underscored by economics. Detroit and all other major older American cities, particularly in the East and Midwest, are being injured because of the change from an industrial-industry base to a service-industry base. You don't have to be an economist to understand *that.* What we've got to do better with Congress and with the national executive leadership is to put our foot down and say, "We're not going to permit any further hemorrhaging of our industrial base in this country." But we've got to educate the local base so they understand what's happening in the nation and to *them,* and to demand change in the federal government policy.

Some kind of national planning should be considered in an economy that's being devastated. We could do like other countries have been doing. Germany has a law of "codetermination," which means that in any company that hires 500 or more employees, 50 percent of the board of directors must be workers. Plant managers are elected by the workers. This is *industrial democracy.* There's a considerable literature on this subject.

222

There's debate within union circles about industrial democracy. Some are against participatory management concepts. They say that the role of unions is to represent workers and they have no business dealing with management. Owners are supposed to run the company, and the workers do the work. My advocacy of industrial democracy is codetermination, German style. For two or three years before I retired we had these discussions with Chrysler management. They became advocates of it. I made speeches to the workers to encourage higher quality in their work to save Chrysler and save their jobs.

We in this country don't think as broadly as we should. We fear the persons who oppose us and the labels they give us. We're intellectually very fearful people. Let's look at health. We should be talking about a national health service in this country. But, man, if you mention a national health *service* you're a mossback communist. [*Laughs*]

223

In 1977, the Community Reinvestment Act was passed. That act mandates banks to put some of their profits back into the communities where they derived those profits, for community improvement loans, home improvement mortgages, etc. I'm presently on the steering committee of a coalition of organizations that negotiated with the ten largest banks in Detroit. Now the banks are competing like hell with each other to get the money out there. Our next project centers on insurance companies. Chrysler Finance and General Motors Acceptance Corporation, among others, are targeted.

We're going to target the administration of the city of Detroit— many are Coleman Young supporters—and find out why all the vacant land in this city has remained vacant for so long. We need to create some industrial parks with attractive buildings within the city. They don't have to be out in a cornfield. We're not going to get involved in the matter of downtown versus the neighborhoods.

Would corporations make a profit?

Oh yes! It's not a welfare operation. We recognize they're not going to pay $18 an hour. They pay what they can afford to pay. Walter Reuther said years ago, "A half a loaf is better than no loaf." Eight dollars an hour is better than *no* dollars. Trade unionists are just as proud today as they were before. The UAW had a million and a half industrial workers. Today there are probably 750,000 industrial workers in the union, but the membership is over one million. Who are the new ones? They're 22,000 white-collar workers in Michigan, for example. All the lawyers in the law department in the city of Detroit belong to the UAW. All ancillary personnel at Wayne State University belong to the UAW, as well as at Wayne County Community College and Cornell University. People in the legal department of the city of New York belong to the UAW. We're replenishing our membership rolls, although we have a different classification of workers as members. The genius of the philosophy of replenishment is not being hemmed in by some narrowly focused worker category. I call this "rejuvenating the spirit of trade unionism."

Mike Kerwin

I was born in Chicago in 1924 and came to Detroit in 1950. To me, Detroit was a better town to live in. The neighborhoods were nicer, the attitudes of people were better. It was more unionized than Chicago. It was a more open town. You could get a factory job with a good wage. Detroit's a city with single-family houses. It's a pretty city. Almost every street had trees all up and down. The Dutch elm disease took many of those out. It's about the same area as Chicago, but with about half the population in the '50s: Chicago had about 4,000,000 and Detroit had about 2,000,000.

I got a press operator's job at the American Metal Products plant on the west side. I got active in Local 174. In 1953 I went on the staff of the UAW education department. I worked for the union until I retired in 1989, except for a period of nine years when I served as Detroit deputy city clerk from 1974 to 1983 under Jim Bradley.

In the last ten to fifteen years I've been angered by media people who come from out of town to do a quick analysis of the problems of Detroit: "Is Detroit flat on its back?" "Is Detroit the sewer of the universe?" They'll show an abandoned factory and a "typical" neighborhood, which will be one of those really devastated places within a mile of downtown where half the houses are boarded up and the weeds are growing everywhere and the dogs are running down the street. They ignore the majority of Detroit neighborhoods with streets of well-kept houses. Some are low-cost, some are high-cost, but the people work hard to keep them painted and there is green in the front of the houses. There are hundreds of thousands of people taking great interest in keeping up their neighborhood. You *never* see that on television.

One thing that hurt us in the late '60s was the "HUD disease." It was an awful disaster. The HUD [Housing and Urban Development] program was part of L. B. Johnson's Great Society program, intended to provide decent housing for low-income people through assisted mortgages. No sooner had the law been on the books than Nixon

Mike Kerwin recently retired from the education department of the United Auto Workers.

224

came in. Our great genius from Michigan, George Romney, was put in charge of the HUD Department. The thing just ran hog-wild. It was corrupt. Everybody was raking money out of it: real estate agents, insurance people, rehabilitation people, inspectors, appraisers. People were pushed into these houses like Latin American countries were pushed into taking loans after the oil crisis. This whole pack of jackals—the appraisers, builders, real estate agents, mortgage agents— often would come through and reap more than one helping. They would falsify many of the details so they could keep a house in play.

By the late '60s some of us began thinking that we had won all the battles that needed to be won. That's about the time the other side began creeping in and preaching their free-market theory that everybody seeks his own advantage, selfishly dedicating himself/herself to personal gain, and the unseen hand would bring about a net benefit to everybody. That's the sheerest hogwash that could be possibly thought of. Gus Scholl, president of the Michigan CIO for many years, had a definition of trickle down: "Trickle down is when the horses eat, the sparrows feed."

If the companies wanted to get away from us in the '50s, they would move down to Mississippi or Alabama, or someplace, and set up a plant there. Under the laws of the United States labor would follow them. Sometimes our organizers would be tarred and feathered, and sometimes they'd be murdered. Race would be set against race more seriously down there. In the '70s they discovered that the technology had developed sufficiently that, instead of running to Alabama or Mississippi, they could go to Taiwan or Mexico or Brazil, or you-name-it, and make the stuff and get it back to our market here just as conveniently as they could have done from Arkansas.

We've lost hundreds of small manufacturing, tool, and machine shops that were in Detroit when I first came here. You can't get them back. You walk down West Fort Street and you can't help but cry. When I first came to town I lived in that neighborhood. At Scotten there was the Yankee Girl tobacco factory. At Clark Street there was the Timken Axle, and further down there was American Brass, Anaconda, General Motors, on and on. They're *all* gone. Whatever criticisms I have of the Big Three, and they would be many, we *need* them. We have to be constantly on them to keep them here and keep those jobs here. It's ten times harder bringing in new plants than saving the old ones.

I have a sticker on my car that says "Buy Union, Buy American." I don't think that's xenophobic at all. If they want to set up automobile plants in Mexico, I say, fine, let's help them set up the plants to sell automobiles to Mexicans. Let's help Mexican workers get enough money so they can buy a Mexican-made automobile. If they're gonna sell automobiles in this country that are 90 percent made in Taiwan, Singapore, the Philippines, and Mexico—where people make 10 percent of *our* wages—then we've got to become protectionist. Free trade applied to labor standards is poisonous.

One of the reasons for the economic dismemberment of this country is that corporations, with the connivance of the federal government, whipsaw states and communities against each other and get them to bargain down. A headline in the *Detroit News* read, "Tennessee and Arkansas come to Detroit to grovel for new Saturn plant." That manifestation of the free market is a poisonous injection into the economic lifestream of this country. You get communities and states degrading themselves to get the scraps off the table.

In the '20s the economic philosophy and atmosphere was very similar to today: *laissez-faire*, free market, private profit enterprise. It fell apart. A program came together that was promoted by Democrats, socialists, cooperatists, progressives, populists. They elected a patrician man as president who had the knack of pulling people together in support of that program. The labor movement, that had been stagnating for decades, found a new life when the CIO organized the unorganized industrial workers and provided political leadership. There also was an active and innovative left outside of the Democratic Party. I think they *can* play a good role to keep jabbing at complacent Democrats, among other things. It would be a very helpful thing today. Detroit could very well be one of the places where that might begin to happen.

We need a national policy to stop the export of good-paying American jobs to wage-slave jobs in other countries where the product is reimported into this country. We need legislation and other action to stop union busting. We need a higher floor on the minimum wage. We need an extension of the plant-closing legislation which we got in token form two years ago. We need to go back to our battle for domestic content laws for imports. We need to give workers some kind of a domestic property right to the job they hold. We need health and safety on the job. We need to continue to fight against racial discrimination and discrimination against women.

Most of mainline so-called Democratic candidates for public office won't go near those policies with a twenty-foot pole. Michael Dukakis was here on Labor Day in 1988 to address a big crowd at Hart Plaza. His people were comparing it to Harry Truman's 1948 campaign kickoff on Labor Day in Detroit when he was the underdog. Truman came to Detroit and gave them hell. He used the word "union" forty-seven times, the word "strike" six times, the word "work-

226

ers," etc. Dukakis didn't use the words union, workers, or strike at *all*. With that kind of *nothing* candidate, where are you gonna go? We were stuck with him. Not since Hubert Humphrey have the Democrats put up a candidate who would talk about stepping on the toes of vested corporate interests and requiring them to civilize themselves.

We need to resurrect an adventurous governmental spirit that uses the powers of the government and the law to become a player in the economy and to act as a counterweight to the free-market forces in defense of the common good of the entire population. The political establishment is discussing noneconomic questions. It's not willing to take on the corporations or the financiers.

Part 7   *Theology for the People*

It seems the "church" has been around forever, but
now it seems like it's maturing in Detroit. Churches are
beginning to say, "Wow, we have people who come
here every day asking us for food, but we keep turning
them away. Is that part of our mission?" People from
the National Conference of Black Churches said that
Black churches in this country deposit ten billion dollars every Monday. I know all that money doesn't go to
run the facility. Some of that money is sitting and waiting. Even a small piece of that pool could have a tremendous impact for economic development. What
good is a church physical structure if the city around
you crumbles and people can't work?

> Angela Brown, Deputy Director, Warren Connor
> Community Development Coalition

SINCE SLAVE DAYS, the African-American church has had a tradition of protection and development of the flock. This mission continues in full force today in Detroit, where survival of the people is a
strong core of theology. That is true also for many of the remaining
churches with white clergy.

In his testimony in this book, James Boggs said there were 2,300
churches in Detroit, excluding the storefronts. That would be about
one for every 435 Detroiters. Some, like Hartford Memorial Baptist
Church, have thousands of members. Most of them, though, are like
Reverend Ron Spann's Church of the Messiah, with a hundred or so
members. Big or small, church life in Detroit is pretty important to a
lot of people.

Many churches in Detroit are special because they advance the
ideas of salvation and survival at the same time. Deindustrialization
and population shifts altered the composition and mission of
churches. There are fewer white Catholics because they moved to the
suburbs. There are more Black Protestants who moved from the Deep
South.

In this section six center-city clergymen express different theological foundations for their urban ministries. They're different by
race (three Black, three white), by church affiliation (Baptist, United
Methodist, Episcopalian, Catholic), and by the affluence of their congregations. But their ministries reflect a common compassion for the
downtrodden. They have not abandoned the secular needs of the
people. They represent the best of the church.

Ed Rowe

I've been in Detroit since I was four months old. My family originally was from Ottawa, Canada. I grew up in about fifteen different places in the city. My father was a boiler operator and refrigeration engineer, first for Briggs and then for Chrysler. I was going to work for Chrysler and raise a family and be like my father.

When I was at Denby High School I dropped out of the church altogether. Then I moved to a house on Seven Mile and Morang that was a block away from the United Methodist Church. One day the John Birch Society was picketing the church. Another day, Donald Lobsinger [right-wing populist] was picketing the church and I said, "Hum, I don't know what's going on in that church, but it can't be all bad." I went over and got to know this pacifist pastor who didn't believe in killing anything, for any reason. Out of the relationship with him, I began to understand Christianity much differently. This was probably in 1959 to 1960.

I went to Adrian College, a Methodist college, and then decided that I would go into the ministry. I became an intern in a church on the west side of Chicago, working for a Black pastor by the name of Ulysses Doss. [Martin Luther] King was killed, Chicago was burned. A group of us—Seminarians Organized for Racial Justice—did a lot of demonstrating. We shut down the seminary so we could get a look at how its curriculum was relating to the reality in the city.

Ulysses Doss used to sit us down on the floor in his office at seven in the morning and study Karl Barth. Then we would go out on the street and try to apply both the biblical and theological teachings. The whole idea was that your head and your feet, and everything in between, needed to be integrated in your ministry. That became a baptism by fire for me. I decided that taking a "normal" church was not where I was called.

When I got out of seminary I went to work for the South Shore Commission on the south side of Chicago under one of the lieutenants of Saul Alinsky. I tried to learn something about community organizing, which I thought was critical to my understanding of the Gospel. I wanted to learn how people receive power, a key theological question. How do you end up feeling less helpless? If you're trying to figure out how the church stands against the gods of the culture and offers an alternative to a community, then you're in the right struggle. We don't need a church that confirms the greed of the world or

Ed Rowe is the pastor of Cass United Methodist Church and Center on Cass Avenue in the Wayne State University area.

flies the American flag on one side of the chancel and the Christian flag on the other.

Does your theology differ from traditional religious organizations?

I think it's pretty solidly biblical and in that sense pretty traditional. I think the church has gotten away from its tradition. The church has become not a sanctuary from the war, after you've been out there fighting for justice and humanity and healing, but simply sanctuary from never having to go to war. We now have budget cuts in the state of Michigan where we've decided that we're not going to pay for poor people's glasses, hearing, oxygen, and physical therapy. I'm part of a faith that follows a Christ that restored vision and people's ability to walk and a God that breathed into people the breath of life. You look for ways to continue to do that for people because you believe that's what, in fact, you're called to do. As a people, we've climbed into the hiding place before we ever had anything to hide from, before we ever engaged the issue. I don't consider myself to be very religious, but more in the struggle to be faithful. "Religious" to me means the institutional church.

We take people, eighty to ninety strong, to sleep in church base-ments. People walk in and say, "I used to work with you, I used to go to school with you; I can't believe it, I thought homeless people were different than me; I've discovered a very scary thing: homeless people are just *like* me; in fact, if I had missed three paychecks I'd be sleep-ing right here with you." People come to me and say, "You know, I've been a member of this church for thirty years and I've finally figured out what it's about; I've finally met Jesus here in this basement."

Christians are called to believe that everything can be converted to Christianity, even the institutional church. But that's difficult. Jesus had the same struggle, you know. We had this text in the lecture today about the widow's mite, about the widow who gave it all, and Jesus, in my reading, is *furious* at a temple that would require that. I suppose Jesus is, if not an anticleric, at least anti-institution. Cass Church keeps me faithful. You can't have this kind of pain in your face and forget. I have a place where people preach to me and keep me honest in terms of the faith.

It's an evangelistic decision to say, "There's bread here! Can't you see people are dying on the street? If you don't take this power that you have and act, you are going to destroy your credibility as a Chris-tian. You're not just going to be responsible for this person's blood, but you're going to destroy your *own* spirit if you don't act." That's a salvation statement.

The Black church changed my life. I wouldn't be doing what I'm doing without the Black church, without the Ulysses Dosses of the world. The liberation struggle of African-Americans in the church . . . my understanding of my own white racism . . . that has changed my life. I wouldn't know the Gospel nor understand crucifixion or resurrection the way that I do without the Black church.

I don't think there are many Cass Churches in the white church. I think there ought to be more ministries where people are doing liturgy in the street, like Jesus. That's not a partisan act; it's a political act. We have a kind of timidity, self-protectionism, and fear. No amount of police or military force, and no amount of money in the bank is going to get you that security you're looking for. Security comes from getting out there and putting it on the line and realizing that you didn't *die*, and even if you *did* die, you're OK.

235

I feel *blessed*. I have *fun* doing this. This isn't drudgery for me; I wouldn't *be* here if it was. I feel sorry for people who have it all but end up with nothing. I talk to those folks all the *time*. We get sucked into, "Where's the next big church you can go to and the next big parsonage you can live in?" I don't need that. There's no place they *have* that's any better than where I am. When I came to Cass they said, "We want a pastor that will keep this church on the street." To go someplace where you have to take ten years to ever get to the point when people would say anything like that to you, now *that's* work. Compared to that, this is a piece of cake. One of the things that's different at Cass than most other churches is that the board of the church is the board of the outreach ministry. The pastors are the administrators and overseers of the projects.

We have a ministry for developmentally disabled adults. We relate to thirty-five adult foster care homes. It's one of the few such social-recreation programs in this area, if not in the state. People who work in sheltered workshops, for example, will come here in the evening and get involved in recreation, arts and crafts, reading and writing, musical contests, writing contests. They discover how to become a community and unravel from their own fears. I've watched people open up who wouldn't talk to anybody when they first came.

Then there's a program for developmentally disabled seniors. People who had retired from a sheltered workshop had no place to go except to their foster care home where they watched TV or looked out the window for the rest of their lives. So we created a retirement center for them. There's a building, a staff, a series of activities, field trips. It has physical therapists and activity staff people specifically trained with and for the developmentally disabled.

We have 300 to 350 people who eat breakfast here every morning. There are 500 to 600 people who eat lunch here on Saturday. There are 70 seniors who eat lunch here every day. We used to have a very active packaged food program that was probably 50 to 60 percent state and federal grants, and then the state cut 40 percent of that. At a time when 90,000 people are penniless with the budget cuts, we have 40 percent less ability to help them find something to eat. We're redoing a piece of our building to store food gleaned from restaurants and food distributors. We're looking to feed several hundred people a week by giving them enough food in a bag for ten meals. They can provide for their own family with some kind of integrity, and not have to bring the kids to a soup kitchen.

Our area had 1,500 people on the city waiting list for home-delivered meals, so we started delivering ourselves. We got some money from the Detroit Area Office on Aging and the Skillman Foundation. The funds that Detroit can get from the federal and state governments is not near the amount needed for the number of people who need the service. We had a huge waiting list and still have one that's still too large. What's the difference if you have to wait for 1,500 or 500 people to die till you get your meal?

We have a senior activities center with traditional recreation and field trips, and also education around insurance and other things that people need to know about the aging process. Many of these people don't have any family that relates to them at all. At their funeral there will be members of the staff, and that's it, because they *were* substance abusers at one time, because they moved to the corridor, because . . . who knows?

One of the most distressing facts came from a report from HEW [Department of Health, Education and Welfare]. It said that 78 percent of people who were homeless had no friends and no relatives who cared. So there's this acute loneliness in the community that we try to relate to through the senior center. We also have a senior citizens outreach program where we go out into the community and try to help people become, or remain, independent as long as possible. The nursing homes where we put poor people are horrendous. We've just had the state cuts for home care services, so more and more people are being forced into nursing homes that are less and less able to take care of people. They weren't staffed adequately to start with.

I hope there's never a time when the church isn't involved in serving the community. On the other hand, I hope there's never a time when the church allows government to say, "We're not responsible for the common good any more; government's job is not to protect the people who are most vulnerable." That's not the way I understand government. That's *exactly* what a government is for. You talk about national security, that's *part* of the national security.

236

When the speaker of the Michigan House said he made a deal with the governor that he couldn't go back on, so he helped him cut out GA [general assistance], I said, "What happened to the deal you made with the people; what happened to your oath of office?" Part of my job is to keep exposing things like this. I need to be making sure that *this* church becomes the *conscience* for a community.

Ron Spann

I'm the sixth generation from Ann Arbor. During the 1960s I devoted much of my life to the civil rights and antiwar movements. I was active in Latin America support activities. I spent time in Guatemala, spent time with [education activist and theorist] Ivan Ilitch in Mexico, spent time with Paulo Friere [Brazilian educator for social change]. During the 1968 police riot, I was in Chicago working with [presidential peace candidate] Eugene McCarthy.

I was a good, mainline, liberally oriented Christian before a charismatic change took place which had do to with a much deeper dimension of the personal experience of Jesus Christ as a person. The Jesus Christ I knew was a very prophetic and compassionate and angry and powerful and loving and just savior. That was deepened for me out of this conversion experience. It fed directly into my experience in the last twenty years in Detroit. The emphasis has been on building community. That has been the whole drift of my ministry.

When I came here as pastor in fall '71, things began to come together very quickly. From early '72 until late '87 we launched a "common life group." That was a communitarian expression of church membership where people formed a very *intentional* form of Christian community. We pooled our economic life and lived together literally out of a common purse. Those on salary like myself and outside income earners combined our economics. We provided the living needs of this community, subsidized things happening in the church ministry, and did outreach things as well. We were like a communal group, though I prefer the term communitarian to distinguish us from the counterculture groups of that period. Most of our membership relocated here to the neighborhood from the suburbs, other parts of the city, and out of state, not because it was the nearest Episcopal church, but because of its mission.

Ron Spann is the minister of the Church of the Messiah, an Episcopal church on Detroit's east side.

237

For a long time we were a predominantly white membership because many were coming out of a movement in a lot of the mainline churches to look for something different. I guess they were the straight-laced, middle-class equivalent of what was happening in the counterculture. They made a rather radical departure from the norms of middle-class life out of a religious motivation. Several of us were Black and we tended to be middle class.

Out of that pool of human resources were people like the woman I eventually married. She was a Detroit public school teacher who left her job to start a church-based school that we operated out of a nearby Catholic school building. It began in 1973 and operated for the next thirteen years. We eventually expanded it to six grades. Its attendance was about two-thirds neighborhood children and one-third church children. At its peak the school had about seventy children, including a kindergarten and preschool.

Relocating into the neighborhood became part of a strategy that later on we would call the 3 Rs—Relocation, Reconciliation, and Redistribution—which we borrowed from a Black church leader named John Perkins, who was schooled in the hard knocks of the movement in the '60s.

"Relocation" refers to moving into the area where you're involved in ministry and witness. The idea behind that is that the best leadership in any situation is going to come out of the community itself. People had to test a sense of calling to be here. The motivation as Christians, and what we understood about the reincarnation, is that Jesus moved into a specific human situation in ancient Palestine and became part of it. He didn't commute from the heavenly suburbs, but moved in.

"Reconciliation," the second R, has to do with the religious significance of reconciliation of the gospel. God offers forgiveness and a new life to us as a human race, as sinners, who brings life and renewal in place of sin and death. But it also has the practical dimension of making a new kind of community possible. So being Christians in the twentieth century in the United States means living with a history of racism and alienation between Black and white, of the class issues of rich and poor, and tensions around gender politics. So that's a motivation for us in the ministry of this church to be an interracial membership, in a location and time in history where the races are polarized. It has lots of risks for whites. There's a kind of Tarzan–Jane dimension to it, you know, coming down among the natives to do a good turn, kind of patronage and condescension. I think our membership has been guilty of that, but we've tried to be very self-conscious about dialogue within our membership.

The communitarian group within our membership officially disbanded itself in 1987. It was an "alternative" congregation, a membership within our membership. Why did it disband? Some people left because of life changes, some middle-class folk were having a hard time dealing with our neighborhood, and some left from the mistakes we made in our leadership and government. Most communitarian experiments don't have a very long life span. I think it was remarkable considering it lasted fifteen years. It was very productive and the source of much of our leadership in the church and the neighborhood. It was a very rich time in our lives and in the evolution of this church's ministry.

Now, 90 percent of our membership *still* lives within a four-block radius of this building. We live in a much more conventional manner, looking much more like our neighbors with single families instead of large households of people. I think we're now a lot more accessible to the neighborhood. We've been able to redirect a lot of our energy into the forms of our outreach.

We're about 110 adults and children. In my first ten years here we grew to over 200. Those now coming to the church tend more to come out of the neighborhood. The bridges that we've built through our outreach have a lot of traffic beginning to come back over. That's providing new leadership in the church. I expect membership to grow. In fact, we're going through a modest but real growth right now. That's encouraging, but it's *demanding* because it means training a whole new generation of leadership.

The third R—"Redistribution"—means that we can have a role in helping this neighborhood form linkages with human and material resources so that we can get investors to give us grants or low-interest loans. That involves a recycling, or redistribution, of human skills to help us train leadership for a community that can then govern itself.

We relate to the same bounds as the Island View Association: Mt. Elliot on the west, Baldwin on the east, Jefferson to the south, and Mack to the north. It's about a 100-square-block area with a population close to 20,000. In the last fifteen years 3,000 parcels of real estate have been demolished. That's why it looks like the prairie around here.

We have a housing corporation that's been developing multiunit apartment buildings. Our aim is to create affordable, decent housing for a low- and moderate-income group. We try to develop the buildings as co-ops which later can be owned by the resident group. Well, that's been a real lesson for us. We perceive that ownership is an important piece of community development. Many times we are up against the difference between our goal and the felt needs of someone who wants decent housing, who applies to get into one of our apartment buildings, but does *not* feel a need to be part of a co-op. So we have to talk about cooperative economics, a very sophisticated and difficult form of community organization which requires constant education and struggle. More recently, people have been given the choice of being ordinary rent payers or co-op members from the beginning.

The other outreaches we do are aimed at leadership development, things like our teen youth ministry and our children's ministry, where it's a combination of religiously evangelizing the people to reach the spirit of the people. What we do is more holistic. Also, we try to develop the community in its cultural life, the academic life of kids, their social experience, their recreational experience, so that they can grow. Our aim is to challenge those that we reach not to leave our community, but in fact to come back into it as indigenous leadership.

Is your kind of church unique?

In Detroit we're relatively unique. However, we're part of a movement which has a national expression and we belong, in fact, to a national organization called the Christian Community Development Association. We're talking about holistic ministries which are largely urban, although some are rural, with the aim of dealing with the entire person—body, soul, and spirit—as well as dealing with the environment. They typically have chartered development corporations as an instrument of their work, something like our housing corporation. They operate health clinics, schools, learning centers with computer banks, tutorial programs, etc. We have a neighborhood outreach tutorial program for about sixty-five kids from first through twelfth grade.

Do these initiatives result from government's failure?

Yes, we're a substitution, but I think we're the only show in town that could have worked anyway. Back under the old OEO [Office of Economic Opportunity], the initiatives that came from the War on Poverty were all top down, and ultimately destined to fail. The big piece that I see happening so differently now is that grassroots communities have actually found a way to institutionalize their work. It's very neighborhood specific. Their role as entrepreneurial groups is to take the risks that no one else will take. Another nonprofit sector, the foundations, along with the for-profit sector, and also municipal governments, are grudgingly coming along. There's still plenty of room for government to do something. But we won't make the mistake that was made in the '60s and '70s to abdicate the initiatives to government.

Now, hopefully the die is cast forever for the initiatives to be coming out of the communities. We're having to bring the bureaucrats down into our communities, educate them, and help them understand.

Some communities, like Eastside Community Investments in Indianapolis, are already beginning to produce businesses. They actually got the city of Indianapolis to cede eminent domain to them for about 1,000 acres of abandoned industrial property in their community. We have an industrial corridor like that right here in our Island View neighborhood. It boggles my mind to think that the city of Detroit might cede eminent domain to us, to have our own strategies for enticing businesses to relocate or get community-based businesses going and create jobs here.

241

Can we assume that capital won't come from outside?

Which is one reason we're interested in creating the co-ops here. Our first successful, all-the-way product was the Mustard Tree Co-op across the street from our church here. It's a twenty-four-unit building that was developed between 1978 and 1984. Then it was taken over by the residents of the building. For the first time in Detroit that we know of, a privately owned apartment went co-op, owned and managed by a low- and moderate-income group. They've been on their own ever since. So they now have a capital stake in this neighborhood they didn't have before.

Economics in America has never been democratized. Hopefully, that's what something like co-op economics can help do. Liberalism has been a prevailing philosophy for two or more centuries, but it just isn't working any more. Everything's up for grabs right now. That's why the community group is such an important source of leadership and a real challenge to the Black community. And I'm hopeful. This is a movement that's come of age. It's both secular and religious, and the two often are not antagonistic, but working very closely together.

I've got to go out on the street. . . .

Eddie Edwards

I was born and raised here on the east side where I now live. I still believe this is a good city. We're going through some very difficult times, like other major urban communities across the country. My

Eddie Edwards is the pastor of the Joy of Jesus Church on Camden in the heart of Detroit's east side.

work is very stimulating, challenging, and rewarding. It is my life purpose. I'm a fulfilled person.

At one time my career was well established with AT&T and I could have gone up the corporate ladder. But I decided I wanted to be more involved in helping people in the community rather than helping a corporation earn millions of dollars. It was good training, especially in the methodologies of organizing and planning. I then went to work in the criminal justice system and got real good exposure to the problems related to the most needy citizens. I realized that if we were ever going to get ahead of the situation we needed to work with the children. I then made a decision to start this organization. That decision wasn't made in a vacuum. I firmly believe that God influenced me and directed me to do it.

We started by working with youth through a summer camp program. Our purpose was to reach youngsters as early as possible to help develop their character and potential. The beginnings were crude, but growth-producing, especially for me. Then we started an after-school program for kids. We formed caravans to pick up the kids. We took them on field trips, counseled them, listened to them. We moved into *this* building to have a daily after-school program for kids in the community.

Then the adults asked us to help them and we developed an outreach program, known as the Ravendale Project, to revitalize the community. It's thirty-eight blocks around this building. We've organized the blocks, rehabbed housing, painted. You name it, and we've done it here.

The reasons why youngsters are in crisis is because the very institutions that God ordained to help these youngsters were in crisis: home, family, school, and church. He said that we must develop surrogate communities that will fill the void. That's what I see my colleagues across this city doing. The surrogate communities have defined boundaries and are working to involve the people in making change, taking responsibility, and being accountable.

We realized that once kids reach age nine, the streets had them. So four years ago we started a private school to reach kids at age five. It's an interdenominational Cornerstone system with 240 school days per year and lots of resources. It has a real solid Christ-centered curriculum. Our teachers have taught in other private Christian schools. We're now constructing a new school building.

We've now come to the conclusion that age five is too late for a large number of our children. So we're constructing another building to start working with mothers at the prenatal stage so that they will have healthy babies and make the right decisions that will impact the rest of their lives. We want to help mothers to help their children as soon as they're born so that by the time they're five they're socially adjusted, already reading, and motivated to want to learn. This is the model we hope to spread across the city.

We've found employment for about 160 people. We have a printing training program. Our Camden House New Start in Life program works with ten dysfunctional families with forty-four children to bring them to productive lifestyles.

Our two buildings under construction were made possible by donations from about thirteen people. It's an indication that there are a lot of people out there who care and who are looking for ways to put their money where it's going to make a difference. Probably 85 percent of our resources come from suburbanites. Many of them are former Detroiters who want to participate and give, but they also want to make sure it will count.

Abandoned and boarded-up homes in this community were dotted all over the place. As a result of a survey we took, the community decided that housing should be dealt with. We've rehabilitated seventeen houses and two now are under reconstruction. We did this by providing opportunities for volunteers to get involved in a very planned way. We arrange with HUD [Department of Housing and Urban Development] to lease houses for $10 a month over three years. That gives us access to the houses and we rehabilitate them. The community helps to plan rehabilitations.

Corporations love it. We get most of the materials and resources donated. One donor gave us $50,000 to buy and rehab houses. Church's Lumber donated $30,000 worth of materials. Church's motivation was to be part of what the community of Christ was doing here. Other corporations are involved with us because it's good public relations. They want to be known as contributors to the community because they've extracted dollars from the community. Corporations are concerned about the workforce of the future, the direction of the country, and the fact that morals and values are dissipated. They want to attach themselves to *credible* community organizations. They're now asking, "What can we do to make a difference?" This is a national trend.

Our philosophy here is not to accept government funds, though all my colleagues may not agree with that. Joy of Jesus is a Christian organization. Just because the government gives us money, we don't want it to tell us not to present Judeo-Christian standards to our youngsters. We believe that God started Joy of Jesus and this was his instruction.

243

Thomas Gumbleton

In the early 1960s I studied in Rome for three years at the time of the Vatican Council. I had a firsthand experience of tremendous changes taking place within the Catholic church, especially in its commitment to be involved in the world. One of the key documents from that council was called *The Pastoral Constitution on the Church and the Modern World*. It was a real call and commitment to interact with the world. It gave quite a significant change to the church's direction away from being a "triumphal" church, apart from the world, superior to the rest of society, complete in and of itself. The church prided itself in having the right answer to every question. The way I learned theology was learning all the right answers.

But the Vatican Council called for the church to be more of a community of people, a church struggling to come to greater integrity and recognizing a lot of its failings from the past, and a church committed to being involved with the problems of people in the world. The first sentence of the *Pastoral Constitution* talks about "the joys, the griefs, the hopes, and the anxieties of people everywhere, especially the poor and oppressed, are the joys, the griefs, the hopes, and the anxieties of the Church."

Shortly thereafter I came home to the United States. *The Other America* [Michael Harrington] had been published and evidently had been read by John Kennedy. I read it while still in Rome. I had been somewhat oblivious to poverty in the U.S., even though I'd grown up in the Depression and thought I had some sense what it meant to be poor. But I really didn't. The federal government began the Economic Opportunity Program and cities were getting more and more involved in it. Detroit, with Mayor Jerry Cavanaugh, was connected to the Democratic administration in Washington, so Detroit was going to be a kind of a model in the War against Poverty.

The archbishop asked me to head up the AOP [Archdiocesan Opportunity Program]. We became an agent of the city to carry out some of the federal programs then being developed. At that time Archbishop Dearden was quite open to this sort of thing. My work in AOP got me involved in lots of things then going on in the city. We built some housing. We got into job training programs. One of our big programs was Head Start, recognized by most people as one of the *best* programs that came through.

At the same time, the civil rights movement was developing. The

Thomas Gumbleton is auxiliary bishop of the Catholic Archdiocese of Detroit whose reputation as a humanist-activist extends far beyond the borders of Detroit.

archbishop's committee for human relations was beginning to function within the parishes to work on people's attitudes. We developed Project Commitment, an educational program to help people understand the situation of Black people with regard to jobs, housing, and discrimination. I connected with all of those things. That's what got me started into activism, while being a churchperson at the same time.

The Vietnam War was heating up at that time and I think it was my connection to the antiwar movement that more identified me as being radical. The War on Poverty was pretty well accepted and wasn't perceived as radical. But my antiwar work was seen by more people as political activity, rather than social service activity.

Martin Luther King, Jr. best symbolized the combination of things coming together at that time. His major speech at Riverside Church [New York City] in April 1967 was an attempt to take the civil rights movement into the antiwar movement. He clearly could see the connections: poor people being killed, a poor nation being destroyed, and tremendous amounts of money being diverted for the war. He saw the relationships of poverty, race, and war. He clearly influenced me, especially as I became more and more aware of his deep religious convictions. His commitment to nonviolence challenged me.

Have we learned much?

I don't think we learned much. In fact, our situation is deteriorating. Sometimes when I speak about this I go back to something Dr. King said in that speech in April '67: "Any nation that continues to spend more of its resources on programs of defense than it does on programs of social uplift is a nation approaching spiritual death." That was a prophesy. Instead of heeding his cry we went the other direction.

We live in a culture of violence. Sometimes I'm overwhelmed by the facts, like the number of kids in Detroit who kill other kids. I read an article by a social scientist that said before a youngster is eighteen he or she has seen 26,000 murders on television. That's incredible. You can't be taking that in from the time you're a baby and not have that influence your attitude toward violence. Our nation so quickly turns to violence as a solution to its problems. When we have a problem in Grenada we *invade*. When we want to arrest a drug dealer in Panama we *invade* and kill thousands of people and destroy thousands of homes, and we think nothing of it. The Persian Gulf war is just another example of how we choose a violent solution rather than try to discover a way to settle conflicts nonviolently.

This culture of violence is destroying us spiritually. In my own tiny parish last week three murdered people were buried, and this is a *tiny* parish. In a little community like that, murder is happening to family members in *those* numbers. We're into a degree of violence in this city and this country that exceeds anything I ever knew. I grew up in Detroit and I know what the streets were like thirty or forty years ago. It's just not the same.

The lack of job opportunities in the city leaves so many young people without any resources. The kind of jobs people used to get without a lot of education and sophisticated skills just aren't around any more. In theological jargon this is called "institutionalized or structural violence" or "social sin." Social sin is a situation in which some level of society is organized in such a way that it works to the detriment of other individuals or groups. An easy example, of course, would be apartheid in South Africa where the whole nation is organized to the detriment of the Black people and the Colored people. Very much of *our* economic system is organized to the detriment of Black people or other minorities or women.

Would the church call the current cuts of 90,000 general assistance recipients from Michigan's social services rolls a social sin?

I would call it that. They're organizing the state on an economic basis that eliminates that segment of society from any chance to participate. They don't have the education or skills, so they can't participate in this "new vision" that Governor Engler is promoting for the state. It's like the "new world order" that George Bush talks about. It's great for people already benefiting from the system, but those who aren't are pushed further out of the system.

Some people will say, "You can't blame *me* for that." But the moral theologian says, "You *are* responsible for social sin if you help to make the decisions as a leader, or if you *vote* for the people who make those decisions. Then it becomes your *personal* sin." This doesn't allow very many people off the hook.

In 1971 the Senate of Bishops meeting in Rome first came up with this analysis of social sin. They said, "Action for justice and participation in the transformation of the world are constitutive dimensions in the preaching of the Gospel." If you're gonna preach the Gospel or live the Gospel of Jesus Christ then action for justice and participation in the transformation of society are essential. So it's a call to enter into the political order. Our task is to keep on trying to transform the social order into one that is just and that brings the benefits of society to all, and helps to distribute goods of the world to all, not just to a few.

Catholic teaching *always* insists that people have a right to private property; however, there are social obligations that go with it, and *no* one has an absolute right to anything. That got lost a little bit during the '30s and '40s and '50s when there was this tremendous effort to stop the "evil empire" from taking over the world.

The Justice and the World document of 1971, and many other Catholic social teaching documents, have tried to bring the whole thing back into balance. The state should regulate the use of private property and the way it's distributed, and we ought to organize a society in which private property is recognized but not absolute. Just the very opposite is happening in our own country.

The U.S. tax laws, especially since 1980, have brought about our shift in wealth ownership. It's a systemic, structural thing. It flies in the face of what would be Catholic social teaching. We haven't heard the Catholic bishops, as church leaders and as religious teachers, saying very much about it. We published a pastoral letter in 1986 on the U.S. economy, but in that letter we never challenged the system. We tried to say how we could make it work more effectively, but we never really analyzed the system itself and what was happening structurally. So the letter was somewhat of a failure.

There's a sentence in one of Paul VI's encyclicals called "On Developing the People" that came out in '67 and is one of the most powerful. He said, "No one has the right to keep for his or her own use *anything* beyond their need when others lack the necessities." Now if you took that sentence seriously, how could you be a millionaire? If you were to say that to a chairman of General Motors who may be a practicing Roman Catholic, he couldn't accept it.

I see the greatest hope for Detroit in strengthening the small community organizations throughout the city. My parish helped to start Core City Neighborhoods. We work on problems like crack, crime, housing, jobs, and all those things. It's more than providing services, it's an empowering kind of thing, trying to get people in the neighborhood doing things for themselves and challenging the city. If we can convince the people that they can make a difference by getting involved in their own neighborhood, and then get a city administration that would reinforce what they're trying to do, we could make Detroit a model city again.

Charles Adams

My family was dedicated to workers' rights and the rights of the African-American community. My paternal grandfather was a minister in rural South Carolina, headquartered in Orangeburg. My maternal grandparents were also from rural South Carolina. My grandfather moved to Augusta, Georgia, where he led a strike against a railroad

Charles Adams is the pastor of Hartford Memorial Baptist Church.

company there in the early 1920s. When all the fellows got called back to work, they left him off because he had been a troublemaker. Since he couldn't find any other work he moved up here and brought his political fight with him. He was one of the first members of Ford Local 600. So the fight was in him.

Local 600 was organized in Hartford Church with the approbation of Reverend Charles A. Hill, who was my immediate predecessor and a real go-against-the-stream fighter for the rights of poor people, working people, Black people, Japanese-Americans. Almost any kind of an oppressed group that you could name found a resting place under his umbrella. He was very cosmopolitan and univeralistic in his view. The meat of his sermons did not seem to me to be tilted in the direction of his ideological commitment. I didn't get that much difference in his preaching than any other Baptist preacher.

But he would comment before the sermon about the political issues and after the sermon he would give political directions to the congregation concerning whom they should support and whom they should avoid. He also would encourage them to be politically active: "You've come from the South, you could not register, you could not vote. You are now in the North, you can register, you can vote, so you need to develop a sense of civic responsibility." He would help them to make that transition.

I came to consciousness under Reverend Hill's ministry. In 1969 I took his ministry after his retirement. My parents chose his church as the church they could identify with. It was a real transition for them to make because he was a northerner. They had never known a minister who hadn't been born in the South and who didn't have all that you would expect in an old-fashioned southern minister, including a certain kind of melodic moan at the end of the sermon which Black people understand and are very attuned to. You can't get that from a northerner, because a northerner is more assimilated into white, majoritarian culture and theology, so you didn't get that type of African emotionalism in his presence or in his preaching.

But they got something else from Charlie Hill. They got a man who was holistic in his theological view. His brand of Christianity demanded activism in society on behalf of the oppressed, the underdog. In that sense, he broke stride with his teacher and trainer, the Reverend R. L. Bradby, Sr., who was pastor of Second Baptist Church, downtown, from 1910 until 1946. Reverend Hill had grown up under Reverend Bradby even as I grew up under Reverend Hill. Reverend Hill agreed with Reverend Bradby that the church should be relevant to the social position and social struggle of the people. But whereas Reverend Bradby wanted to accommodate them to certain structures

248

upon which they were dependent, such as Ford Motor Company, Reverend Hill came in on the side of the labor movement, the worker, the underdog.

If you go all the way back, Black churches—particularly the Baptist church and the African Methodist Episcopal Zion church and the Christian Methodist Episcopal church—always have been distinct because they had to be more than a sacerdotal or purely religious institution. They had to be social from the very beginning. They had to educate, they had to be the focus for the education of the slaves and for those who were set free from slavery because the predominating society did not do it. If you look at Morehouse, Spellman, Benedict, Morris, Florida, Baptist College, Florida Memorial Baptist College, Arkansas Baptist, Leland—all of those colleges in the South grew out of   **249** the Black church. That was the only institution that was dedicated to the education of Black people. Also, the burial societies and the charity funds—the safety net for those who were going to fall through to utter ruin—the church provided that.

At a later time when political opportunities were made available to us, it was the church, and sometimes the minister himself, who would get out there and run for office because he was the one the people could identify with and trust. All the way from its beginning, no Black church in slavery could be aloof from the issue of freedom. They had to pray for it, and work for it, and keep the people together, and sing. As I read Black history, the early conventions of Black people were usually held at churches because they were big enough to hold a great number of people, and the commitment was there to a faith that was relevant to the struggle for freedom.

Today Black people do not have ownership and control of any other institution than the church; not the schools, banks, factories. The church is still the only institution that can really galvanize and organize the race. We're having to provide a certain self-esteem for our people that they have not been able to achieve in any other sphere. A person can be quite outstanding in the church who has not achieved distinction in any other sphere of endeavor. The church still is sort of the only thing we've got. Therefore, it cannot be aloof to our basic human, psychological, emotional, and economic needs. So people do come to church with their economic problems and the church has to do something about it in terms of charity, building and rehabilitating housing, creating jobs, buying up land and making sure that that land can and will hire people, can and will enhance our neighborhood, can and will add to the economic viability of the people. You just have to do it. There's no way you can back out of it now.

Agape House (a New Testament noun for "love") took off here

ten years ago with such great fire and fervor. It's a social service ministry across the street that provides medical services to the afflicted, legal counsel for those who can't afford it. I said, "Now look, we're out here on James Cousins now (we used to be down at Hartford and Milford in a nice cozy, quiet community), at the crossroads, and people are suffering. I have all of you beautiful middle-class people (we have a good number of those) who have made it in medicine, law, education, industry, or business, so now I need you to help build an Agape House so that those who have fallen through Reagan's safety net can be sustained." If they need food, we'll feed them; if they need clothes, we'll clothe them; if they need medical treatment, we'll give it to them; if they need legal advice, we'll provide that; if they need counseling, we're here for them.

As a stopgap measure, I would like to see churches and community organizations in the job-creation area. But I think we need more than mom 'n pop movements and little neighborhood things. We have to have some megaeconomic activity going on in Detroit. I don't think it's going to take place by industry alone. It's not going to take place by churches or community organizations alone. It certainly can't take place by government alone. I don't see any model for this anywhere in the country, but it will require big industry, in cooperation with local, state, and perhaps federal government, with community organization or church to trigger it. The church has to somehow organize the neighborhood to approve the activity and the acquisition of the land. So you get everybody working together to make something happen in a very large way.

Fourteen years ago the purchase of Hartford required participation from a white bank and a majority-white religious denomination. That's the only way we're going to make much happen today. We may give considerable support to a Black institution, to a Detroit-only institution, but we better have a hand in some other institutions so that we can bring them together to make something happen on a large scale. The Black churches should begin to be very intentional about that. We're going to have to be collaborative. We're not doing anything together and we're not sitting down together to see what we can do to make Detroit whole, not just what we can do to make Hartford or some other church outstanding. I said that from my pulpit last Sunday. Here we are knocking each other down, competing for members and support, when we need to build each other up.

Let me do a little dreaming. Suppose, rather than Hartford having a housing corporation, why don't we have one megachurch housing corporation that wants to produce housing, here this time, over there that time? Maybe it wouldn't be in my neighborhood, but

250

I'm part of what's happening on the far east side and maybe it would happen next time in *this* neighborhood and the far east side can take some pride in what has happened on the west side.

You'd have to have a corporate structure of churches joining together to form a nonprofit or for-profit corporation that can do business: housing, factories, hospitals, etc. They'd have to raise money through donations. We'll probably have to leverage because you're not going to be able to mortgage the church properties since the churches aren't going to let you do that.

Detroit is going to turn around. The land is valuable. We're on an international border. We have plenty of water. We have fine volunteer organizations. I think the question is, Will those of us who are Black and poor have any stake in it at all, or will it turn around in such a way that we are left out of it? Those of us who have anything, had better hold on to it and maintain it well. We must not panic and sell the land that we do own. We're going to have broad interests and commitments that take us beyond the narrow working of our own selfish, individualistic institutions. When Hartford does more of that and Greater Grace does more, and we meet somewhere out there working on the same agenda, then I think we're going to get somewhere.

251

Hugh White

I'm a fourth-generation Scotch-Irish Detroiter. My maternal grandfather was the captain of *The City of Cleveland, III,* one of the great passenger ships of the Detroit-Cleveland Navigation Company. My paternal grandfather was a pipefitter for forty years with the White and Fisher Plumbing Company at Fort Street and Third Avenue in Detroit. I was raised on Detroit's west side between Linwood and Dexter. As an early teenager, I was a part of the Buena Vista gang. We each had a knife in our hightop boots. The gang was a mix of Anglo-Saxons and Jews. Later I was a day student at Cranbrook Academy for five years and built up a prejudice against those "rich brats," and I *still* have a healthy prejudice against them. I've always thought dialectically about the business of capitalism and poverty and what that does to people.

I consider myself a serious theologian. I did a fair amount of work

An Episcopal priest, Hugh White occupies an office in the headquarters of the Episcopal Diocese of Michigan, near Wayne State University.

under Reinhold Niebuhr at Union Seminary. I've also been interested in the connection between thinking and acting. I've always been disgusted that they separated those two. I always felt that theory must come out of practice.

The Scripture, the Koran, the holy words wherever you meet them, are anecdotal. Out of that comes the theory which can only be understood if you know the context. The meaning is not in the theory, it's in the action. For some reason, we Anglicans messed that up. [*Laughs*] I could never be a fundamentalist. I'm a great admirer of [Italian socialist theorist] Antonio Gramsci.

My work in the DIM [Detroit Industrial Mission] is a good example of this. We had eleven missions around the country at one point. There's still one going in Peurto Rico. I was part of DIM for seventeen years and then became national director. DIM was entangled in affirmative action for Blacks, women, and in the rights of workers to control their own work and sharing in the faults and successes of the work, both economically and socially. If you're going to have a good workforce, you have to allow workers to decide what it is they do best. When we first got into that it was looked down upon. It is now recognized and accepted practice.

The anomie in Detroit assembly plants is worse today. The ideal for production in almost every shop, including commercial establishments like J. L. Hudson's, is the computer and the control room. If you go way out Jefferson Avenue to the "Seven Virgins" [smokestacks] and go into that old, lovely Detroit Edison power plant, there are no people. There are still twenty-six toilets. Ten or twelve people run that whole damned unit, including the incoming coal. And those people are bored to death. We must be fair about the pluses of technology, how it takes hard work off the back of workers. The new technology saves a lot of arms and legs. That's the dialectic.

The problem is that we have not dealt with the way people are stuck, particularly if they're unemployed or underemployed or have no place to go. One effect of all of this on the body politic is the gap between the rich and poor. I'm astounded by the substantive numbers of rich people.

I think we're in a terrible religious bind right now. I went to church Sunday and was so upset by hearing, "Jesus is the king of everybody and he's the—" I just can't do that any more, and I'm a Christian. The historic Jesus is important to me and always will be. Faith has become a very important thing to me: to have faith in who you are yourself, to have faith in others, to have faith in ideas. Belief doesn't mean much to me any more. The Trinity is poetic, but I can't take it any other way. I don't want to waste time in feeling that I have to convert people to my faith and belief. I see the various faiths of the world making a constructive contribution to the new world order if they will decloak themselves and offer faith, rather than insisting on people having the same belief.

The *hard* work is dealing with what is corrupt and what is truth, whether it's capitalism, communism, religious faith, or nationalism. That's where our heavy work should be done.

The "new world" today is *very* new. It's not what we were talking about in the '60s. It still has race issues, but we should not use race as the singular issue, like it became for many of us in the '60s. It's still very prominent and you can't discard it, but it's not the singular issue.

Is there a singular issue?

Yes. We've got to become more comprehensive and know that is not a difficult thing to do. Even ignorant people have the capacity for comprehension. It's like a bird was born to fly. The human being was born for comprehension, that's our genius, and it's the most lacking.

Part 8   *The Changing Visions of
Detroit's White Male Left*

IN THE 1930s AND 1940s, WHEN DETROIT was predominantly
white, the left had a powerful presence in the union movement and
later in the civil rights movement. This Old Left paved the way for the
white activism of the early 1960s, which developed in tandem with
Black Power.

In the 1960s and early 1970s a number of progressive-minded
whites came to Detroit to join up with similar-minded native-born
white Detroiters. They wanted to mold a political movement, in cooperation with Black progressives, that would incorporate the latest synthesis of thinkers like Marx, Lenin, Mao, Fanon, and Malcolm X.
Their vision was the total reformulation of American society. Detroit
would be one of the opening shots in a protracted war with the holders
of power—maybe the Fort Sumter of the late twentieth-century people's movement. Detroit would be a testing ground for experiments in
social-political change and the tactics and strategy of mobilization.

As people evaluate the results of such bold ambitions, there are
fragmented conclusions. Few places in this country could boast a
greater commitment to the struggle to gain power for the downtrodden. In light of the current racial divisions and lowering of the quality
of life in Detroit, some question whether much was gained. Others,
less cynical in their view, will say that lessons were learned from the
Detroit experience and that it was but a foray in the long-haul struggle to build a society based on justice, freedom, and equality.

To further explore this assessment, this section presents the testimony of leaders and cogent observers who were involved in the heyday of the Detroit radical experiment. They approach the subject
from the perspectives of mature, talented, and experienced white
males. There's a certain eliteness in their real-life status today—most
are directors, professors, lawyers, or authors—the product of their
skills and talents and of the privileges the political culture has invested in their gender and race.

The testifiers have paid their movement dues. They have been in many battles. They studied hard. They took risks and delayed gratifications. They were activists in the radical or reformist activities of the 1960s, like Students for a Democratic Society and People Against Racism. Some hardy souls gravitated into groups like the Motor City Labor League that linked late 1960s politics with the do-or-die, deeply serious politics of the 1970s. A few became cadre in the small revolutionary parties that matured in the 1970s, to try to bring a logical closure to their practice and theory.

But white left politics in Detroit eroded by the end of the 1970s in response to Detroit's economic drummer and the onslaught of the police agencies that represented a threatened ruling class. There was an attrition of forces and difficulty in developing a long-range strategy. Also, some goals—like Black Power in Detroit—seemed to have been achieved.

None of the testifiers is the same today as during the movement days. Most live in the suburbs or in somewhat protected enclaves in the center city. One could judge that nobody has sold out. Perhaps they've mellowed. Perhaps they'll be available for consultation to the new left that will emerge in due course.

Ron Aronson

I was born just a few blocks from where I work, in a place that's now Hutzel Hospital. Every day when I drive to my office I pass my father's old office building where he used to sell insurance, at 3049 West Grand Boulevard, a couple of blocks from the General Motors Building.

It seems that we've gone through an irreversible transformation of the city. It happened to a lot of metropolitan areas, but it happened in Detroit with a hemorrhaging of the middle and upper middle classes and their kinds of employment in the center city. Like a lot of people who were born here and who bleed for the city, I've been watching this hemorrhaging and wondering when and how it would reverse. I'm like many political activists who have absorbed a sense of inevitable progress while waiting for the inevitable reversal. It doesn't seem like anyone can figure out how to make it happen. Each major historic event seems to put another nail in the coffin.

I was just talking to someone yesterday about the cross-district busing decision in the early '70s, which was going to be a pairing of city and suburban schools. We were living in Highland Park [a municipality inside Detroit] at the time. If cross-district busing had gone through, we would continue to live there. It would stabilize that neighborhood. Indeed, whites would move in. The houses were cheap and big, and it was close to downtown. What the hell, if you were paired with Bloomfield Hills, it didn't matter if you lived in Bloomfield Hills or in Highland Park. Your kid would go to one school part of the time and the other school part of the time. The Bloomfield Hills people would make sure that your district would be solid educationally. When cross-district busing was overruled by the Supreme Court, busing was imposed *within* Detroit, which led to the opposite result. Many of the remaining middle-class whites moved out. That was one of the last nails in the coffin.

I live in Huntington Woods, two miles north of Detroit, but Detroit is my home. I'm living in a small, semiprivate bedroom community which has certain features I like. If I had found them in Detroit, I'd be living in Detroit. When I left Highland Park in 1979 the schools were impossible, so we decided we would send our kids to Berkeley schools and move to Huntington Woods. I had a hard time making this decision, but then I said, "Look, in the real world you don't get all of what you want, even the most vital things you need."

A Detroit activist for years, Ron Aronson is a professor at Wayne State University and one of the key scholars of Sartre.

Middle-class Blacks, who now have more nearly equal opportunity as a result of the civil rights movement, move out if they can. They move to places like Southfield and Oak Park, and send their kids to Detroit Country Day School or Roeper if they can afford it. They make use of the mobility that a society of equal opportunity promises them.

What used to happen in ghetto neighborhoods was that because of systematic racial oppression the middle-class Blacks—teachers, lawyers, doctors—lived in their communities. In the ghetto school system the Blacks who became teachers were those with high aspirations and a sense of discipline which they could impose on kids. The most recent layer of the hemorrhaging has been middle-class blacks who can move out, who want better schools, who want safe neighborhoods. What that tends to leave behind in the city are the poor without the "talented tenth," as they were called. So there's more despair than ever. Jobs have moved out, the tax base has moved out, factory employment has moved out.

Among the big cities, Detroit is second to Baltimore in the lowest percentage of high school graduates. Most of the poor are inside the city. Most of the poor are Black. It didn't seem likely that the city could be totally abandoned, with the medical center, the university, business infrastructure downtown. Southfield has more office space now than Detroit. No bank will now loan money for rehabilitation of downtown buildings. But it's not an abandoned city. One million people live there: one-quarter of the metropolitan population.

I take visitors to Detroit on a tour from the airport. We start at Ford Rouge and then go by the Ford world headquarters. We go through the integrated neighborhoods of Southfield and then into Huntington Woods. As we go down to the university we pass through Palmer Woods. Then we go by the old Ford plant in Highland Park and to Chrysler world headquarters, Hamtramck, the Poletown plant. You have the sense of the circle. You see old Detroit, falling-down Detroit, and efforts like the Poletown plant to retain some industry. Every time I do it I sort of reflect. My reflections have now gotten past this deep pain of someone who's showing people around his home, feeling that "Gee, this isn't being fixed." It's clear that this is a long-term, stable condition.

To understand Detroit, you have to drive out to Novi, West Bloomfield, Sterling Heights, Auburn Heights, Mt. Clemens. You have to see what's beyond. It's no longer commuting distance from Detroit, like we used to measure it. Forty to fifty miles from Detroit there are housing developments or individual houses built on two- to three-acre lots.

Depending on the weekend, I go from Point Pele to Windsor, to downtown, to Bloomfield Hills where my daughter takes dancing lessons at the Jewish Community Center, to where her doctor is in Troy. Just look at the sweep of my own movement around the city. I can go from fifty miles in one direction to thirty, forty miles in another direction. That's the place where I live, and that's the city. It's divided into 168 different communities, a vast number, with 168 private school systems. They're not public school systems. They're private school systems, all democratically operated.

By the way, I'm very much into South Africa. When de Klerk finally decided to abolish apartheid, it was clear to me he began spending a lot of time studying the United States. He figured out how you can have democracy, local control, civil rights and liberties, and still have privilege firmly ensconced and protected. In the Detroit area it's expressed in the Birmingham schools, Bloomfield schools, whatever. Simply by virtue of that local, democratic control, class priviledge is firmly protected.

When I show South Africans around here I say, "If you don't watch out this is your future." That's to say, political power, a political bourgeoisie being built up, a political class, freedom of opportunity to move, and the vast bulk of the population still stuck in the [South African] townships with inferior schools and housing. Those who can afford to move out do so, and the rest are left behind, but now no longer with political leadership.

Today we can use the term that Mandela and the ANC [African National Congress] uses: nonracial society. I've learned a lot about Detroit from being in South Africa with ANC activists. Apartheid is seen as intimately connected with capitalism. One of the reasons why de Klerk chose to negotiate early was because he understood that the future articulate majority, making its presence felt ever more strongly, will be anticapitalist and demanding fundamental change. If he wanted to preserve what could be preserved, he'd better negotiate while they were still less, rather than more, organized.

That's what's happened in the United States. The civil rights movement unfolded within the context of the liberal promise of equal opportunity, civil rights, civil liberties, and voting rights. It created opportunity for those prepared to take advantage of it. That's been a signal success. But the majority of Detroiters have needs that require a much more *radical* solution, or even a social democratic solution, in which jobs are provided, housing is provided, medical care is provided. Those people have been left behind here.

And what de Klerk has understood is that the American model is a model for a future, stable South Africa with the whites keeping their position. But not all the whites. From his point of view, the dumb whites, the whites without skills, the lower- and working-class whites with only their skin privilege, will sink. What's novel about de Klerk is that he has said, "I'm willing to let you, my fellow Afrikaaners, sink. You'll have to compete with those talented Blacks. You'll have to find your own level. We're creating a new order based on talent, skills, property, capital."

We have to start thinking how Detroit's problems can be dealt with in the larger metropolitan space. Then we have some interestingly conflictful thoughts on Black power. There are extremely important reasons for Black Power, including psychological, empowerment, and development of a middle-class political cadre. But the problem is original. The problem of Detroit is the problem of a city within a region.

Unlike West Germany, where a business simply cannot move from one place to another, at least before reunification, we have free capital movement with no consequences. Businesses get tax abatements, or threaten to move from Detroit, or *do* move. There's no control over keeping business facilities in Detroit.

There is a need for regional government and regional control over simple things like capital movement and development. It can only happen with some surrender of political power from the Black community in Detroit. That poses tremendous difficulties for the present administration. What's going to create a demand to live in Detroit? You need some massive changes in the larger economic processes and people coming in because they have a reason to come into the city in large numbers.

There are four and three-quarter million people in the Detroit metropolitan area. Once we've included the 800,000 Blacks and a certain number of UAW workers, is there a working-class majority? What is the basis for a possible future movement? White radicals have tended to be stymied on this question all the way back into the '60s because the majority in Detroit was Black. OK, we could be supporters, and in the end there was a fairly large movement of white radicals. But it wasn't a critical mass, and couldn't be. As long as Blacks were in motion, I think we were sort of fixated on that reality. There's an advantage now in not having to deal with that. There's a need to regionalize our thinking about the city and to begin to look critically at the radicals' usual preference for old urban areas.

Most of us who are raising kids and sending them to schools have done what most people have done, which is move out to the suburbs. Three and three-quarter million people live in the suburbs. Is it thinkable that vital regional issues could be decided on the basis of common interests across racial lines? When we got involved in the Black movement originally, it was not a Black people's movement *exclusively*, but a civil rights movement. It represented a vision of a whole different society that whites and Blacks together could work for and build and that would be meaningful to all. That was King's vision, or SNCC's vision. We've achieved that in the United States and in Detroit, and that's what we're suffering from.

For white radicals the challenge is how to create a nonracial movement that demands that opportunity be made real by having excellent schools, adequate housing, adequate health care, jobs, and so forth, as the responsibility of the whole society.

For us, as white radicals, the concept of being supportive of Black politics is not only obsolete, but it's an obstacle to creating some kind of wider nonracial movement for more basic changes. We have to try to find the white audience for those demands. The majority in this country is not really financially comfortable. It's a potential political force that now doesn't engage in electoral politics. They're racist, at least in their immediate response to issues. What are these people demanding that I can support? Where are they in motion?

The working class has been demographically shrinking over the past twenty years. More and more workers are in smaller, more individualized work environments. Things that upset and oppress people are a more complex mixture than simply issues arising at the point of production. A movement today has to be much more complex, pluralistic, and multilayered. That's part of why we need to be looking out of the city into the suburbs.

I talk to friends about this, but we're not sure what to do. I remember a meeting of DSA [Democratic Socialists of America] in the Ferndale Community Center, maybe in 1984, which was part of deciding that most of us weren't in Detroit. To be in Detroit was impossible in terms of political activity anyway since we were whites in a Black city. Politics had become racialized in a way that was impossible to deal with.

One of the things we might think about doing is to organize a group of Oakland County progressives from a variety of organizations to deal with Oakland County issues: open housing, racial steering, economic development, housing development. We should tie ourselves into whatever organizations are out there: the ACLU [American Civil Liberties Union], the Democratic Party, school boards, human relations councils, PTAs. Then you'd have to do the same thing in Wayne County, which is almost equally divided between Detroit and the western and eastern suburbs. Then in McComb County. If you were serious about developing a countywide political organization, eventually whites would sit down at the table with Blacks under conditions of equality. There are very articulate and increasingly older, bright and sophisticated people out there. My guess would be that most of the 300-odd people who go to the Buck Dinner [annual progressive fundraiser] live in Oakland County.

It's necessary to think conceptually about what a regionalized progressive politics would look like. There are some theoretical matters that have to do with my rethinking of Marxism. The working class simply no longer is the majority. People committed to Marxism need to understand that a working-class transformation is only possible in a larger coalition. I would call it a radical coalition. The question is, coalition with whom and on what basis?

We don't have enough trade unionists and we have a smaller and smaller number of industrial workers. To talk about basic changes means including allies in other groups who have their own ways of defining themselves and their own reasons for entering a political coalition. We're going to have to listen to them and find out what basic changes they need and figure out how we can come together.

Workers' movements and workers in movements have alternated between arrogance and despair. The arrogance is, "We're the people who make things happen and control the means of production and really do the work." The despair is, "They're kicking our butts left and right, we're shrinking in size, unions are becoming fewer and fewer, there's nothing much we can do." They turn inward. What I'm suggesting is a pathway between the despair and the arrogance. Radicals relate to a fundamental layer of the social formation. No change is going to happen without us. But there are other fundamental layers. Who's going to say which is more important? Who should even waste their time arguing which is more important?

That opens us to looking around in the widest possible way for allies. I'm not sure where that leads, but it sure as hell leads out of the city into the suburbs. For the past ten years I've been involved in South Africa, Jewish peace politics, NAM [New American Movement], DSA, the Cockrel organization and campaign. I teach adult workers at my college. I'm a theoretician and that's the main thing I should be doing.

Rick Feldman

I was born in 1949 and raised in Brooklyn, New York. My grandfather was in the Workmen's Circle, a Jewish secular organization for progressives from Eastern Europe and Russia. I lived a life very similar to

Rick Feldman is the co-editor, with Michael Betzold, of End of the Line *(Weidenfeld and Nicolson, 1988), an oral history of Detroit autoworkers, and an officer of UAW Local 900.*

the TV show *Brooklyn Bridge*. My family was liberal. As a junior in high school I gave a speech about the war in Vietnam. I went to Andover prep school.

In '67 I went to the University of Michigan and told my parents there's no way I'm going to cause trouble. I was going to be a lawyer or doctor. In a matter of six weeks my life turned on its head. I went to some SDS [Students for a Democratic Society] meetings and got involved with Students for McCarthy. I heard Reverend Cleague at the U. of M. speak on racism. He shook the hell out of me; made me think about the difference between guilt and wanting to care. The significance of racism and knowing that there was a Black movement came into my life. At John Sinclair concerts pot was passed around the audience.

For about nine months I traveled around the country working on McCarthy's national staff. I believed this was the last hope for electoral politics in America. I began to befriend people in all different political arenas. I had political discussion with strangers around the country who had a love and hunger for peace. It was a great educational experience. My life changed in Chicago in '68 [Democratic national convention], seeing the viciousness of the police and the bankruptcy of the Democratic Party. And I learned some organizing skills.

There was a funny story in Nebraska. Dustin Hoffman's movie *The Graduate* had just come out and at that point I looked a lot like him. Hoffman was working on the campaign. People would come up to me, carry my suitcase, and ask for my autograph. I went along with the trick.

In '69 at U. of M. we had an "independent" chapter of SDS. We welcomed people from different cultural and political backgrounds. We did some study of Marxism-Leninism with people from Youth Against War and Fascism. It was exciting to read about how Cuba was solving problems of health care and literacy. I got arrested a number of times in Ann Arbor at anticorporate recruitment, anti-ROTC, and anti-DuPont actions. It was an exciting period.

We got involved in the movement, not so much based on the ideas of democracy and participation, but more based on anger toward the government, the war, and the assassinations of Martin Luther King and Malcolm X. Militancy and tactics and stragegy were much more important than ideas and personal transformation.

In the spring of '70 I moved to Detroit as part of the "Ann Arbor 35." This was a time when there was a massive movement of students from SDS into the cities. We believed that if there was going to be a revolution it had to be among "real" people, not among students any more. We had "graduated" from the student movement. We sent out

265

scouts to go around the country to see which cities we would move into.

In Detroit we set up small houses around the city. We put out the newspaper *Red Times* that was directed at young people and talked about rock and roll, fighting in the streets, the Vietnam War, the struggle of the Palestines. We were going to make the revolution in Detroit. We were welcomed and challenged and criticized by everybody who was here before us.

We were all white. About nine of the thirty-five were women. Eventually, all the women split from the organization and became a women's collective. We had to search our souls and understanding of what women's liberation and male chauvenism meant. That period was about constantly challenging your thinking on what it meant to be a revolutionary, let alone being a human being. We wanted to be the best we could be and we wanted to link process with result. Hypocrisy was a driving force in the '60s against our government in Vietnam, so we weren't going to lie in our relationships or our politics.

The problem was that we began to think that we could control every part of ourselves, that free will could determine everything, and that social evolution and history could be totally transcended. That's what revolution taught. The Russians, Chinese, Cubans could transcend and change everything, and we were that extension. The arrogant confidence of our nation in the '50s and '60s, being the world's only economic and military force, was also part of *our* confidence in believing that we could change the world. There was that dialectic. We were in a period of hope, not only because of the change that *was* taking place, but because we were the wealthiest nation in the world, and we were raised with that.

The Black Panther Party met with us on Commonwealth Street and asked if we were going to take care of the technical equipment— guns and stuff. We were in support of the Black liberation struggle, whether it meant the nationalists, the Panthers, or whatever. Mike Hamlin from the League of Revolutionary Black Workers introduced us to the city in a very warm, embracing style. You really felt as though you were needed, a different tone from the Black Panthers.

The Ann Arbor 35 had different views of what to do. Some would do youth organizing, some would get jobs in the plant, etc. The 35 had many splits, but many of these people are still very active. Over the years they became activists in many Marxist-Leninist organizations: Revolutionary Communist Party, October League, Workers World Party, International Socialists, all of those folks.

Some of us went into the local branch of the Workers World Party. At one point the women in the organization expelled us. The national leadership in the party who had been involved in politics

266

since the '30s came to Detroit and supported the women. They also gave us ways to begin to talk about it and read about women's oppression and male chauvinism.

I thought our central responsiblity was to organize white working class people rather than to focus on African-Americans in the city. We would go into the parks and leaflet the kids. I'd never before seen ten- to twelve-year-old white kids talking about "spearchuckers from Africa." It became clear to me that the Marxist-Leninist view that the working class is divided by the media and the bourgeoisie didn't work. I thought it was something much deeper in American culture than political manipulation.

Then I formed a group called Down the River in the Ecorse–Wyandotte–River Rouge–Lincoln Park area. There were maybe twenty people with backgrounds in the peace movement or the womens movement, etc. We handed out newspapers. Once I was arrested for handing out a paper in front of River Rouge High School about young people burning down their school. The bail was rather high. They wanted to know if we were related to Bobby Seale or Jerry Rubin or Abbie Hoffman.

We thought we could recreate the spontaneous movement of the '60s. But as we came up more and more up against the questions people were raising, we had to begin to think again.

What were people asking?

In '71 I hired into the Ford truck plant. People were asking, "What is socialism?" All I could talk about was what it was like in another country. They could understand what was wrong here and even agree with the criticism and anger, but they couldn't understand what our solutions were. The Vietnam vet in the plant who had just come back was as angry as the young kid off the street who had been doing drugs in the plant. To both, that supervisor was dirt. People wanted to know how it would affect their lives at *this* moment. They didn't want to know what was going to happen after we took power and changed all the institutions.

I told people in the plant that I had come there to do organizing. I never hid my politics. I knew you couldn't trick people into anything. From '71 to '74 we put out a newspaper in the plant, we led walkouts over paint shop conditions, we picketed Solidarity House [UAW international headquarters].

By '73 I was wondering whether I was saying anything profound in the plant. I was learning what people in the plant were thinking. The most fundamental thing was that people in the plant were no different from me. Their concerns were the same.

At that point I bumped into Jimmy Boggs and Grace Boggs. They emphasized how significant racism was in this country. They understood that it was a race and class analysis, rather than a class analysis. Jimmy Boggs had written this pamphlet *What About the Workers?* in which he described auto plants to a T. I bought fifty pamphlets and gave them out to everybody to read. They said, "Yeah, this is *it;* they're talking about me." I was flabbergasted. Here was an African-American who challenged relationships and behavior. He didn't challenge a person's color. He was going to another stage. So at that point I began to relate politically to Jim and Grace. We formed a white and Chicano organization called Alternatives and we studied their book *Revolution and Evolution in the Twentieth Century.* Jimmy and Grace were saying we needed to study American history, which was as exciting as it could be. I knew if I was going to stay in the plant and be revolutionary I needed to take a leap in my analysis and understanding to have something to offer people.

At the plant I was trying to fit in. I always said what I believed, but I also wanted to be liked. I would play basketball with the Black guys. I like playing basketball, but they took it so *seriously;* it was bloodthirsty basketball. I'd go drinking with white guys. I didn't mind a beer, but they'd get drunk as skunks. We'd play cards and they'd lose their paycheck. What the hell am I going to do? I don't want to be part of this. I was even winning and giving them back their money. It wasn't who I was.

I remember crying one evening as I drove home and asking myself, "Where do I fit in"? I saw myself as a political person, as a revolutionary, but what was I offering them? This was an important period for me because it began to link the concept of cultural transformation with the political struggle for power. What was the relation between the two? In the '60s I used to make fun of my friends who baked bread or talked about relationships or wanted to be healthy. That wasn't what politics was.

In *Manifesto for a Black Revolutionary Party,* Jimmy Boggs and his co-authors proposed that the charismatic leadership that had dominated the Black movement had to be overcome, that young African-American leadership had to be developed, that disciplined cadre-type organizations had to be developed, that biological thinking should not be the basis of politics. Blacks would be in the vanguard of this transformation and had the responsibility to develop the ideas to govern the entire nation, and not just take care of Black people. Biological thinking means you're just thinking about race as the issue. They were going to lead an American revolution because Blacks had been at the bottom of our nation.

Jimmy and Grace understood in 1969 that the movement was finished because we didn't ask the question, "Where do we go after rebellion?" They wrote pamphlets on what things like health care and education would be like. Whites were making commitments with an analysis and a philosophy that was similar to the Boggses', combining dialectical materialism and dialectical humanism, or human transformation and political power. This was great.

I stayed working in the plant because it was very convenient. I would work three days a week and do politics four days a week. I would get phony doctor's notes. I didn't care if the company had people working or not because what I was doing was important. I could take two weeks off on personal or medical leave to travel with Jimmy or to do organizing in West Virginia or wherever in the late '70s to form branches for NOAR [National Organization for an American Revolution].

Though the national Marxist-Leninist formations formed parties very quickly, Jimmy and Grace thought we should make sure that we had the core of cadre that were rooted in communities before we became a national organization. We used to ask ourselves the question, "What would we do if we were governing?" Radicals are *always* good at pointing out problems, but the question is, How do you resolve the crisis? We would have constant educationals, asking questions like, What does it mean to be an American? What is an *American* revolution? What is democracy? What is freedom? What is community? What is work? We were never satisfied with the answers.

From '73 to '83 I worked with people throughout the country, predominantly African-American, and step by step tried to build NOAR locals. We would go to Dayton, Ohio, on Saturday morning, for example, and meet with people and try to form a branch. I learned a tremendous amount about the country and talked with some of the brightest people I ever met.

But the organizational form of a Marxist-Leninist cadre-type organization in the '70s and '80s was not one that facilitated transformation. It facilitated getting things done. We didn't know how to break out of that. When the organization dissolved, the question of what kind of organizational form helps people to develop as well as relate to grassroots activities and cadre development was not resolved. These are still important questions.

I met my wife Janice in '78 when I was between organizations, between Alternatives and what was to become NOAR. My son was born in 1984. He had special health problems which took a lot of my time and energy. So we left Detroit in '89 and ended up out here in Huntington Woods because of the special education program in the school system.

269

So we now live in Ozzie and Harrietville—an amazing place—where my son can walk to school and the library, where he can take a sleigh ride to the children's concert on Saturday, where he goes to the secular Jewish Sunday school, where there's an integration of community. It's almost how life should be. What's very much missing is the cultural diversity and the crisis of America. So the question for me is, How much does that dominate what I think and what I do?

Fortunately, being in the plant continues to keep me in touch with a certain sector of the American population. I'm a member of Detroiters Uniting. I work with SOSAD [Save Our Sons and Daughters]. These are organizations that I think embody the grassroots activities of people who say they have to be responsible for changing the city. I march with them against crack houses. I march with them to rebuild our cities, to make the streets safe, to create a new economy in our city, and to rebuild every institution because they are as corrupt as the whole system is. Any institution that was built in a dying America has got to be yucko. Just as people marched and organized in the South in the '50s, we have to organize in our cities. As race was the question of the twentieth century, the questions of the twenty-first century are going to be, How do we rebuild our cities? What is the purpose of cities? How will people work?

What about "class" as the question of the twenty-first century?

One of the lessons from the '70s and '80s is that government will no longer provide services and financial support to resolve the crisis. There is no political will and no financial capability to do it. Corporations are not coming back to Detroit or to Youngstown, Ohio. I guess I've never understood when people say that "class" is the issue. That simplifies it to such a point that I don't know what you do with it. When I say cities, or wherever people live, we have to figure out how to start living differently. We have to transform those abandoned factories into greenhouses so that people can grow food. In the relationship between the cultural revolution and the political struggle for power, the side is much more toward cultural transformation. At this point, that's more critical than how to get people to oppose the rulers. We're so unclear on where we're going. I don't think we can get people to be angry or involved enough until we can show them that life can be different. Some of us think that we're in a transition from capitalism to whatever we're going to call it or whatever it's going to become. It's evolutionary as well as revolutionary.

I'm involved in a project—Detroit Summer—that's based on Mississippi Summer, when folks went down South for voter registration and focused national attention on the crisis of segregation and race.

We want to focus national attention on the need to rebuild our cities. We want to bring in several hundred young people from around the country to work with young people here on community projects: rehab homes, plant flowers, do murals, do theater work, etc. When they leave here they will have participated in workshops as well as concretely changed the face of part of Detroit. It's extremely exciting.

Also, we continue our discussions on work, family, patriotism, democracy, economics—all those issues we've been discussing in the last fifteen years. Future discussions on these issues need to include people actively engaged in their community.

Jim Jacobs

In 1967 I was going to school at the University of Michigan. I knew very little about Detroit. You could feel in Ann Arbor that there was something going on in Detroit that you had to relate to. We got a call in the REP [Radical Education Project] from somebody saying, "Could we hide people coming from the rebellion?" We had this big debate, whether they had guns, etc. We agreed to it, but he never showed up. [*Laughs*] But for the first time, this was a *major* issue; not something that you read about, but something that was happening.

The same week, because I was involved in SDS [Students for a Democratic Society] and REP, I was asked to speak to a class at McComb County Community College. The second day of the rebellion I drove into Warren, Michigan, spoke on SDS, and was offered a teaching job. I was only twenty-three at the time and wore blue jeans. I drove in from Ann Arbor two nights a week. I've been associated with McComb now for twenty-four years.

I remember using *Rebellion in Newark* by Tom Hayden as a text. People were just astonished. Somebody said, "I knew Tom Hayden. He went to Dondero High School with me, and he was always a jerk." [*Laughs*] It was no-nonsense stuff. They weren't interested in theory at all, they were interested in what's going on around them. If you couldn't be concrete, you couldn't last a second in the class.

Donna and I got married in 1968 and we moved to Detroit. Because I taught in McComb County, we gravitated toward the east side. We rented a place on Lennon Street, off Jefferson. That morning I went to the grocery store and asked, "Do you have any bagels?" The

Jim Jacobs is an instructor at McComb County Community College, is on the staff of the Industrial Technology Institute in Ann Arbor, and is a trustee of Wayne County Community College.

woman looked at me and said, "You're on the wrong side of town." [*Laughs*] Very few progressives lived on the east side of town.

We got hooked up with these people who were coming out of SDS called the National Organizing Committee. By then, a lot of people in SDS had begun to think about organizing the working class, particularly young workers—a kind of analogue to the Black Panther Party. There was a huge debate in 1968–'69 over the Weathermen. It was personally a wrenching experience because a lot of my close friends joined the Weathermen. I remember sitting up all night in Oakland, California, trying to convince my friend not to join the Weathermen. He was told that he had to give up his child because children were considered fetters in the underground. I was unsuccessful. I swore that from then on I would never allow political debates to assume such a highly personal character. When people actually do things like giving up their children, it's sick. Later on in Detroit, similar self-righteousness and manipulation of people occurred.

We had no one with experience in organizing. The Old Left was totally absent from these debates. We had nowhere to go but books, and we were turning to models like China and Vietnam, which were completely different cultures. We were so immature. We thought that power was going to come once we took over something. We also didn't realize the tremendous *leverage* we had. Our ideas had, in fact, moved a lot of people. I began to realize that those of us on the left have a profound effect on lots of people. But if you try to force an issue, a lot of people will be against you. If you allow people the space, they may support you.

Detroit was different in 1968. At least 20 percent of my students lived in Detroit and another 30 percent had direct, concrete experiences in the city. Today, much to my sadness, I'd say 85 percent of the students at McComb have *no* contact with Detroit. They know how to get to a concert at Cobo Hall, they go to Greektown, they ride the People Mover. But they have no direct experiences with Black people.

Now there are racist attitudes that are totally ephemeral and based on listening to rap music and watching television. The view of Black people is so one-dimensional that reading a book on Malcolm X goes over the heads of most white kids. On a whole today, most whites may be less racist, but they're so ill-informed of the Black experience and so willing to stereotype Black people. It's *incredible!* I say to Black guys in Detroit, "You guys don't realize how little people really give a shit about you any more."

A problem the white left has now is that it's highly concentrated within the city. It takes on issues in the city because the Black community takes those issues on. For most whites in Oakland County, Downriver, and McComb County, those are nonissues. The mayor's a source of delight and interest, but no one really gives a shit if the city falls apart. That's a scary thing to me. We can't even mobilize racist contempt and hatred for the city.

Because of the centralization of the auto industry, the issues were always fairly clear. Armchair Marxism works very little here. One of the nice things about the intellectuals from Detroit is that they're *real* intellectuals. If they're gonna write stuff, they'll write about workers and about Black people. This city probably has produced less academic Marxist theoreticians than anywhere else. But we've produced a lot of empiricist Marxists: people who believe that you concretely identify issues, gather data, and come up with solutions. This is a place where the left has a toehold. Even though the mayor has made his peace with capitalism, there are people within his administration who are clearly leftist. This city has been affected by progressive struggles, and made a better place for it.

In the late 1960s the Black movement had coalesced around questions of political control of Detroit. There was no way you could address *any* issue, from the Vietnam War to housing, without the component of race emerging. This is a city where the Black liberation struggle is an objective reality. Being a participant in struggles with that movement is a great educational experience. It demonstrates to those of us in the white left what a multilayered struggle is all about. Watching sophisticated Black activists, you got a sense of the interrelationship between cadre and mass; the interrelationship between tactical and long-range demands.

There was a clear Marxist, working-class perspective in the left leadership of the Black community. Many Black activists had experience in the auto plants. The kind of cultural nationalism that emerged in other cities did not emerge here. This was clearly a proletarian-led nationalism. I remember a famous leaflet passed out at Dodge Main in 1970 during the DRUM [Dodge Revolutionary Union Movement] election that had a big picture of the black, red, and green flag, and it said, "Take the flag with you to the ballot box." Nationalism meant that you voted for Black candidates in the plants, it wasn't necessarily that you supported a struggle in Africa, etc. There was a clear emphasis on power for Black people at school board or city elections, or control over the police.

When my mother, who lives in New York, comes out here, she sees a difference in the attitude of Black people. Black people in the city of New york finally got a mayor this year, and they're still struggling for political power. Black people in Detroit have had political power for twenty years. There's a large multiclass Black movement

273

which is far more complex than many of the other eastern cities. Detroit Black people are far less uptight around white people because they are, in fact, in control.

The mayor of Detroit heavily depends on Black nationalists to do his organizing in the Black community. He tells the Black masses that it's in their interests to support downtown development. The mayor gives business some stability for long-term investments downtown. He knows he can extract from them support for his own works, and a very interesting silence on issues that the Black community is particularly concerned about. Community control over the police is not opposed by the business establishment. They like affirmative action programs. Detroit was one of the last cities to get cable TV. They had to wire the entire city and couldn't just cherry-pick the more affluent areas and wire them, which they do in most cities. As a result of waiting around, they finally found a Black firm.

A number of people emerged in the late '60s and early '70s who set the parameters to certain debates. They were interracial in their interests. Even the leaders of the League of Revolutionary Black Workers who were active in nationalist causes, clearly saw the need to have an organized white left, and would work with people. Similarly, the white left was so influenced by race that there was a great deal of interest in making sure that whatever was done around the war in Vietnam or student activities, etc. was always related to the Black struggle.

Detroit was the place where John Sinclair started the White Panther Party. That was an attempt to organize white people, as Black people had been organized. At least the belief among hippie and psychedelic people was that they had something in common with Black people. They clearly were affected by Black culture and the Black struggle. PAR [People Against Racism] was organized in 1968 by people from Royal Oak and southern Oakland County with fairly wealthy backgrounds. They organized around an antiracism perspective. The *Fifth Estate,* an underground newspaper, in comparison to other underground newspapers, had a far closer connection with the Black movement. Where else would a campus newspaper, *The South End,* have as its banner, "One class-conscious worker is worth a thousand students"?

The Detroit area was *always* more sensitive to the Palestine and Middle East issues. In 1973 Arab workers closed down Dodge Main to protest the UAW buying Israeli war bonds. As activists, most of us were going to Arab dinners and activities in the Arab community.

Emphasizing local struggles has helped us enormously embed ourselves into this community. We don't go away. I suspect you find more people in Detroit than in any other city who have spent their entire political lives here. Many émigrés who came here in the '60s never left. Why are they staying now at a time when there aren't groups that are disciplining us to stay, or there aren't enough jobs? Part of the reason is the feeling that you do, in fact, control certain things. You're not alienated from the city.

Over the last decade, there's been a polarization in the Detroit suburbs. Oakland County is increasingly becoming the locomotive of the whole area while McComb County, Downriver, and western Wayne County suburbs increasingly have second-rate status, suffering income and land value declines. This might provide the material conditions for someone in Roseville to say, "As a suburbanite, I really can't identify with that person in Birmingham. *My* problems are more like that person in Detroit." That won't be a Black and white, unite and fight thing, but it does mean there may be far more willingness of white suburbanites in places like McComb County to see their interests lying with what happens with Detroit.

The regionalist approach of the ruling class is to use the democratic process to isolate the problems of Detroit and to control the city through a variety of means. That has started to happen. The response among progressives and leftists cannot be, "Well, we'll take the opposite. If they're for regionalization, we're for nonregionalization. We're for the city running its own stuff." Since the city is so bankrupt of resources at this point, that would play into a racial argument. Only Black nationalists who want to run soap-making factories could believe that Detroit can develop by itself. The issue is, how are people to recognize the particular needs of the city, which include Black control over certain things, within a metropolitan area which is heavily white?

It makes sense for white leftists to live in the suburbs and do political work in the suburbs because that's where whites live. Leftists can help them understand the issues affecting the city and how suburban schools can't develop unless Detroit schools develop; how they can't solve their economic development issues by simply luring plants out of Detroit. That doesn't solve anything; it just restacks the deck.

Most people viewing themselves and their families are not solely materialistic in making decisions. One does not choose to buy a house *solely* on resale value or to send their kid to school *solely* because that will get them into an Ivy League school. Except for a band of maybe 5 percent whites who are hard-core ideological racists, the majority of white people know that they have to deal with the city and the future of their children is at stake. Begrudgingly, if the proper alternatives are posed, they *will* accept it.

If you make a narrow economistic argument on racism, while it may sound logical and be somewhat useful, it really isn't the way that white people are going to be convinced. The fears of white people should not be discounted. Those same fears are inside the Black community. At the same time, a higher view must be promoted: there is strength and good things about diversity; the richness of the difference is what should be recognized.

I'm just about ready to move to Grosse Point. I thought a lot of people would say I'm selling out, but they haven't. I now have to say honestly that I'm leaving the city because of schools, etc. But we're committed to working within the city, to interracial issues, and we will fight racism wherever we are. The reality will be that there will be more and more white people living and working in suburban areas.

Frank Joyce

I continue to amaze people outside of Detroit when I tell them I'm a hard-core, native Detroiter, but indeed I am. I've lived in the Detroit area continuously all of my life. I graduated from the Royal Oak–Dondero High School in the class of 1959. Dondero produced a number of 1960s activists of whom the most well known was Tom Hayden in the class of '57.

For whatever reasons, as children of the '50s and products of the Ozzie and Harriet generation, some of us became "rebels without causes." We were good students and active in student affairs. I was the president of the student government in my senior year. But we were troublemakers of a sort. Tom and some others started a publication called *The Daily Smirker,* which was really a forerunner of the underground press.

I got involved in perhaps the earliest civil rights demonstrations in Detroit at the Crystal Pool, a whites-only swimming pool at the corner of Greenfield and Eight Mile Road. Following the upsurge in the South that began with the lunch-counter sitins in Greensboro, South Carolina, the poor became a target of activity here, and I joined those demonstrations. That led to some conflict at home, and I found myself living on my own shortly after getting out of high school.

Then I got involved in an organization called the Northern Student Movement, which had sprung up partly to support the student

Frank Joyce is the director of public relations for the United Auto Workers.

civil rights movement in the South. It developed a tutorial assistance program in northern cities in which white college students were recruited to work in inner-city environments. It was a paternalistic program, but at the time it didn't particularly feel that way. It was an inherently radical thing to do simply because it was against the segregated mores of the time. It's something of an understatement to say we were naive.

I think what happened to myself and a lot of other people as we became more involved in the life of the city was that our sense of injustice deepened and we began to understand that there was something fundamentally wrong at the core of American life. There was a lot of interaction between whites and Blacks in Detroit. It was an exciting time. There were marches, demonstrations, social change. It was one of those periods in history not unlike the labor activism that characterized Detroit and all of Michigan in the late '30s.

277

The Northern Student Movement concluded that it was appropriate for whites to concentrate *our* energy on the white community itself. *That* was where the core of racism was located. So I was involved with founding an organization called PAR [People Against Racism]. For a time it was an extensive and effective organization, with chapters in several cities from coast to coast. Organizationally and theoretically we developed some real understanding of the power of race, dating from before the days of slavery.

Then we became distracted and sidetracked in other issues. The antiwar movement, for example, intersected in *my* life and in the organizational life of PAR as a part of the social and political movement of the late '60s and early '70s. As it was in the civil rights movement in the South, the decision of what to do about the war was controversial in PAR. But ultimately we concluded that the war was an extension of the same racist attitudes and practices that characterized domestic policy.

We got swept up in very powerful events that we didn't understand, that we now need to assess, not for reason of nostalgia but to clarify what the questions are. I don't think anybody has the answers. We need to try to come to terms with the past and what happened, as well as with the present and future and the great descrepancy between the way we had *hoped* they would be and the way they turned out to be. We need to revisit these issues.

That said, I reached a couple conclusions some time ago and that I still hold to: we *lost*, we were defeated. We were a spontaneous political force. We took a multitude of directions and forms. We were essentially the dominant ideology of anarchism—very common in American history—regardless of all the rigorous, disciplined vanguard parties. I don't mean to say that *I* was an anarchist, or anybody else was, but there was a great deal of rebellion for its own sake. We knew what we were for. There *were* political forces opposed to us and they knew what they were for and against. They *prevailed,* and we didn't. As I continue to talk to people who were involved in that earlier time, I find quite a bit of naiveté on that point. There *was* COINTELPRO, there *was* the FBI, there *was* the CIA, there *was* the Republican Party and elements of the Democratic Party. There was an establishment in this country that said, "This stuff is dangerous and we're gonna put a stop to it." They *did,* and they didn't hesitate to use violence.

Our impact, such as it was, doesn't look that good today. It doesn't appear that there has been any significant transfomation of the attitudes of huge numbers of whites that you can trace to that period, given the reality that we see in Detroit and elsewhere today. That's a source of considerable pain and regret to me. Given the need, why isn't there a descendant of People Against Racism today in white communities across the country?

The most stunning thing to me about the movements of the '60s and '70s is that we failed to institutionalize much of anything. This applies to virtually every organization that appeared on the scene in the '60s, with a few notable exceptions like the National Organization for Women. For the most part the organizational forms that were created were not sustained. I don't mean there was no lasting impact and nothing endured, but certainly what did *not* endure was an institutionalized base from which there would be a continuing, ongoing struggle, whether it was antiracism, economic justice, or whatever.

It's not an accident that many '60s activists like myself now find ourselves in one way or another working with or for the labor movement because that remains the single most potent, institutionalized, progressive force in American life.

Another thing I'm struck with, and I guess this is a self-criticism, is that, for a combination of reasons, I've not done as much as I would like. One of the disturbing things about the present situation is the absence of continuity with the movements and organizations of the past and a new generation of leadership that is springing up. We used to bemoan the fact that there wasn't more of that in the '60s, but there was a lot more *then* than there is now. One thing that would be desirable today would be a book club and study groups and a more cross-generational, cross-geographic, cross-experiential involvement.

Elements of the "coalition" involved in the election of Coleman Young as mayor and Justin Ravitz to Recorders Court and Ken Cockrel to City Council are still around and are very well-connected, experienced, and talented people. They're out there looking for some-

278

thing to do. Periodically, there *have* been discussions about the resurrection of some kind of forum that develops the kind of leadership necessary to do the planning and logistics and organizational details. It should have some sort of national appeal. The book club—Control, Conflict, and Change—at its peak involved hundreds and hundreds of people on a regular basis. A lot of people needed it then, and it clearly is still needed.

There *is* a morale problem out there, that's for sure. How much of that derives from people being discouraged about the outcome of past activities, and how much derives from the direction of people's personal lives, and how much from depression about the current situation, I don't know. This kind of a discussion is a recurring theme of my life.

Detroit's negative conditions cut two ways. They are very demoralizing in the sense of "Boy, this town is *so* far gone, I don't know how the hell it could ever be fixed." But that's opposed by a sense of "Well, *Jesus,* I didn't bust my butt for all these years to have *this* be the end result; this is not acceptable." [*Laughs*]

The kind of isolationalism of the city that has emerged over the last decade or so is unacceptable. The alternative must be to find a way to reverse that. Maybe that's regionalism, maybe it's not. There is a faction that says the city is the Black man's land so people are going to have to come to terms with that. I'm not even sure whether that's the antithesis of regionalism. But if this means an enduring split in which the city is going to see itself, and be seen, as quite distinct from the rest of the region, the nature of that relationship doesn't have to be what it is now. It doesn't have to entail the kind of disarray and poverty of resources and misallocation of resources and the kind of decay and decline that we're seeing now.

In the UAW we're involved in a critically important, life and death struggle for the defense of the auto industry in particular, but more broadly for the defense of a strong industrial core as a component of the economy of the United States. I don't see an improvement in the prospects for the city of Detroit proper or the southeast Michigan region without some progress on that front. I'm talking about issues of industrial development, trade, and how the nation and its economy adapt to a post–Cold War world and a world in which the economic arrangements amongst industrial blocks are very different than they were coming out of the 1960s.

I think the '90s are going to be different from the '80s. The evidence is already clear that what we used to refer to as "objective conditions" are going to assert themselves. We're going to see a different quality to debate and discussion. Whether some of us get off our butts or not, there probably will be some new forums emerge and some new ideas out and about. We're at quite an extraordinary point in world history. We can sit here and bemoan what's not going on, but the fact is that this is a period of intense and deep change.

I hope this doesn't sound condescending, but it's kind of sad if people think that events in the world are so big and overwhelming that they're going to stay focused on their own block. The world is going to intrude on that block. We're not going to build an economy based on flipping hamburgers. I hate to sound like a PR person for the UAW, but that ain't gonna work. If it *did* work we wouldn't be in the situation we're in. Fast food has been one of the few proliferating businesses within the city limits of Detroit. That's not adequate to the creation of an economy that can sustain people in a decent way.

We've had a decade plus of the dominant ideology: government is inept, cumbersome, inefficient, intrusive. This is a profoundly anti-democratic idea when you stop to think about it, particularly in a country that starts from the notion that the government is of, by, and for the people.

Dick Lobenthal

Detroit in the '70s had a stronger radical base than most other communities. Detroit also was the center of virtually all the antiracism stuff going on in the country: People Against Racism, Center for Resources on Institutional Oppression, International Black Appeal. Detroit had a reputation as the revolutionary capital of America, and that could have pointed out the sad state of the revolution. [*Laughs*]

Detroit also had another kind of history. It had the inherited history of the Students for a Democratic Society. It is one of those two or three cities in the country which is a border city. It also had a strong antiwar movement which helped draft dodgers or deserters to go into Canada. Almost simultaneously it was one of the centers of support for revolutionary movements in Latin America. All of that was a kind of unique confluence of events at a unique moment in time.

There was a perception that Detroit might be up for grabs. There was a perception that there were enough cracks in the armor that maybe you could wrest control from the elites. The Ravitz-Cockrel group was part of it. Linda Ewen was going to expose it, and did so in her book about how power intermarried [*Corporate Power and Urban*

Dick Lobenthal is the director of the Michigan Anti-Defamation League of B'nai B'rith, with offices in Southfield, Michigan.

Crisis, Princeton University Press, 1978]. The Communist Labor Party thought they actually had a chance in electoral politics. And many others. It all meshed with what was going on nationally: civil rights, ecology, feminism, and all those late '60s issues that split or galvanized the country, depending on how you want to view it.

This place was fantastic. It was phenomenal. There was more energy here, more ideas, more activity, more struggle, more commitment. My guess is that during five or six years of the '70s decade anyone who slept more than three hours a night was a laggard. There was a lot of burnout and heart attacks.

Detroit in the '70s was *inherently* valid. In my lifetime it may have been the only moment of democracy I ever will experience. It was democracy in its truest sense. It was participatory. It was theoretical and philosophic. It was self-consciously directed action. It probably involved more people in some component of the political process than anything else I've ever seen. In 1970 you probably had close to 75 percent of the people in Detroit frenetically involved in politics. You had a sense that you were relevant. Today, *nobody* feels relevant to the political process. 281

Of course, we didn't think of ourselves in those terms. We saw ourselves as besieged and beleaguered. We saw ourselves as against an oppressive elite and a dangerous police state. We saw ourselves as victimized by the rawest and most venomous forms of exploitation. But all around, there were the struggles in the plants, high schools, universities, on the streets, or even in the ballot. I would describe it as a unique opportunity to be lucky enough to be at the right time, place, and age. And it never will happen again in my lifetime. *Most* people never had the chance. It was bigger than life. How lucky I was! There's not a day that I don't have a part of that period with me on a conscious level.

How do you define what the question was in the '70s? Was it a civil rights question? Yeah, there was a civil rights component to whatever it is you want to call the '70s. Were those civil rights goals met? Sure they were; civil rights goals included antidiscrimination. As we began to look at antidiscrimination we said that we had to look at racism. After we looked at racism we said we had to look at oppression. After oppression, we had to look at capitalism, and then imperialism. It's a continuum.

I worked in the establishment with a slightly liberal middle class constituency, and I pushed to the limits. I was the ADL [Anti-Defamation League] director who was the joke around the country, coming to work in dashikis and jeans and boots. I did know that I had to have a tie on when I had a television interview. I felt squeezed. I was totally committed to the movement. We were most afraid of being co-opted by liberalism. That was the seduction that kept threatening us all the time. That was that door in the corner, and God forbid that someone would open it. We didn't know who'd go in it.

But there's a downside. The '60s and '70s gave me a worldview I would never have been capable of otherwise. It made me *far* more sophisticated and sensitive to the interconnections. The downside is that, having acquired this, I redefined my goals in 1990 in ways that are much more frustrating. I wouldn't be nearly as frustrated in 1990 if I didn't have all that damn sophistication. We got through anti-discrimination laws, and we just passed an ethnic intimidation law. Rah! Rah! We had a victory. But then you have to say, "Bullshit, there's more to it than that."

When [Black progressive] Dick Simmons left the Urban Studies Center at Wayne State I went to a sendoff party that was held by his friends. It was a reunion of a mostly Black crowd who Dick knew for twenty-five or more years. I knew many of them over that time. It was fascinating to look around. There was not an ensemble in the room, including blue jeans, that cost less than $300. I'm remembering fifteen years before when there was nobody in that room who owned *anything* but blue jeans, and they were not the $300 designer jeans. We were kind of kidding around about it: "Hey man, that's not the way I last saw you."

This was not illegitimate. These were people who were recognized. They had not sold out. They were people like *me* who changed their style a little bit because they got tired of living on the fringe. They had the same agendas, but maybe in different arenas, different ways. They had become older and more middle class, and had some things now that they wanted to hold on to. We're not talking about selling out at all. Those 1970s really *did* produce some empowerment. If it *hadn't* been for the 1970s, nobody in that room would have had a job earning more than $15,000 to $18,000 per year. I don't think there was anybody in that room earning *less* than $40,000.

Certain objective realities forced the institutions to, at least, accommodate. They're accommodating like crazy today though they're not radically changing. I got to tell you something, I'm busy as hell, and I'm not soliciting anything. I'm *besieged* by requests. Fifteen years ago I was begging somebody to listen to me and I couldn't get in the front door. I wanted to do training on multicultural issues, affirmative action, sexism, racism. I'd be pounding on the door of the damned administration building saying, "Will you buy a *pamphlet*, at least, that says Blacks aren't subhuman?" And they said, "No, we don't have a need for it." Now I'm a consultant to school districts, on retainer.

Did the people's movements end?

I'm inclined to say yes. We went into the "me" generation and those kinds of things. I don't know, technology may have done it. The promise of high-tech seduced our recruits. Maybe in Detroit it got harder to define the enemy since there was Black political empowerment. Maybe we asked too much of ourselves. We were enclaved. We kept asking of ourselves to get out of the enclave and go do the radical organizing in an impossible place, and we didn't have a place to go. Maybe we swallowed each other and ourselves up. Look at the splits in the Motor City Labor League and From the Ground Up. These splits cannibalized the movement. Maybe there were *other* ways we cannibalized ourselves.

283

I don't think the demands of these groups were too radical. If anything, I had the sense they got too doctrinaire. One thing we started doing with a certain desperation was petty monitoring of each other. We got caught up defining correctness, like lots of radical movements did. I remember in a study group I was in for two or three years that the circles kept getting smaller. Finally, I began to feel, "It's not productive; I'm not growing any more." I felt an increasing defensiveness.

Where is the Ku Klux Klan costume that was in the downtown office?

It's still here, in the back room. It's still being shown. I don't want that forgotten. [*Laughs*] I got a death threat downtown, which I thought was a real one. I called the police. Two Black cops came. They were standing in the door of my office reading this death threat and looking at this Klan uniform. Finally, one of the cops said, "What the hell kind of place is this anyway?" [*Laughs*] I said, "No, no, we're opposed to that, we're fighting them." The guy looks at me fisheyed. "Yeah, sure, buddy." When they walked out I said, "Let me give you a photocopy of the letter." I figure that was one death threat that nobody ever took any action on.

Ron Glotta

I come from a very poor background in Kansas. I had rickets, a disease of starvation. Kansas was the center of the Bible Belt. *Elmer Gantry* was a very influential movie on me. Kansas also has a progressive

Ron Glotta is a partner in the law firm of Glotta, Rawlings and Skutt known for defending the legal rights of workers.

populist tradition. The newspaper in Hutchinson where I went to high school supported the anti-segregation case of *Brown versus Topeka Board of Education.* The newspaper was important to my maturation. It put forth positions that were *fair* in those days of McCarthy.

I was recognized as a dumb athlete in high school. There were progressive teachers who encouraged me to go to college. At the University of Kansas I started getting high grades and ended up with an opportunity of going to law school at Michigan, Harvard, or Kansas. I didn't have any money. Michigan offered a real nice scholarship, so I came up here in 1963 and have been here ever since.

When I got here it was like a breath of fresh air. In Michigan there was this rich labor tradition that allowed you to express your own viewpoints and have your own opinions. I felt like there was a heavy load off my back. At the University of Michigan I really started moving in a progressive direction. From '63 to '66, Michigan was the center for the SDS [Students for a Democratic Society] movement. I was distributing the *Port Huron Statement* and meeting activists like Ezra Hendon and Carl Oglesby.

After I graduated from law school I got a job with a labor firm in Muskegon. That firm represented almost all the unions in that area and did workers' disability compensation work. I helped to organize a rent strike and wrote a paper on it which was presented at the Radicals in the Professions meetings in 1967. The book *Unsafe at Any Speed* by Ralph Nader really convinced me that there had to be a complete overhauling of the system.

I moved to Detroit in July 1968 and joined the law firm of Philo, Maki, Moore, Pitts, Ravitz, Glotta, Cockrel and Robb, a firm that ended up having a big impact on the city for the next twenty years. I organized the workers' disability compensation section in the firm. I recruited Michael Adelman, who had a lot of labor experience, into the firm. Between the two of us, we represented DRUM [Dodge Revolutionary Union Movement], FRUM [Ford Revolutionary Union Movement], and ELRUM [Elden Avenue Revolutionary Union Movement], all of which were included in the League of Revolutionary Black Workers.

DRUM was involved in a lot of wildcat strikes. The international union is opposed to wildcatters almost as much as the company is opposed, so wildcatters have no representation. In 1973 I represented people in wildcat strikes at Jefferson Assembly and Chrysler Forge, as well as the Mack Avenue plant when the international UAW took ball bats and beat the workers back to work. This was a watershed point in the development of the movement. It was written up by Heather Thompson. Wildcat strikes were in violation of the contract. In contrast, we would always base these strikes on safety violations and not on questions of race or representation for Blacks on the plant floor. The safety strike, involving immediate hazard to life and limb, is *not* in violation of the contract. The answer of the UAW was that a safety strike can only be sanctioned by the UAW. The propaganda that DRUM would superimpose on those strikes was to bring up the lack of representation for Blacks on the shop floor, the lack of representation for Blacks in the international UAW, the lack of any Black foremen, etc. The first DRUM strike was started by white women and then was joined by General Baker, who gave the strength to the strike.

In July 1970 Mike Adelman and I organized our own firm. I was able to use that as a financial base to support a lot of activities for the MCLL [Motor City Labor League] and the National Lawyers Guild. I was making attorney's money, and you were able to make *money* in those days.

Early on I had a position that if you're a lawyer you should make money and support the struggle. I was the treasurer of Chuck Ravitz's first campaign [for judge of Recorders Court] and really the treasurer of the MCLL. I set up a program requiring attorneys, and everybody else for that matter who had any money, to make contributions. You should make a commitment to pay a certain amount of money every week that would be enough to hurt. And I went around and collected the money. I made a lot of enemies because I was the hammer.

I set up a program within the guild to raise money and got law firms to make contributions to the guild. Dean Robb and I, and many other people, began to revitalize the guild. I took a position that lawyers should not make more than a skilled trades worker makes. I thought, rather than being in a collective where everybody's equal, people should recognize that unequal positions exist in this society and make those up by requiring contributions to the movement. This was a political position inside my law firm and in any organization I belonged to. It provided a really solid financial base. We were able to pay for full-time organizers.

Retrospectively, I would have made some alterations to that political position. I think that it was extreme and did the opposite of what I had intended. In the initial enthusiasm from '68 through '71, it was a great tactic. The problem was you just gotta be more flexible in a movement, and I wasn't. In the law firm it allowed for people to make excuses for why they weren't being productive as lawyers. In the movement it allowed for a lot of people to sit on their ass and collect money without any requirement that they produce politically. It gave the full-time people a lot of power without any method of control or accounting. Within my law firm it was destructive of a lot of things.

The MCLL split in 1972 right after Chuck Ravitz won the primary election. There were serious political differences and we had no system of resolving them. We had no political leadership to look to. All we had to look to was battles between Trotskyists and communists and socialists and social democrats, and on and on. There was a tremendous history of factionalism, and we more or less mimicked that history, unfortunately.

None of us had any training in Marxism. When you first learn something you're very rigid and very dogmatic. If we'd had theoretical leadership from the older generation, we could have worked through our differences and avoided the violence. We carried guns and threatened people. I carried a gun for three or four years and actually believed my life was in danger.

The other side of that was the program of COINTELPRO, initiated by the FBI and CIA, which generated a tremendous amount of that violence. We were very naive about the sophisticated tactics that the government brought to our movement which helped destroy us, most of which the older generation already knew about. We had to find out through bitter experience. They didn't explain to us what "double jacketing" was or what *agents provocateurs* were. To this day I can't specifically tell you who the agents were. When you get your Red Squad files all that's blacked out.

We had a lot of study groups, but they were organized by people who were not very sophisticated in Marxism. If there had been a tradition of Marxist intellectual work, we would have been much less rigid and more able to resolve theoretical differences and absorb the tremendous intellectual ferment of the time into the Marxist movement.

We set up the book club Control, Conflict, and Change which was a combination of groups like the MCLL and the Black Workers Congress. It was a good program with fantastic intellectual energy. The limitations of it were *our* limitations. Had we had a more sophisticated approach to Marxism we could have taken it further. I always felt that Michigan had the most lively intellectual environment anywhere in the country. I still believe that.

I was instrumental in having the Communist Labor Party enter the Democratic Party in 1978 when General Baker ran for the state legislature. We raised a lot of money and generated tremendous support. You can tell that it's still a good idea today when you see the religious right, the Klansmen and David Duke, all entering the Republican Party. Why? Because that's the only way you're going to get those ideas across. We did exactly the right thing, but we couldn't sustain the movement.

If Kennedy had lived, the relationship between the left movement and the liberal movement would have been far more fertile, and would have produced a whole different kind of movement than what we ended with. There would have been compromises which would have set the basis for a different and stronger movement.

How about the old-new left reaching out to advise the current generation of Detroit activists?

The old-new left is barely surviving, just from an economic standpoint. I know that I have never worked so hard and made so little. I'm working eighty to ninety hours per week, and not making a surplus. It used to be that I could work forty to forty-five hours a week in law and forty to forty-five hours a week on politics, and economically support the politics. Every law firm is under the gun. In fact, just the survival of the representation of workers is a day-to-day struggle. **287**

One of Governor Engler's primary targets is the Michigan Trial Lawyers Association, which at one point was considered kind of an establishment organization. It's considered by Engler as some kind of radical group of lawyers trying to feather their own nest. Lawyers have sued Engler, but the ability to support those suits is much more limited than it used to be. We're under attack all the time. I'm in battles every day; not battles for victories, but battles to avoid losses.

In the late '40s it was the progressive lawyers who got together to build a bar association, to represent injured workers, to handle malpractice cases, to handle personal injury and product liability cases. These were all lawyers with ideology who created a base to support the movement and protect people who were in struggle. Progressive lawyers had a corner on the market in their representation of workers because nobody but progressives would represent them. That's not true today. There are attacks on that type of law. The system doesn't want ideologically committed lawyers, they want crooked lawyers.

The same thing is happening in the plants. I represent more comrades today than I did twenty years ago. People are getting hurt, being laid off, being fired, they have no protection, they're broke, they're just trying to survive. Whereas before we were building and growing, today everybody's fragmented and under attack.

We used to make criticisms of the Soviet system, but we didn't know where to go with them. We really didn't believe that it would collapse. We thought that there were serious flaws in Soviet socialism. My position was that it just reflected the backwardness of the country. It's only in the last five years that I think that it reflected flaws in Marxist theory along with weaknesses in the country.

What we need is some serious intellectual work right now. With the collapse of socialism, we have to rethink what were the theoretical problems in Marxism. I think Marxism contains a rigid view of the labor theory of value and it needs to be altered. We have to accept certain concepts of the theory of marginal value which recognizes some realities in terms of the market. We have to begin to think about how to integrate feminist and nationalist ideology into a socialist perspective.

These things have to be done before we can set the base for another progressive movement. What we need is a new Karl Marx, and I don't know who's gonna fill that role. We need people trained in capitalist economics who have a progressive perspective.

There is no question that class struggle is the motive force of history. *Capitalists* don't disagree with that. They are in a vicious class struggle today. The Laffer Curve [relationship between tax rates and revenues] is nothing but the reserve army of the unemployed restated. The basic concepts of Marxism—class struggle is the motive force of history, capitalism cannot exist without a reserve army of unemployed, capitalism inevitably leads toward monopoly, monopoly distorts the market for people in privilege who are not productive—have to be distilled out so that people understand what Marxism is about.

How are people to be brought together to study these matters?

It requires leadership. I just haven't been willing to show the leadership at this point. If there were the right constellation of forces, I would participate. We need a younger generation of intellectuals who may not necessarily be the activists. There are two different groups, one not being superior or inferior to the other. Both have skills that are absolutely essential. The two have to work together and respect each other. The younger intellectuals, if they have the breadth of vision, will seek out the older activists and intellectuals. Through that process they'll formulate more substantial theories for action.

Everybody says that Coleman Young is from the old school and we're never going to get capital here until he goes. I really don't buy into that. Ultimately, the market is going to determine what happens to Detroit. Look at the history of capital: it destroys an area, reduces the prices of the property, and then flows back in because a lot of money can be made. And that's what's gonna happen. Detroit's going to be revived because it's a central area and Michigan can't exist without a city like this. The power structure is much less rigid today about allowing Blacks to make some money.

Detroit is not going to die any more than the United States dies. The rich people and the upper-middle-class people in this country who believe that they can wall themselves off from the poverty and destitution that exists in this country are just wrong. Their quality of life is going to be destroyed if they continue to function like that. The ideology of the '80s was, Make your own and forget about everybody else. That ideology is collapsing. How fast it will happen, I don't know. I suppose it depends on the degree to which the right wing continues to develop. I'm very worried about fascism in this country.

But the movement can only go as far as the theory allows it to. Right now we have none. We, the people who have involved themselves in past progressive movements, have a responsibility to start providing an overall criticism of capitalism as it exists in this country. Those people who have the desire, understanding, and energy to do the intellectual work gotta get off their asses and start doing it. Detroit has always been a center for that and should continue. It's got people with experience and basic knowledge. It's just gotta happen.

289

Dan Georgakas

I was born in Detroit and grew up on the east side in a working-class environment. My father was one of three partners in a bar on St. Jean and Jefferson across from the old Hudson plant. The neighborhood I lived in had a wide mix of peoples, including Chinese, Jews, Arabs, Mexicans, Cubans, and even Ethiopians, but no African-Americans. My family was horse collar, New Deal Democrat and very pro-union, mostly meaning the UAW.

When I began at Wayne State University the last socialist organization had just been kicked off campus as part of the McCarthy purge. Some friends and I started going around to listen to different political speakers. We were more curious than rebellious. As a lark, we even went to hear Gus Hall speak in a Hamtramck hall. I had completely forgotten that until I got my Red Squad files where our presence was duly recorded. What struck me at Wayne State was that nearly every professor was insistent that Marxism was dead and should be of no interest to anyone. Being a contrarian, I always assumed that whatever people didn't want me to know about must be valuable. I had become a de facto atheist in junior high after reading Thomas Paine's *Age of Reason*. At Wayne State they assigned us *The God That Failed* by Rich-

Dan Georgakas is the author or editor of twelve books, including Detroit: I Do Mind Dying *(co-author Marvin Surkin, St. Martin's Press, 1975) and* The Encyclopedia of the American Left *(co-editors Mari Jo Buhle and Paul Buhle, Garland Press, 1991).*

ard Crossman. My reaction was great interest in why so many intelligent and gifted writers had been communists.

I soon came into contact with three political organizations. One afternoon I was in the Detroit Institute of Arts where they had just put an Edsel automobile on display in the Diego Rivera room. A guy, Morgan Gibson of Wayne State, came up and asked me what I thought. I replied, "This is an abomination," and he invited me to a meeting of the News and Letters Committee, Raya Dunayevskaya's group. I was appalled by the way they treated me. I was pro-labor and pro-integration, but if I said something positive about the UAW they would rake me out as a middle-class, college-educated, privileged freak. It seemed to me that the group was a personality cult. There was something rigid about the setup that I just didn't like.

Shortly thereafter I attended an open lecture by James Boggs and I was quite impressed. I began going to lectures of the Facing Reality group that he belonged to, but it seemed I had come into the middle of a story. I always felt they were at letter *M* or *N* and I needed to get back to *A*. But they were very nice people and they knew how to listen. They seemed to exist mainly to support C.L.R. James, who was in England. I loved his *Black Jacobins* and *Mariners, Renegades, and Castaways,* but I did not feel political urgency in the group.

With Ernest Nassar and other long-time friends I began to attend the Friday Night Socialist Forums sponsored by the SWP [Socialist Workers Party]. Again, people like Frank Lovell were very nice and some of the lectures were very informative, but the SWP seemed trapped in the discourse of the 1930s, what we would later call Old Left politics.

Concurrent with these local developments, the Cuban Revolution had transpired and the Chinese Revolution was becoming more and more important to us. All my contemporaries were pro-Cuba and pro-China. We were thrilled that socialist revolution had occurred in our hemisphere and that it promised to be antiauthoritarian. As for China, we thought it was far more progressive than the USSR and we wanted to know more. To be a Maoist then didn't mean anything other than you were interested in China and you thought it was a positive revolutionary situation.

Most important politically, however, was the civil rights movement. That overshadowed everything. The first group I remember was the Robert Williams Defense Committee. Williams disagreed with King about nonviolence and had been set up on a kidnapping charge in North Carolina. I became active in his defense committee. It was there and at the various lectures that people who became prominent in the late 1960s first got to know one another. I remember John

290

Watson, Luke Tripp, and Charlie "Mao" Johnson best. I was teaching in the public schools by then.

We then formed the Negro Action Committee [NAC]. Our first effort was a sitin at a Detroit bank which had only a handful of Black employees. We struck at the branch in a Black neighborhood where most of the Black employees were, in order to point up the hypocrisy of the bank. We created chaos at an intersection of Grand River near Fenkell. An assemblyman backed us surreptitiously with some money. NAC did not have a martyr complex. After we had started the sitin, some FBI men came in and told us we were going to be arrested. We had no lawyers or bail money set up, so we decided the demonstration was over and walked out. We had disrupted the bank. We had gotten the press we wanted. The point had been made. That was one of the things I liked about working with Detroit Blacks who I got to know quite well. You had an objective that was specific for the day. If you accomplished that objective, go home. You can fight again tomorrow.

In those days culture confluted with politics. In my case I had some poems published in the paper put out by Facing Reality and in *The Minority of One* published in New Jersey by M. S. Arnoni. I also started a literary magazine at Wayne titled *Serendipity*. Of the six people on the editorial board, two were Black, quite unusual at the time. The magazine was not political in any way. Later I worked on *On the Town*, an attempt at an interracial popular entertainment guide that was Black owned.

Coffeehouses played an important cultural role in those years. The Unstabled was started by Edith Carol Cantor, who belonged to the Western Socialists. She had a vision of having an integrated theater company and social-cultural center in the center of Detroit. Through the course of three or four years, that theater produced plays by Tennessee Williams, Ionesco, Jack Gelber, Samuel Beckett, and Detroit's Ron Milner. We also wrote and performed a play for the UAW which was presented to the Flint autoworkers on the twenty-fifth anniversary of their great strike. Tuesday nights we had literary events and Thursdays it was chess or a hootenanny. Saturday nights after midnight there was jazz. After I left the Unstabled, Lily Tomlin came in.

After Woody King, Jr., left the Unstabled, he went to New York where he became director of the Franklin Settlement House Playhouse and produced a number of plays that made it to Broadway. Tony Brown was doing Black beauty pageants when we had the Unstabled. Then he left Detroit and eventually created *Tony Brown's Journal* for PBS. An all-Black spinoff from the Unstabled started the Concept

291

East. There was no schism. It was like, "Oh, Dave Rambeau wants to have a theater of his own and he wants to do all Black stuff." It seemed a natural evolution, just as NAC was followed by the all-Black Uhuru [Swahili word for freedom]. Why shouldn't Blacks run their own organizations if they wanted to? There were other coffeehouses as well: the Retort, which was Black owned and operated out of a hotel basement and featured music, and the Cup of Socrates, which was near the university and had literary events.

I think Detroit radicalism ran ahead of the national pace. In the early 1960s a group of Black Detroiters went to New York to meet Che Guevara when he was at the United Nations and others were on the first flights made to defy the travel ban to Cuba. All of those guys belonged to a broad social circle I was connected with. The Cuban missile crisis drove the last liberalism out of people like myself. I remember attending a lecture by Reverend Albert Cleague and going home thinking we might be dead by morning.

In 1964 I went to teach at the Overseas School of Rome where I got involved in anti–Vietnam War rallies. But that's another story. When I came back to Detroit, John Watson had started *The Inner City Voice* after studying with Martin Glaberman and reading Lenin's pamphlets on the importance of a press. Shortly thereafter, I moved to New York, but I contributed to *The Inner City Voice* and I helped give it some kind of national visibility.

From my time in Italy I knew people who eventually became involved with *Poterio Operia* [Workers Power] and *La Lutta Continua* [Continuous Struggle]. These were extraparliamentary groups much to the left of the Communist Party. When the League of Revolutionary Black Workers began in Detroit by the guys I had known since the late 1950s, I supported them whatever way I could long distance. Since they wanted international contacts, one thing I could do was put them in contact with radical Italians of like mind. When the League made the film *Finally Got the News*, I helped bring it to Europe where we sold segments to Italian and German television.

I'm not going to go over all the territory in *Detroit: I Do Mind Dying*. I'll just say that I think the League of Revolutionary Black Workers was a serious attempt to move beyond King and SNCC with certain Marxist perspectives. At that time a lot of people flocked to Detroit to get in on the action. I think it's perfectly fine for people to move to a city and become politically engaged, but many of the newcomers were highly authoritarian and sectarian. The effect was that the movement splintered into ever-smaller groups more interested in political correctness than effectiveness. I believe there are limited windows of opportunity in politics and if you don't go through the window when the time is right, you may be stranded for decades. You're lucky if the window appears and you're super lucky if you get through.

Most of the people I have known in the Detroit movement who stayed in Detroit remain unrepentant leftists. They're disheartened in the sense of they don't know what to do in practical terms, but they do not think they were wrong. They think, "Well, we didn't win, but all the bad things we said were going to happen here have happened." Many of them are involved in the infrastructure of the Detroit system: unions, educational institutions, city government. What they do personally is good, but their actions reinforce the very institutions that they question.

The other thing that happens, and I see this everywhere, is that you tend to forget your bigger vision in trying to solve the immediate problems in front of you. An example is affirmative action. You can argue affirmative action backward and forward, but whatever it is, it is not a principle of socialism. The socialist principle is that everyone works, everyone gets educated. You have a level playing field. From each according to his abilities, to each according to his needs. But if you get too involved in the infrastructure, then things like affirmative action can become the end, rather than one of many means to move your social agenda. That's one of the major problems that all of us face who are trying to give some immediate relief. We get so caught up in the terms the establishment has set up that we fail to convey our broader vision.

Racial gaps are greater today than when I first became politically active. There are fewer points of natural conjunction. To put it another way, you have to say, "Okay, I'm going to be sure to go out and make this contact." During my formative years, such relationships just evolved out of joint political and cultural interests.

I am quite pessimistic about Detroit reviving as a city. The capitalists seem to have abandoned it. Since it is now predominantly Black, if they are going to revive any center, it is not likely to be Detroit. I'm kept from the brink of despair by something I was taught by the C.L.R. James groups. They said, "You've got to approach each day as if the revolution is going to happen tomorrow." They didn't mean that literally. It was a reminder that when you can't see any stirrings, when the system seems invulnerable, there may be turmoil right under the surface.

I remember James speaking in Windsor, Ontario, in 1965 after I came back from Italy. He said there was going to be a great student movement soon because it was needed. We all laughed and thought age had fried his brains a bit. A couple of years later we saw millions in the streets in France, Italy, and Czechoslovakia; we saw the revolts at Columbia, in Newark, and the Great Rebellion in Detroit.

The old Detroit rebels who are in the infrastructure have not changed their views. I can't think of anyone who defected to the other side. The next time around, when the next wave of young rebels begins to emerge, there are people inside the structure waiting to embrace them. That political window could open tomorrow.

Chuck Wilbur

My earliest political experience was in the '50s in Ferndale when I came home one day and repeated the word "nigger" that I heard a kid down the street say. My mother, not even slightly a political person, said, "We don't say that word, period." My family had a basic sense of fairness. When we moved to Warren I was the only non-Catholic kid amongst the kids I hung around with and didn't understand what they were doing when they crossed themselves. I was sometimes called a "nigger lover" in this all-white neighborhood. At an early age I got used to being a little different. By junior high I was pretty conscious of being either an atheist or agnostic. I was a pretty straight kid—no drugs, no sex—and pretty much your national honor society–type student who also happened to think he was a socialist.

At age fifteen I organized the Eugene McCarthy campaign in my part of the world, McComb County. I had some sense at that time that hard work was necessary to make political change. A new set of friends emerged. We took what we had learned about politics and became student activists at high school. We raised all kind of ungodly hell. [*Laughs*] Student leaders were no longer the cheerleaders and the jocks, but the political activists. I had this basic sense that if you didn't have socialism that the rich would always run the political culture. A number of older people were trying to organize the youth. But my sense at the time, and I still retain this, was that you should organize a constituency. We were learning how to do this around student issues. Those were wonderful times.

When I went to the U. of M. I was kind of overwhelmed. I became less radical, but studied a lot. In '74 the Human Rights Party got organized and it made sense to me. I got involved in their rent control and city council campaigns, and the ballot initiative for public ownership of utilities. I gravitated to the kind of populist organizing

Chuck Wilbur is the news director at WDET, Detroit's public radio station.

that was going on in the '70s. This got me exposed to community organizing.

In the meantime I was a teacher in Inkster in a racially troubled high school. This burned me out pretty fast. Those kids related to high school as something like a prison they were trapped in. They were right in a lot of ways. I had a sense that the left had to learn to communicate with those kids.

I thought the left very often had no idea how to talk to regular people. The only time I was exclusively in a group of all middle-class people was when I was with the left. The left was "preaching to the choir." Even those I considered allies had trouble connecting. If Americans ate beef, the left ate vegetables. There was a counter-cultural remnant that said that radicalism meant being *different* from the American people. There was a "holier-than-thouism." I wasn't interested in politics as a way of self-definition.

Politics to me was to get something done and to move a constituency. I always thought that what I did in politics had to move *Warren* or it wasn't going to be real. Here I am, twenty years later, still grappling with that same question. I tended not to join ideological left organizations, even one as nice as NAM [New American Movement] was at the time. It frustrated some people I knew, but I saw those experiences as a cul-de-sac. I guess I made a lot of mistakes and was ridiculously arrogant about it.

Then I went to work for ACORN [Association of Community Organizations for Reform Now] for four years. The ACORN community organizing model was, is, based on the idea that you don't organize coalitions, you organize people directly. And you do it the hard way: you knock on doors. In the organizing world it had the image of the Marine Corps bootcamp approach to organizing.

When I first did an ACORN drive in early '81 I was a white person organizing in an almost totally Black neighborhood around Six Mile Road and Livernois. In six weeks I knocked on about 1,300 doors, asking people to join the *idea* of an organization that was committed to giving power so the neighborhood could solve some of its problems. It was the most basic exercise in organizing you could imagine, that power came from the collective experience of people. You asked people to join the organization for $16 per year. You knocked on thirty, forty doors a day and hoped to get two people to join. The quota was $25 per day. We were living off the land, not much different than a Maoist model. It taught you to deal with issues in a direct and sincere way. You looked for leadership. The neighborhood would define the issues. More than ten years later, some of the people I organized are still active.

295

I was taught some things about politics. Some people spend their entire lives on the left without really learning. They relate to the left as a sanctuary from America. I don't want to be part of *that* left. Organizing has to have faith that the ordinary American can make a difference. I learned that organizing is a little bit like enjoying a movie: you have to suspend your disbelief. I learned that in a film class. Because the rewards are long term, organizing in this country is long term, and sometimes your disbelief catches up with you and you have to take a break. I now have some doubts about the model. Maybe we believed in it too much and weren't able to see some of its limitations. Still, if you look at the movements around the world, it *does* take a direct organizing of people rather than just borrowing other organizational forms.

One of the things we learned from the Vietnam War was that while the Vietcong had ten people in the field for every person they had in the rear, the American army was exactly the opposite. I used to think that the U.S. left was kind of based on the American model: for every person we had doing direct contact with constituents, we had five lawyers, eight academics, two doctors, and whatever. We were a middle-class, intellectual movement. I'm not being judgmental about that, but it did really affect our ability to impact society.

There were a lot of mistakes made in the past. I think that socialism became this kind of crutch that the left used to deal with our disillusionment with America and its politics, and anchor ourselves in some kind of world tradition that could make us feel rooted. I don't consider myself now to be a socialist, even though some of the socialist concepts still interest me and still may be the way to solve some of our problems as a human race.

Is your core belief still the more equitable distribution of resources?

Yeah! I still want to live in a society that's just. Maybe I'm a social democrat, closer to the western European capitalist countries where they harness the profit-making instincts of the society to create a society that's relatively just.

Mike Smith

I came to Detroit with a draft deferment in September 1967 after graduating from the University of Wisconsin Law School. I choose Detroit via VISTA, rather than the infantry in Vietnam. VISTA gave

Mike Smith is a lawyer in New York City and the author of Notebook of a 60s Lawyer *(Smyrna Press, 1992).*

me the choice of Chicago or Detroit, and I thought that you could do more politically in Detroit.

I found myself a little apartment for fifty bucks a month on Willis Avenue. Formerly, it had been a whorehouse. It was across the street from the Willis Showbar, a topless joint. I could glance out the window and see a neon sign blinking on and off twenty-four hours a day: "Welcome Delegates, Welcome Delegates."

I was assigned to Community Legal Services, a part of the War on Poverty. There were ten would-be lawyers. All of us had graduated from law school and had passed the bar, but none of us knew what we were doing. The program was headed up by Warfield Moore, a Black attorney, who's now a judge in Detroit.

We were supposed to represent community organizations. If they needed a lawyer we were there to service them. I was there with a lot of time on my hands. I read all three volumes of Trotsky's *History of the Russian Revolution* and I really got to understand the revolutionary dynamics of the national question. I read much of Lenin. I also read Earl Ofari's *The Myth of Black Capitalism,* which is what Nixon was advocating at the time.

Along with Ron Reosti, who became the head of Community Legal Services after Warfield left, I represented a guy named Fred Lyles, who formed the United Tenants Union with headquarters on Grand River near Twelfth Street. The first time we met Lyles he was lying sick in bed. The incinerator in his building was spewing up smoke that went into his room. The walls of his room were gray from this stuff. You could imagine what his lungs looked like.

We went from his individual problem, to the building's problem, to organizing a whole number of buildings. Lyles became the president of the organization, and we were his lawyers. We got to the point where we had a number of buildings on rent strike. When the landlords would move to evict the tenants, Reosti would have the tenants call up the city enforcement arm. When the landlords moved to evict them for nonpayment of rent, our defense was, it's a retaliatory eviction based on our exercising our constitutional rights to complain to a governmental agency about an illegality. We'd get a stay on an eviction until the place was straightened up. Well, the landlords didn't want to spend money fixing up the buildings.

We wound up engineering the purchase of thirteen buildings, owned and run by the tenants themselves. The thing that forced the owner to sell was that we told him that we were going to take a couple of busloads of his tenants out to his country club. Next week we met with him in his office. This guy was a wonderful creep. He had a beautiful walnut-paneled office with floor-to-ceiling bookshelves. Not only is this guy an entrepreneur and real estate man, he's an intellectual. We learned later that a decorator bought his books by the pound.

The tragic note on all this was that soon after the sale, Lyles was up in his office one night standing in front of a window. A car cruised by and a rifle came out of a window and somebody shot him through the neck. It severed his spinal cord and he became a quadriplegic. The last time I saw him before I left Detroit he was in a hospital bed, totally paralyzed.

In early 1969, I got elected as chair of the Detroit Committee to End the War in Vietnam. I was asked to go down to Columbia, South Carolina to be the assistant of Leonard Boudin, who was at that time, and twenty years hence, *the* great constitutional lawyer in the country. He was chief counsel for GIs United Against the War at Fort Jackson, South Carolina, a group of Black and Puerto Rican GIs with one white guy. They had organized a huge antiwar group on the base. These guys were being trained to go to Vietnam. The group was organized against racism in the army, and for the right to communicate their opinions on the war in Vietnam to their elected representatives. They were circulating a petition around the base. The night they got arrested they had called an antiwar rally between two barracks, and 250 men in uniform attended. The Pentagon went crazy and put nine leaders into the stockade. I went there to help represent these men. We won the case.

Later in Detroit I went to work for NLS [Neighborhood Legal Services], part of the poverty program, with offices on Grand River. We had this experimental law office that was paid for by the government. We were a think tank and could do what we wanted. I remember my first assignment. Arthur Kinoy and Morton Stavis, who are very fine consitutional lawyers, had a firm out in the East. They had sued the police department in Newark who had savagely put down the Newark rebellion. They had argued that the police department was politically and morally bankrupt and should be put in receivership. I was sent by NLS to Newark to interview Morton Stavis to find out how they did it because we were going to sue the Detroit police department to put *them* in receivership. There was a real wave of police brutality.

When Nixon was elected, all of us at NLS saw the handwriting on the wall. We knew he was going to clip the wings of NLS or try to destroy it. In fact, Nixon, and later Reagan, pretty much crippled it. We bought an old house in the New Center area, just behind the GM building, and fixed it up. Lafferty was good at carpentry. We established the law firm of Lafferty, Reosti, Papakian, James, Stickgold, Smith, and Sobel. Linda Nordquist wasn't a lawyer, but she functioned in every respect as a partner.

We represented just about every movement group in the city. A lot of what we did related to the war in Vietnam. Lafferty became one of the experts in America on draft law. He was published in a book and taught the subject at the University of Michigan. Mark Stickgold did draft law. Dennis James was a wonderful draft-law counselor. We became famous. There were articles about us in *Time* and various newspapers. Before we knew it, we had more clients than we knew what to do with. Nobody else did draft work. We represented Freddy Perlman, an anarchist, and we donated the money for him to buy his first printing press. We were totally nonsectarian.

And we made a living at it. I think we grossed $250,000 our first year, a lot of money then, a lot of money now, because of our draft work. I remember somebody came to us from Grosse Pointe whose father was an arms manufacturer. Dennis James reported at our partnership meeting on Friday that this guy was our client and we were going to charge him so much. We thought about it for a second and we said, "No, let's charge him twice as much." The father called up and yowled about it, and we said he could go somewhere else if he liked. We got the money. Then we turned around and financed a lot of the movement with the money we made. We never *thought* about making money. We were interested in building the movement.

This insurance agent came over to sell us life insurance. We put Mark Stickgold on him. Stickgold never wore a suit. I used to tell Mark, "You know, you can't get a decent fee unless you look like you're worth it." But Mark didn't abide by that. He was very open and casual with his clients. This life insurance agent came in with his attaché case up to Mark's third-floor office, and Mark met him in his blue jeans. I was in the office next door, so I could hear the conversation. The guy gave Mark the pitch for the insurance. Mark listened to him and then said, "You know, the reason we're not going to take the life insurance is because we think there's going to be a revolution in this country and it's going to take care of widows and orphans and elderly people and anybody who would otherwise need life insurance." I saw the guy walk out of our door shaking his head like he couldn't believe it. But that was our attitude.

I joined the SWP [Socialist Workers Party] in 1968. The SWP had been in Detroit since the '30s. Its origins were in the leftwing of the Socialist Party under Debs, and the IWW [Industrial Workers of the World]. I had been influenced by the IWW and their notion of industrial democracy and their free speech fights.

I knew I was a socialist. I didn't think that what existed in the Soviet Union was socialism. I knew they had replaced capitalism, but they didn't have the kind of democratic rights and humanistic society that I was for. So I didn't support the regime in the Soviet Union, although I was very much influenced by and supportive of the Cuban revolution. I was attracted by the SWP because it had opposed the degeneration of the revolution in Russia. The SWP was very active in the antiwar movement, which was where my heart was ever since law school.

There were about twenty-five members when I joined. They had the Friday Night Militant Labor Forum, a real institution in Detroit, where they invited people of different political persuasions to speak and engage in discussion. I got quite an education from them. The forum started in 1954, when the Communist Party was disintegrating, when there was an attempt made to pull things together in an open forum. It was a good idea then; it's a good idea now.

The other thing that was very important to me was Black nationalism. SWP had been early supporters of Malcolm X. George Breitman, who had lived in Detroit until 1967, had edited *Malcolm Speaks* and had written the book *Malcolm X: The Evolution of a Revolutionary*. I had read his works. I had heard Malcolm speak in Wisconsin and was very shaken up when he was murdered. In Detroit, you could really see Black nationalists. There was this feeling of dignity and energy that I had never experienced before.

The SWP degenerated after a time, I think mainly because the political situation in America was just so adverse to any left-wing organization. It affected *all* of us. We were all in the same boat, but in different seats. The SWP turned inward and got real sectarian and expelled a lot of its people, including me. I was the first one kicked out in New York because I disagreed with what they were doing and I didn't keep my mouth shut.

It's always important for socialists to be up front in what they think, in what they say, and in their vision of what a future society would be like. And it shouldn't be in utopian terms. Also, I think it's important for us to treat each other as comrades in a decent way.

I stayed in Detroit from 1967 to 1971. Those were very good years. If there was one lesson I learned from being in Detroit it was seeing how people could come together and make a difference.

Part 9   *Analyze and Regroup: The Left Against All Odds*

The American ruling class is very resourceful. We did not go through that period without facing counter-measures. There were agents out there. People were killed. Nixon developed a strategy to promote Black capitalism. I think we were as legitimately committed as anyone. Che Guevara said, "In revolution you win or die." Well, we didn't die physically, but we didn't win.

There are thousands of people, millions maybe, across this country who would like to see a different system. Creative people have to come along who can organize and mobilize and energize those people, and I think that will happen again.

Mike Hamlin

TODAY CONSERVATIVES EXTOL THE FREE enterprise system
and delight in the decline of socialism worldwide. Today it is almost
seditious to consider the redistribution of wealth as a worthy social
goal. In spite of this, a serious left still thrives in Detroit, against all
odds. The people involved are still dedicated to core left concepts like
class struggle and rebuilding society according to socialist principles.
This left has emerged out of Detroit's historical configuration of
trade unionism, Old Left Marxism-Leninism, New Left Progressivism,
and the variants of oppressed people's struggles. Detroit's left has
taken on the difficult task of understanding the theory and practice
of the past so as to forge a movement that's relevant today. These are
determined people.

What is left, and what's left in Detroit? The word *left* applies to a
fairly sizable body of people in the United States, and proportionately
more in Detroit, who believe in the principles of socialism. These
principles include an equitable distribution of wealth and power, democracy in the social organization of society, and full equality for all
historically oppressed people. Left principles grow in proportion to
the new issues that emerge in this era of rapid change, such as the
social impact of technology and environmental degradation.

Along with being astute in analyzing political economy, the left
that's left, that lives and organizes in Detroit today, is very class conscious. If the word *proletarian* can be used, Detroit applies aptly because of its historical labor struggles and, more important, because of
the immiserated condition of its present working class. Many believe
that Marxist thought is as apt today as it was seventy-five to one hundred years ago. By all that's logical, the Detroit left should have some
success in a place where the human throwaways of unrestrained free
enterprise abound. The organizing focus of some parts of Detroit's
left is on the survival struggles of such displaced workers.

Detroiters deeply want change in their income flow and the security of their persons. They understand that those changes can result only from changes in their opportunity to have a good job and develop their families in a safe and supportive community. But there's a catch-22 that Detroiters also understand: for the rest of their lives they likely will be part of a system which will not, or cannot, facilitate such required changes. That gruesome understanding characterizes urban America and most of working-class America. This contradiction is intriguing and challenging to Detroit's left because it is the grist of left politics, of what the Marxist tradition was all about.

This section presents a small and eclectic set of the unapologetically left. They present some of their experiences for inspection and review, and share what they have learned from them. They are very different people and often see things differently. But they share things that have characterized the left for a long time: a vision of a better life, an analysis of reality, and a will to struggle.

General Baker

My family moved to Detroit from rural Georgia in 1941. They came from a basic sharecropper background. My father came first and got a job in the auto industry. Then he sent back for the family. When my mother arrived here she was carrying me. I was born in September 1941. My family lived on the east side in Black Bottom, which was the part of Detroit where minorities concentrated. My father worked as a welder at the Midland-Ross steel plant where there were a high number of minorities. My family lived on the ups and downs of the auto industry like most working-class families in Detroit. The politics of that day included a lot of union activity. The UAW was so predominant in Detroit that even as a child you were drawn into union politics at family picnics or Labor Day parades.

We knew about discrimination because in every trip South to see Grandmomma and the family members in Georgia my father would take us through basic training about what we had to do traveling south. It wasn't just a casual trip, you know; we had to prepare a certain way: who to speak to, who not to speak to, and what to say when addressed. We had to carry everything in the car, be prepared not to have bathroom facilities, ask for the colored [water] dipper, say yes sir and yes ma'am when addressed—you know, behavior codes.

When I finished high school the civil rights movement was on the rise and I became quite interested in it. I enrolled at Highland Park Junior College in '59. Malcolm X and Elijah Muhammad were in the news. I was hit with the question of how the Black Muslims existed all this time and I didn't know about it. I went through all this schooling and didn't have a smattering of Black history nowhere. I was outraged. The Muslims were fathered in Detroit and had the first mosque over on Linwood Avenue.

To find literature on Blacks you almost had to go to the *National Geographic* and find a picture somewhere, rather than any written material. When Malcolm X came to town in '61 or '62 the Muslims would open little booths selling things like African artifacts and dashikis. But the critical thing was books. One of the things that attracted me was Mark Twain's *King Leopold Soliloquy*, a book on the Congo. Another was a book called *The God Damned White Man*. I can't remember who wrote it.

We were able to get our hands on *The Crusader*, a publication that Robert Williams printed from Cuba. He went on exile there from

General Baker, recently an official with Local 600 of the United Auto Workers, does hard manual work on the midnight shift at Ford's River Rouge plant in Dearborn.

North Carolina after being chased out of the country by the FBI for alleged kidnapping. He had a shortwave radio program on Friday nights called "Radio Free Dixie" that you could pick up from Havana. We would gather around at each other's houses and talk about what kind of activity we could develop in Detroit around the edge of the civil rights movement.

Then I transferred to Wayne State University. We created a little organization on Wayne State's campus called Uhuru, which meant freedom in Swahili. We produced newsletters. We went to SWP's Militant Labor Forum and got introduced to people that was coming around the country on circuits. There was a lot of talk about the 1955 Bandung Conference—you know, the nonaligned nations. A lot of nonwhite nations came together and prepared an agenda in terms of a neocolonial world. That popularized all of the colonial revolutions: the Chinese, the Vietnamese, and struggles all over Africa.

Our first arrest came when we picketed because Detroit didn't have open occupancy laws. There was a big rally downtown held by people who were trying to bring the Olympics to Detroit. We'd figured that Detroit wasn't deserving of the Olympics because it didn't have open occupancy. It was going to be broadcast all over the world. We were singing and hissing. They attempted to strike up the police band playing the national anthem and we were told to be quiet. After the rally one of the leaders, Luke Tripp, was called by the prosecutor's office that they wanted us—CORE, NAACP, and other groups— to come to their office and apologize. Luke sent a message that we didn't apologize for anything. I think the other groups did apologize. So they sent warrants for our arrest for disturbing the peace. That was *my* first real antagonism with the law.

Then we met some Ann Arbor students who went on a trip to Cuba the previous year in defiance of the ban on travel that was instituted in 1962. They specifically needed to get some Blacks, so we were offered the opportunity to go and accepted. I particularly wanted to talk to Robert Williams. In this period, the polarity of the struggle between violence and nonviolence was constantly debated in the Black community. Williams's book *Negroes with Guns* was a popular early reading for us. He was removed from being head of the NAACP chapter in Monroe, South Carolina, because he advocated armed self-defense.

I didn't have enough seniority at Ford to take a leave of that length, and I couldn't let them know where I was going. So I had to take what was available, a one-week leave. We went to Cuba through western Europe. In real cloak and dagger, we left in little groups of four or five. We got a plane from Paris to Czechoslovakia and then transferred to a Cuban plane. Of the eighty-four in our group, eleven were black. Of the blacks, four were from Detroit: Charles Johnson, Charles Simmons, Luke Tripp, and myself.

I had read Che Guevara, Fidel Castro's *History Will Absolve Me*, and Frantz Fanon's *The Wretched of the Earth*, but I still went to Cuba with a half-baked outlook and no set theory. I really was fantasizing about revolutionary theory. Going to Cuba was a real sobering experience and a real turning point in my life. Cuba was open to revolutionary fighters from everywhere. You met freedom fighters from Angola and South Africa; some had been wounded in battle and were convalescing. You met Vietnamese, Indonesians, and South Americans in struggle. It was a laboratory of revolutionary fervor.

A couple things happened that deeply affected me. A plane with U.S. markings had bombed a sugar mill while we were there. It was shot down. We believed they were counterrevolutionaries from Miami. The Bay of Pigs was a couple years earlier. There was still a lot of hostility and threats to Cuba about a new invasion. In the Cuban people's minds they had to be prepared to resist that. In the bombing a mother and her child was killed. We visited the site and saw the plane markings. The very next day the *New York Times* denied anything like that had happened. In another incident a Cuban militiaman was shot and killed at the Guantanamo Marine base. We had a chance to witness that and at the same time read in the *Times* that it wasn't true.

These events made me question *everything*. It was a sort of rebirth. I had to physically shut myself off in a hotel room for a couple days so I could regroup. If they lied to me about *these* things, then they've taught me lies all my life. I went through a sort of metamorphosis.

When we got back from the trip we found the level of surveillance had been stepped up on us. We had made a lot of militant statements from Cuba which were in the newspapers. I got in line at Dodge Main and hired in there. I had forsaken student life. It became clear to me that if you could get workers to move they had much more to sacrifice than students did.

At this time I received a notice to show up for a physical for the draft. In the fall of 1964 I wrote to the draft board saying I wouldn't serve. Then they sent me a letter saying I was dodging the draft. So I went personally to the draft board down at Fort Wayne and said I was not dodging the draft, I was just not going to be drafted. I believe in fighting, but I'm not fighting *this* fight. I had come to know the difference between just and unjust wars. They drafted me anyway.

The date of my draft was September 10, 1965, so we created the September 10th Movement around my draft resistance. We planned a

307

big demonstration at Fort Wayne. Our strategy was that I would go in and take the physical and then refuse to take the oath—if you don't like it call the police. I went down that morning and passed the physical. At the point where you swear in I told them I wouldn't do it. They took me in the back to Captain Cox's office. He asked if I had changed my mind. I told him I'm not fit for the army and I'm not going in. They ended up sending me home as a security risk. My draft status was changed to 1-Y.

We worked with antiwar activists and used to have joint peace marches. We were awkward in the marches because of the racial matter. Sometimes we would demand to march up front, and found that didn't work cause when we got downtown Lobsinger and the right-wing groups would be there. So we'd go and bust them up side the head and break through the line. Soon as we'd do all the fighting, here come all these little ladies with Easter lilies. So damn, looked like even though we marched up front we got mistreated. Then when we would march at the back of the line you got the old historical "back of the bus" status. [*Laughs*] We couldn't find a happy medium.

We took a direct action fight to the factories. All our tactics were direct action struggles: demonstrations, leafleting, agitation. Strikes at the shops were based on the question of discrimination, the way we were treated as Black workers by supervision, by the medical center, by our ability to get skilled trades positions or supervisory positions.

DRUM [Dodge Revolutionary Union Movement] was formed in May 1968 by a group of Black workers that had come together after various strike struggles and discharge cases. We put out a little weekly newspaper that was consistently trying to mobilize workers in the shops. Dodge Main was our main base of operations. It was so huge: 12,000 employees working three shifts. People started demanding that we take some action. That led to little rallies out at the back of the plant, then to demonstrations, then to the first strike.

We were in a period in the '60s when you had a massive upheaval of national liberation struggles throughout the world that were setting a general kind of framework in the battle against imperialism. Clearly, Vietnam was principle. We spouted "smash imperialism" and "struggle for socialism" alongside the daily agitation that we did inside the shop. We were often accused of being ideologically confused because we were asking for minority people to be put on the board of directors of Chrysler and become supervisors all the way down the line, while at the same time spouting some loose goals about socialism. Most of the workers understood that we wanted *more* than just narrow reforms. We tried to bring in educators from around the country who we thought were more astute than ourselves to teach the principles of socialism to these workers. Most of those efforts fell on their face.

Our successes at Dodge Main and the actual explosion of the RUM groupings after the Dodge Main strike in '68, brought us a lot of workers who forced us to take on other battles. We had workers from *Detroit News* (NEWRUM), United Parcel (UPRUM), Chevrolet (CRUM), Ford (FRUM), nurses at Lafayette Clinic (LARUM). It was mainly Black oriented.

We were thrown into broad coalitions on various fronts, from ad hoc committees within the UAW to broad united-front work in the Black community. We were a key part of all that activity. To a degree, that helped *sap* some of our ability to continue to fight on the work-force front. We solicited the help of youth to leaflet plants in the morning so that workers would be protected from being fired. The students took the same tactics back to the schools. We ended up giving political guidance and leadership to a broad-based Black student united front in high schools and community colleges in Michigan and Detroit. Those broadened frameworks threw awesome responsibility on us. We got a lot of national and international attention. After a few *Wall Street Journal* articles about our activity, trips were available for us to go various places to learn about other experiences.

The League of Revolutionary Black Workers was formed after the Eldon strike in 1969. It was an amalgamation of little groups. Under a fierce frontal attack from the police and courts, we were forced to pull all the community organizations and plant groupings together under some kind of general command. We existed side by side with the Black Panthers and the other organizations in the Black community like the RNA [Republic of New Africa]. We pretty much dominated the politics of Detroit. If you look at the police documents from the Red Squad files, I think the Panther file, the RNA file, and our League file were the largest.

The UAW *and* Chrysler Corporation had made some fundamental changes to try to alleviate the contradictions we'd talked about, but they'd never give us credit for it. Chrysler created an urban affairs department headed up by Al Dunmore, who was given the task of trying to figure out some kind of way to bridge the gap between Black autoworkers and the corporation. Walter Reuther came and offered to help us take over Local 3. Minorities began to get elected in local plants. There was a new Black vice-president at Dodge Main. They upgraded a lot more Blacks in staff positions. They gave us a Black regional director, Marcellus Ivory, on the west side, Region 1-A. Our general line of development around the union was "We finally got the news how our dues is being used." That expressed the fact that we

309

hadn't been getting the social benefit from all these dues we had paid. The film *Finally Got the News* was named after that slogan.

We were under such harassment and intimidation by the police, FBI, Internal Revenue Service, that personally I never did think we were going to live very long. We had too many close calls. Fred Lyles, who just recently passed, was head of the United Tenants Union and was shot and paralyzed right after the Dodge strike. We thought the shot basically was aimed for me. We were standing together in the office on Grand River. Fred and I was talking and we just moved and the shot rang out from somewhere across the street. You didn't sleep the same place most nights. You just tried to build whatever organizational strength you could and educate as many workers as you could to try to keep the struggle on course.

By 1971 the League split. We were being drawn off into too many other things instead of plant agitation. We had Black Star Productions, Black Star Printing, two Black Star bookstores, Black Conscious Library, and all these other facilities that we'd gathered around us. In the split we lost our intellectual wing that we relied heavily on to be our spokesmen. Not having these spokesmen, then, there developed a great sense of collectivity which became the basis for us to become tolerant of the educational process. We went on a kind of retreat. We had to.

We were fortunate to meet up with representatives from the CL [Communist League] and have classes. We withdrew totally from all participation in mass activity and began the tedious process of struggling with a Marxist education. After a short period of study about sixty of us joined the CL.

We studied Leninism, political economy, and organization. We hadn't had an overall analysis of the auto industry or a national focus. We hadn't had a comprehensive sense of American history or the revolutionary process in America. The more you learned, the more conservative you became in choice of tactics. We didn't participate in *any* mass activity, including Coleman Young's election and the effort to get rid of [police anti-crime undercover unit] STRESS [Stop the Robberies, Enjoy Safe Streets] and the other big movements in the city. We had our own reluctance and druthers about communism.

By 1974 we decided that we needed a national party that could assess the situation we just come through and because most of the earlier syndicalist groupings had gone as far as they could. The Communist Labor Party was formed in 1974.

By the time we get to '79–'80, capital had a market all over the globe, except in the socialist countries which it's encroaching on now. When the capitalists here at home have no further place to expand it turns inward on its own working class. We've seen these inward attacks with the massive concessions that came in 1979–80 and hit a crescendo in 1985 with the big Hormel strike in Austin, Minnesota. Each step of the way the ruling class learns something. We haven't had another big fight on concessions because the ruling class learned that when it cuts *everybody's* wage it unites the working class. Now they cut one section and lay off the other section. Automation got rid of half of the working force, and the half that's working won't say shit. Unions today are bribed.

Our party's estimate now is that *tools*—the instruments of production—always change first in a society. When archaeologists look backward to discover the level of a society, they first look for the tools. We've seen a change from electromagnetics to electronics. We've been having discussions with computer experts, talking about nuclear fusion and stuff. They don't know what to call this new technology, but they recognize it's something new and different.

Electronics is eliminating the need for human labor and offering the ability to free up working people from the burden that work has always placed on life. The critical factor is that it produces a commodity that has no value. A commodity is exchanged on the basis of the amount of necessary labor embodied in it. A car produced by a robot don't have no socially necessary labor, so it's valueless. Ultimately it will glut the market. Since it has no value it won't be exchanged. Without human labor inputted into the commodity, nobody has the wages to buy the commodity back.

Now, workers quickly understand that when you talk to them, without understanding Marxism. They tell you quickly that a robot can't buy no car. Then we say, "Well, you've hit on the key of political economy." Profits are realized in the marketplace. The commodity produced by that robot is an antagonism on the marketplace. It's incompatible with the social organization of capital. That's what can't be reversed. But capital is compelled by competition and the profit motive to become the most efficient and cheapest producer. The Marxist interpretation is more valid than ever.

The overwhelming majority of people in this country are working class, whether they're selling mental or physical labor, whether they're paid by the hour or all at once, whether they work in the town or the countryside, whether they don't work at all and are given some kind of dole by the state as a supplement for *not* working. All these people make up the working class. It's not a *lumpen*, it's not a "declassed" element, it's a class that's strictly proletarian cause it doesn't own anything. Only with classwide unity are we going to be able to be victorious in the *social* revolution. A social revolution is a response to the contradictions in the economy, and it's gonna take place. The strategy of the communists is to guarantee that it's going to be a *proletarian* revolution.

Some say that the failure of socialist societies prove the inadequacy of Marxism. How do you handle that?

That chapter's not over. In the Soviet Union the dictatorship of the proletariat inherited a society that hadn't even made the transformation from manual labor to mechanics. Under Stalin's leadership it pretty much done that. It did not go too much further in the development of electronics. Khrushchev had begun leaning toward the production of consumer goods instead of the commodities that make machinery that makes machines. Also, a certain social bribe developed under the socialist state. People had privileges on the basis of their positions. That became an institution. The bureaus had become bureaucracies. The struggle is still for the Soviet people to develop electronics. But it takes a certain level of sacrifices to do it.

You ran for the Michigan state legislature in 1976 and in 1978.

Yes. I ran first on the Communist Labor Party ticket and then on the Democratic Party ticket. We tried to develop a program and campaign that was quite practical for the ninth state legislative district. The main issue was redlining by the banks and insurance companies. The representative for this district was the chairman of the state banking and finance committee. The district wasn't well enough off for him to live in it. We raised the question whenever we could of property relationships and who should be served. We didn't lean a lot on the ideology. It was a hard vote to get. In the '78 Democratic primary we ran second out of a field of nine candidates. The electoral struggle still has a lot of merit.

Clearly, the ruling class's main task is to continue to cut, cut, cut. From 1980 on, the little halfway boom in the economy was based on the fact that they took from the welfare recipient, took from the Medicaid patient, and turned it over to themselves—you know, the old trickle up. Their tactic now is to make sure the working class stays divided on the color question. As we find more and more solidarity and economic equality, they find every issue they can to divide us on the basis of color. This is the trump card that's been left to them by American history. In Howard Zinn's book *American Ideology* he talks about the question of civil rights and fairness in America. The ruling class keeps narrowing the scope of who should be the benefactor of these things.

Clearly, the task of revolutionaries today is the intellectual development of this working class. Objectively, the working class is already revolutionary. They've gotta do *something* to get the necessities of life. What *we've* got to do is help the working class develop the intellectual capacity to understand what's happening. And we've got to be there with them as participants in strikes and whatever. The main thing is to overcome the color question.

The rulers-that-be have said they don't need or want the working class educated. The few people they'll need for a narrow society with fewer people in production they'll get through private schools. We've got to have working-class education, but it's going to come out of fighting police brutality, drugs, etc., more than it being education per se. The same people who decided they don't want you educated also have decided a systematic way to get rid of you: Just let you kill each other. It's genocide.

313

Today's youth don't have things to hold onto as a driving force, except in some kind of historical context. They're groping in the blind trying to find leadership. In my youth there were a lot of leaders and a lot of broad forums. Fewer youth are entering college campuses and they don't work in the factories where they could be politicized. They just hang on the streets. Somebody's going to organize them. Either they'll be organized by us or by the fascists. Our ability to propagandize gotta be broader than ever before.

Gene Cunningham

While I was still in high school, we made contact with the Black Student United Front, an arm of the League of Revolutionary Black Workers. We had become increasingly frustrated with what we discerned was the limited scope of what loosely falls under the rubric of Black nationalism. We called it "porkchop nationalism." We considered the more bourgeois elements—in terms of thinking, not necessarily income—as being involved in the Black struggle only for their own ends. To deal with this frustration with Black nationalism—which was like a limit, a wall—we began to seriously look at Marxism-Leninism.

When I went to Wayne State there were few opportunities for us to grow politically, other than turning our attention to the student structures. Because a lot of us were writers, we gravitated toward the *South End* [student] newspaper. We put together a plan to take con-

Gene Cunningham is an assistant to Kay Everett, Detroit City Council member.

trol of the *South End* and make it serve the Black community, rather than the student body at Wayne State, though where the two could be combined we tried to do that. My involvement in the *South End* and the Black Student United Front led directly to my involvement in the *Inner City Voice,* where I got a much wider range of perspectives of what a newspaper is for and how far a newspaper can reach.

The university administration and the local power structure would insist on playing hardball with us. At the same time, though we weren't aware of it, the FBI was conducting the COINTELPRO operation where they infiltrated the League, the Panthers, and the Republic of New Africa, and began to systematically tear those groups up from within. There were splits and purges, all in the name of so-called ideological clarity. Actually, the object was just to bust these groups up and turn people one against the other.

One of the big issues in '72–'73 was the struggle against STRESS [Stop the Robberies, Enjoy Safe Streets] and the pursuit of John Boyd, Mark Bethune, and Hayward Brown. In a sort of vigilante-type action, they tried to singlehandedly clean drugs out of the neighborhoods. We had become aware of books like *The Politics of Heroin in Southeast Asia.* We learned that there was a direct connection among the revolutionary activity of Black people, and drugs coming into our community to subdue that struggle and retard the progress of the people. It was heroin then. Today it's crack cocaine which, in a lot of ways, is even more insidious.

I was very good friends with Hayward Brown. He lasted the longest of the three. He was pulled out of the progressive struggle into that seamy underworld that he began to inhabit because he had no other place to go. But I know his heart was always progressive because I talked with him. Due to some unfortunate turns of circumstances during the time that I was driving a taxicab, I had the good fortune of spending jail time with Hayward Brown. [*Laughs*] I always knew when the political police were very active in sweeping the city because it always coincided with me and Haywood being in jail at the same time on trumped-up charges.

We saw things being possible to do in Detroit that couldn't be done anywhere in the country. We looked at Detroit as a social laboratory, particularly with Detroit's rich history of labor struggle and Detroit's concentration of heavy industry. We felt we had been steeled in struggle. We had struggled through the conditions we had to come up with. We were influenced by the late civil rights movement, the early Black Power movement, and the labor movement. We felt we had many resources and people to draw on, and we had almost a fresh canvas upon which to brush our own strokes. For a time we felt that there were no limits.

Then, around the time of the end of Vietnam War and Watergate, the atmosphere began to change. The right-wing backlash that had been building up since the early '60s began to manifest itself on the American political scene with the election of Nixon and with the Democrats digging in their heels, particularly LBJ, on Vietnam, the Dominican Republic, the Panama Canal. We began to realize how all these things were linked together.

We began an intense period of study. We studied generic Marxism and Third World authors like Ho Chi Minh and Fidel Castro. We tried to ground ourselves in as much history and theory as we could, and accumulated as much knowledge as we could. We were waiting for the next wave of social activity. That may actually be just beginning today.

After the right-wing reaction set in, everybody was happy that they had a Black mayor. The Black middle classes were bought off with jobs and favors. The more radical elements were told, "Thanks for your help in getting us here, but we don't need you now." A lot of us were jettisoned. I know of so many people who weren't able to get employment, and were hounded and jailed. Some, like Boyd, Bethune, and Brown are even dead.

A lot of people thought, and probably still think—certainly within the Young administration—that given the history of Black people in this country, maybe that's as far as they could go, and this was the best it was going to get under the circumstances. Of course, those same people went further than the Black leadership of the '20s and '30s. If they *hadn't*, we would not have made the progress we did today. As they had overthrown *their* fathers, we only felt it our duty to overthrow them. They had reached the limits of where they could go today, and we knew things had to go further.

Many of us see now that we are in a neocolonial situation. It's a painful reality. You see the same things in other cities: an enclave of Blacks, an enclave of Hispanics, businesses in the neighborhoods run by middlemen or outsiders. Our small urban bantustan finds that it is under the stresses and strains of the economic powers that *really* control it. Almost no matter who you elect, unless they're very focused, tough, and uncompromising on certain principles, they wind up bowing to the will of the corporate structures which want to suck Detroit dry, suck *America* dry, and take all their money to other areas of the world where they can get cheap labor and resources. One of the first things I learned from Marx is that capital always flies to the place where the most profit can be made. It's so apparent today.

Not only that, they took the things that are public—took public money—and used it for private purposes. A lot of people are beginning to open their eyes to the travesty of Tiger Stadium. We're going to pay $200,000,000 to $300,000,000 to house a baseball team when we can't house the homeless.

Then there's the tax abatements, something which Kenny Cockrel fought when he got on City Council and was outvoted every time. The man was a prophet. He kept saying, "The more you give them, the more they'll want." There was Chrysler: "Give us a big tax abatement, give us the land, give us the money, you'll get the jobs." There was Poletown: same thing—big plant, one shift. Where did all those Cadillac and Fleetwood jobs go? They're in the *maquiladoros*, that little stretch along the Mexican border, about twenty-five to fifty miles either way, where there's heavy industry, and the Mexicans perform the labor. They ship the cars across the border duty-free, and the American workers slap the name plate Cadillac on them, put the tires on them, and it's "American made." That's one of the scary things about the free trade agreement.

The trade union movement right now should be sending down labor organizers to assist Mexican workers in building their *own* powerful unions to counterbalance the corporate structure in the U.S. that is driving the wages and jobs of *both* of our working classes down to the floor. The competition is not between the labor of Mexico and the labor of the United States. It's with the corporate structures who want to sell the products at super-high prices which the American working class is less and less able to afford.

One great phenomenon of the '80s was that people's pension funds were *raided* right and left. A growing number of Americans are going to wake up and realize that they have no future, they have very little present, and that the only thing that's going to save them is to get up off their asses and do something for themselves. All of us have got to come out of our shells.

There's another great, dark dilemma lurking in the background: the thing that people like [ultraconservative politician] David Duke represent. There is fertile ground in this country, in *any* country that's faced with these kind of conditions, for the emergence of authoritarianism. Is the word *fascism* too strong? Probably a lot of the American working class, with their xenophobia against the Japanese, the French, the Germans, blame everybody else but their own corporate structures.

We've now found out that for the last two or three years, maybe longer, the corporate structures in Detroit, through some kind of mechanism they call the Citizens Research Council—what a misnomer— has had the ear of the Young administration and has been advocating for the city to get out of public housing. Once you understand that, you understand why it is that public housing goes unrehabilitated, and in some cases why it may be sabotaged, and why the power of the police is set upon these people to forcibly evict them and tear down their tents.

Some neighborhood groups have been around for a long time. They're very worried about the deterioration of their neighborhoods, about jobs, about education, about quality of life in the city. But they have a very limited vision. I see them as being embryonic at this point in terms of their consciousness penetrating beyond city limits to forge a new urban agenda. A lot of them see things that need to be done, but where they're really frustrated is how to go about doing these things and how to achieve long-range results with memberships that are constantly changing and with a real paucity of resources.

In almost every local municipal election only about 16 percent of the registered voters actually vote. There are a lot of young African-Americans in this city who are *completely* turned off by the political process. As more and more of these neighborhood groups come into political maturity, and realize what their real interests are, they will begin to look at these people as focal points for mass registration to support the groups' aims and candidates. This is where the electoral process threatens to get away from the powers-that-be. The city administration deliberately wants to lower the number of people who are participating in the electoral process, in favor of more middle-class citizens in Detroit who are more tied into the system. They're actually very frightened of the poor, working-class, underemployed, unemployed, and homeless people exercising their franchise.

One of the ways out for Detroit, particularly because of its geography, is world trade. Where the corporate entities are not prepared to give these people jobs through the expansion of world trade, people will begin to see how to do these things for themselves. They will form workers' cooperatives. Through purchase or tax default, they will take over the rotting, underutilized infrastructure—the empty warehouses, factories, office buildings—and turn them into trade zones. They will make contact with countries in Europe and with underdeveloped countries in Africa, Caribbean, and Latin America. Through the exchange of goods and services, they can build these cooperatives into independent economic structures that will be able to fend for themselves on a world level.

Detroit is uniquely situated for that. The French put it here because it was in command of the Great Lakes. No matter how many jobs and industries they move out of Detroit, they can't change Detroit's geography. I see the St. Lawrence Seaway as a giant funnel with Detroit at the very bottom of it. By pooling resources, by expanding the franchise to every eligible voter, and by *forcing* governments to acquire infrastructure that the corporate entities are no longer using—and would prefer to see destroyed, rather than anyone *else* use it—people will begin to take these things for themselves before they're destroyed. Then they'll use their sweat equity to build them back up for their own benefit.

I won't say that we're necessarily moving toward a one-world government, but people will recognize that their economic interests lie in total free trade everywhere with as few encumbrances as possible for the mutual profit of all. Marx's theories from the 1840s to the 1870s will become part of everyone's vision. We're moving toward that now as the world becomes more and more one market. The way to maximize productivity for people and their neighborhoods and cities is to cut out the middleman and do it yourself.

Today's restructuring of science and technology, as applied to the means of production, has the potential to be *truly* revolutionary. We're talking about the emancipation of human beings from labor. There's the scientific applications of phenomena like superconductivity: the friction-free flow of electrons. In Japan they're already using superconductivity. They're starting to build magnetic levitation trains, hovercraft and hydrofoils. Nissan recently came out with an electric car that can be charged in fifteen minutes and will run for half a day, or more.

How would this technology be applied to Detroit and the production and trade program that you foresee?

It's going to be resisted by the present corporate entities who don't want to see a lot of restructuring and are making good profits now—Detroit Edison, Michigan Gas, etc. But that's where the neighborhood groups will really have to rise to the fore. This is the information age now. If you can tap into a computer and have access to information, they can't stop these things. They can delay you from implementing these things, but they can't stop you from having access to the technology and having people understand how these new technologies can be applied. Once people get political empowerment and mass enfranchisement of the voters who don't vote, once these groups acquire the world vision to see how all these things can be brought together to make their lives better, the corporate powers-that-be are going to catch hell if they keep people from demanding and using these things for themselves.

Once people take their political destiny in their own hands, they will take over entities like the Board of Education, the City Council of Detroit, the mayor's office, the Wayne County government. America is that kind of country. Once you get people past their fears and frustrations, and give them a vision of hope for better things, and possibilities of better things, the pressure on the corporate and political bodies-that-be will be *relentless* and brutal. Because their methods of organization and social control of the means of production will be rendered so brutishly *primitive* by the things that are right on the horizon, they will be smashed to pieces unless they make some kind of new social peace with the people in this country.

Pat Fry

I was born in Highland Park Hospital in 1947 and have lived in Detroit all my life except for five years when I went to Eastern Michigan University in Ipsilanti. My twelve years of Catholic education was a serious influence on my life. I seriously entertained going into the nunnery after high school to be a missionary nun. My parents were honest, hard-working people. I never remember overtly racist talk. My mother came here from Iowa to work in the plants.

My first political movement was antiracism and the struggle against discrimination. In high school I began to question the assumption that everyone was equal in the U. S. In 1963 Viola Liuzzo, from my parish, went south to help break segregation and was killed at gunpoint by a carload of KKK members. The reaction to her death from the parishioners was, How dare she leave her children and go down south with "them" people? I was horrified by that reaction even though I wasn't very aware of the civil rights movement. I had a kind of antirich attitude, but I didn't understand the issue of equality. I *did* have a strong reaction to discrimination; it repelled me.

After about three years of college I stopped going to church. But it really was not until I read and absorbed dialectical and historical materialism that it all fit together for me. I could understand the world as a nonmystical world, that all phenomena were interconnected. It just became unreasonable that there was a supernatural being. For the first time I was at peace and understanding.

In 1967 the Detroit rebellion took place. That fall on campus, a Black woman won the contest for homecoming queen and she was disqualified. I was outraged. I began to see something was not right. The student senate formed a human rights committee, which I joined. We began exploring discrimination in housing on campus. All kinds of things came together. The following year Black students took

Pat Fry is a correspondent for the People's Weekly World.

over the admissions building. Police were called in and the head of the Black Student Association was arrested. Ken Cockrel was his lawyer. I also heard Frank Joyce and Reverend Cleague speak on campus. It was important to my development to see a white person speak out against racism. I became very involved in antiracism work among white people. We did guerrilla theater in dormitories and went door to door talking to white students about how they needed to be involved.

Were you anxious in these new unconventional roles?

Well, I was pretty much convinced of the righteousness of this movement. I *did* have problems with men in leadership roles. It was always a struggle to assert my leadership. But I never had any problems with doing that. I was attracted to the women's movement, although not radical feminism. I was kind of repelled by that. I never had an anti-male view. I quit my sorority because they would not accept Black women. My sorority sisters thought I had just gone crazy. I didn't feel bad about myself as a woman, or that I should be a "proper" woman and think more about raising a family.

After nearly two years of active leadership on antiracism issues, I began to question the role of the U. S. in Vietnam. I began to better understand U.S. corporate interests and imperialism in general. Then I and four others were expelled from school in 1970 for passing out an outlawed underground student newspaper. They got a court injunction, which enraged the student population. This led to a sitdown in the streets the day before the massacre at Kent State and a number of people were arrested, including my sister. This began a three-day siege of the campus by the Washtenaw County police. The jails were filled. Tear gas was used indiscriminately throughout the campus. My apartment was the key target because that's where the mimeograph machines were that produced leaflets for each day's activities. It was probably the biggest campus disturbance anywhere in Michigan in that period.

I got a job teaching school in Detroit at Post Junior High. This was the center of activity for the youth wing of the League of Revolutionary Black Workers. A number of the cadre were students in my classes. They were tremendous students, the brightest and most disciplined. They would help discipline the class, as well. I would have Black Panthers come into the class to speak. I enjoyed the teaching experience, but it was completely overwhelming to me. I had five classes, each with forty kids, many of whom couldn't read or write. I gave up.

I was confused what I should do politically. So a friend and I called Jim Jacobs to find out what was going on in the city. That's how I joined DOC [Detroit Organizing Committee] and began political education classes under the leadership of John Solenberger and Hamish Sinclair. The experience in DOC brought together, for the first time, a cohesive understanding of the world and my first contact with the working-class movement. DOC was a political collective that studied together, put out newspapers for the plants, was on picket lines with DRUM [Dodge Revolutionary Union Movement], and had contact with the League of Revolutionary Black Workers. DOC was very important formatively for me, but there was a lot of political turmoil and the collective fell apart after a while. It was very male dominated, so a lot of issues arose around sexism.

DOC was like many small, local political collectives that I had a lot of experience with. What they can do is very limited. I think it's impossible to build something like that outside of a political party. How can a small political collective help to move the trade union movement in a progressive direction? You need a national political organization to do that. We *attempted* to go beyond our small collective. We had many discussions with other political organizations such as the Sojourner Truth organization in Chicago. But the internal dynamics became dominant and tore us apart.

However, I was very active at the time. I learned to print at the Revolutionary Print Co-op, Freddy Perlman's shop. I loved that. In '71 Phil Hutchins came into town to organize a local chapter of the Venceremos Brigade. I became regional coordinator for the brigade in Detroit and helped organize people who went on the fourth brigade. In 1972 I went to Cuba with the fifth brigade and was there for two months. Working with the committee here was one of my finest political experiences. We studied U.S. imperialism together in preparation for going to Cuba.

When I returned from Cuba I became a part of a political collective organized by James and Grace Boggs. Up until the point I joined, there were no white members. Two other white women and I formed a cell of this organization. We studied the American revolution and tried to come up with creative ideas about strategy. I left that organization on the basis of some rigid and dogmatic views of Marxism-Leninism. I believed in the dictatorship of the proletariat and they were against that concept. They also emphasized individuals transforming themselves personally. I never was attracted to that. I always was an activist and believed that people transformed themselves and came to class consciousness through their activity in movements.

Then all kind of study groups began to grow. The so-called pre-party formations began: the October League, the Revolutionary

321

Union. I also got involved in the U.S.–China Friendship Association since I was very much influenced by Maoism. That was a very well-organized organization here under the leadership of Janet Gold-wasser and Stu Dowdy. I was in three different study groups at the same time: on the national question, a study of revisionism in the Communist Party, and Dave Riddle's "One Hundred and Forty Years of Near Misses," which inquired into why there hadn't been a successful revolutionary movement in an advanced industrial country.

By 1975 many of us who had been in DOC had formed an organization called DMLO [Detroit Marxist-Leninist Organization]. We were anti-ultraleft and antirevisionist. DMLO could never successfully recruit other members. We were very commited to Marxism-Leninism, though we didn't do much practical work. There were numerous groups like us around the country. Most of the political lines of these groups mirrored the Communist Party, USA. The only point of departure was the question of the Soviet Union. We also thought the CP tailed after the labor movement.

Then a national formation was formed called the Organizing Committee for an Ideological Center. As it should have, it distintegrated quickly. But it was personally destructive to many people in it. It could have been very well led by agents. We began a campaign against white chauvinism that was completely internal and divorced from the working-class movement. Like me, many people came to the movement through the fight against racism. Talking about white chauvinism must be done mindful of the working class and the connection to the mass movement, and not directed at individuals. This was a difficult period for me. It was emotionally destructive. The organization quickly folded. I left in early '81 and was not politically active for about two years while I tried to recoup my personal life. I quit smoking and started training for the marathon. I ran with friends on Belle Isle. Many of them were recoving from their own experiences, especially alcoholism.

I can't ever imagine myself disconnected from the revolutionary movement. This comes, of course, from my intellectual self. But mostly it comes from my gut feeling that I have some scores to settle with the ruling class. One of these was the suicide death of my brother. He got burned out on drugs—LSD—emanating from the conflict around the Vietnam War and facing the draft. It led to three years of schizophrenia in mental hospitals. At about the same time I went to Cuba and visited a mental hospital there. What a contrast. It showed me that socialism is a more humane system. I will *never* forget the humanity that was the guiding light of that hospital.

For a while I was floundering politically. So I sought out a friend who who was a reporter for the *Daily World* in Detroit. In the spring of '83 I went to a club meeting of the CP [Communist Party] and heard a presentation on the attack on Coleman Young when he was under survelliance by the FBI. The FBI was trying to connect him up to corruption in his administration. Most of the left took a negative view of Young. But Jim Jacobs wrote a good piece in the *Metro Times* that pointed out the role of the government in undermining Black leadership in the state. That was also the view of the CP. The analysis was very sharp. I signed up that day. [*Laughs*]

I became active in the peace movement through the U.S. Peace Council. It brought together all the questions of peace under one organization: South Africa, Central America, the nuclear arms race. I also became active in the electoral movement. Gus Hall and Angela Davis were running for president and vice-president in '84. The party was rooted in the trade union movement at different levels and paid very much attention to building Black-white unity in the organization. It shined in its ability to bring together coalitions, primarily from labor and the African-American community. Most of that work is not done in the name of the party.

The [Joseph] McCarthy period just about destroyed the party in Michigan. For a left organization, the membership of the party is quite big. Compared to what it was, it's very small. At the height of the party's activity in the early '40s, there were eighteen shop clubs, each with about twenty people, inside the Ford Rouge plant's Local 600. The House Un-American Activities Committee was brought right inside the plant. But many people survived that and are important people in leadership roles in the trade union movement in the city. Even people who left the party still support it in various ways.

The world communist movement has gone through tremendous change. Many working people ask me why I am a communist today when it's failed around the world. I joined the party because of concrete conditions *here*, not because of socialism in eastern Europe or the Soviet Union. A lot of people who've been in the party their whole lifetime might be having a more difficult time around decisions about Czechoslovakia or Hungary and reassessments of Stalin. But I think it's more important to draw lessons from the experiences of other parties: questions of democracy and centralism, and what were the errors that were made.

If there were any illusions or drift toward social democracy among left forces in this country because of what's happened worldwide, the Gulf War, the new world order, certainly should have put an end to any illusions that imperialism was changing its spots. We've launched a barbaric war in the Middle East, spending half a billion

323

dollars a day in armaments, while our cities are falling apart. The crisis domestically is becoming much sharper. Our party talks about concentrating more effort on the economic crisis and organizing at the grassroots level. Organizations of the unemployed are going to become crucial along with building coalitions to challenge the rise of racist violence.

Communism is not a dirty word any more with the end of the Cold War. To see what the demise of socialism in Europe is meaning for working people, in that their gains are being taken away from them, for the first time it's becoming understandable what socialism is all about. I think we're going to see the working class in eastern Europe and the Soviet Union defending their gains. They're going to have to take up the class struggle for the first time. That's going to be a democratizing experience. I'm hopeful there will be a positive experience.

Democratic organizations like the NAACP and the labor unions play an important role in Detroit. But their weakness is that they don't organize at the grass roots. They don't organize the unemployed into militant fight-back action. The left will have to help organize this, to fight on key legislation to extend unemployment benefits, to win back all the cuts that have been made. The legislative front is going to go only as far as the mass movement pushes.

Dave Riddle

I was raised in Kansas City where there's a lot of wheatfield wealth and a lot of factory workers. My father owned a small civil engineering firm. We had no hardships and the kids all got to go to college. Every summer from the time I was fifteen I'd get a job away from home and do different kinds of work. One summer I dug potatoes on an island in the middle of the Missouri River. Another time I worked on a construction gang in Iowa.

In the early '60s I went away to school at DePauw University. It was very conservative. They had de facto segregation. There were no Blacks in the fraternities. A bunch of us lived as kind of "outcasts" in town. My first political act was to help picket the goddamned rush week and we nearly got our asses kicked for it. Nobody did that kind of thing. We were responding to the civil rights movement, trying to

Dave Riddle is a staff person with the Red Squad Notification and Distribution Compliance Program, and doctoral candidate in history at Wayne State University.

do our bit. Some of the professors we admired were going down to the barbershops with Black people and sitting in.

I accidently drifted into some contact with Marxism. I did an honors paper on the confrontation between Marx and Bakunin at the First International. As I was reading for that paper I moved home for the summer and worked in a corn products factory. I was reading Marx's *1844 Manuscripts* at the time. Mostly I did manual work, but on this one night job I sat by a feed processing machine that occasionally clogged up with cattle feed and you'd have to spray it out with a pressure hose. So I was tied to this machine and reading this book about the alienation of labor and how man is the appendage of the machine. It felt like there was something in this guy Marx.

Then I went out to graduate school at Berkeley right after the Free Speech Movement. The thing that radicalized me there had to do with living in an all-Asian rooming house. A roomful of us would watch the evening news on Vietnam. There was an Indian engineering student who used to ask me, "Why does the United States do this?" One student was a Vietnamese guy who came from the landlord class, whose parents had everything to gain from the U.S. presence. But he couldn't handle it. He was a brilliant guy, but he dropped out of school. It was hard to defend the role of the U.S. in Vietnam.

I thought there was a dichotomy between what we were supposed to be doing at school intellectually and all this horror of the war. Some of us did some crazy things. We founded a journal for the history graduate students called *Bullshit and Society*. We printed all kinds of situationist literature and manifestos. It got us a bad reputation and I don't think any of us got our Ph.D.s either.

I came to Detroit from Berkeley in 1969 after I turned twenty-six and was no longer draft eligible. Got tired of the tear gas out at Berkeley and kind of burned out on the ethereal culture of California. Someone showed me a "movement job" pamphlet. One entry said Radical Education Project. I hooked up with them at the Austin, Texas, SDS [Students for a Democratic Society] convention in '68. I agreed to work with them, dropped out of school, and drove across the country to Detroit.

I was part of that generation of '60s radicals who saw Detroit as a very significant place. We looked at it as a labor center and a center of the movement for Black liberation. Times were still good. Waves of people were coming to Detroit, like the Revolutionary Union, the Maoists, the folks from Ann Arbor. People looked at themselves, almost consciously, as Narodniks—the young Russian student intellectuals who wanted to bring the word of revolution to the peasant masses. There was a *real* intellectual arrogance.

The emigrés brought certain intellectual baggage to Detroit which shaped the way we functioned once we got here. We thought big labor was almost as much a problem as big capital. My own trade union experience in Detroit has been a process of running with that theory for a while, and then coming to criticize it. Big labor has got its ass kicked for so long. There was an adolescent labor movement and then they passed the Taft-Hartley Law, and then the Landrum-Griffin Law, and then the industries all moved out and the unions got smaller. A lot of us thought the union leadership was the primary enemy. I think we, the émigrés, had a bad reading on the labor movement and where it was at.

The other thing we came to Detroit encumbered with was a sycophantic view of the political leaders of the Black working class. Much of *this* came out of our view of Third World revolution. You know, our generation in many ways felt the Vietnamese could do no wrong. And if a person was speaking as a member of the Black Panther Party or the League of Revolutionary Black Workers, basically you listened to it and took direction from it, but didn't really evaluate it much. That is not to say that both the Panthers and the League were not coming from a real place, analyzing things the best way they knew how, and making a sincere, principled effort to improve Black people's condition, as well as the condition of the rest of the people in this country.

My story in Detroit for the last twenty-three years is a story of trying to get rid of the myths of big labor, the infallibility of the Black movement, and the revolution viewed primarily in the Third World model; that, and trying to find the right organizational form where Blacks and whites could work together. Much of the story of the movement in Detroit has been the story of failures to really deal on an equal basis between so-called white revolutionaries and Black people who saw themselves as revolutionaries, on a level of true equality in a nonpatronizing, nonsycophantic way.

I worked a couple of years printing pamphlets for the Radical Education Project on Michigan Avenue near the Clark Street Cadillac plant. Then I worked a year for the *Fifth Estate* newspaper as a reporter. I got tired of no money and got a job at Dodge Truck plant on Mound Road, worked there for eighteen months, and got fired for insubordination and also helping to put out a newsletter which was equally critical of the union and the company. The same shit: big labor was as bad as big capital. I hung out with these people from the RU [Revolutionary Union] until I finally saw through it and split with them. Before I got fired I wrote a long paper saying "you people are full of shit."

In Detroit the Maoists and the anarchists had this purest view of what a union was. The Maoists thought *they* should be in charge. The anarchists thought it should be this communitarian, utopian kind of working class in a continuous state of self-activity. Both thought, If it isn't that then fuck it. I always wrote these resignation letters. Somewhere I have a file of resignation papers. I think my last one is going to be my suicide note. [*Laughs*]

Eventually I ran into a truck driver who told me it was easier to drive the trucks than to unload them. So I went to truck-driver school in 1974, but couldn't get a job for a couple years. So I taught sociology and history at community colleges around town. Eventually, in 1977 jobs opened up and I got a job hauling cars. I did that for thirteen years. I got involved in TDU [Teamsters for a Democratic Union] and went through the *same* thing again having to do with the union. TDU was fundamentally concerned with corruption in the Teamsters Union and lack of democracy. I supported that because there certainly are big problems. But eventually I came to the conclusion that they *also* could not distinguish who the main enemy was, so I left them.

The Marxist movement, both Black and white, had been here for decades. I'm really getting a sense of this, working this job at the Red Squad files. There's a reason they call it the *Red* Squad files. It's mostly communists and there's a hell of a lot of them, little and big people. It's like walking through Woodmere Cemetery and seeing those little gravestones. You go through those files and see those old raggedy yellowing folders containing little memoranda from these cops regarding so-and-so who went to a Communist Party picnic at such-and-such a park in 1949 and was seen in the company of so-and-so and driving these license-plate cars. There's just a lot of people like that.

I belonged to a group called the Detroit Marxist-Leninist Organization which was associated with a national body called the Organizing Committee for an Ideological Center, which never came to anything. This was one of a number of preparty formation groups all over the country. Whatever corner of politics you happened to be involved with, you were trying to do national preparty formations in order to form a revolutionary party.

I was part of a number of study groups. It was the first time I studied Black people in terms of oppressed nationhood. I'd always seen it as a question of racism. About 1974 the first study group we formed was called "140 Years of Near Misses," which was the study of why revolution never happened in the industrial West. The Vietnam War had ended. Joan Baez was already pissed off at the Vietnamese 'cause they didn't form a hippie commune or whatever she wanted them to do. We were wondering how far this model of Third World revolution was going to get *us*. What do we do *now*? We read a bunch of Marx and stuff on the Russian Revolution. Marx said that the most economically developed countries would be the ones where the contradictions of capital would assert themselves and there would be an immiseration of the working class, a polarization of classes, and there would be revolution. Why hasn't that happened?

When we studied the United States we dealt with basic, crude, but interesting, rehashes of the old question of American exceptionalism. Does the frontier thesis in American history mean that the people just pick up and move to Idaho, rather than confronting class oppression? How has racism divided the working class? Is the working class just terminally stupid in this country? We entertained questions from Marcuse and Gramsci. What is it about culture, especially mass culture, that seems to have such an enervating effect on class consciousness? We were quite eclectic.

When we came up with a study group it wasn't, "Well, let's get together and study." It was more like you'd be sitting around, drinking beer, or doing whatever you were doing, and . . . Jeff Goodman, who died since, was a guy you'd sit up all night with and you wouldn't think about studying, you'd think about real questions like where's the movement at or what's happening to this city?

Most of the people I hung out with were Marxists, but we also were into having a good time. We were hippies who were, by definition, self-indulgent. You're talking to a self-indulgent Leninist. It's a contradiction, but it's kept me sane. We did what we did more or less 'cause we *had* to do it, not because we wanted to do it. We really didn't do much externally. As far as actual work among the masses, I didn't do much. Maybe a few contributions. Mostly just observed.

I don't feel weird about my life. As a matter of fact that's the source of my political optimism. I don't feel the least bit strange. I figure if someone can come up the way I came up and end up thinking what I think it must be possible because I'm not insane. Other people can do that. This is not a fair society and most people are aware of that. And it has a lot to do with the way the economy runs and the way people are divided from one another.

I think there is the possibility of fascism. This is the first time that I've said that. We have to confront the fact that the main bulwark against fascism in this country is the working class. This country is headed for severe internal contradictions, crises of overproduction, and declining profit rate—all the stuff that Marx said. Given the nature of the crisis in the old socialist states, how do you, with any credibility, tell workers that American socialism will have to combine socialism and democracy and bring it to a new level?

Pete Camarata

I was born and raised in Detroit. Dad came to the United States from Sicily in 1913, when he was about seven years old. Mom was born in Detroit on the east side. There was always a union background. My dad was active at Packard where he helped organize the union. He was off on strike as much as he used to work.

In high school, I came in contact with a teacher named Terry King, a social activist, who was involved with a homeless shelter, mostly older males, and he used to take us down to this shelter on 14th Street not too far from Tiger Stadium. We would go out and beg day-old bread from some of the bakeries. I began to develop a social consciousness at that time.

I started working at Earl C. Smith in 1968 on the truck docks. Smith used to use a lot of college kids as extras. They had a right-wing boss there who used the college kids to intimidate the workers. Well, I got to be pretty good friends with the workers. I didn't intimidate them, just had the kind of normal instinct that I'd learned from my dad about unionism.

I got put on as a committeeman for the afternoon shift just six months after I went to work there. And I started to read the contract. A lot of people came up to me who just wanted to know what the contract said on this issue or that issue, and I spent all my lunch and coffee breaks reading the contract.

We were always upset over the fact that we were under the master contract. The way Hoffa had it set up was that you would vote on your master contract, but the supplements, which were your local conditions, were not voted separately—how jobs were bid, how your starting time was determined, how many sick days you got, all these kind of local conditions. We always thought that was pretty undemocratic. Hoffa's dream was that sooner or later everything would finally be standardized, that there would be no separate local conditions.

In 1970 I was elected steward. I had committeemen on every shift. I had a safety representative on every shift. I'd try to have meetings with these guys over lunch. If we had a grievance, I'd never research

Pete Camarata is a truck driver and member of the Teamsters for a Democratic Union (TDU).

the grievance myself. I made sure everybody had contract books. We'd always try to do collective things.

When Hoffa disappeared in the summer of 1975, it created a leadership vacuum in the local. [Interim head] Johnson desperately wanted to retire, and the bureaucracy wanted him out too. The Fitzsimmons and the Bobby Holmes faction were kind of against Hoffa. They wanted Johnson out. They blew up his boat down in Florida. They broke his leg while he was in office at the union hall. He was only hanging on for Hoffa, and it was a big disappointment when Hoffa disappeared. There were all these people organizing these Hoffa dinners—those How Old Friends Feel Active dinners.

When Hoffa disappeared, we were all organizing in the hopes that he would come back. We called ourselves the ARF [Action Rank and File]. Then there was the Action Committee of Teamsters.

In the late '60s and early '70s, the IS [International Socialists] had decided there were a lot of radicalized students coming out of the antiwar movement. Part of the IS's political perspective was that they would send these working-class radicalized students to get jobs in the Teamsters, auto and mine workers, heavy industry. They felt there was going to be an upsurge in heavy industry. They tried to start organizations and caucuses around the contract struggles that were coming up. In the Teamsters, they called themselves Teamsters for a Decent Contract. At UPS they called themselves UPSURGE.

In April 1976 when the master freight agreement expired, we had a wildcat strike in Detroit. I was really radicalized to left ideas out of the wildcat strike. I started to see the way that forces line up, whose side the bosses ended up being on, and what kind of role the union bureaucrats play. I was able to feel in a real intimate way the power you have if the workers get together. I mean, we were able to shut down the whole of Detroit. It was amazing. There were about 300 of us who were active in the beginning of that wildcat strike, and we shut down the whole city. There wasn't a truck that moved. The union bureaucrats were against us, and we had to fight them too.

Plus, having a radical person around like Steve Kindred. Steve was honest with me from the very beginning. He said, "I'm a socialist. I don't want this to come as a big shock to you. If you want to talk about politics, we can talk later. But I'm here to work with you on this wildcat strike, and I'll help you out any way I can." I thought he had a real good approach. Naturally, then I started to be interested in it. What is this socialist stuff? And I started to ask those questions. But I guess I had an understanding of the class struggle and the power of the working class before I understood the whole idea of socialism.

Most of the key people who have been longtime activists in TDU are people who came to develop their radical ideas out of those wildcat strikes.

After the master freight contract was signed, sealed and delivered, people who were active in the freight agreement in TDC had a meeting outside of Cleveland, Ohio. There were about 250 people asking, What shall we do? We hadn't really been successful in having a huge impact. We had a wildcat strike in Detroit, but we weren't able to spread it. Should we continue to build this organization in an ongoing way? All the activists there said, We should continue to build our organization so that in three years when the contract expires again, we'll have more of an impact.

We were already on the outs with the international bureaucracy over the farmworkers question. At that time, the Teamsters were in the field raiding the farmworkers. We were shown a video of the Teamster goons beating the shit out of these poor farmworkers, and we were against that kind of thing.

Folks felt it was time for us to put our agenda for change in the union on the chopping block. So we put them on notice that we were going to be at the next Teamster convention. I got elected as a delegate, out of the wildcat strike. A lot of the activists got together and hammered out proposed changes to the international constitution, and submitted them in a timely fashion, to be presented at the Teamster convention.

So I went down to the convention, and that was another eye-opener for me. I had been elected as a delegate to the convention. I was the top vote-getter out of my local, Local 299, Jimmy Hoffa's old local, and I felt I had a right to have something to say down there. I was a representative of the rank-and-file members. So I made all these proposals. I tried to get them on the floor. I didn't have any allies down there, nobody that I knew. None of the delegates in Local 299 would have anything to do with me. They said, Look, just keep your mouth shut. I said, No, the members voted me in to present these changes and I'm going to present them.

As it turned out I was able to get the thing for the right to vote for our international officers on the floor because they were proposing a change in the 1976 convention constitution in the procedure for electing the international officers. I think they had included a change to allow the executive board to appoint a successor if one of the principal officers dies or has to give up his office midterm, rather than hold a new convention vote for that office. That was in response to Hoffa. But that opened the door for me to get the right-to-vote amendment on the floor of the convention. And, naturally, at every convention they always propose increases in their salaries and wages, so I was able to propose the limit of $100,000 on the officers' salaries.

The only way that I was able to get a second on the floor was that one of the delegates from the 299 delegation got sick and my cousin John ended up being seated. Otherwise, I would never have had a second to any of the amendments that I proposed. I found out that it wasn't just like a hostile attitude, they were physically hostile. They were like mad dogs. These people were really pissed off. I didn't expect it. The intimidation was so intense. The convention was designed to be a rubber stamp for the international bureaucracy. It did not present a forum for people who were dissenters from the bureaucracy.

I learned more lessons about the working-class struggle, and what role the bureaucracy in the unions play in that. At that convention, they had all the bosses from UPS, Roadway and all the major carriers. And I thought, God, we're supposed to be enemies on either side of the bargaining table, and here they are coming to the Teamster convention as honored guests. The mayor of Las Vegas, the governor of Nevada, a right-to-work state, are speaking at the biggest Teamster convention. Even then they were supporting all the Republican candidates for office. They supported Nixon.

At that point I felt like, Well, maybe they can be changed. I felt that the international bureaucracy did not represent all the local officials. Since that time I've come to realize that the union bureaucrats actually end up being cops for the employers. The first three or four years at TDU, I was under constant attack. They tried to expel me from the union a couple of times. There was physical intimidation. There were charges being brought and leveled.

In 1978, we started our campaign for the 1981 Teamster convention. I went to the Marble Palace—that's what we called the International Brotherhood of Teamsters headquarters in Washington, D.C.— and I announced my candidacy for the presidency of the international union. I ran against Roy Williams at the 1981 convention. We worked together very hard on that convention and made all those same proposals—the right to vote for the international officers, limiting their salaries and no multiple salaries, and on and on.

So then I learned the value of having the TDC network. I was able to contact rank-and-file members to find out what's going on in places like California that I could never do before. There were people I could talk to who were truck drivers just like myself out in Los Angeles who could tell me about the struggle they were going through.

I really didn't have a chance to win in the '81 convention. We just did it to gain publicity around the idea of the need for a right to vote. I always joked that I came in second in that race, because nobody else would run. I think I went on record as getting about ten or twelve votes. Roy Williams, the official candidate for the international, was already under indictment for trying to bribe a senator with pension fund money. Now he was actually bribing him for a good reason: he wanted the senator to vote against deregulation of the trucking industry. Within a year and a half, Williams was out. Shortly after that, Jackie Presser came into power.

Since that time, TDU has slowly and steadily grown. In 1976 when we had our founding convention, 250 activists from around the country were there. By 1979, we went to 3,000 members. I don't think we ever got past about 8,000 members, which is where we're at now. But the numbers thing is kind of divisive. There are a million and a half members of the Teamsters and you're only 8,000; you're just a pimple on an elephant's butt. I think the key thing about TDU is that it's an activist organization. We've got people in thirty-five states who do TDU work on a weekly basis.

I think the ones who have stuck with it the longest, the people who are the stalwarts of TDU, are the people who have come to some kind of worldview. That's not to say that all of these people became radicals and joined the IS or joined the Communist Party or some political group. But they've come to understand it with more of a worldview, seeing how our struggle in the Teamsters fits into the struggle by workers all over the world.

I've been elected to the international steering committee of TDU all but one year. I didn't run two years ago; I decided that I would concentrate on building the Detroit chapter. When things really started to downturn here in Detroit, the chapter itself started to fall apart. For a long time Detroit was the core, but now there are areas that have bigger memberships than Detroit.

I end up being the double dissident. I'm dissident inside the Teamsters, and then I'm dissident inside TDU. I guess through my experiences in 1976 and the understanding of how important rank-and-file organization is, I end up being on the left fringe of feeling that the organization's major priority has to be in building at the grassroots.

There's always a tendency in the TDU kinds of organizations to say, "If we can get this guy elected to office, we'll democratize our local and then the TDU network will grow." The sad answer is that it doesn't work. It's happened over and over again where you'll get your best people to organize for TDU and they get elected to local office, they'll be so overwhelmed by just trying to keep their head above

333

water being a local officer that TDU disappears. They don't change their principles about TDU; it's just that they don't have the energy to be major activists.

People recognize TDU. In Detroit, they recognize an alternative to the way things are run in the union. I've not been successful in winning a local office and I ran numerous times. I've told the members it's the best thing in the world for them that I haven't won. I said, "Because you guys aren't ready for me. When I get elected to office, that's not the end of the war; that's the beginning." People identify me as a socialist, a communist. I've been called everything in Detroit. People tell me my political career suffered because I was honest enough to tell people that I had socialist ideas, because it's just the death knell for working-class people.

Our master freight agreement is expiring the end of this month, and there's very little activity around it. People are pretty much complacent, pretty much job scared. They don't feel like there's any real alternative being presented.

The employers are much more meticulous about trying to keep people under their thumb. Even in these trucking jobs. They've got the drug-testing aspect; they want to drug test you, every turn of the wheel they're going to scrutinize you. They want to get into your bladder to find out what kind of person you are. On my job I have to clock in and out at every stop. We've had people fired for having a seven-minute discrepancy, spending two minutes extra in a coffee stop, being ten minutes late getting off their break.

How do you see your role in the next five years?

I'm looking for that twenty-five-and-out pension, and I'd like to go to work for TDU and organize full time and build some worker fightback all over the country. Then too I think it's my job as a person with socialist ideas to spread those ideas to other people. Not to make it seem so foreign and sounding like communist Russia, but to understand that you can be a socialist and be an American and be proud of being part of this country too. You may not be proud of what the government does, but you can be proud of the people and respectful of the working-class people in this country.

I believe that people are looking for an alternative. They really do want another explanation of the way things are. I feel there's going to be potential for those of us who have radical ideas. I think people are going to be more open to those ideas, and I think working-class people are going to be willing to want to struggle to fight back a little bit. I can't believe that they're just going to take this continually.

There's got to be a break from the Democratic Party. Even in the progressive wing of the labor bureaucracy, about as far as they go to the left is the Democratic Party. And there's got to be a break from that, because the Democratic Party, after all, is a capitalist party. They're going to do what's best for the employers. I'm optimistic about a potential for radical ideas, for people to look for an alternative to explain what's going on. That might not mean that they're going to be in a union. But they'll understand that organizing their brothers and sisters on the job is important, and that understanding the class struggle is important.

INDEX

339

341

347